Peter Beer is a retired schoolmaster and author with an interest in the interplay of temperament and circumstance in public lives, which is also the all-too-common pulse of our conflicting selves. His first book was a collection of biographical essays, *A Turning of Keys: Poets and Norfolk 1460–1991*. *The Playboy Princes* is his second book.

The
PLAYBOY PRINCES
The Apprentice Years of Edward VII and Edward VIII

Peter J. Beer

PETER OWEN
London and Chicago

PETER OWEN PUBLISHERS
81 Ridge Road, London N8 9NP

Peter Owen books are distributed in the USA and Canada by
Independent Publishers Group/Trafalgar Square
814 North Franklin Street, Chicago, IL 60610, USA

First published in Great Britain by Peter Owen Publishers in 2014

PAPERBACK ISBN 978-0-7206-1590-6
EPUB ISBN 978-0-7206-1836-5
MOBIPOCKET ISBN 978-0-7206-1837-2
PDF ISBN 978-0-7206-1838-9

A catalogue record for this book is available from the British Library

Typeset by Octavo Smith Publishing Services in Baskerville MT

Printed and bound in the UK by
CPI Group (UK) Ltd, Croydon, CR0 4YY

To Christopher

Acknowledgements

Quotations from archive collections and private papers are cited from secondary sources. I am greatly obliged to those who have given their written permission: to Sir John Aird in respect of the period when Major John Aird was Equerry to the Prince of Wales (later Edward VIII); to the Syndics of Cambridge University Library for permission in respect of an extract from the Baldwin Papers; to Lord Howick in respect of the Earl Grey Papers; to Mrs Caroline Erskine in respect of Sir Alan Lascelles's Papers; to Lord Newton for permission to reproduce extracts relating to his great uncle, Piers Legh; to the Chatsworth Archives; to Mr Roger North for permission to quote words of his father, Admiral Sir Dudley North; to the Collections and Archives at Hatfield House in respect of the papers of the 3rd Marquess of Salisbury; to Mr John Wood for permission to quote words of his grandfather, Sir Lionel Halsey; and to Huntingdonshire Archive and Local Studies.

I am grateful to the respective authors (or their personal representatives), publishers and agents for permission to quote from the following copyright works: Anthony Allfrey (copyright © Anthony Allfrey 1991) *Edward VII and His Jewish Court*, the Orion Publishing Group Ltd; Michael Arlen, *The Green Hat*, David Higham Associates Ltd; Georgina Battiscombe (copyright © Georgina Battiscombe 1969), *Queen Alexandra*, Constable and Robinson Ltd and A.M. Heath and Company Ltd; Laura Beatty, *Lillie Langtry: Manners, Masks, Morals*, the Random House Group Ltd; the Duke of Beaufort, *Memoirs*, Country Life Books; Michael Bloch (ed.) (copyright © Michael Bloch 1986), *Wallis and Edward: Letters 1931–1937*, Curtis Brown Group Ltd, London; Philipp Blom (copyright © Philipp Blom 2008), *The Vertigo Years: Change and Culture in the West, 1900–1914*, the Orion Publishing Group and Perseus Books Group; Piers Brendon, *The*

Dark Valley: A Panorama of the 1930s and *The Decline and Fall of the British Empire 1781–1997*, the Random House Group Ltd; Gordon Brook-Shepherd (copyright © Gordon Brook-Shepherd 1975), *Uncle of Europe*, HarperCollins Publishers Ltd; James Brough (copyright © 1975 James Brough), *The Prince and the Lily: Edward, Prince of Wales and Lillie Langtry*, Hodder and Stoughton; Thomas E. Brown, *Attention Deficit Disorder: The Unfocused Mind in Children and Adults*, Yale University Press; David Cannadine, *History in Our Time*, Yale University Press; Sir Kenneth Carlisle, *Wyken: The Life of a Small Suffolk Estate*, by permission of the author; Lord Chandos, *From Peace to War*, by permission of Viscount Chandos; Randolph S. Churchill, *Lord Derby: King of Lancashire*, (copyright © Randolph S. Churchill), by permission of Curtis Brown Ltd on behalf of the Estate of Randolph S. Churchill; Pierre Crabitès, *Victoria's Guardian Angel: A Study of Baron Stockmar*, Taylor and Francis Books (UK); Richard Davis, *The English Rothschilds* (copyright © Richard Davis 1983), HarperCollins Publishers Ltd; the Donaldson Papers and Frances Donaldson, *Edward VIII*, by permission of Peters Fraser and Dunlop on behalf of the Estate of Lady Donaldson and the Orion Publishing Group Ltd; James Pope-Hennessy, *Queen Mary 1867–1953* and *A Lonely Business*, the estate of James Pope-Hennessy c/o Artellus Ltd; J. Ellis (ed.), *Thatched with Gold: The Memoirs of Mabell, Countess of Airlie*, by permission of the Earl of Airlie; Roger Fulford (ed.), *Dearest Child: Letters Between Queen Victoria and the Princess Royal 1858–1861*, *Dearest Mama: Letters Between Queen Victoria and the Crown Princess of Prussia 1861–1864*, *Darling Child: Private Correspondence of Queen Victoria and the Crown Princess of Prussia 1871–1878*, by permission of Lord Shuttleworth; Rupert Godfrey (ed.) (copyright © Rupert Godfrey 1998), *Letters From a Prince, March 1918–January 1921*, Curtis Brown Group Ltd, London, and Little, Brown and Company; Peter Gordon and Denis Lawton, *Royal Education: Past, Present and Future*, Taylor and Francis Books (UK); Robert Graves and Alan Hodge, *The Long Weekend: A Social History of Great Britain 1918–1938*, Carcanet Press Ltd; Elizabeth Hamilton, *The Warwickshire Scandal*, by permission of Michael Russell; Simon Heffer, *Power and Place*, Capel and Land Ltd; Christopher Hibbert, *Edward VII: A Portrait*, David Higham Associates Ltd; Robert Rhodes James (ed.), *Chips: The Diaries of Sir Henry Channon* and *Memoirs of a Conservative*, by permission respectively of Sheil Land Associates Ltd and the Orion Publishing Group Ltd; James Lees-Milne, *Harold Nicolson, Vol. 2*, David Higham Associates Ltd; Anita Leslie, *The Marlborough House Set*, Doubleday and Company; Susan Lowndes (ed.), *Diaries and Letters of Marie Belloc*

Lowndes, by permission of Ana Vicente; Oliver Lyttelton, Viscount Chandos, *The Memoirs of Lord Chandos*, by permission of Viscount Chandos; J.M. Mackenzie, *Propaganda and Empire*, Manchester University Press; Compton Mackenzie, *The Windsor Tapestry*, the Society of Authors as the Literary Representative of the Estate of Compton Mackenzie; David Marquand, *Ramsay MacDonald*, David Higham Associates Ltd; Donald McLachlan, *In the Chair: Barrington-Ward of The Times*, Artellus Ltd; James Morris, *Pax Britannia: The Climax of Empire* and *Farewell the Trumpets: An Imperial Retreat*, Faber and Faber; Juliet Nicolson, *The Perfect Summer: Dancing into the Shadow in England in 1911* (copyright © Juliet Nicolson 2006), by permission of John Murray Press and Grove/Atlantic Inc.; S. Orwell and I. Angus (eds.), *The Collected Essays, Journalism and Letters of George Orwell* (copyright © George Orwell 1971), reprinted by permission of Bill Hamilton as the Literary Executor of the Estate of the Late Sonia Brownell Orwell; Harold Nicolson, *King George V: His Life and Reign*, Constable and Robinson; Stanley Olson (ed.), *Harold Nicolson: Diaries and Letters 1930–1964*, by permission of Sheil Land Associates Ltd; Michael Partridge, *The Royal Naval College, Osborne*, the History Press; Martin Pugh, *We Danced All Night: A Social History of Britain Between the Wars*, the Bodley Head and the Andrew Lownie Literary Agency Ltd; Kenneth Rose (copyright © Kenneth Rose 1983), *King George V*, the Orion Publishing Group Ltd; Jonathan Garnier Ruffer, *The Big Shots: Edwardian Shooting Parties*, (copyright © Debrett's Peerage and Baronetage 1977); Richard Shannon, *Gladstone: Heroic Minister 1865–1898*, David Higham Associates Ltd; Osbert Sitwell, *Left Hand, Right Hand, Laughter in the Next Room* and *Great Morning*, David Higham Associates Ltd; Diana Souhami, *Mrs Keppel and Her Daughter*, Capel and Land Ltd; Lytton Strachey, *Eminent Victorians*, the Society of Authors; A.J.P. Taylor, *Lloyd George, A Diary*, David Higham Associates Ltd; Dan Todman (copyright © Dan Todman 2007), *The Great War: Myth and Memory*, Hambledon Continuum, by permission of Bloomsbury Publishing Plc; John Vincent (ed.), *The Crawford Papers*, Manchester University Press; Gloria Vanderbilt and Thelma, Lady Furness, *Double Exposure*, Frederick Muller Ltd by permission of the Random House Group Ltd; A.N. Wilson, *The Victorians*, The Random House Group Ltd and W.W. Norton and Company; A.N. Wilson, *After the Victorians* (2005), The Random House Group Ltd and Farrar, Straus and Giroux; the Duchess of Windsor, *The Heart Has Its Reasons*, Penguin Books Ltd; Cecil Woodham-Smith, (copyright © Cecil Woodham-Smith 1972), *Queen Victoria: Her Life and Times*, by permission of A.M. Heath and Company Ltd; G.M. Young, *Daylight and Champaign, Victorian England: Portrait of an Age* and *Early Victorian England 1830–1865*, the Codrington Library, All Souls College, Oxford; Philip Ziegler (copyright © 1991 Philip Ziegler), *King Edward VIII: The Official Biography*, HarperCollins Publishers Ltd; Emile Zola, translated with an introduction by Douglas Parmée (1992), *Nana*, Oxford University Press.

Every effort has been made over a long period to contact owners of copyright. If there are acknowledgements which I ought to have made I hope that the authors and publishers concerned will accept my apologies and my plea of an absence of *mens rea*. All omissions brought to my attention will be rectified in future editions and reprints.

I am greatly indebted to Christopher Bromley-Martin, who read every chapter in typescript and made fruitful recommendations to the betterment of the book. To him the book is dedicated. Notwithstanding his kindness, I must take full responsibility for any imperfections that remain. My grateful thanks also to Simon Smith of Peter Owen for his steadying hand on the tiller; to David Miller, who dispelled some shadows; and to Eunice Glass, for perspicacious and timely encouragement.

Contents

Illustrations

between pages 160 and 161

EDWARD VII

Prince Albert Edward, aged twelve, and his brother, Prince Alfred, with their tutor, F.W. Gibbs *Royal Collection Trust/© Her Majesty Queen Elizabeth II 2014*

Sandringham House, Norfolk, which the Prince of Wales acquired in October 1862

Queen Victoria in mourning dress seated before a bust of the late Prince Consort in 1863 with the Prince and Princess of Wales *Royal Collection Trust/© Her Majesty Queen Elizabeth II 2014*

The Prince of Wales standing over the carcass of a wild Chillingham bull, *c.* 1879 *Getty Images*

Lillie Langtry, the Prince of Wales's mistress

Le Ciel (Heaven) and L'Enfer (Hell), adjacent cabarets in Montmartre, Paris, the city which the Prince of Wales enjoyed at the height of its allure

EDWARD VIII

The future George V with Prince Albert, Princess Mary, Prince Edward and Prince Henry, Sandringham, 1902 *Royal Collection Trust/© Her Majesty Queen Elizabeth II 2014*

Prince Edward as a naval cadet, 1908 *Topham Picturepoint*

Aged eighteen, the Prince of Wales strides out with his tutor, Henry Hansell, at Auteuil, Paris, 1912 *Getty Images*

The Prince of Wales with his friends Rosemary Leveson-Gower and Diana Capel at the Duchess of Sutherland's hospital in France during the Great War *© Imperial War Museum (Q2585)*

The Prince of Wales takes a fall at the Arborfield Cross point-to-point in 1924 *Getty Images*

Freda Dudley Ward with her children, 1918 *Illustrated London News Picture Library, London, UK/Bridgeman Images*

Wallis Simpson, dressed for her presentation at Court, 1931 *Topham Picturepoint*

Introduction

The privileges of rank aside, the formative years of Albert Edward and Edward, Princes of Wales, were strained affairs. Plainly the stakes were high, as they had been for royal heirs before them. For want of a happy template for grooming an heir to the throne, the Princes suffered enervating supervision that was light in sympathy and patience, and sparse in praise. A good deal of princely goodwill was lost in the process. Indeed, the Princes came to manhood (Prince Edward the more so) all too aware of disharmonies between their personal likings and their royal duties. And so, in certain essentials, Princes Albert Edward and Edward were of a pair: they had troubled and unfulfilling educations, their adolescent years were crushingly prescriptive, and childhood and adult expectations were hard to bear. (Censure was proverbial. In a letter written to mark the eighth birthday of their nearest predecessor as Prince of Wales, later George IV, Queen Charlotte wanted him to imitate fully his father George III's virtues: 'Look upon everything that is in opposition to that duty as destructive to yourself,' she told him.)[1] The weight of obligation rendered them keenly vulnerable to parental disapproval, until such time as they were able to pursue their leisure as they pleased and the criticism mattered less.

Neither man set much store by his training in the duties of a king. At no stage did Queen Victoria express the slightest confidence that Prince Albert Edward would use his time profitably if given an official role in public affairs, an opportunity which Gladstone, among others, could not persuade her to sanction; her crude dismissals (which were never to be forgiven) he banished in a welter of social distraction. It was grist to the mill of his detractors that Prince Albert Edward filled the void with shallow interests.

His grandson, Prince Edward, took a jaundiced view of matters of state and his interest in them swiftly evaporated. As man and as boy he looked upon duty as an impoverishment. Yet for extended periods Prince Edward's record was hardly passive. There was the enduring, if dull, war service; the close concern for people's welfare in mining village, town and city; the overseas tours that kept him long from home. But all the while he suppressed his yearnings with punishing physical exertion and with maudlin letter-writing at all hours, notably to his lover, Mrs Dudley Ward. The more his father, George V, used him as a workhorse abroad, the more evident became his reluctance to commit himself to the royal enterprise at the cost of the private, non-ceremonial life he craved, and to which by inclination and temperament he was proving better suited.

The Princes set much store by time that was their own. Prince Albert Edward became the exemplar of a lavish style of living which was denounced as vulgar by depleted landowning wealth, a style sustained by the financial acumen – and personal generosity – of a cosmopolitan coterie, which kept him afloat. In their company he liked most to listen, content when he did not have to pull the strings. For salacious interest he turned to Paris, the New Babylon, unmoved by moral censure. Prince Edward's social pleasures, once the years had diminished his legendary stamina on the dance floor, were less flamboyant, more self-effacing. He preferred discreet settings, nightclubs for choice, with a female companion, their presence familiar to a proprietor who spared them attention and fuss. The challenging pursuits continued: riding to hounds was to be at one with the democracy of the field.

Presenting the Princes independently of their respective performances as King has allowed full weight to be given to the record that each would bring to the role of monarch – to portray, indeed, the temper of apprenticeships conducted in anticipation of a troubling unknown.

EDWARD VII

1
'Make Him Climb Trees!'

The boyhood diary of Albert Edward, later Edward VII, which he maintained at the insistence of his father, Prince Albert, was little more than a reluctant exercise in compliance; his parent saw it grow more 'bald, ungrammatical, and badly penned' with every passing month.[1] Once, though, the boy let rip. Aged nine, he had visited the Great Exhibition (1851) in Hyde Park where, among the intimidating array of exhibits he was expected to admire, was a display that truly enchanted him. In a setting of huts and bamboos of an Indian village, members of the fraternity of murderers known as the Thugs were portrayed (in waxwork) in the act of strangling a traveller from behind with their hallmark yellow silk cloth – a rite they perpetrated, the Prince learnt, as votaries of their patroness, the Hindu goddess Kali. Their victims, moreover, were well mutilated to ensure that no swollen body could displace the earth and reveal its place of burial. This vision the Prince committed to his diary in macabre and exuberant detail, and awaited, as usual, the verdict of his mentors. He received only censure. He 'was born in a Christian and enlightened age in which such atrocious acts are not even dreamt of'.[2]

The Prince was no stranger to cautions whenever he gave the least hint that he might not become the 'most perfect man', the ideal which the Bishop of Oxford, Samuel Wilberforce, advised his young parents should be 'the great object in view'.[3] To which end, everything should be done to ensure that the failings of his Hanoverian great-uncles George IV and William IV were not visited upon him. The means – unquestioned principles of education applied with Teutonic rigour – were no panacea in the past, and would not be now. (Lord Melbourne's pragmatic advice, for one, went unheeded. 'Be not over solicitous about education,' he counselled Queen Victoria on 1 December 1841, when her son was a mere four weeks old. 'It may be able to do much, but it does not do as much as is expected from it. It may mould and correct the character, but it rarely alters it'.) [4] Surround him with persons of formidable rectitude, and the Prince, like some rare, hothouse plant, would grow to be a paragon of his species. So his father believed, who prided himself on being largely untainted by the world – even indeed by the example of his own unprincipled father, Ernest I, Duke of Saxe-Coburg and Gotha.[5]

Prince Albert looked to his former tutor and mentor, Baron Stockmar, to help shape his son's education. Everything that this physician of subtle mind proposed came with sedulous justification; as his biographer iterates, he was determined 'to save . . . the Prince of Wales from the contagion of a dangerous heredity'.[6] On 6 March 1842, when the Prince was just four months old (and Princess Victoria, the Princess Royal, was in her sixteenth month), Stockmar submitted his 'Memorandum on the Education of the Royal Children', a thesis he was to amplify four years later. 'Whatever was thought blameworthy' in the sons of George III (George IV, the Duke of York and William IV apart) 'was sought for in their foreign education': their vices were imported ones. So the Prince's education 'should be thoroughly *moral* and thoroughly *English*'.

> [It] should . . . nowise tend to make him a demagogue or a moral enthusiast but a man of calm, profound, comprehensive understanding imbued with a deep conviction of the indispensable necessity of practical morality to the welfare of both Sovereign and the people . . . Above all attainments, the Prince should be trained to freedom of thought, and a firm reliance on the inherited power of sound principles, political, moral and religious, to sustain themselves and produce practical good, when left in a fair field of development.[7]

Troubled at the revolutionary landscape in many European states, Stockmar wished above all that the Prince should become an embodiment of stability, a monarch stamped with 'an impression of the sacred character of all existing institutions'; if not actively resisting change, he should not 'take the lead' in it, but 'act as a balance-wheel on the movement of the social body'.[8] It was the Prince's lot, then, to be prepared for so pivotal a calling, yet no concessions were made to temperament, or to his commonplace intellectual abilities. When his governess, Lady Lyttelton, told the Queen how the four-year-old liked 'violent exercise and enjoyment of life',[9] her comment was meant as strong criticism. As to winning his father's regard, the Prince always fell short of the mark. He would carry his father's ambitions, but could do nothing to allay his jealousy: after all, Prince Albert's influence as Consort – indeed as King in everything but name – would be as dust should the Queen die before him.[10]

The royal nursery was witness to attrition from the beginning. The Prince's arrival there, to join his sister, Princess Victoria (Vicky), was enough to see off their worthy governess, Mrs Southey, whose regime was considered lax. The Princess greeted the arrival of her successor, Lady Lyttelton, with screams of 'unconquerable horror', although the Prince appeared unaffected by the change and was in 'crowing spirits'. However, the new governess was soon deploring his 'passions and stampings', which presaged the violent frustrations to come.[11] He would never prove tractable. The Prince could not stomach the unremitting concentration demanded of him from an early age. And there were early signs of learning difficulties. Although his sister Victoria was only eleven months his senior, he was soon way behind her in learning. The Queen was quick to make unfavourable comparisons: the Prince was not articulate like his sister, 'but rather babyish in accent' and 'altogether backward in language'.[12] By the time he was four, Lady Lyttelton was exercising considerable patience over his wilful inattention and incessant interruptions. These were frustrations of a kind strikingly similar to those we associate today with attention deficit disorder. As an expert in the field explains:

> Some children are not only uncooperative; they are intensely oppositional . . . often mouthy, argumentative, and extremely demanding . . . quick to mount a protracted temper tantrum . . . outrageously presumptuous and brazen with parents and siblings alike, acting as though their every wish must immediately be fulfilled.[13]

All the while, the Prince was adding to his own catalogue of outbursts. Lady Lyttelton told of him escaping under the table, upsetting his books, and 'sundry other *anti-studious* practices'.[14] His attention span was disconcertingly short, particularly when asked to learn something new or difficult: he would hang his head, the Queen recorded, whereupon there would 'invariably' follow 'one of his fits of unmanageable temper'.[15] At ten these were described by his father's librarian, Dr Becker, as eruptions of 'blind destructive rage', during which 'he takes everything at hand and throws it with the greatest violence against the wall or window, without thinking the least of the consequences of what he is doing; or he stands in the corner stamping with his legs and screaming in the most dreadful manner'.[16] Yet, a tutor reported, when the fury burnt out the Prince 'always evinced a most forgiving disposition'.

Evidently, Prince Albert's interventions were both firm and grave. When the Prince once chose to stand drumming his fingers on one of the schoolroom windows (which reached from ceiling to floor) rather than learn his tutor's lesson at his desk, he took violent exception to the remonstrations of his governess, Miss Hildyard. 'I won't learn . . . and I won't stand in the corner, for I am the Prince of Wales,' he protested, whereupon he kicked out a pane of glass. As Miss Hildyard reached hastily for the bell-pull to call for assistance, he kicked out a second. When his father saw the wreckage he resorted to Bible and birch rod. St Paul, he decided, would serve his purpose well. 'Now I say, that the heir, as long as he is a child, differeth nothing from a servant, though he be lord of all; but is under tutors and governors until the time appointed of his father,' declared the apostle. Whereupon Prince Albert elucidated: 'It is true that you are the Prince of Wales, and if you conduct yourself properly you may become a man of high station, and even after the death of your mother you may be King of England. But now you are a little boy who must obey your tutors and governors.' Then, in summary justification of the beating that followed, he took his cue from Proverbs: 'He that spareth the rod hateth his son, but he that loveth him chasteneth him betimes,' he pronounced over the Prince, who found himself thrust across a footstool.[17]

At the age of seven and a half the boy's education was 'taken *entirely away* from women'[18] (as the Queen had proposed when he was still an infant) and put into the hands of his first tutor, a thirty-year-old Eton master, Henry Birch, who was forbidden to meddle with Prince Albert's educational regime in any regard. Every day excepting Sunday, Birch taught English, arithmetic and geography within a five-hour timetable. (The Prince never enjoyed reading; it was said that he rarely read a book right through in later life.) He was tutored in German and French, each of which he had studied for an hour a day since the age of six; he could read a German book and converse in the language by the age of five – an early assimilation which bequeathed him a guttural burr in pronouncing the letter 'r', something he never lost. And there were further lessons in handwriting, drawing and music. His father, meanwhile, expected tutors to send him regular, detailed reports on all the Prince's schoolroom activities.

All his tutors had their trials. Birch, in his first year, was close to despairing of the Prince's rages and general excitability, which would dissolve into displays of dumb insolence, or leave him too exhausted to work. Even when a mood lifted he was rarely predictable: his tutor found it 'almost impossible to follow out any thoroughly systematic plan of management or thoroughly regular course of study' because his pupil 'was so different on different days'.[19] Yet even as the Prince was enduring his studies with ill grace, Birch could see much good in him ('a very keen perception of right and wrong' as well as '*numerous* traits of a very amiable and affectionate disposition')[20] and recognized the budding charm that became the man, and went far to compensate for what amounted to a mis-education. Though later he felt he had failed the Prince in the schoolroom, he was able to tell Stockmar: 'I seem to have found the key to his heart.'[21] (Lord Fisher said of the future king – by way of valediction: 'He wasn't clever, but he always did the right thing, which is better than brains'; Fisher thought the King's charm 'some magnetic touch'.)[22]

Though Birch recognized early signs of social instinct, the Prince had no contact with boys of his own age until his tutor pressed for it, but was continually in the company of older persons with whom he was 'the centre round which everything seemed to move', a circumstance that mirrored the Queen's own friendless – in her case sibling-less – childhood. (Out of fear that another might win her affection and undermine her mother's, the Duchess of Kent's, authority, she was allowed no society – indeed, saw no one unless a third party was present. Instead, her adult dolls were her surrogate friends – 132 of them – dressed to represent characters in the plays and operas she had attended.)

Birch felt that the Prince needed some 'standard by which to measure his own powers'; he knew that nothing a tutor, or even parent, can say 'has such influence as intercourse with sensible boys of the same age, or a little older, unconsciously teaching by example'.[23] Yet a public school education for the Prince was never considered: such places were held in deep distrust by his parents as being centres of doubtful rectitude and jungle law. When visits by a number of Eton boys were arranged (albeit grudgingly), Prince Albert was always present. The Etonians (among them William Gladstone, the future prime minister's son, and Charles Wynne-Carrington, one of the few friends the Prince would later address by their Christian names) would call the Prince 'Sir'; then, when his father's back was turned, he would likely abuse them. Yet he craved companionship, and whenever his younger brother, Prince Alfred (b. 1844), joined him in the schoolroom the Prince was always calmer for his being there.

Into the third year of his appointment Birch was 'like a colt let out of a dark stable into a green field' whenever he took a break from his duties.[24] He was soon to resign in favour of ordination and the rich living of Prestwich-with-Oldham, in the gift of Lord Wilton. Neither parent was inclined to regret his going. Prince Albert was a closet agnostic who objected to the future Defender of the Faith learning his catechism. To him the Bible was merely a useful repository of ethics; as for the Churches and their 'formularies', they 'ought to be discouraged'.[25] The Queen, who was ill at ease in the presence of austerity, found it expedient to assume that Birch was harbouring High Church views: she had thought it necessary to advise him against declining 'innocent amusements'.[26] Though Stockmar in his 'Memorandum' advocated that the Prince '*must unquestionably* be trained' in the doctrine of the Church of England, he was none the less equivocal on this point, advocating at the same time 'a sound morality' founded upon 'the deductions of philosophy', not upon 'mere religious belief'; he would sooner have the Prince taught by a man of scientific mind in tune with 'the spirit of the age'.[27] It was a Whiggish aspiration. There were no absolutes in 'the March of Mind' – only 'debate, doubt, contradiction and examination', as Lord Melbourne understood; rational natures 'could never be warmed by belief'.[28]

The ten-year-old Prince took Birch's departure badly. 'You can't wonder if we are rather dull today,' he told his successor. 'We are very sorry Mr Birch is gone. It is very natural, is it not? He has been with us so long.'[29] The new tutor, Frederick Waymouth Gibbs (a Trinity Fellow), was a dry-as-dust barrister and religious dissenter. His regime proved utterly unsympathetic. Instruction now lasted seven hours, not five, and included riding, exercise and drill. Within days of his appointment Gibbs was confiscating a paper knife with which the Prince had threatened his brother Alfred; there was hair pulling, anger and general disobedience. These early weeks became eight years under the tutelage of a man the Prince grew to detest. Indeed, Gibbs's diary entries testify to a failing educational experiment:

> Began better – we finished the sums left unfinished yesterday – but walking, [The Prince] was excited and disobedient . . . going where I wished not to go . . . and breaking and plucking the trees in the copse. I played with them but it only partially succeeded. On the Terrace he quarrelled with, and struck,

P. Alfred, and I had to hasten home . . . A very bad day. The P. of W. has been like a person half silly. I could not gain his attention. He was very rude, particularly in the afternoon, throwing stones in my face . . . Afterwards I had to do some arithmetic . . . he became passionate, the pencil was flung to the end of the room, the stool was kicked away, and he was hardly able to apply at all. That night he woke twice. Next day he became very passionate because I told him he must not take out a walking stick . . . Later in the day he became violently angry because I wanted some Latin done. He flung things about – made grimaces – called me names, and would not do anything for a long time . . . During his lesson in the morning he was running first in one place, then in another. He made faces, and spat. Dr Becker [his German tutor] complained of his great naughtiness. There was a great deal of bad words.[30]

The range of the Prince's studies would no doubt have taxed the most willing public schoolboy. As well as mastering Latin, he was expected to write historical and biographical essays in any of three languages – English, German and French. Reading was restricted almost entirely to prescribed literary masterpieces. Moreover, some of his learning appears to have been piecemeal. Gibbs explains how, rather than follow 'the strictly logical Course of Mathematics followed in the Schools', the first principles of algebra and geometry were skimped in favour of their precise application to 'Gunnery, Fortifications and the Mechanical Arts'. True to Prince Albert's appetite for scientific enquiry, everything should be done to foster a like interest. The Prince was put to 'regular' study of 'Chemistry and its kindred sciences, with the Arts dependent upon them'. Eminent scientists were brought to Windsor solely for his benefit; and he attended the Royal Institution, where, among others, he heard Michael Faraday lecture on metals and William Ellis on political economy.

Even Gibbs would acknowledge that too much was being expected of his pupil: pursuits that other boys might have welcomed because they provided light relief only added to 'the strain of exhaustion'. There was gardening and housekeeping (in the children's kitchen at Osborne House, his parents' holiday palazzo on the Isle of Wight), forestry and farming, carpentry and building. The only activity to promise delight was dancing, which became a proud and defining accomplishment of his manhood – a pleasure he would indulge with uncommon panache. But even this social grace drew parental caution: to counter any effeminacy in bearing which dancing might encourage, both Princes did regular military drill under the direction of a sergeant so they would be sure to develop 'manly frame[s]'.[31]

All this irksome activity was proving counter-productive: the Prince was constantly as 'a person who has had too strong a tonic', Gibbs declared.[32] When an anxious Prince Albert consulted a phrenologist, Dr George Combe, even the Prince's physical comfort was due for upsetting. Combe's reading of the princely cranium confirmed what was already clear to everyone – that the Prince was a person of unexceptional intellect. This of itself, the doctor confirmed, could lead to 'strong self-will, at times obstinacy', behaviour which he advised could be redressed by exposure to salubrious air – though not apparently to the sun, and not in flat places, or where the soil might be wet; cold baths and a firm bed he deemed essentials.[33] Dr Voisin, the Prince's sensible French tutor, distained all such sophistry: 'Make him climb trees! Run! Leap! Row! Ride!' was his uncluttered advice.

Dr Becker mixed kindness with severity, the latter being Prince Albert's preference, which merely provoked violent fury in the Prince. His startling prognosis, which he hoped would persuade Prince Albert to modify his son's regime, evidently cut no ice; after all, in everything concerning the Prince's education the stakes were high. Yet Dr Becker was witnessing a weakness that

> is in frequent cases increased to such an extent as to produce a total incapacity. A mental pursuit for about five minutes may sometimes be possible in such a case, but after this an exhaustion ensues, in consequence of which any attempt towards making an impression is just as unsuccessful as with a sleeping person. Neither kindness nor severity can succeed in such a case . . . To anyone who knows the functions performed by the nerves in the human body, it is quite superfluous to demonstrate that these outbreaks of passion, especially with so tender a child as the Prince of Wales in his moments of greatest mental exhaustion, must be *destructive* to the child.

Dr Becker's reading of the Prince's psychology was not without empathy. His parents should give '*encouragement* of every kind . . . to a high degree', and not resort to mockery, which was their wont.[34] ('Poor Princey,' thought Lady Lyttelton, when a naïve effort to please was howled down: 'Mama, is not a pink the female of a carnation?', he had told her.)[35] In later life he could not tolerate chaffing.

There was much to encourage a feeling of inadequacy. It was not in the Queen's nature to bestow approval on a son whose shortcoming was a constant reminder of her own failings as a young girl.[36] And whenever she compared him to Prince Albert, the result was invariably unfavourable: '*None* of you can *ever* be proud enough of being the *child* of such a Father who has not his *equal* in this world – so great, so good, so faultless,' she insisted.[37] It was a familiar refrain. But what his mother withheld was beyond his father's capacity to grant. If his growing son increasingly feared him, so be it: little, indeed, might be wrought through sentiment. Someone who attested to the Prince's fear was his Etonian friend, Charles Wynne-Carrington, who thought Prince Albert 'a proud, shy, stand-offish man, not calculated to make friends easily with children'; he recorded how, 'for sheer alarm at seeing him', he had himself once fallen off a see-saw, nearly breaking his neck.[38]

While the young Prince countered the overweening demands of his tutors by resorting to cussed silence – Gibbs deplored a habit of refusing to give answers he knew well enough – his ignorance found no hiding place once he reached adolescence. Examined in ancient and modern history at the age of sixteen, he mustered a mere six and a half lines in the two and a half hours allowed him, but even this brevity was unconvincing: 'The war of Tarrentum, it was between Hannibal the Carthaginian General and the Romans, Hannibal was engaged in a war with it, for some time . . .' he began. Often, expectations were absurdly unrealizable, as when Sir James Stephen, Professor of Modern History at Cambridge, thought it proper that he should improve his spelling by mastering the etymology of every Latinate word basic to English. As Elizabeth Longford, the Queen's biographer, suggests, 'the nadir of futility' was the Prince's attendance at a Latin play performed by the boys of Westminster School. It was the Queen's decided opinion that he 'understood not a word of it'.[39]

What flattered this unenlightened educational experiment was the 'incorrigible amiability'[40] which survived it. The Prince came to manhood lacking intellectual or spiritual interests, yet with immense psychological reserves against his parents' vitiating disapproval. But other gifts he would find amply rewarding, not least when enjoying the peripatetic, great-house hospitality that largely sustained him – notably an unfailing memory for names and an appetite for miscellaneous knowledge with which to amuse his hosts. Resentment – if it figured at all during the long wait for accession – was not something to get the better of a surprisingly well-adjusted disposition. And if after his mother's death on 22 January 1901

27

(when he was fifty-nine) he saw to the removal from the royal residences of each and every one of his parents' effects, so that he would never have to look again upon reminders of either of them,[41] he had been scrupulous during her lifetime in matters of courtly deference, and had even made a fist of appearing affectionate.

There had been spontaneity enough in the Prince's childhood to belie the supposedly stuffy partialities of a young, yet somewhat matronly, Queen. Indeed, she found the nursery 'irresistible'.[42] Prince Albert would haul the Prince (called 'Bertie' within the family circle) and his sister Victoria ('Pussy') around in a basket, crawl with them on the floor, or dandle them each on a knee. Birthdays and festivals were full of family benevolence and were never overlooked. Seasonal junketing invariably comprised sledge-rides, skating (at Frogmore) and the making of snowmen in winter, one of which measured twelve feet high. It was built at Claremont House, near Esher, home of the Queen's uncle, the eccentric King Leopold of the Belgians (who, to the children's delight, sported a wig and feather boa). The Queen's 'missed' childhood she could now enjoy vicariously: she fell in with the children's games, danced quadrilles with the seven-year-old Prince and caught moths with him on summer evenings.[43] In summer, too, there was riding and sea-bathing in a contraption moored offshore at Osborne House. And in the spirit of the Great Exhibition, the exotica of a shrinking Victorian world were brought to Windsor as entertainment: for example, 'General' Tom Thumb, the American midget, made an appearance, as did Wombell's famed menagerie (performing in the Quadrangle) and a group of Red Indians, naked to the waist and in war paint.

There was family yachting at Cowes, journeys by yacht and train to Ireland and (from 1848) to Balmoral, the Queen's and Prince Albert's new residence on the Tweed, when the Prince would be seen wearing the sailor suit which set the fashion for many another boy of his age. And it was on occasions like these that his wilful behaviour would sometimes receive a public airing – as when, on deck with his parents at Aberdeen dock when he was five, he would not stop playing with the tassels of a sofa on which the family were seated to receive a welcoming party. Anticipating yet another pull at a tassel, the Queen took him 'by the scruff of the neck', so a spectator recorded, 'hoisted the youngster over her knee . . . and gave him a sound spanking', during which the Prince 'kicked and bellowed quite as lustily as children of lower birth are wont to do'. The crowd's startled silence soon broke into laughter, and a blushing Queen repaired to the cabin to restore her dignity.[44]

Once, on the beach at Osborne, the Prince purposely upset a boy's basket of shells. 'You do that again and I'll lick you,' threatened the boy, at which the Prince held his ground (as the *Birmingham Journal* reported some time later): 'Put the shells into the basket, and see if I don't,' he retorted. Whereupon the stranger renewed his challenge: 'Now touch 'em again if you dare!' His temper now flaring, the Prince spilled the basket again and a fight ensued, which left him well bruised and bloody. When he returned to the Queen and confessed all, the local lad was summoned. The Queen could see for herself that justice was adequately done and told the Prince so. 'You have been rightly served, Sir . . . When you commit a like offence, I trust you will always receive a similar punishment.' She would make amends by providing for the local boy's education.[45]

In December 1847, when the Prince had barely outgrown his infancy, Prince Albert envisaged a future in which his son would be 'accustomed early to work with and for us, to have great confidence shewn him'.[46] It was never to be. Indeed, five years later, when the Queen needed to clear up an evident confusion in the ten-year-old Prince's mind about his place in the succession, this was one of few instances of either parent taking much account of their failing son's interest in his inheritance; 'he had always believed Vicky would succeed, but now he knew that in default of *him*, Affie (Prince Alfred) & another brother, if perhaps we have one, would come before Vicky'.[47] Yet short-lived as were Prince Albert's intentions for the Prince as he expressed them at the close of 1847, the spring that followed – one of revolutionary appetites in Europe – had all the royal families fearing for their futures. Political upheavals of differing intensity were affecting kingdoms as various as Hanover, Bavaria, Saxe-Coburg and Gotha, Naples, Portugal, Spain, and the multifarious peoples of the Habsburg Empire. On 17 March the Prussian King Frederick William IV (whose son was to marry the Princess Royal) bowed to bloodshed in the streets of Berlin and accepted an elected Parliament. Some weeks earlier, subterfuge was required to bring Louis Philippe and his queen safely to England after Parisians forced his abdication. 'They both look very *abbatu* . . . In short, humbled poor people they looked,' the Queen told King Leopold of the Belgians, whose own position remained secure.[48] When she wrote again in July, her family's prospects were foremost in her thoughts. 'When one thinks of one's children, their education, their future – and prays for them,' she admitted, 'I always think and say to myself: "Let them grow up fit for *whatever station* they may be placed in – *high or low*. This I never thought of before, but I *do* always now." '[49] On 10 April in London the planned gathering of some 20,000 Chartists to present their Third Petition to Parliament had so alarmed the Whig government as to have the royal family dispatched by train to safety on the Isle of Wight. (It turned out that forty supposed Chartists reported to have arrived at Cowes in June were a harmless party of Oddfellows on a Whitsun outing.)

In outcome, the English way of doing things survived the convulsions so securely that the Great Exhibition (with which our story began) was tantamount to a 'pageant of domestic peace'.[50] Yet almost immediately there were intimations of further power games to be played out in a Europe that the Prince would frequent keenly in later life. He was present (aged twelve) when the first troops were inspected before embarkation for the Crimea in February 1854, and in Hyde Park to see the Queen make the inaugural awards of the Victoria Cross. Nor did his parents balk at having him with them when they visited the wounded.

Two years earlier, on 18 November 1852, the Prince stood with his family on the new balcony at Buckingham Palace as the Duke of Wellington's bronze funeral car – a massive configuration of lions, symbols of victory, battle honours and arms[51] – was drawn towards St Paul's. It was as though a curtain was falling on a past fit for such a hero. The subject, as we have seen, of acute misgivings, the Prince would prove benignly suited to the demands of an age less 'peopled with Immortals'.[52]

2
Seeds of Approval

On a nine-day visit with his parents to Paris in August 1855 as guests of Louis Napoleon (III) and Empress Eugénie, the thirteen-year-old Prince had his first taste of the charms that would sweeten the dullest duty. He found the scented radiance and deep *décolletage* of the Empress's ladies-in-waiting, whom he partnered at a Versailles ball, utterly captivating.[1] The Empress outshone them all – a striking woman (recorded the Queen on her wedding day) of 'beautifully chiselled features . . . marble complexion . . . exquisitely proportioned figure and graceful carriage . . . the whole like a Poet's Vision'.[2] The Queen, who wore unfashionable poke bonnets and plain dress and habitually carried a voluminous white satin bag (embroidered with a poodle), could only appear dowdy by comparison.

The hospitality, unmatched by Windsor's best, was irresistible. On the night of the ball, Versailles was a blaze of reflected light from torches and from the chandeliers that seemingly multiplied in the palace's vast mirrors, while outside were fountains and a triumphal arch, surmounted with the arms of the two nations. A firework representation of Windsor's towers and battlements marked the opening of the ball.[3] What the Prince appreciated above all was the telling magnanimity of his hosts towards him, something he had no intention of going unrecorded when he made his farewells. 'I would like to be your son,' he confided to the Emperor.[4] Undoubtedly, the unbuttoned gaiety of the French Court provoked appetites that, in manhood, he would have slim cause to forgo. When he asked the Empress to persuade the Queen to let him and Princess Victoria extend their own stay, the Empress felt bound to insist that their parents could not do without them in England. 'Not do without us! Don't fancy that! They don't want us, and there are six more of us at home!' was a heartfelt retort.[5]

Gaiety had its price. On their return, when his parents went to Balmoral, the Prince was put to his studies at Osborne House to make up for lost time, with the promise of a walking tour in Dorset in the autumn which, it turned out, had to be cut short. In the uncongenial company of Gibbs and a groom-in-waiting, Colonel Cavendish, he stayed incognito at various inns, but his identity as Lord Renfrew was discovered. (A second tour the following year to the Lake District was happier for his having, in addition to three of his tutors, the company of four Etonians of like age.) But if Prince Albert had come to accept that there might be benefit to the Prince in having periods away from the family, this sop to independence was seen as yet another opportunity for improvement – an impatiently awaited sign of which his father noticed in an essay the Prince submitted before the West Country walk, entitled 'Friends and Flatterers'. A friend will 'tell you of your faults', but a flatterer 'lead[s] you into any imaginable vice', he opined in a piece that his tutor considered 'not fully worked up', but which he commended because 'the judgement shown was . . . right-minded'. Improvement or not, the father was always anticipating the son's backsliding. When he returned from the Lakes in May 1857 and was dispatched for four months to Königswinter on the Rhine to extend his knowledge of German language and literature, Prince Albert (on whom the title Prince Consort was conferred on 25 June) resumed his carping: 'In the absence of lessons,' he wrote, '. . . write to us a little more at length and give us your impressions of things, and not the mere bare facts.'

Many who met the Prince abroad thought well of him, including his father's equerry, Colonel Henry Ponsonby, who found him 'one of the nicest boys I ever saw, and very lively and pleasant'.[6] When, having dined well on the first evening of the visit, the Prince was seen to impart a kiss to a pretty girl, Ponsonby was not inclined to report the lapse to Windsor. On the other hand, William Gladstone, Chancellor of the Exchequer, who came to hear of it in a roundabout way, saw the meaningless kiss as a 'squalid little debauch' and evidence of a failed education; 'this sort of unworthy little indulgence is the compensation,' he told his wife Catherine.[7] It was not a stricture to trouble the Prince – who remained ignorant of it – yet it presaged a widespread view, reported by *The Times* on the day of the Queen's death in 1901, that in his private life the Prince had fully deserved censure for having been 'importuned by temptation in its most seductive forms'.

*

The Prince's transition to manhood filled the Prince Consort with such foreboding that he settled on removing him to White Lodge in Richmond Park, where, he said, 'away from the world' and in the sole company of picked men, 'no point of detail' was to be thought 'too minute to be important' in grooming him in the characteristics of a gentleman.[8] He now had a governor, Colonel Robert Bruce, a man 'full of ability', and the services of three equerries in Major Christopher Teesdale and Major Robert Lindsay (each of whom had won the VC in the Crimean War), and 'the moral and accomplished' Lord Valletort.[9] Their control over the Prince's movements was absolute. In a memorandum he received on 9 November 1858, his seventeenth birthday, he learnt that he was forbidden to leave the Lodge without his governor's permission, and that Bruce alone would determine who should accompany him. Henceforth he should understand that 'life is composed of duties, and in the due, punctual, and cheerful performance of them the true Christian, true soldier, and true gentleman is recognised'. (To mark his birthday, he received a new allowance of £500 a year, an increase on the £100 received since he was fifteen, and he was gazetted a lieutenant-colonel, although he had taken no examination and was not attached to a regiment.)

Rarely will the responsibilities that fall to a prince's equerries have been delineated so gravely. In a confidential memorandum to them, the Prince Consort places his reliance on the Prince founding his gentlemanly persona 'upon what he daily sees in them'; they will justify their 'flattering selection' insofar as the Prince's habits of life are 'inculcated and strengthened by association'. They, too, should be on their mettle. Putting aside consideration of the 'higher attributes of mind and feeling of a gentleman', the Prince Consort urges an awareness of what, in their own conduct and demeanour, may influence the Prince for good:

> The appearance, deportment and dress of a gentleman consists perhaps more in the absence of certain offences against good taste, and in a careful avoidance of vulgarities and exaggerations of any kind, however generally they may be the fashion of the day, than in the adherence to any rules which can be exactly laid down. A gentleman does not indulge in careless, self-indulgent, lounging ways, such as lolling in armchairs, or on sofas, slouching in his gait, or placing himself in unbecoming attitudes, with his hands in his pockets, or

in any position in which he appears to consult more the idle ease of the moment than the maintenance of decorum which is characteristic of a polished gentleman . . . He will borrow nothing from the fashions of the groom or the game-keeper, and whilst avoiding the frivolity and foolish vanity of dandyism, will take care that his clothes are of the best quality, well made, and suitable to his rank and position.

What might appear 'unobjectionable' in deportment and dress in the equerries' ordinary lives would be 'dangerous examples' for the Prince to copy; it should not be forgotten that theirs was an exceptional responsibility. (In manhood the Prince was punctilious in all matters of dress, and woe betide a member of his entourage who sported the slightest irregularity.)

As to manners, the Prince should practise those exacting skills by which the royal demeanour is universally recognized; no one, after all, 'will be more watched'. He must understand that

A prince should return every mark of respect, not only with the most punctilious exactitude, but with an appearance of goodwill and cordiality. A salute returned with the air of its being a bore is rather an affront than a civility. [He] should never say a harsh or a rude word to anybody, nor indulge in satirical or bantering expressions, by which the person to whom it is addressed may be lowered. As soon as the conversation of a prince makes his companion feel uncomfortable he is sure to have offended against some of the laws of good breeding.

In conversing with the Prince, his equerries should 'mark in their manner any approach to want of civility or rudeness towards themselves' if ever the Prince should attempt to take a liberty with them. Any kind of practical joke should be deemed unworthy.

What had long been his father's mantra – that the Prince should waste no opportunity to 'exercise the mind' – he reiterates here in urging upon them intelligent conversation and a knowledge of 'those studies and pursuits' which 'adorn society', among which he cites music, the fine arts, poetry, 'amusing' books or plays read aloud. More than likely, he grants, the Prince will show resistance in favour of 'mere games of cards and billiards, and idle gossiping talk', but if they will persevere in these improving interests themselves, then they may encourage the Prince to join them. Of this wholesale counsel of perfection – 'these minute points to be attended to' – the Prince Consort readily admits that his chosen three have been entrusted with what he calls 'something beyond the mere attendance of an Equerry'.[10]

Intimations, at first private, of failing health soon lent despairing urgency to his efforts to have the Prince prove the worth of the regime he was pursuing: he would exercise unremitting control to the last. Colonel Bruce – in whom was placed 'momentous trust' – must 'regulate all the Prince's movements, the distribution and employment of his time, and the occupation and details of his daily life.' No mentor's calling was more austere. Bruce was to instil in the Prince 'habits of reflection and self-denial, the strictest truthfulness and honour, above all, the conscientious discharge of his duty towards God and man'.[11] Even the Prince's religious observance was subject to scrutiny. When, aged sixteen, he had the worthy intention of receiving the sacrament three months after his confirmation, his father advised against what would be a precedent, since his parents did so only at Christmas and Easter.

There were further foreign visits, notably to Potsdam and Rome, with men handpicked so as to allow the Prince to gain every educational advantage from these travels. However, the presence of his accompanying tutors made a visit in November 1858 to his elder sister, Princess Victoria (lately married in London to Prince Frederick William of Prussia), less than fully gratifying. The couple's embarkation at Gravesend early in the year – all 'tears and snowdrift',[12] the Prince Consort recalled – had been a painful parting for the Prince, who, despite being a reluctant writer, was to maintain a regular correspondence with his sister, whom he knew to be his father's favourite. But with Prince Alfred earlier gone to the Navy, close sibling relations belonged now to the past.

The Prince appeared untroubled that both his parents were encouraging in his sister a degree of surrogate influence with him. While Bruce kept the Prince to several hours' serious study each day, his sister obeyed her father's wish that she hear him read aloud from improving books. Writing to her on 17 November, the Prince Consort made early mention of her brother's blossoming vanity:

> You will find Bertie grown up and improved. Do not miss any opportunity of urging him to hard work. Our united efforts must be directed to this end. Unfortunately, he takes no interest in anything but clothes, and again clothes. Even when out shooting he is more occupied with his trousers than with the

game! I am particularly anxious that he should have mental occupation . . .
Perhaps you could let him share in some of yours, lectures etc.

Instead of lectures there were dinners and balls. His hosts were charmed; and he took an immediate liking to his brother-in-law (the future Emperor, Frederick III), a man ten years his senior. On his return, the Queen was irritated that, in relating his experiences, the Prince would speak only of 'parties, theatres, [and of] what people said'. While his father now agreed that the Prince possessed 'remarkable social talent', he thought his intellect usually 'of no more use than a pistol packed in the bottom of a trunk if one were attacked in the robber-infested Apennines'.[13] He promptly dispatched him to Rome.

The Prince had done precious little to ameliorate the Queen's anxiety; she long held his prospects to be barely redeemable:

> I tremble at the thought of only three years and a half before us [she admitted to Princess Victoria shortly after her daughter's marriage] – when he will be of age and we can't hold him except by moral power! I try to shut my eyes to that terrible moment! He is improving very decidedly – but Oh! it is the improvement of such a poor or still more idle intellect. Oh! dear, what would happen if I were to die next winter. It is too awful a contemplation. His journal is worse a great deal than Affie's [Prince Alfred's] letters. And all from laziness. Still we must hope for improvement in essentials; but the greatest improvement I fear, will never make him fit for his position. His only safety – and the country's – is his implicit reliance in everything, on dearest Papa, that perfection of human beings![14]

Rome brought an iteration of schoolroom routine. Before breakfast each day he learnt by heart; Italian and classics tutors attended in the morning; an hour in the late afternoon was given to French. Otherwise there were enervating tours of classical sites, churches and museums in the company of guides recommended (in the main) by the President of the Royal Academy, Sir Charles Eastlake. Nor was the Prince to neglect the opportunity to read in archaeology and art, by which his father set much store – as he did in having eminent men at the Prince's dinner table, much of whose discourse will have passed effortlessly above his head. Notwithstanding, there were moments his father might have cherished. He made a good impression when conducting Major Teesdale round St Peter's and the Vatican, and he talked freely one night after dinner with the

American historian, John Lothrop Motley, about 'German literature, Goethe and Schiller, and objects of art in Rome'. Indeed, Motley's impression of the seventeen-year-old Prince was entirely favourable:

> [His] profile is extremely like that of the Queen. The complexion is pure, fresh, and healthy, like that of most English boys, his hair light brown, cut short, and curly. His eyes are bluish-grey, rather large, and very frank in his expression; his smile is very ready and genuine; his manners are extremely good. I have not had much to do with royal personages, but of those I have known I know none whose address is more winning, and with whom one feels more at one's ease.

Among unfamiliar faces, almost none were youthful. The Prince liked the company of a thirty-year-old diplomat, Odo Russell, who became a long-standing friend – as did the black-bearded young artist, Frederick Leighton, upon whose death the Prince told of 'knowing him . . . ever since I was a boy (at Rome)'.[15] And it was through Leighton that he had something material by which to remember the visit. In his studio was a delectable portrait of a model, Nanna Risi, at ease in a harem. 'I admired three beautiful portraits of a Roman woman each representing the same person in a different attitude,' he tamely mentioned in his journal. The canvas was already sold, but the purchaser agreed to let the Prince acquire it if Leighton would make him a copy. The Prince was delighted.[16]

Home again at the end of June 1859 (he had been away seven months), the Prince was installed a Knight of the Garter. By late summer his father had tightened the academic tourniquet. While his parents holidayed at Balmoral, the Prince was to endure intensive cramming at Holyroodhouse in preparation for a spell at Oxford – being 'whipped to the Isis', *Punch* thought it.[17] He was to read history, law and applied science. As the Prince Consort envisaged, 'the only use of Oxford is that it is a place of *study*, a refuge from the world and its claims'. He wished to have the college system set aside, ostensibly to keep the Prince free from overmuch association with his fellow undergraduates, a case he presented with his usual, high idealism. Given that the Prince's 'position and life *must* be different from that of the other undergraduates', he must be seen to belong to the university as a whole, as he 'will always belong to the whole nation'.[18] However, at the insistence of the Vice-Chancellor, Dr Francis Jeune, some concession was made to Oxford's 'traditional airs'[19] and the Prince was admitted to Christ Church on the understanding that he attend college lectures – specially prepared for him – in the company of six chosen undergraduates. (He was known to fellow undergraduates as 'Wales of Christ Church',[20] but they would always rise to him when he entered a room, even at the Union of which he was elected an honorary member.) He was seen occasionally at university lectures and was regularly in chapel, but lived independently with Major-General Bruce (recently promoted) and Major Teesdale at Frewin Hall, an uninviting residence off Cornmarket. General Bruce was to be 'entirely master' of the society the Prince should keep.

The rapport that the Prince's university mentors established with him cast in a poor light the regard of those who had reared him. He made what proved to be long friendships, for example, with Dean Liddell of Christ Church and his wife and with Arthur Penrhyn Stanley, Professor of Ecclesiastical History (with whom the twenty-year-old Prince would tour Egypt, Palestine and Syria). Dr Liddell's assessment of the Prince's character at Oxford was unequivocal: he thought him 'the nicest fellow possible, so simple, naïf, ingenuous, and modest, and moreover with extremely good wits; possessing also the royal faculty of never forgetting a face'.[21]

While the Prince's pleasures were undoubtedly circumscribed, it appears he was not entirely restrained. For physical recreation, his parents suggested tennis and racquets, at which he performed poorly, but with the encouragement of two members of the raffish Bullingdon Club, a philanderer, Frederick Johnstone, and a son of the cloth, Henry (later Viscount) Chaplin, he rode to hounds with the South Oxfordshire. His girth was already attesting to the effects of good dining – from the age of fifteen he was allowed his own chef – and he had no difficulty in keeping from Bruce the existence of agreeable smoking companions. (It was said to be on the voyage home from Rome that he smoked the first of the cigars that we associate with his style of life.)

'H.R.H. acquitted himself admirably, and seems pleased with everything, himself included.'[22] This was General Bruce's tart opinion during the Prince's tour of Canada and America in the summer of 1860: the die, it seems, was cast. While his entourage manoeuvred with tact whenever the Canadian visit provided excuse for a flexing of sectarian muscle (in a land not yet settled into Confederation), the Prince lapped up the attention, much of it duly recorded by *The Times*, the

Illustrated London News and the *New York Herald*. It was a way of filling the Long Vacation and saved the Queen – who disliked venturing far – from the obligation to cross the Atlantic herself. For the Prince, who was naïvely ripe for the razzmatazz of celebrity and performed accordingly, these few months must have been the time of his life. ('God bless his pretty face and send him a good wife!' exclaimed the wife of the Archdeacon of St John's, Newfoundland, in a letter to relatives in England.)

He delivered countless short speeches, written by his father or the Duke of Newcastle (Secretary of State for the Colonies), and had inescapable opportunity for exercising the prerogative of patient listening: at St John's alone, his first Canadian landfall, then little more than a fishing station, he sat through fourteen speeches of welcome at a Government House reception. His duties (he became adept with silver trowels), the constant travel by steamer or train and the soaking Canadian weather apart, he cherished the limelight. The royal routes were garlanded; fireworks lit the sky; the Prince's name or face, or his feathers, appeared on innumerable cheapjack collectables – even, a journalist recorded, beneath the gravy on your plate as you dined out. Few matched the Prince's stamina on the dance floor. On one occasion he stood out for only two of twenty-four dances; on another, as the *New York Herald* reported, 'he whispered soft nothings to the ladies as he passed them in the dance, directed them how to go right, & shook his finger at those who mixed [up] the figures'. Safe to say, the *New York Herald* was not read at Windsor: 'His Royal Highness looks as if he might have a very susceptible nature,' the writer contended, 'and has already yielded to several twinges in the region of his midriff.'[23] Of more overt excitement had been a hurtling descent down some rapids in a barge at a timber slide by the Ottawa river, a heart-stopping moment for those who watched it, one which his parents saw reproduced in the pages of the *Illustrated London News* when it was too late to matter.

In October, during a stay at a dour White House as guest of President Buchanan (who allowed no dancing there), the Prince was conducted to Mount Vernon, there to plant a chestnut tree at George Washington's grave. In a letter to the Queen at the close of the tour, the President was full of praise for the Prince who

had passed through a long ordeal for a person of his years, and his conduct throughout has been such as became his age and station . . . In our domestic circle he won all hearts. His free and ingenuous intercourse with myself evinced both a kind heart and a good understanding. I shall ever cherish the warmest wishes for his welfare.[24]

After Washington, he travelled south to Richmond, Virginia – where his hosts thought it politic to cancel a slave auction (Abraham Lincoln of Illinois, the champion of abolition, was destined to be little known no longer) – then, by way of Philadelphia to New York, which lionised him in the manner New Yorkers do best. Wearing his colonel's uniform, he rode up Broadway in an open barouche accompanied by 6,000 militiamen; an estimated 300,000 lined the route. The Duke of Newcastle told of the crowds 'worked up almost to madness and yet self-restrained within the bounds of the most perfect courtesy'. All of which smacked of the emotional contagion, which, in our own time, sustains the cult of celebrity. 'I never dreamt that we should be received as we are,' he told his mother.[25] The Prince had merely set the precedent – as a versifier and witness to the New York frenzy testified:

> They have stolen his gloves, and purloined his cravat;
> Even scraped a souvenir from the nap of his hat.
> In short, they have followed him, hustled and shoved him,
> To convince him more fully how dearly they loved him.[26]

Contrary weather in the Atlantic meant that only four days were left to him once he returned home in November before he must be at Oxford to complete his term. In January (1861) he transferred to Trinity College, Cambridge. Rooms were available to him during the day at the Master's Lodge, but he resided four miles from the city at Lady King's Madingley Hall. Its saving grace was a private staircase adjacent to his quarters, which he used to strategic advantage. This prolongation of university life was merely fostering ennui, something he challenged, at least once, by escaping by train to London. 'I fancy the little spirit he has is quite broken, as his remarks are commonplace and very slow,' reported a fellow undergraduate, Nathaniel Rothschild, who told his parents that the Prince was allowed only a single horse for the hunting field (while his equerries had none). Rothschild mentions the Prince's interest in riddles and his fondness for strong cigars. Given that the Prince's allowance was unexceptional, what followed was ominously prescient: 'If he followed the bent of his own inclination, it strikes me he would take to gambling and certainly keep away from the law lectures he is obliged to go to now.'[27] The Queen, meanwhile, continued her carping, on one occasion criticizing his posture. He had 'got into the habit of sitting quite bent, on one side, or lolling on the table . . . This dear child will NOT do for *any* person in your position . . . I feel quite *pained* at what has the effect of ill breeding or nonchalance.'[28]

By the summer the Prince Consort had little fight left in him. He was barely sleeping, through overwork on the Queen's behalf following the death of her mother, the Duchess of Kent, a loss which saw her relapse into a characteristic, grief-stricken torpor, punctuated by bouts of hysteria. The Prince Consort's other ailments – lost appetite, fits of shivering and general debility – were to invite, as his condition deteriorated, a varied diagnosis that encompassed typhoid fever and pneumonia. Amid this quotidian blend of grief and ill health, the young Prince's seduction by a young actress, Nellie Clifden, was considered by his mother to have precipitated the Prince Consort's death.

The Prince first met Clifden in Ireland. Against his better judgement, an ailing Consort had granted him a spell of army service – something he had earlier opposed, believing that life in a regimental mess would invite moral contamination. After a guest night at the Curragh camp near Dublin, his brother Grenadier Guards officers saw to it that the girl awaited him in his bed. (It was said that he later brought her to Windsor.) By the time his parents got to hear of it from a gossipmonger, George Byng, 7th Viscount Torrington, then a lord-in-waiting, the affair was already going the round of the London clubs. Inevitably, a nervous, weary Prince Consort could not accommodate a sowing of wild oats in the manner of many an aristocratic father, but professed moral outrage. Writing to the Prince on 20 November, he spelled out what he feared might be the consequences. What, he posited, if Clifden were to claim that a child was his?

> If you were to try and deny it, she can drag you into a Court of Law to force you to own it, and there with you in the witness box, she will be able to give before a greedy Multitude disgusting details of your profligacy for the sake of convincing the Jury; yourself cross-examined by a railing indecent attorney and hooted and yelled at by a Lawless Mob!! Oh, horrible prospect, which this person has in her power, any day to realize! and to break your poor parents' hearts![29]

Suitably shaken and contrite, the Prince assured him that the affair was at an end. 'The past is the past,'[30] his father owned with uncommon magnanimity to a son he was capable of liking, but whom he never understood.

The Prince Consort had told the Queen of their son's predicament a week earlier, sparing her 'the disgusting details'; it was 'the *one* great sorrow which cast [the Prince Consort] down', she recorded.[31] 'Oh! that boy – much as I pity him I never can or shall look at him without a shudder . . .'[32] It was an established position, which the Prince gave her little cause to mitigate through the forty years left to her.

The Prince Consort died on 14 December 1861. By January, the Queen was writing to Princess Victoria in familiar vein:

If you had seen what I saw, if you had seen Fritz struck down, day by day get worse and finally die, I doubt you could bear the sight of the one who was the cause; or if you could not feel, as I do, a shudder. Still more, if you saw what little deep feeling about anything there is . . . I feel daily, hourly, something which is too dreadful to describe. Pity him, I do . . . But more you cannot ask. This dreadful, dreadful cross kills me![33]

3
Marriage

The liaison with Nellie Clifden had an immediate consequence. When the Prince was first introduced to his prospective bride, the sixteen-year-old Princess Alexandra of Denmark, at Speier in the Rhineland in September 1861, his close family were at a loss in the weeks that followed to account for a lukewarm response to an 'outrageously beautiful'[1] young woman. His sister, Princess Victoria, felt a 'great sadness when I think of that sweet lovely flower . . . which would make most men fire and flames' having made so slight an impression. 'If she fails to kindle a flame – none will ever succeed in doing so.' The Queen put the Prince's hesitancy down to 'a sudden fear of marriage' and of having children while so young.[2] But then, she did not think him 'capable of enthusiasm about anything in the world',[3] an opinion Princess Victoria would not gainsay; she understood how readily his head appeared to rule his heart. 'I love him with all my heart and soul,' she wrote, 'but I do not envy his future wife.'[4]

The Prince Consort, who thought the Prince's priorities 'a little confused', felt it necessary to spell out the tortuous diplomacy that had been exercised on his behalf in bringing about a meeting with the Princess. If she and her parents were to be invited to England – as the Prince Consort wished – further hesitancy would be unacceptable: '*We* must be *quite sure*, and *you must thoroughly understand*, that the interview is obtained in order that you may propose to the young lady.' Moreover, were she to return home without the Prince having made his intentions plain, he will have brought 'public disgrace upon [himself] and us'.[5]

*

Princess Alexandra's late arrival in the reckoning as a possible bride for the Prince was due to a cocktail of antipathies casting the Danish Court in an unfavourable light. The Queen was known to support the Prussians in their hereditary claim to Denmark's largely German-speaking Duchies of Schleswig and Holstein (an issue of simmering complexity), and she later appeared unmoved when, in the tenth month of the royal marriage, Prussia turned aggressor and secured a gateway to the Baltic seaboard and the port of Kiel. (Later, the elderly Lord Palmerston declared the 'Schleswig-Holstein question' to be one which only three men had understood: the Prince Consort, who by then was dead; a Foreign Office official of questionable sanity; and he himself – who could remember nothing about it.)6 Furthermore, the Queen had no wish for closer ties with a family she thought tainted with decadence – among whom the drunken King Frederick VII (Princess Alexandra's father, Prince Christian, was his heir) had contracted, after two divorces, a morganatic marriage to a third wife. Equally unacceptable to the Queen were Princess Christian's Hesse-Cassel relations, whose lively summer gatherings at the castle of Rumpenheim, near Frankfurt, were renowned for fomenting matrimonial intrigues.

Meanwhile, mere suspicion of a betrothal detrimental to German interests could be relied on to breed fabricated stories intended to disparage the Princess's family. Louise of Prussia (Crown Princess Victoria's sister-in-law) insisted that Prince Christian was himself a drunkard and that his wife 'bore a very bad reputation'.7 Duke Ernst of Saxe-Coburg and Gotha was not alone in peddling the accusation that Princess Alexandra's father had sired illegitimate children and that she was a flirt. When the Duke raised his objections with his brother, the Prince Consort, on 22 July 1861 (a little over a year before Princess Alexandra accepted the Prince's proposal of marriage), they were curtly dismissed: 'What has that got to do with you? We have no choice.'8

Indeed. The bevy of Germanic candidates were an unattractive lot, apart that is from the '*quite lovely*' Princess Marie of Hohenzollern-Sigmaringen, who, as a Roman Catholic, could not be considered. Baron Stockmar favoured the dowdy Elizabeth of Wied (the poet Carmen Sylva, afterwards Queen of Rumania), whom Crown Princess Victoria did not consider 'at all *distinguée* looking'. Princess Marie of Altenburg was 'shockingly dressed' and 'always with her most disagreeable mother'. Others, like the Weimar princesses, were either plain or too young or, not being '*distinguée*' (Crown Princess Victoria's judgement again), were 'certainly the opposite to Bertie's usual taste'.9

With the trawl of Northern European princesses complete, it was a photograph of Princess Alexandra that began the dismantling of the Queen's misgiving:

I send you now a photograph of Prince Christian's lovely daughter [wrote Crown Princess Victoria]. I have seen several people who have seen her of late – and who give such accounts of her beauty, her charm, her amiability, her frank manner and many excellent qualities. I though it right to tell you all this in Bertie's interest, though I as Prussian cannot wish Bertie should ever marry her . . . I must say on the photograph I think her lovely and just the style Bertie admires, but I repeat that an alliance with Denmark would be a misfortune for us here.

The Queen thought the Princess 'indeed lovely', but her reply carried a barb: 'what a pity she is who she is!'[10] Sir Charles Phipps, Keeper of the Privy Purse, put her regret in telling perspective, pointing out to the Queen that 'the misconduct of relations' ought not to receive undue consideration when in all other respects there was none to rival her. 'It is of the *first importance* that the Prince of Wales's wife should have beauty, agreeable manners, and the power of attracting people to her,' he told her; these were attributes he believed the Princess possessed 'in a remarkable degree'. Perhaps the Queen might consider how, 'with a virtuous and well-educated girl, the ill-repute of some members of her family usually adds to her horror of vice'.[11]

The couple's first meeting – orchestrated by Crown Princess Victoria – took place in the cathedral at Speier in the presence of the Princess's parents on the morning of 24 September 1861, just short of a year before their engagement was made public. Looking at frescoes with the Bishop at a discreet distance, the Prince's sister contrived to keep the party in view, noticing how 'the reverse of indifference on both sides soon became quite unmistakable'. She was able to tell her parents that in 'a quarter of an hour [the Prince] thought her lovely'.[12] However, when the Prince next visited Balmoral (on 30 September), the Queen was noticing how nervous he seemed 'about deciding anything yet'.[13] On 9 November, a week after his twentieth birthday, the Prince Consort was writing to him 'with a heavy heart',[14] having heard the gossip associating him with Nellie Clifden.

The Prince's dalliance and the illness that hastened the Prince Consort's death – events inseparable in the Queen's mind – left her wishing to put immediate distance between herself and her heir: in place, she said, of their 'constant contact which is more than ever unbearable to me',[15] he was sent on a five-month tour of Palestine and the Near East in February 1862, with Arthur Penrhyn Stanley acting as guide (the Arthur of *Tom Brown's Schooldays*, ridiculed for saying his prayers), a journey his father had planned to complete his education. (In the marshes of the Upper Jordan, the Prince's governor, now General Bruce, contracted a fever from which he died soon after their return in London; '[his] death has been a terrible blow to me . . . I have lost in him a most useful and valuable friend,' the Prince told Dr Henry Acland, his physician when at Oxford.)[16] When she next saw the Prince at Windsor, the Queen found him not only much improved, but evidently ready to marry: he showed her 'a number of pretty things'[17] he had bought for Princess Alexandra in Paris.

It was then that the Queen's cousin, the mischievous Duke of Cambridge, made the Princess's family aware of the Nellie Clifden embarrassment. On hearing of it, the Crown Princess's lady-in-waiting, Walburga Paget, found Princess Christian in tears, the Duke's letter in her hand. '*Wicked wretches* had led our poor innocent Boy into a scrape,' the Queen later explained; it had caused his parents 'the deepest pain'. Nevertheless she was confident that he would make a 'steady Husband'; she 'looked to his wife as being his salvation'.[18] Princess Christian, it appears, was not unaware of the familial chill afflicting the Prince at home and was soon reconciled; her daughter's match after all, once it was sealed by a formal proposal, would make her the envy of Protestant Europe.[19]

On 2 September 1862 the Queen travelled to Laeken, near Brussels, to vet the Princess in person at the country palace of her uncle, King Leopold of the Belgians. For the meeting the Princess dressed in black and without jewels, out of respect for the Queen's mourning: 'Alexandra is lovely, such a beautiful refined profile,' she recorded. The Prince arrived three days later and told Prince Christian of his intentions. On 9 September, alone with the Princess in the palace garden, he offered her 'his hand . . . and heart'. The account he gave the Queen conveyed his pleasure, though its tone was somewhat perfunctory:

> She immediately said *yes*. But I told her not to answer too quickly but to consider over it. She said she had long ago. I then kissed her hand and she kissed me. We then talked for some time, and I told her that I was sure you would love her as your own daughter . . . I told her how *very* sorry I was that she could

never know dear Papa. She said she regretted it deeply and hoped he would have approved of my choice. I told her that it had always been his greatest wish; I only feared that I was not worthy of her. I then . . . saw the Prince and Princess and their daughter alone in a room and asked their permission that she should be my bride. They consented at once, and then I kissed Alexandra, and she me. We then went to luncheon . . . I cannot tell you with what feelings my head is filled, and how happy I feel . . . May God grant that *our* happiness may throw a ray of light on your once so happy and now desolate home.[20]

What was required now, the Queen decided, was to have Princess Alexandra willingly submit to a course of Windsor treatment – time alone with the Queen in which to temper her family's influence and to press for detachment in the political sphere (something the Princess's fierce patriotism would never allow) without which she would likely encourage anti-German sentiment in the Prince; time, too, to refine her English accent and to instruct her in the niceties of Court procedure. The Prince must agree to be away – and Princess Christian must remain at home. No invitation was extended to Prince Christian, who, after accompanying his daughter to England, was obliged to stay at a hotel. Nor should Princess Alexandra be allowed the companionship of her lady-in-waiting, or the attentions of a Danish maid. The Prince was dispatched early in October to cruise in the Mediterranean, where he was joined by the Crown Prince and Princess of Prussia, for whom the holiday offered respite from criticism at home for their hand in promoting the marriage – while in Berlin their absence was perceived to be a protest against Bismarck's constitutional sabre-rattling.

The wedding – on 10 March 1863 – was arranged uncompromisingly on the Queen's terms: it would be held not in London, as would delight the public, but in the relative privacy of St George's Chapel, Windsor. She chose the date without consulting the couple, and dismissed the counsel of the officiating clergy that a Lenten wedding was contrary to customary practice.)[21] True to form, the German relations of whom she disapproved were not invited, while the Prince was allowed just six personal friends, among them Charles (Lord) Carrington, who inherited Nellie Clifden from him. Two others were Viscount Hinchingbrooke (later Earl of Sandwich) – like Carrington, one of the boys who visited the Prince from Eton – and the budding high churchman, Charles Wood (later Viscount Halifax), the Prince's Groom of the Bedchamber, who had been of Gibbs's party in the Lake District in 1856. The Princess, on the other hand, had no one to witness her union other than her immediate family.

Though nothing would persuade the Queen to sacrifice her sorrow for the sake of the couple's joy, the public would not be deterred from putting a shine on the occasion. From the moment on 6 March, when the Prince abandoned protocol and ran up the gangway of the royal yacht *Victoria and Albert* at Gravesend to greet the Princess and enfold her in a very public embrace, until their departure for Osborne after the wedding breakfast some four days later – when a group of Eton boys did their best to keep the train from leaving – their progress, in bitter cold, was a popular, often haphazard affair. (When an escort's horse, in kicking out amid surging crowds near the Mansion House, trapped a hoof in a wheel of the royal carriage, the Princess bravely leant out and extricated it herself.)

For the ceremony, the Queen barely allowed the Royal Family release from Court mourning, the women wearing lilac and white, or white and grey. A diarist, Lady Geraldine Somerset, thought the gowns 'pretty', but the wreaths 'hideous'.[22] The Prince was in general's uniform beneath Garter robes and a gold collar; he 'looked . . . more *considerable* than he is wont to do', recorded Lord Clarendon.[23] For patriotic reasons, the Princess was obliged to forgo wearing a dress of Brussels lace, a gift of King Leopold of the Belgians, the Queen's uncle; Lord Granville criticised its replacement as being 'too sunk in greenery'.[24] The artist W.P. Frith's depiction of the scene has the Queen looking down from the dark interior of Catherine of Aragon's gallery closet above the altar, as the bridal couple exchange their vows before Archbishop Charles Longley. She is in her black widow's cap with white veil, and wears the Prince Consort's Order of the Garter; she came and went by a private way leading from the deanery. The previous day the Queen had conducted the Prince and Princess to the mausoleum at Frogmore where the Prince Consort was buried: '*He* gives you his blessing,' she assured them.[25] And there was much else relating to the marriage which attested to her grief. A wedding photograph has the Queen seated in front of the couple, but sideways to the camera, her eyes fixed piously upon a bust of her late husband. 'Ah, dear brother,' she wrote to King William of Prussia, 'what a sad and dismal ceremony it was!'[26]

The marriage merely exacerbated the Queen's tyranny of disappointment. 'I fear Bertie and she will soon be nothing but two puppets running about for show all day and night,' she complained.[27] But hers was a perspective lost on the Prince, who, freed from the restraints – as well as the near presence – of his mother, was enjoying the heady adulation of Society that wished him to assume social sovereignty unclaimed for half a generation. The Queen merely condemned the pleasure-seekers, while expecting the Prince and Princess to keep up 'that tone . . . which *used* to be the pride of England'.[28] Yet the Prince was unmoved. He could see new elements claiming recognition: men of enterprise making their fortunes through commerce (and its financing), property development and industry (and the mining interests at home and abroad that sustained it) – a case of 'new money' usurping old landed wealth lately depressed by falling rents. It was a catholicity the Prince understood. Money might be a vulgar thing, but it was the leaven dismantling the social exclusiveness of the past and creating an ineluctable shift in which a man's individuality would count for more than his origin.[29] He unashamedly chose his friends for their unstuffy, cosmopolitan sociability, many of them drawn out of self-interest – from the most rarefied stratum of rich men, whose superlative hospitality he could never match.[30] The liberal realist, Walter Bagehot, for one, had no patience with the Queen's killjoy tone. 'All the world and the glory of it, whatever is most seductive, has always been offered to the Prince of Wales of the day,' he acknowledged in his contemporary study, *The British Constitution* (1867); it was not irrational 'to expect the best virtue where temptation is applied in the most trying form at the frailest time of human life'. [31]

For her part, Princess Alexandra was propelled into an adventure of parties and adulation, the stuff of fairy tales for a young woman whose home life in Copenhagen has been likened to one of aristocratic want. (The Princess had shared a room with her younger sister, Princess Dagmar, who would marry Tsarevitch Alexander of Russia; belying its name, the family residence, the Yellow Palace, was an unpretentious town house whose front door and ground-floor windows adjoined a public pavement.) The prolonged and frantic social whirl – a public honeymoon, Disraeli called it – was fed by near-hysterical admiration of the Princess, such as would have turned the head of many a winsome eighteen-year-old lacking her secure dignity. Among the many to compliment her, Disraeli and Canon Arthur Stanley recognized immediately why all eyes were drawn to her. She '[is] most simple and fascinating, so winning and graceful, and yet so fresh and free and full of life',[32] the Canon wrote. Disraeli captured the defining quality that, no matter how great the effort, cannot be acquired: 'She has the accomplishment of being gracious without smiling; she has repose.'[33]

But the Prince could not mask the play of frustration for long. He was easily bored, a torment which the barrenness of his wife's conversation merely confirmed; she had been reared in grey domesticity, and it had left its mark. (The Princess's sympathetic biographer, Georgina Battiscombe, believed her poor education had rendered her 'an almost complete ignoramus'.)[34] In comparison, the Prince's intellectual limitations mattered little: he could always count on brilliant minds to distract him, and could change his company at will. And though he might overlook palpable ignorance in a wife otherwise universally admired for her sympathy and charm (and undoubted intuition), he would come to value the virtues of clever women rather more.

In a major regard, his sympathies were found wanting. The Princess had inherited from her mother a form of deafness (otosclerosis), barely noticeable at first, but made worse after the birth in 1867 of her third child, Princess Louise (later the Princess Royal), by a severe bout of rheumatic fever. While his wife was coming to terms with an irreversible handicap, as well as suffering extreme pain from the disease, the Prince satisfied his craving for distractions with long absences from her sickroom at Marlborough House, their London home.

This untimely indulgence was a trait the Princess would learn to accommodate; it came, not least, of his having no role to call his own. Time and again the Queen frustrated his wish to be educated in matters of state. Nor would she allow him to perform much in the way of public engagements, for this would trespass upon the former preserve of the Prince Consort, whose influence she honoured as if he were still at her side. '*Upon no account*', she told the Liberal statesman Lord Granville on the day of the Prince's wedding, should he 'be put at the head of any of those Societies or Commissions, or preside at any of those scientific proceedings in which his beloved Father took so prominent a part'.[35] She instructed the Prince to hold drawing rooms on her behalf, solely because she was not prepared to end her mourning.

While many saw candour as a refreshing quality in a Prince (Napoleon III's cousin, Princess Mathilde, thought him 'open . . . not like other princes, who always give the impression that they have something to hide'),[36] the Queen saw only a weakness for indiscretion, which justified forbidding him from having access to Cabinet papers. To a man with strong feelings about dignity, such exclusion was deeply hurtful.[37] Not until he was fifty-seven did he preside at a Privy Council. When representations – even those of Gladstone and the Foreign Secretary, Lord John Russell – failed to achieve an easing of the Queen's prohibition, the Prince was reduced to gleaning what he could from his circle of political and diplomatic friends, habitually within the privacy of the smoking room at Marlborough House or by importuning ministers by letter. 'Would you consider it very indiscreet if I asked you to let me know . . .' began a letter of 1873 to Lord Hartington, the Chief Secretary for Ireland.[38]

In the matter of Prussia's predatory designs on his wife's homeland the twenty-two-year-old Prince's outspokenness was surely understandable. No sooner was there an incursion upon Schleswig soil in January 1864 than an exasperated Prince was free with his criticism of the government. In a letter of 17 February to Mrs Bruce, his former governor's wife, he thought it '*very* wrong' of the government not to have intervened; as for Lord John Russell's 'everlasting Notes' to continental foreign ministers, he thought they would 'probably light their cigars with them'. On 5 May he was to tell Lord Spencer, his Groom of the Stole (and later First Lord of the Admiralty) 'that if we had sent our fleet to the Baltic at the beginning, all this bloodshed might possibly have been avoided, and we should cut a much better figure in Europe than we do at present'.[39] When the Italian revolutionary leader, Giuseppe Garibaldi, came to London with the aim of raising support for the Danes as their battlefield losses mounted, the Prince thought nothing of abandoning protocol, choosing to pay him a visit at the Duke of Sutherland's Stafford House. 'For a quasi-crowned head to call on a subject is strange, and that subject is a rebel!' Disraeli remonstrated. The Queen called the visit 'incredible folly and imprudence'. Through the Prince's Comptroller and Treasurer, General Sir William Knollys (whom she blamed for allowing it), the Queen insisted that the Prince take 'no step of the *slightest political importance*' without consulting her. For his part, the Prince could but accept this timely reminder that independence of action was not his automatic right as heir to the throne; but, as for Knollys having any degree of surrogate influence with him, he would stand his ground. Knollys 'is not, and cannot be, responsible for my actions', the Prince told the Queen. 'I have now been of age for some time and am *alone* responsible, and am only too happy to bear *any* blame on my shoulders.'[40]

*

The Queen's wish to be present at the birth of Princess Alexandra's children was thwarted either by circumstances or by the Prince contriving that it should not be so. Their first child, Prince Albert Victor, known generally to the family as Eddy (he predeceased his father in 1892), was born two months prematurely on 8 January 1864. His parents had returned in haste the day before from Virginia Water, where, in intense cold, they had been watching hockey on the ice. With no time for proper preparations, the Windsor town doctor delivered the child, whom Lady Macclesfield, a lady-in-waiting, received into her flannel petticoat. (When a bevy of royal doctors arrived too late to be of much service, the Princess gave way to laughter.) The delighted parents were later seen crying in each other's arms. As to naming the child, the Queen – who wished the Prince's descendants to bear the names of either Albert or Victoria in perpetuity – had her way. It annoyed the Prince that the Queen 'had settled what our little boy was to be called' before he had spoken to her about it. In a letter to King Leopold some two months later, she was to insist on her 'strong right . . . to *interfere*' in the management of her grandchild.

The arrival a month early, on 3 June 1865, of the couple's second son, George (later George V), again precluded the Queen from attending the confinement. 'Alix and I never will or can be intimate; she shows me no confidence whatsoever especially about the children,' she complained some nine months later. The Queen's affection for the Princess was ambivalent at best. To her face she was lovingly disposed; behind her back there was a deal of sourness. The Princess, after all, was an outsider – 'from the enemy's camp *in every way*'[41] [author's italics], as the Queen once put it. She might be dutiful, but she would not sacrifice her self-esteem by toadying to a mother-in-law whose affection for her own children appeared so obviously to be conditional upon what they were prepared to do for her.[42] While the Prince had acquired a wife of determined will – the attribute that his mother thought to be of greatest value to him when she began seeking a wife for him in late 1858 – just occasionally the Queen would reap the whirlwind. When it was proposed that the Queen's third daughter, Princess Helena, should make what proved an unpropitious match with the dull Prince Christian of Schleswig-Holstein-Sonderburg-Augustenburg, the Princess vehemently encouraged the Prince's opposition to it on the grounds that the bridegroom's family had openly sided with Denmark's enemies in the recent war. The pleas of three siblings, Prince Alfred, Princess Alice and Crown Princess Victoria, prevailed with the Prince in the end, who reluctantly agreed to attend the ceremony. 'I cannot tell you what I have suffered . . . It will be long, if ever, before she [the Princess] regains my confidence,' wrote the Queen in the broil of the moment.[43] Princess Alice's perspective on the family dilemma would surely have weighed with the Prince:

> Oh, darling Bertie, don't let you be the one who cannot sacrifice his *own feelings* for the welfare of Mother and Sister. Mamma knows and deeply regrets what you feel, but, nowhere would she find another [husband], and as she almost broke with Papa's only brother and all her other relations and friends for you and Alix, saying never should political feelings stand between her and her son's happiness do you both dear ones repress your feelings for a Mother's sake and let not political feelings towards Alix's relations stand between you and your own sister's happiness.[44]

There was little to test the integrity of the Prince's marital devotion during the first four giddy years of marriage, but this was to change. He returned from the Russian imperial wedding of the Princess's sister, Princess Dagmar, to the Tsarevitch Alexander, and its attendant junketings, to a wife brought low in her third pregnancy by fever and severe pain in her limbs: five days before the birth of Princess Louise (on 20 February 1867) it was confirmed that she was suffering a severe attack of rheumatic fever. Careless, it seemed, of the symptoms – acute and unrelieved pain in her leg, knee and hip – the Prince chose to attend a steeplechase on 15 February, after which he went to dine at Windsor. Three telegrams were sent before he returned to Marlborough House at noon the next day. By then the doctors knew it would be unwise in the Princess's weakened condition to administer chloroform during delivery. The Prince, in everyone's eyes but his own, was found wanting. The death of his father had been an inevitable, unhurried rite of passage, hardly to be compared to this life-threatening streptococcal infection in a young, spirited wife, prostrated by fever and migratory arthritis, and whose heartbeat was worryingly irregular.[45] Furthermore, she was getting no natural sleep, and her mouth was so inflamed that she could not eat. (It would be two years before she would risk her inflamed knee on the dance floor, a period when the 'Alexandra limp' was copied in Court circles.) Unable, then, to mistake the evidence of pain, the Prince accommodated the emotions that must surely have been thrust upon him by taking refuge in a delusion: better to live as if his wife's condition was not serious after all. This was not a mature response from one shielded from the caprices of the human condition since childhood. He would sit for a while writing letters at his desk, which had been brought into his wife's room, until restlessness drove him to find congenial company away from Marlborough House, a pattern of behaviour to which an exasperated Lady Macclesfield – the Princess's chief support throughout her illness – testified. 'The Princess had another bad night,' she wrote on one occasion, '*chiefly* owing to the Prince promising to come in at 1 a.m. and keeping her in a perpetual fret, refusing to take her opiate for fear she should be asleep when he came! And he never came till 3 a.m.!' Lady Macclesfield was hearing 'nothing but general indignation at [the Prince's] indifference to her and his devotion to his own amusements'. Inevitably, perhaps, given the Prince's inadequate powers of imagination, there were moments of crass insensitivity, as when, against all advice at the end of a day during which the Princess underwent a painful examination of her knee, he would not postpone distressing her with news of her grandmother's death until morning. 'He really is a *child* about such things,' Lady Macclesfield observed.[46]

Nor, after the illness, would the Prince's proper attentions be restored. The exhaustion of convalescence would pass – the Princess was still using a wheelchair in July – but advancing deafness and the insidious isolation it would impose, however expertly she might mask it, began to diminish her appetite for the social calendar on which the Prince's fulfilment so depended. Increasingly, he sought his pleasures without her. For her part, the Princess had no choice but to extend the limits of her patience. She would learn to disregard the regular rumours of his peccadilloes, believing that the ties of affection which made for a strong marriage were best secured by employing a light hand.[47] If the Prince chose to seek sexual favours from others, she would not let it become a cause of estrangement: discreet infidelity – as understood by most of her class – was a sufferable adjunct to marriage, and she did her best to ignore it.

The Princess left her bed for the first time on 20 April, two months to the day after her daughter's birth. On 10 May, still using a wheelchair, she attended her child's christening, after which the Prince travelled to Dieppe at the invitation of Lord Cranborne, and on to Paris – then 'the New Babylon' (so-called) of Second Empire frivolity and 'fleshly pleasures'[48] – ostensibly for the opening in May of the Universal Exhibition (L'Exposition Universelle). When his Comptroller, Sir William Knollys, wrote of the Prince going to supper 'with some of the female Paris notorieties [*les grandes horizontales*] etc. etc.', he left much unsaid.[49] The Prince was enjoying the city at the apogee of its promiscuous, vulgar allure, before political events in the shape of the Franco-Prussian War, a five-month siege and subsequent revolutionary Commune brought nemesis. Nothing mirrored the carnival of titillation more than the wild fury of the can-can danced nightly in the city's theatres – not the mildly saucy routine it later became, but a high-kicking 'sexually predatory ritual': 'Everybody followed their own demon,' complained the *Revue et Gazette Musicale de Paris*, the women (most went without knickers) challenging the men 'to thrust and enter, as the dance became hotter, faster, louder'. Naked expectation was nowhere more apparent than in the ballet, at the Opéra and at the Théâtre des Variétés, as the brothers Jules and Edmond Goncourt witnessed:

> From the stage to the auditorium, from the wings to the stage, and from one side of the auditorium to the other, invisible threads criss-cross between actresses' smiles, dancers' legs, and men's opera glasses, in a network of arousal and liaison. One couldn't gather together in less space a greater number of sexual stimuli, of invitations to copulate.[50]

The Prince did not waste the opportunities. He paid court backstage at the Variétiés to the leading singer in Offenbach's *La Grande Duchesse de Gerolstein*, Hortense Schneider, whom Emile Zola envisaged as the eponymous *Nana* (1880) in the novel he set in this same year, 1867. There were also assignations in the Jardin des Plantes and visits to Le Chabanais, which was the Prince's brothel of choice. (When the notorious whore 'La Barucci', Giulia Beneti, was introduced to him at the Maison d'Or restaurant, she curtsied and dropped her skirts. 'I showed him the best I have, and it was free,' she told the Duc de Gramont, who felt obliged to remonstrate with her.)[51] In *Nana*, the Prince (renamed the Prince of Scotland) and his friends are shown into a gas-lit, stifling theatre dressing room, heady with *odore di femmina*, half-nakedness, greasepaint and champagne, where they are 'surrounded by a vulgar entourage of dressers, tarts, stage hacks . . . and exhibitors of women'. Nana (as Venus) attends to making up 'with particular care for her nude appearance in the third act', as the Prince, 'a sturdy man of pleasure', alone now with just two companions, witnesses 'the intimate details of a woman's *toilette*, amid a clutter of jars and basins, in this air heavy with soft, rich perfumes'. 'So it's agreed . . . Next year you'll come to London and we'll give you a welcome you'll never forget, and you'll never want to go back to France,' he says, looking 'very much at his ease' on her divan.[52] A fiction, of course; yet no one better than Zola had the measure of theatre- and brothel-based male sexuality as it played out among the cast of kept women in Second Empire Paris. He expressed as much in his notes for *Nana*, where he spoke of 'sex on an altar with everybody [the Prince included] offering sacrifices to it'.[53]

4
Marlborough House

In a cartoon of the early 1920s, Max Beerbohm depicted the adult Prince as an archetype: the recalcitrant schoolboy, stood in the corner in the presence of an unyielding mother – a caricature that aptly conveys a damaged dignity that no amount of social poise could redeem. If his pride required tempering, he told the writer Laurence Oliphant, all he needed do was take a short walk to Buckingham Palace (although it was at Windsor that the Queen habitually resided).[1] But if the Prince suffered her snubs in silence, he was understandably touchy at the least hint of presumption or disrespect on the part of those he knew; even a favoured member of his set might find himself peremptorily dismissed for an instance of ill-judged familiarity.[2] Sir Frederick Johnstone, for one, was ordered to have his bags packed before breakfast for chaffing the Prince, who had objected to his drunkenness. Johnstone's imitation of the Prince's voice as he hazarded his nickname ('Tum-Tum, you're *verrrry* fat!') had frozen the Prince's affability in an instant. Numerous such blunders have been recorded. When a bad shot at billiards was greeted by a jocular 'Pull yourself together, Wales!' the offender's carriage was promptly at the door.[3] If caught off guard, the Prince's composure could snap, as a Jewish friend, the 'flashily foppish' Reuben Sassoon, discovered when, daring to put a playful arm round the Prince's shoulders as they walked downstairs, he found himself pushed violently down.[4]

Practical jokes, then an unexceptional diversion of country house life, were much to the Prince's taste, but, again, his friends were wise to observe the boundaries: they knew they would never get away with perpetrating one against him. As is commonly the way of men who lack self-confidence, the Prince liked to spice his with a dash of cruelty. His nephew, Kaiser Wilhelm II – who, like the Prince, endured an overbearing mother, Crown Princess Victoria –

was notorious in this regard, making his generals perform demeaning antics. Of the Prince's own japes, two examples must suffice. The lugubrious Christopher Sykes was so used to being the butt of the Prince's amusement – he was to bankrupt himself in the cause of entertaining the Prince – that onlookers could anticipate his 'As your Royal Highness pleases', the self-abasing mantra which invariably followed the tricks played upon him. One of these the Prince repeated a number of times. Told to look into his eyes to see whether smoke was coming from them, the Prince would stab his cigar into Sykes's hand, which had the company roaring their laughter.[5] Similarly greeted was a trick the Prince played on the blind Duke of Mecklenburg. Placing the Duke's hand on the grossly fat arm of Helen Henneker, a friend of the Duke, the Prince asked the bewildered, aged man: 'Now, don't you think Helen has a lovely little waist?' Henneker was amply amused.[6]

Plainly, there is nothing that upholds the dignity of the monarchy quite as effectively as the exercise of precedence, and the Prince was a stickler for it. He once insisted that a minor Indian rajah ranked higher than an English duke. And when German pride was offended because the sovereign of the Hawaiian Islands, Kalakaua, instead of the Prince's brother-in-law, the Crown Prince of Germany, opened the dancing with the Princess of Wales at a Marlborough House ball, the Prince's reasoning appeared flawless. 'Either the brute is a King or else he is an ordinary nigger, and if he is not a King, why is he here?' he retorted.[7]

Commonly presented as the Prince's clubbable, masculine headquarters, it is easy to forget that Marlborough House was also the Princess's equally favoured London home, until she reluctantly accepted the move to Buckingham Palace on the Prince's accession. Writing at the time to Prince George, Duke of York, she confided: 'All my happiness and sorrow were here, very nearly all you children were born here, all the reminiscences of my whole life are here, and I feel as if by taking me away a cord will be torn in my heart which can never be mended again.'[8] Given the Prince's roving attentions, there were occasions enough in the course of thirty-eight years' residence when she would swallow her pride in the privacy of her cluttered apartment, only to devote herself the more to raising her children, attended by her spirited Pomeranians, Pekinese and pugs.[9]

The Wren residence behind high walls in Pall Mall (built in 1709–10 for the first Duke of Marlborough) had been the home of Queen Adelaide, William IV's widow, until her death in 1849, since when some £60,000 was spent on adding to it. There was now space for the whole of London Society – served by a household of more than 100 – to be entertained at a single ball. Away from the reception rooms, there was much panelling and the ubiquitous Victorian accumulation of framed photographs, *objets d'art*, and flowers on every available surface. In the Prince's private quarters, walls were hung with swords and guns, military paintings and Scottish scenes. There was no library. Only the smoking room contained books, but many of them were dummies, though the *Westminster Gazette* and *Pall Mall Gazette* were laid out in the anteroom.[10] A story recounted by Sir Sidney Lee attests to the Prince being un-bookish. (He was little in the company of writers or artists, and was ill at ease with those he thought intellectual.) The occasion was a dinner the Prince had been persuaded to give at Marlborough House to celebrate the publication of the *Dictionary of National Biography*, at which the learned Lord Acton sat next to him. Lee recounts how, on seeing a clergyman among the guests – Canon Ainger, the man responsible for the entries on Charles and Mary Lamb in the *Dictionary* – the Prince asked, 'Who is the little parson? Why is he here?', whereupon it was explained to him that Ainger was 'a very great authority on Lamb'. The Prince was instantly bewildered. 'On *lamb*!' he spluttered.[11]

When not in the company of his friends at Marlborough House – his 'wicked boys', he playfully called them – they would habitually join him at the Marlborough Club, which he founded in 1869, close by at 52 Pall Mall, ostensibly in protest at the smoking restrictions imposed at White's Club. The club's eventual membership of 400 were all vetted by him and known to him personally: plutocrats and parvenus (the grocer, Sir Thomas Lipton, and the furniture store proprietor, Sir John Blundell Maple, among them), English and foreign diplomats, serving officers, Jews and Roman Catholics, as well as numerous members of the aristocracy (prominently, the Prince's Sandringham coterie). But it was the uninhibited 'small evenings', attended by younger members of the set at Marlborough House, which pleased the Prince most and could be relied on to provide the competitive horseplay – 'roaring fun', Charles Carrington called it – without which the Prince's evenings would have been uncharacteristically tame affairs. 'Their Royal Highnesses like nothing so much as a romp,' opined a guest. Indeed, some high jinks never palled, such as playing wetting games with soda siphons (then newly invented) or tobogganing on trays down a flight of stairs. Charles Carrington recorded how the Prince 'had a tremendous spill' when one of the poles of a sedan chair snapped as he was being 'carried in triumph round the house'. The Princess, too, would enter into the spirit of things as pregnancies allowed, but she eschewed the late-night baccarat sessions, the card game much favoured at the time by rich gamblers, despite its prohibition in law. (We shall see later how the Prince was seriously compromised by a lawsuit brought by Sir William Gordon-Cumming in September 1890 in defence of an accusation of cheating.)

While it was generally agreed that the Prince preferred the company of women, he was no less fond of easy and unabashed male confidences. Alluding, we may assume, to sexual performance, the Prince advised Carrington on one occasion: 'You won't I am sure forget those few hints I gave you respecting *certain* matters, and I have not forgotten those you gave me at the same time.' Writing to him again on 22 April 1866, the Prince was in teasing mode, trusting that he was enjoying himself in Paris 'and not committing *too* many atrocities etc'. Letters to Carrington tell of their shared interest in pornographic books. 'I think you still have in your possession the 3rd Vol: of "Les Amours de N." and "La Femme de Caesar",' the Prince reminded him early in his married life. Two years later, in November 1867, he was telling him: 'I find that the 4th volume of "Les Amours de Napoleon" has not yet come out so I send you another French book, which is said to be amusing.'[12]

Denied the opportunity to test his prowess through service in the army, albeit a less painful frustration than was the lot of his immediate predecessor as Prince of Wales, the future George IV, the Prince similarly delighted in wearing uniform to meticulous effect. His military wardrobe occupied much of the top floor at Marlborough House. Here were the trappings of the honorary titles he had accrued, which encompassed military and naval ranks of all the monarchies of Europe, to set alongside British honours as Admiral of the Fleet, Field Marshal and Colonel of several regiments. (It was that most strutting of militarists, Kaiser Wilhelm, who nicknamed his uncle 'Old Peacock'.)[13] But if, on the evidence of a too brief spell at the Curragh Camp, the Prince missed the ritual rumpus of the officers' mess – as he once hankered for a taste of rough equality with schoolfellows – he would not forgo an opportunity for surrogate camaraderie such as was presented to him as a consequence of an accident, and which came laced with real danger: he would turn out – strictly as the mood took him

– with men of the Chandos Street Fire Brigade. His first encounter with Captain Eyre Massey Shaw of the Metropolitan Fire Brigade – the Captain Shaw of W.S. Gilbert's libretto for *Iolanthe* ('Could thy Brigade/With cold cascade/Quench my great love, I wonder!') – occurred when the captain attended a fire at Marlborough House and found the Prince chopping at burning floorboards with an axe, having organized a human chain to bring buckets of water to the scene. Encouraged by the pyromaniac Duke of Sutherland, the Prince at once asked to be told when a good fire was in progress; he would then desert his guests, don fireman's uniform and ride the next available engine. Forty-one years old – and already corpulent – at the time of the Alhambra Music Hall fire of 1882, the Prince and Sutherland were playing their hoses from the roof when a section fell in, killing two members of the brigade.[14]

There were precious few public engagements to occupy the Prince's time and only a few levees and drawing rooms which, solely on account of the 'Queen's invisibility' (Gladstone's phrase)[15] at Windsor and Osborne House, the Prince and Princess hosted in her stead. Apart from attending twelve formal committee meetings, the Prince's diary for 1879 (his thirty-seventh year) listed a mere twenty (mostly minor) engagements, not an untypical number, in the course of a year:

14 April	Open Convalescent Home at Hunstanton, Norfolk.
26 April	Dine with Royal Institute of British Architects.
12 May	Attend Grand Military Assault at Arms and Gymnastic Display at Albert Hall in aid of Widows and Orphans of Zulu War.
24 May	Drive in procession over Lambeth, Vauxhall, Chelsea, the Albert and Battersea bridges, pausing to declare each one free of tolls in perpetuity.
17 June	Lay foundation stone of Norfolk and Norwich Hospital.
21 June	Visit Plymouth and lay foundation stone of new Eddystone lighthouse [the ceremony was cancelled at the last moment owing to bad weather].
24 June	Open new school and other buildings of Alexandra Orphanage at Hornsey Rise.
26 June	Preside at annual dinner of West London Hospital.
27 June	Attend conversazione at Royal Colonial Institute.

30 June	Inaugurate International Agricultural Exhibition at Kilburn.
5 July	Conduct Queen round International Agricultural Exhibition.
7 July	Attend Fancy Dress Fair at Albert Hall in aid of French charities in London.
8 July	Lay foundation stone of new wing of Royal Hospital for Incurables at West Hill, Putney Heath.
9 July	Visit Royal Normal College and Academy of Music for the Blind, when Princess presents prizes.
15 July	Visit National Orphan Home, Ham Common, when Princess presents prizes.
17 July	Lay foundation stone of new wing at Hospital for Consumption and Diseases of the Chest at Brompton.
18 July	Visit North London Collegiate School for Girls, where Princess presents prizes.
22 July	Stay with Lord Yarborough at Brocklesby House and unveil new statue of Prince Consort at Grimsby.
26 July	Visit Royal Hospital School at Greenwich and present prizes.
3 November	Visit St Bartholomew's Hospital; open new museum, classroom and library; and lunch in Great Hall.[16]

So there was time enough – however hard the Prince chased distraction – to regret a want of inner resources. Being alone was a prospect sure to unsettle him. Faced with gaps in his social programme, he proceeded on the canny presumption that close members of his circle would be the means of escaping his own company. It was their loyal duty to oblige him, and they did, frequently at short notice and at the cost of their own plans. Given that the Prince invariably functioned on very little sleep, it could be an irritating sacrifice. Out of London, he took 'unscrupulous advantage' of country house hospitality and of hosts who feared their arrangements might not meet with his approval. To the chagrin of some, 'he came over and over again. And on Monday morning other people would read of it in the *Morning Post*.'[17] Plainly, complacent country house rituals were no substitute for a purposeful life, and the Prince was increasingly prone to intervals of lassitude and irritability, although he was adept at masking the royal mood. His facile 'Yes, yes, yes!' was commonly all he offered publicly by way of satisfaction; displeasure elicited silence and an assumed 'air of martyrdom' (as his biographer Philip Magnus lucidly puts it).[18]

Silencing his demons – for such they seemed – meant keeping to strict routines, around which the day's activities never flagged. The Prince's meals, for instance, were an unfolding ritual of orchestrated tension between compulsive feeding and the (self-imposed) strictures of the clock. He was a determined trencherman, intolerant while eating of all but the lightest conversation: banter, a little gossip, nothing intellectual.[19] Guests who could not adapt to the Prince's tempo (there were seldom fewer than twelve courses at dinner) would find their plates removed abruptly from before them as flunkies kept the meal to its allotted sixty minutes.[20] (The Prince never liked to be away from the ladies for long, once they had retired.) He ate his five meals a day with equal relish (mastication being an avoidable inconvenience): the Princess called it 'terrible'[21] gormandizing, but she appeared helpless to influence its hold on him. Fish, chicken, bacon, eggs and toast were typical early fare on a morning in the country, to be followed by luncheon (at half past two) and tea – itself a substantial repast of 'poached eggs, *petits fours*, and preserved ginger as well as rolls and scones, hot cakes, cold cakes, sweet cakes . . . and Scotch shortcake'.[22] After dinner at eight thirty, an evening was incomplete without midnight supper, frequently a dish of grilled oysters or quail. Of the Prince's favourite dishes, *Cotelettes de bécassines à la Souvaroff* (of Russian origin) was one of boned snipe stuffed with *foie gras* and forcemeat, grilled in a pig's caul and served in Madeira sauce with truffles; pheasant would invariably be stuffed with snipe or woodcock, these stuffed with truffles, and the whole in a rich sauce.[23] At table he commonly drank pink champagne, decanted for him into a jug; other drink – a little wine, nips of brandy, a favourite cocktail (champagne, whisky, bitters and maraschino), but rarely neat spirits – was habitual. Smoking was the inveterate pleasure that would kill him. (In photographs, his cigars and Egyptian cigarettes are as ubiquitous as his hats.) He smoked two cigarettes and a cigar on waking – a choice of Corona y Corona, Henry Clay's or Upmann's – and the slow exhalations of at least a dozen more large cigars were the comfort of his days; in sum, then, an astonishing liberality for the royal constitution to bear. By his early thirties the Prince was measuring four feet (all but an inch) around the belly and weighed over 200 pounds – this of a man five feet seven inches in height.

Meanwhile, he had acquired the 'dull, heavy, blasé look'[24] (his mother's description) that could fairly be taken as confirmation of self-indulgence and complacence. Sir Charles Phipps, Keeper of the Privy Purse, saw his defect plainly: 'it [is] impossible for him to deny himself anything that he desires'.[25]

He dashed with friends – frequently importuned at short notice – between club, theatre, private rooms, the opera, wild parties; to Cremorne Gardens at Vauxhall and Evans Music-and-Supper Rooms in Covent Garden – often travelling incognito in hansom cabs. 'What a bore the Prince is!' Lady Carrington had cause to complain when her son was once again unreasonably called away.[26] Before photographers with their instant cameras stalked royalty, and 'royal watching' became a free-for-all a century later, the discretion of one's friends was enough to ensure that visits to the racier haunts of the metropolis went largely without remark. There were, in effect, no barriers to the Prince enjoying disreputable pleasures in the company of such bloods as the spirited Henry (later Viscount) Chaplin, Lord Royston and the consumptive and improvident Marquis of Hastings. Hastings would take his friends to hangings at Newgate, to (illegal) cock fights at Faultless's pit in Endell Street and to 'ratting matches' to lay bets upon the number of sewer rats a terrier could kill in an hour.[27] Chaplin, by all accounts, was incorrigible. One drunken night he drove his four-in-hand into the closed gates of his family seat, Blankney Hall, killing two horses; it was told how he and the Prince, as an old estate woman was passing them, pulled her skirts up over her head, whereupon Chaplin tucked a £5 note into her underclothing.[28]

Taking his pleasures freely, the Prince was dancing to Society's tune, and Society loved him for it. The balls hosted at Marlborough House were on a scale to match those of an earlier age at Carlton House. In July 1874, for instance, the Prince held a *ballo in maschera* to which 1,400 guests were invited – ostensibly the entire complement of Society – an event which *The Times* archly proclaimed to have proved the Prince's descent 'from Kings whose Courts have never been wanting in splendour'. The Prince dressed as Charles I, resplendent in a costume of velvet and satin, embroidered with gold, beneath Cavalier curls and wide-brimmed hat, topped with a white feather; the Princess appeared lavishly jewelled as a Venetian. The entire company supped together in a pair of grand, scarlet marquees.

An earlier ball, at the height of the 1871 season, was overshadowed for the Princess by the death, aged one day, of Prince Alexander John Charles Albert on 6 April. Among those looking for a cause, the Prince did not escape censure for neglecting his wife, and it was said that the Princess, bent upon silencing whispers about the state of the marriage, had exhausted herself in being seen to keep pace with his wishes. The Dean of Windsor, Gerald Wellesley, who conveyed the Queen's concern to the Prince, reported that he was 'evidently deeply attached to the Princess, despite all the flattering distractions that beset him in Society'; the Dean 'hopes and believes that [the Prince] will be more careful about her in future'. Prince John was laid to rest quietly at Sandringham, the Prince placing the infant in the coffin himself and laying white flowers on the pall, with which he covered it. Whatever their private thoughts at the time of this 'Waverley Ball' (the Prince appeared as Sir Walter Scott's 'Lord of the Isle', the Princess as Mary Queen of Scots), no one read anything but contentment in their manner as they led the dancing. Yet the infant's death may have marked the end of their sexual union: true or not, the Princess, at twenty-six, had given birth for the last time – and from then on the Prince's roving attentions held sway.[29]

When the German Chancellor, Prince von Bülow, noted Edward VII's 'marked predilection for very rich people', he had his Jewish friends in mind. As Prince of Wales, the devotion of a group of meritorious financiers to his social well-being – mainly Rothschilds, Sassoons, Cassels and Hirsches – effectively underwrote his unaffordable extravagance. It was to their mutual benefit. These were incomparably discreet men, perfecting their networks of influence in Europe and beyond through the 'raw power . . . of the purse'[30] (while the Prince made do with no worthwhile sphere of influence), who saw their largesse as a modest investment towards securing the elusive grail of Jewish emancipation. But the collusion of money and rank in English society in the second half of the century set teeth on edge. 'Certainly *money* is a vulgar thing, and money is what rules us now,' lamented the Dowager Countess Cowper in 1874. 'What right have such people to force themselves into our society?'[31] One who viewed the matter dispassionately was the Prince's at times tempestuous mistress, Daisy Brooke, Countess of Warwick (see Chapter 7). 'We resented the introduction of the Jews into the social set of the Prince of Wales,' she wrote, 'not because we disliked them individually . . . but because they had brains and understood finance. As a class we did not like brains. As for money, our only understanding of it lay in the spending, not the making of it.'[32]

For many years the Prince's income (including what came to him from the Duchy of Cornwall) did not exceed £110,000 a year, lean fare compared with the incomes of the country's richest men, whose metropolitan rent-rolls alone far outstripped his own revenues. Of the forty-four landowners owning more than 100,000 acres, the Duke of Devonshire received close on £180,000 from 200,000 acres, whereas the Prince's Sandringham rent-roll was a mere £7,000 from a similar number of acres. Taking into account his initial outlay at Marlborough House (some £100,000 on such items as furniture and carriages) and the purchase of Sandringham Hall (later House) as a family home (see Chapter 5), expenditure which had severely depleted his capital, it was to the credit of the Prince's advisers that they found ways of limiting his annual deficit for a long period to about £20,000 a year.[33] That said, gambling debts, racing interests and provision for his mistresses became so much of an additional strain upon his resources that his private capital was exhausted by the time he came to the throne.

The extent of the 'Jewish Court's' benevolence should not be underestimated. We know that a loan to him of 15 million francs (some £15 million in today's money) was never called in. It was arranged in the spring of 1890 by the socially ambitious Baron Maurice de Hirsch, whose fortune was made financing railways in the Balkans and Turkey, and on the surety of the Prince's sister, the Dowager Empress Frederick. It was widely assumed that Hirsch's widow waived the debt when the Baron died in 1896, although the French Ambassador in London, Paul Cambon, believed that its guarantee was taken over by the English Rothschilds. Before Hirsch agreed the loan, the Prince was clearly inconvenienced: he had failed to negotiate one for £40,000 (the terms were too severe) with a Parisian money-lender, the sum to be put up by a champagne merchant whose product the Prince would endorse.

Confirming the Rothschild ascendancy in particular were the country houses, both built and acquired, that peppered the Home Counties. Of the heads of the family, Sir Anthony (of Aston Clinton in the Vale of Aylesbury) was the first of the clan to use his financial acumen in the Prince's service and provide him with advances. Baron Meyer Rothschild of the Prince's own generation employed Joseph Paxton (of Crystal Palace fame) in the building of the Jacobean-style Mentmore. ('I don't believe that the Medici were ever so lodged in the height of their glory,' opined Lady Eastlake).[34] Nathaniel, the first Lord Rothschild, enlarged Tring Park (amid its 200 acre deer park), and his brother Leopold, settled at Ascott, near Wing. Like Mentmore, other houses seemed conceived as totems of competitive ostentation. Gladstone's secretary, Sir Algernon West, described Nathaniel's brother Alfred's gilt and gold (interior) extravagance,

Halton House near Wendover, as 'an exaggerated nightmare of gorgeousness and senseless and ill-applied magnificence'; their cousin Ferdinand took fifteen years to complete the house and fine collections at nearby Waddesdon Manor, where Mary Gladstone felt 'oppressed with the extreme gorgeousness and luxury'.[35] These residences, and the Rothschild London houses in Piccadilly ('Rothschild Row') and close by in Hamilton Place and Seymour Place, were retreats of indispensable indulgence for the Prince, where the tiresome limitations of his own means could be ignored without hint of embarrassment.

Needless to say, this charmed circle's manner of life was entirely cushioned from the painful consequences of mid- and late-century economic instability from which even the largest agricultural estates were not immune. As a modern commentator lucidly puts it, to the landowner 'the countryside seemed a place where one spent, rather than earned, money'.[36] Farming – fast becoming just another 'industry' – vainly competed, for example, with cheaply grown and transported wheat from the American prairies. (The cost of transporting a ton of grain from Chicago to Liverpool was £3 7s in 1873; eleven years later it had fallen to £1 4s.[37] After 1877, home-grown corn never reached 50s a bushel; after the harvest of 1894, 'a year of panic', the price fell to 19s.)[38] Driving the agricultural poor from the land were outbreaks of cattle plague (1865–6 and 1877), a run of wet seasons (1878–82) and a foot-and-mouth epidemic (1881–3).[39] None of this obtruded upon 'Rothschild Row' ostentation, certainly not to the point of eliciting much in the way of philanthropy, though the 'bitter cry' of the desperate poor at the heart of the capital was well publicized. Among notable contemporary guides were *How the Poor Live* by George Sims, *Bitter Cry of Outcast London* – a guide through 'a dark continent that [was] in easy walking distance of the General Post Office'[40] by the Reverend Andrew Mearns – and *Darkest England and the Way Out* by the Salvationist, William Booth. Lady Eastlake, meanwhile, recorded her wonder at a latter-day Medici, and Daisy Brooke confirmed how the Rothschilds entertained the Prince and herself to 'undoubtedly . . . the best dinner parties in London and . . . established a taste for the refinements of luxury. They had the best chefs and bottomless purses.' So impressed was the historian Thomas Babington Macaulay by a Lionel Rothschild dinner that he purloined the menu to show to friends. He shall have the last word: 'Surely this,' he wrote, 'is the land flowing with milk and honey. I do not believe Solomon in all his glory ever dined on *Ortolans farcis à la Talleyrand*.'[41]

5
The Sporting Life

'We are rather cold as all country houses are.'[1] Amid preparations at Sandringham Hall (as it was then called) to receive the Prince and his bride in the third week of their marriage in March 1863, this would seem an unexceptional gloss from the pen of the Prince's Comptroller, General Knollys, but for the fact that the housekeeper was short of some fifty blankets. Not that the Princess will have much minded the Norfolk chill, as she took stock of a landscape not so very different from Denmark's. But her Lady of the Bedchamber, Lady Macclesfield, was bleakly unconvinced. 'No fine trees, no water, no hills, in fact no attraction of any sort or kind,' she deplored:

> There are numerous coverts but no fine woods, large unenclosed turnip fields, with an occasional haystack to break the line of the horizon. It would be difficult to find a more ugly or desolate-looking place, and there is no neighbourhood or any other countervailing advantage. The wind blows keen from the Wash and the Spring is said to be unendurable in that part of Norfolk. It is of course a wretched hunting country and it is dangerous riding as the banks are honey-combed with rabbit-holes. As there was all England wherein to choose I do wish they had had a finer house in a more picturesque and cheerful situation.[2]

The particulars of an earlier sale (in 1836) saw matters differently, sparing no effort in presenting the estate's expansive sense of scale and its sporting attributes. The 'mansion', it declared, '[is] replete with every accommodation for a Family of the first respectability, standing on a beautiful lawn and surrounded by a Deer Park and Pleasure Grounds, varied with ornamental Oak, and other thriving Timber and Plantations . . . [in] one of the finest sporting districts, regularly hunted by the Norfolk Fox Hounds and Harriers . . . and abounding with Game of every description'. Privacy was assured. As the Prince first knew it, the 179-acre park was enclosed by stone walls or paling, and screened by a number of estate plantations. Moreover, within the compass of sixteen miles were neighbours of agreeable pedigree: Sir William Folkes (Hillington Hall); the Marquis of Cholmondeley (Houghton Hall); Lord Townshend (Raynham Hall); the Earl of Leicester (Holkham Hall).[3]

The Hall, which the Prince acquired for £200,000 in October 1862, closely resembled the three-storey residence completed about 1771 – an unremarkable 'huddle of [slate-roofed] blocks, as if a giant had rammed . . . oblong boxes of uneven length side by side', set in an untamed landscape of heath, gorse, pine woodland and red carstone outcrops. After its sale in 1836 to a sporting landowner (John Motteux of Beachamwell Hall, near Swaffham, some fifteen miles away), the Hall was long unoccupied, although Motteux enlarged the estate from 4,500 to 7,000 acres and established the shrubberies and plantations, which so gratified the Prince. By way of whimsical embellishment, the Prince's immediate predecessor at Sandringham, Charles Spencer Cowper (Motteux's legatee), added a two-storey porch on the east front, designed by the fashionable architect, Samuel Sanders Teulon – a confection in the High Gothic style more readily associated with expressions of Victorian municipal pride. Contrasting with the white stucco of the façade, this was unashamed ornament in white and red brick and cream stone. Also of Teulon's design was a brick and carstone conservatory on the west front, as well as balustrades (topped with urns) and a number of mock-Tudor chimneys, which cured the smoky fires.

For a while, in the 1860s, the Prince was content with providing the necessities of a well-managed estate: model cottages and villas, a home farm, lodges and park gates, a game-store with adjoining ice-house – even a private gasworks. Inevitably, the demands of hospitality required new domestic arrangements by way of a larger kitchen and scullery, a servants' hall, footmen's rooms, confectionery and pastry rooms, pantries and a laundry. The Prince had a billiard-room built within Teulon's conservatory, extending it to house a sunken bowling alley. But if the constraints of the private accommodation alone were bound to encourage grander ambition, the Princess's rheumatic illness in th spring of 1867, for which her surgeon, Sir James Paget, was prepared to blame Sandringham's dampness, convinced the Prince that a complete rebuilding of the Hall should be postponed no longer. His architect, A.J. Humbert (the co-designer of the Prince Consort's mausoleum at Frogmore), had already submitted grand designs for a red-brick wing, flanked by Jacobean-style towers, to stand at right angles to Teulon's conservatory, and a further design encompassing a sweeping forecourt that would have enlarged Sandringham 'beyond all reason'.[4]

What we see today is largely what the Prince settled upon – a not over-ambitious, many-gabled house in brick and creamy stone (favourite Norfolk materials), built by Humbert between 1869 and late 1870. By 1884, a ballroom, to a design by Robert Edis (best known as the architect of the then Grand Central Hotel at Marylebone Station), was added as a projection to the eastern front; its mullioned windows looked on to the sweep, where a turreted entrance porch enabled guests to attend without disturbing the privacy of the Hall. An adjoining conservatory (the 'Flower Court') was completed in 1887.[5] The Prince saw fire damage in 1891 as an opportunity to extend the frontage to some 500 feet, a length unrivalled among English country houses. Into the new century, the garden aspect in particular – with its numerous bay windows, summer awnings and terrace – merely invited criticism for appearing indistinguishable from grandiose Edwardian hotels aping the Sandringham style.[6]

In truth, Sandringham House was a 'thoroughly liveable and comfortable' home (the words of a mistress, the actress Lillie Langtry, seemingly at ease under her lover's matrimonial roof)[7] – a hub of family informality and clutter, filled with 'sentimental paintings, plush-covered furniture, mounted animals' heads [and elephants' tusks], suits of armour, display cabinets [of] china, tables crammed with ornaments and photographs';[8] everywhere palm fronds and *bijouterie*, and the makings of the Princess's fine Fabergé collection. Visiting cards were placed on a hall salver held in the paws of a stuffed baboon. To these items of contemporary taste, the *Strand Magazine* of 1893 noted there were tigers' skins and stuffed birds and, in the centre of the large drawing room, a construction of rockwork with ferns and roses, topped with 'a marble figure of Venus',[9] an example of decorative hyperbole not untypical of its time. Below stairs, the Prince was all for innovation (although he could never match such enterprise as was displayed at Cragside in Northumberland, where the armaments tycoon Sir William Armstrong's hydraulic electricity lit all the rooms, powered central heating, sounded gongs for meals and turned the spit in the kitchen).[10] That said, a tramway ran almost the length of the Sandringham cellars, conveying fuel and other necessities between a series of hydraulic lifts serving hatches on the corridors above; most rooms were gas-lit. The incorporation of iron girders and concrete to strengthen the floors made possible a truly egregious indulgence – sunken baths of solid marble (the Prince's was jet-black) in the couple's separate bathrooms, with marble floors to match and gas-lit globes set in recesses. The taps were of German silver.[11]

The Prince well knew that his *affaires d'amour* placed domestic harmony largely in the Princess's gift. She declined to assume the role of betrayed wife ('Jealousy is the bottom of all mischief and misfortune in this world,' she once told her sister-in-law, Princess Louise),[12] but welcomed the Prince's lovers to the house, seemingly without demur, and by her dignified conduct won his unshakeable respect. Indeed, the Prince's solicitude in fulfilling his wife's wishes in regard to the family home can only have nurtured their mutual affection for the house. When the Princess insisted that her private sitting room be replicated in Humbert's new building, the Prince saw that this was done exactly, even down to the fine rococo detail of the original plasterwork.

As a comment on the Prince's often disarming attention to his guests, Lord Redesdale's encounter shortly after the accession was not without its like. Writing in his room one day, he observed the King enter on tiptoe, test with his hand the temperature of the hot water a servant had brought, and leave, as he thought, unobserved.[13] On another occasion the formidable Sir John (or Jackie) Fisher (later Admiral of the Fleet) was unpacking – he had brought no servant ('Never had one . . . couldn't afford it') – when he heard what he took to be a footman trying the door to his room. 'Come in, don't go humbugging with the door handle!' he admonished, only to see his royal host standing before him and enquiring where his servant might be. What followed Fisher's explanation was equally forthright: 'Put those boots down; sit in that armchair,' he was told, whereupon he was engaged so long in conversation as to make them almost late for dinner.[14]

Regular guests were accustomed to a mood of playful informality, particularly as the royal children were allowed to mix freely with them. As at Marlborough House, the grand staircase would double as a carpeted toboggan run, while the ballroom was the ideal place for tricycle races on wet days. Disraeli recalled a mischievous princess pinching his legs beneath the table at dinner; he assumed the child was put there for that purpose.[15] Evidently, the repressions that sullied the Prince's own childhood were not to be visited on his children. 'If children are too strictly or perhaps, too severely treated, they get shy and only fear those whom they ought to love,' he wrote in an attempt to reassure the Queen. But the Queen was unconvinced. 'They are such ill-bred, ill-trained children I can't fancy them at all,'[16] was her uncharitable judgement on one occasion. The diarist Lady Geraldine Somerset thought similarly, finding the boys 'past all management' and the girls 'rampaging'.[17] However, a friend of the Princess, Victor Montagu, who wrote of Sandringham's social life as being 'very jolly . . . very unstiff and only a certain amount of etiquette',[18] would seem to have had the fairer measure of a confident family circle.

In somewhat saccharine vein, the *Strand Magazine* of 1893 did its best to uphold the notion of the Prince as exemplary 'squire' of Sandringham, intent on succouring his tenantry:

> How often have we seen [the royal party] squeezed into one wagonette, looking like a jolly village squire and his family . . . Our Prince is a country gentleman, deep in agriculture and the welfare of his tenantry; and his wife and children pass their time in visiting the schools, the poor, and the sick, working in their dairy, or at their sketching, art and useful needlework etc.[19]

It was in large part an equivocal harmony, brought into question by the publication some six years earlier of a tenant's prejudiced account of her struggle to make a living under the shadow of the sporting gun. Made a widow soon after taking the tenancy of Appleton Farm in the hamlet of West Newton, close by the park, Mrs Louise Cresswell blew the whistle on an unyielding system of game management conducted in the Prince's self-interest. 'Game, game, nothing but game was to be the order of the day,' she disclosed in a memoir, *Eighteen Years on Sandringham Estate*, an interference that confounded her attempts to return 'utterly exhausted' land to modest profit. During a dry, hot summer, 'when the ground game . . . seem[ed] almost to grow out of the earth', she awaited the Prince's arrival with apprehension:

> The Prince came down and all hope of relief vanished; he was infatuated with the shooting; it became a perfect passion with him, and nothing made him more angry than the slightest opposition to it . . . [A] newly-imported head-

keeper, with an organised staff of officials, took possession of the place in military style, and parcelled out my farm like policemen's beats, some of the battalion being told off in charge, and a cottage built for them at either end, whilst I had been entreating for necessary accommodation for my labourers without success. Without either 'with, or by your leave,' strips were cut across some of my fields like a gridiron, and planted for game shelters, and until the trees were sufficiently grown to smother them, a mass of noxious weeds grew, seeded and blew all over my crops and the newly cleaned land, no one being allowed to cut them down for fear of disturbing the nesting.

Further depredations – of hares and rabbits – were spoiling Mrs Cresswell's livelihood well before the first autumn shooting parties, with their loaders and their beaters, took to the fields. She writes of 'crying over the havoc with mingled rage and grief' as she took stock of the growing shoots of swedes and mangolds devoured just as 'the saccharine matter begins to form in the joints'; of seeing the sainfoin (an expensive planting) eaten down to the ground and the maturing wheat so ravaged that she could gather up the ears in bundles. Just occasionally her exasperation softens to whimsy. She never 'want[s] for company' when inspecting the fields, because the hares would run like a pack of hounds at her pony's feet; others would stand upright 'with an air of irritating self-possession', as if they knew themselves to be under the Prince's protection. But grittiness predominates – in the face of increasing debt and 'an under-current of mischief-making', whose source she can never trace. She suspects the land agent and his gamekeepers (the recipients of her many complaints) of playing on the Prince's 'fatal habit of listening to tales from any quarter, without taking the trouble to inquire into the truth of them', so that she 'lived in a sort of chronic disgrace'.[20] Her *Eighteen Years* were to end in the summer of 1880, when the King's Lynn bank called in her debt; she, with her son, would attempt a new life in Abilene, Texas.

So well did the Prince transform the shooting that Sandringham's killing fields soon rivalled Lord Leicester's at Holkham: by 1900 the annual Sandringham bag had risen some fourfold, to 30,000 birds.[21] Yet the early years appeared inauspicious. Writing of Sandringham in the early 1860s, Lord Walsingham described the coverts as 'scanty . . . the stock of game very limited, and the woods ill-adapted for that system of beating which has become the hall-mark of the well-driven pheasant'.[22] Lord Leicester's encouragement notwithstanding, the catalyst for change was the introduction of sanctuaries (remises) for the rearing of birds, which Baron Hirsch was perfecting on his estates in Hungary – arrangements which the Prince and his head gamekeeper, Mr Jackson, saw for themselves. Hirsch's breeding stock was always sufficient to outlive the carnage: a shooting party that the Prince attended in 1891 dispatched 11,300 head of game in a five-day period; again, a month of (presumably) sustained fusillade in 1894 accounted for 22,996 partridges alone.[23] The Prince developed four remises at Sandringham varying in size between twelve and twenty acres, planted in the main with buckwheat and mustard, interspersed with controlled densities of gorse. So well did this system concentrate the game, according to Lord de Grey (by repute 'a near phenomenal shot'), that Sandringham's Captain's Close remise, to take an example, often saw 300 partridges taken 'without the guns moving from their places'.[24] The coverts were as carefully planned. Writing of Dersingham Wood, a Norfolk shooting man of a later generation described it as it earlier was – 'a dense semicircular thicket of broom, snowberry, privets and the like, around which were planted at intervals wide screens of clipped evergreens about seven feet high', conditions which reduced the pheasants to a state of barely sporting compliance. Behind those screens, surmised the sporting gun, Aubrey Buxton, will have 'lurked complacently guns and loaders, some of them only just more mobile than the pheasants from which they were hidden'.[25]

Complementing the successful remises was the battue method of driving birds (another European import), which the Prince employed for the convenience of the guns. The opening scene, against a background of autumn hues and lowering light, would have appeared stagy, as Mrs Cresswell explains:

> A complete silence having been secured for miles round, the day was ushered in by a procession of boys with blue and pink flags, like a Sunday School treat, a band of gamekeepers in green and gold, with the head man on horseback, an army of beaters in smocks and hats bound with Royal red, a caravan for the reception of the game, and a tailing off of loafers to see the fun, for H.R.H. is very good-natured in allowing people to look on at his amusements, provided they do not interfere with them, and, if it could be conveniently managed, would perhaps have no objection to everybody's life being 'skittles and beer' like his own.[26]

The wide semi-circle of boys and beaters would begin the first drive towards the guns (concealed behind fences and shelters) at 9.45 a.m. Sandringham 'time' – always thirty minutes ahead of Greenwich Mean Time, to make best use of the light.[27] Mrs Cresswell records the eager climax: birds bursting in a cloud over the fences, then falling in all directions, or wheeling about in the confusion of flags; those that escaped did so by veering out of range, or by flying through the flags into the fields beyond – the frenzy repeated some sixteen times in the course of a day, with the guns retiring in stages to new lines of fire. A pheasant-only battue offered the least 'sport', particularly when birds were brought to the woods in hen-coops and released to be shot down tamely in their thousands.[28] Of other game, woodcock and snipe were plentiful and hares were regularly imported from Europe in lots of 100.[29] The Prince experimented unsuccessfully with Virginian quail (they strayed from the estate); for one season (1878–9) red grouse were imported, but they never acclimatized to Norfolk conditions.

Clearly the size of bag was governed largely by the efficiency of one's firearm. Into the 1850s, sportsmen were still using muzzle-loaders – percussive guns of violent recoil that were slow to prime and consequently made for intermittent firing. The later breach-loaders, familiar to the Prince's shooting parties, had the benefit of gentler recoil, but not until the advent of the hammerless gun (and the later ejector and single-trigger gun) in the 1870s was the rate of firing transformed. In the following decade the use of Schultz smokeless powder meant that the field of vision no longer resembled a battlefield.

Indulging the Prince's itch for the trigger ('anything that moved received the royal salute') was – if they knew their man – the first consideration of hosts at home and abroad.[30] (No sooner had the young Prince arrived at a homestead in Dwight, Illinois, on his American tour, than he was calling for a gun to bring down a screech-owl that was interrupting a quiet sunset. The following year by the Nile he was popping at vultures, lizards and crocodiles; in India for the winter of 1875–6 (as is mentioned in Chapter 8) he had the run of elephant, cheetah, tiger, even flying fox (a red-haired bat with a five-foot wingspan) and jackals at dawn.[31] Lord Walsingham thought the Prince a good shot because he maintained 'a steady average of 30% kills to cartridges'.[32] Lord Warwick agreed: the then King 'could not be considered a first class shot' but 'he was at least a good one', particularly when the sport was driven partridges.[33] What qualified the Prince as 'eminently human' among the sporting fraternity, Lord Rosebery recalled, was his readiness to give his guests the best of the sport. On pheasant shoots the Prince would commonly exclude himself from the process of drawing lots for position in the firing line and insist on keeping the outside of the line while his guests moved a place to the right after each drive.[34]

Attended strictly by royal command, the weeks that coincided with the birthdays of the Prince (9 November) and the Princess (1 December) were Sandringham's most formal, well-nigh austere affairs, dedicated almost exclusively to the Prince's shooting obsession. What there was of indulgence was limited to evening brandy and cigars and a little billiards or American bowling; the ballroom was not used.[35]All members of the house party were required to follow the day's sport, the women from luncheon onwards. The meal was eaten out in the fields in a tent with its flaps rolled up, however hard the weather. 'With the north wind blowing straight from the sea,' as the Duchess of Marlborough complained, the women would suffer the elements through the afternoon, only the lee of hedges affording them shelter.[36] Bleak photographs attest to the hardihood of these occasions. They invariably show the Prince wearing an Inverness cape and flanked by the entire house party, the women understandably grim-faced in fur hats, scarves and greatcoats against the cold. The day's kill is laid out ritually before them, soon to be taken to the game larder, the capacity of which (at 7,000 birds) was bettered only by Baron Hirsch's. Although the London markets received large quantities of game from shooting estates, the rearing of game birds was only ever conducted for pleasure, not gain. 'Up goes a guinea, bang goes a penny halfpenny, and down comes half-a-crown' was held to be the economics of the sport. The difference (after paying gamekeepers) went on entertaining your guests.[37]

While any shooting day was foremost the exercise of her landlord's rights of property, Louise Cresswell saw it as bringing 'personal loss and inconvenience', a twofold bane of interrupted work and damage that compounded the embarrassment of being in arrears with her rent. She explained how

the fields were cleared for action early in the morning, and I had to stop the work and keep the men at home, field machinery, &c., at a standstill. One year I lost part of the turnip crop in that way, for having engaged a gang of thirty hands from a distance to 'pull, top and tail, heap and mould up' by the acre, they were ordered off the fields for three days in succession; a frost set in, and the roots remained out in it, exposed to the weather and game.

Partridge-driving days were the worst, not so much for being to the discredit of the royal party, but because they were a (utilitarian) free-for-all:

[T]he village boys made it a Carnival, enjoyed trampling down all before them, breaking fences and gates, and doing as much mischief as they could, unconsciously carrying out the latest philanthropic craze, of the greatest happiness of the greatest number, the sacrifice of the few to the many, the elevation of the masses and other benevolences with which I had no sympathy.

When Mrs Cresswell applied for compensation through the Prince's servants who ran the estate – she 'never heard of the Prince receiving or listening to any of the [tenants] on business matters' – her temerity met with skilled condescension. But she countered with a deal of pluck, one summer laying down a damaged mangold (a 'bludgeon', her supporters called it) on the table before the land agent and lawyer determining her complaint. That year she was paid less than half the agreed compensation of £575 16s by way of sparing the Prince's embarrassment at having proof of damages in full laid 'before the country'. (Finding her 'quite impracticable, they paid less than half [the money] into my banker's account, without my knowledge and consent, obtained a receipt for it, and so completely circumvented me, with the advantage of having a virtuous-looking document to file up in the royal offices,' Mrs Cresswell explained.) Next she turned for advice to the Norfolk MP, Clare Sewell Read, who chose to read out her confidential letter in the House – after which the Prince 'scowled at me in true Henry the Eighth style whenever he chanced to meet me'. Soon she was finding him capable of 'some very despotic tendencies'. She was falsely accused of allowing a litter of foxes, which she was asked to rear for the hunt, to account for seventy-one Sandringham pheasants, and only after formal inquiry before the Lord Lieutenant of the County and her supporter 'Mr Onslow', the Prince's Domestic Chaplain (and Rector of Sandringham), was she fully exonerated. The Prince sent word afterwards that it had all arisen from a 'misconception of facts'.

The pumping station episode raised the Prince's ire considerably more. 'Prince Albert Victor [Prince Eddy] has typhoid and it's all your doing,' the land agent informed her in July 1877, the supposed calumny coming just days after the foundation stone was laid for a water tower and pumping station that would bring spring water to Sandringham House from a wood close to Appleton Farm. Mrs Cresswell was allowing the farm drainage to poison the water, it was alleged, when clearly it was newly laid pipes that were at fault. Earlier, a new road Mrs Cresswell had made became badly rutted and holed by the constant passage of carts carrying materials for the project. The Prince, who thought it *his* road, complained to her in person. He had to take her reply on the chin: 'It is *my* road, Sir, and your Royal Highness's carts have cut it all to pieces.'

Before the Prince's tenant withdrew from the fray and left for Texas, Princess Alexandra drove out to wish her farewell. Mrs Cresswell should not go, she believed, and she spoke of 'what could be done'. On the point of departing in her pony carriage, the Princess sent back a last word: 'Tell her I *am* so sorry for her, so *very* sorry.'[38]

More than a decade after the Prince registered his racing colours with the Jockey Club (purple body, scarlet sleeves, black velvet cap with gold fringe), little had occurred to lift his prospects above running a few middling horses for pleasure, but little profit. Speaking as an owner of racehorses early in 1866, he was at his most sanguine: 'To be neither unduly elated by success nor discouraged by reverses has always been considered the first attribute of a good sportsman,' the Prince told a friend. Although he hoped 'some day' to own a Derby winner bred by himself, he was in such poor luck that were a horse of his to be winning a race he rather expected that 'it would drop dead before passing the winning post'.[39] (A filly, Counterpane, duly disobliged him, dying instantly of heart failure in the course of a race.) But a change of trainer after the 1893 season and the earlier purchase of Perdita II for the new Sandringham stud – soon to be the dam of three outstanding progeny – marked the turning point in the Prince's fortunes and confirmed his passion for what he called 'the glorious uncertainties of the Turf'.[40]

None relished the uncertainties more than the Prince's 'oracle'[41] in racing matters, Lord Marcus Beresford, or better epitomized the camaraderie of the turf, or was as adept at trimming his sails to the precise tenor of the Prince's disposition. 'His wit came from him like lightning,' recalled the trainer, Richard Marsh. 'He never let an opening pass and could at times be as savey [*sic*] and daring as at others he could be innocent of his mirth . . . no one was more sensitive of the moods of his royal master.'[42] Lord Marcus Beresford first bought horses for the Prince in 1878 (eighteen years before his first Derby victory), namely two established steeplechasers, Congress and Jackal, the former having run in five Grand Nationals, coming second in two of them. He broke down days before running in his first National in the Prince's colours (in 1879); Jackal, who finished second in the race, beaten by ten lengths, broke down that autumn and was shot.

What truly whetted the Prince's appetite for flat racing was witnessing St Blaise's final Derby trial on John Porter's Kingsclere gallops near Newbury in 1883, the year of his victory. But ten years' association with the Berkshire trainer brought little financial reward. The Prince would travel to Waterloo station in a hansom from Marlborough House, catch the 11.15 a.m. express to Overton, then be taken by fly to hack on the downs and view his horses, before lunching at Porter's residence, Park House.[43] But each visit meant a long day's outing, and, with the Prince's stud established at Sandringham, Lord Marcus Beresford had little difficulty in persuading him to transfer his horses to the Newmarket trainer, Richard Marsh, at Egerton House. The Jockey Club Rooms in the town were familiar to him from his having attended the races and from visits to buy yearlings. Before long he would be provided with a private entrance at the club – an ingenious arrangement whereby his comings and goings passed entirely unobserved, since they took place literally over the heads of members who used the carriage entrance below. He would pass to his rooms by way of a corridor built across the carriageway at first floor level, having only to climb a comfortable flight of steps (flanked at the top by a pair of fine Ionic columns), out of sight from behind the high carriageway wall.

Moving his eight horses to Egerton House (on New Year's Day, 1893) brought the Prince little immediate success: even Porter's purchase on his behalf of the highly regarded Perdita II had failed to pay off on the racecourse, for she was only a modest performer. ('One must have patience,'[44] the Prince assured his son, Prince George, who later was a better judge of a horse than his father during an earlier eight-year period which won him less that £6,000 in prize money.) But also among the batch of (at best) moderate horses newly arrived at Egerton House was an unraced two-year-old, Florizel II, Perdita II's offspring sired by St Simon, who would show exceptional promise that autumn. He would go on to win five races worth £3,499 as a three-year-old, including the prestigious St James's Palace Stakes at Royal Ascot, and counted the Goodwood Cup among his six victories as a five-year-old stayer.[45] However, it was the success of Florizel's younger full brother, the 1896 Derby winner Persimmon, that put Perdita on the way to justifying her later moniker, 'the Goldmine'. Indeed, three sons and a daughter of Perdita would win between them £72,847 in prize money.[46]

Persimmon's Derby credentials were challenged by a rival of similar ability: Leopold de Rothschild's St Frusquin (sired, like Persimmon, by St Simon), whose more telling two-year-old career made him winter favourite for the June classic. Moreover, Persimmon was slow in coming to his peak in the spring when an abscess under a tooth and some unimpressive gallops meant that Marsh would not run him in the Two Thousand Guineas. The Prince wrote to Prince George expressing his disappointment:

> I was also at Newmarket where the weather was very cold. Persimmon is so overgrown that he is only half-trained . . . It is as much as Marsh can do to get him fit for the Derby! And he won't stand knocking about. St Frusquin is what is called a 'set' horse and is now perfectly fit. Thais [*sic*] is looking very well and will I hope run next week.

In the same bitter, blustery cold, the Prince's Thaïs, 'a highly strung and delicate filly',[47] duly won the One Thousand Guineas against a field of nineteen by the narrowest of margins, a short head.

Persimmon's journey to Epsom on 2 June did not at first bode well. The horse was so uncontrollably restive at Dullingham station that Marsh offered a sovereign to everyone who was prepared to manhandle him into his box. But the tantrum passed. The race itself, run on parched ground, became a tense duel over the last hundred yards, Persimmon's longer stride holding off St Frusquin's challenge by a neck. When Counterpane achieved a rare early success in the royal colours some ten years earlier, the Prince had received, as he put it, 'quite an ovation from the public afterwards'.[48] Now, the *Sporting Times*'s correspondent reported, there was a 'gathering roar, like the rumbling of a storm, long before the winning number was hoisted; and then the thunder pealed forth, and a scene took place which we have not the power to describe'. Only Persimmon's jockey, the imperturbable John Watts, appeared unmoved as the Prince led his horse to the unsaddling enclosure: he had ridden all but the last two hundred yards of the race 'as though carved in stone'.[49]

Witnessing the unaccustomed adulation was a large royal party, among them the Duke and Duchess of York, the Duke of Cambridge, the Princesses Victoria and Maud of Wales, and Prince Edward of Saxe-Coburg. The Queen sent a telegram from Balmoral, to which the Prince replied without emotion: 'Most grateful for your kind congratulations. The scene after the Derby was a most remarkable and gratifying sight. Albert Edward.'

If the quality of an owner's hospitality can truly reflect his pleasure in achieving the finest sporting success, the dinner the Prince gave that evening for the Jockey Club at Marlborough House was exemplary. As the racing man and wine expert Michael Seth-Smith highlights, the 1875 claret belonged to the outstanding vintage of the past hundred years and that of 1864 was almost as good. In the context of the Prince's exacting preferences, the dinner will not have disappointed

DINER DU 3 JUIN, 1896

Turtle Punch	*Tortue Clair*
	Consommé à la d'Orléans
Madeira, 1820	*Petites Truites au Bleu à la Bordelaise*
	Filets de Soles froids à la Russe
Marcobrunner, 1868	*Cotelettes de Volailles à la Clambart*
	Chaud-froids de Cailles à la Lucullus
Château Margaux, 1875	*Hanches de Venaison de Sandringham,*
	Sauce Aigre Douce
	Jambons de York Poëlé au Champagne
	Sorbets à la Maltaise
	Poussins rôtis au Cresson
Moët et Chandon, 1880	*Ortolans rôtis sur Cânapés*
	Salades de Romaine à la Française
	Asperges en Branches, Sauce Mousseuse
Still Sillery, 1864	*Croûtes aux Pêches à la Parisienne*
	Petits Soufflés Glacés à la Princesse
	Gradins de Patisseries Assorties
Chambertin, 1875	*Casquettes à la Jockey Club*
	Brouettés Garnies de Glacés variés
	Gauffrettes [sic]

Royal Tawney Port (50 years old): Royal White Port (50 years old): Sherry,
George IV: Magnums Château Lafite 1864: Brandy 1848.[50]

The Prince now rode his good fortune, albeit interspersed with a racing man's setbacks. Persimmon won the final classic of the 1896 season (the St Leger), in a year that won the Prince £26,819 in prize money. In 1900 another full brother to Persimmon, Diamond Jubilee, gave the Prince his second Derby win, to go with the Two Thousand Guineas, the Newmarket Stakes, the Eclipse Stakes and the St Leger the same year. The applause that greeted the victory of his five-year-old, Ambush II, in the Grand National that spring made the Prince feel he had attended 'Persimmon's Derby all over again'.[51]

His appetite for racing wavered little during even the lean years: by the end of September 1890, for example, he had attended twenty-eight race meetings, although inevitably there were times when the call of the turf was an inconsiderate priority. As we have seen, he left his wife's bedside in favour of a steeplechase when she was ill with rheumatic fever. When his mentor (and friend of the Queen) Dean Stanley died in 1881, he wanted the funeral at Westminster Abbey brought forward a day because it clashed with racing at Goodwood, an unforgivable conceit that deeply shocked the Queen. To her it was a shabby reminder that the Prince could so lightly put pleasure before duty – in this instance his duty to a man who had given him exemplary service and had earned, as the Queen believed, an 'immortal name for himself . . . above any Bishop or Archbishop'.[52] The trait was again in play a year before his accession (in 1900), this time exposed in terms of brazen manipulation. Shortly before a grandson's christening (that of the future Duke of Gloucester), he wrote to Prince George:

> [Diamond Jubilee] runs again on 16th for the Newmarket Stakes which he will probably win. That is the day Grandmama has fixed for your little boy's christening. I could not be absent on that occasion from Windsor but I want you to write her a line before you leave tomorrow to beg her to have it on the *17th* instead as a favour to you – as it really *cannot* matter to her – and you could also come down for the day to see the race – as when one has a really good horse it is a grievous disappointment not to see him.

After writing to his grandmother Prince George understandably told his wife, Princess May of Teck: 'It was not an easy letter to write as you can imagine . . .'[53]

When the Prince spoke of his annual visit to Lord Savile at Rufford Abbey to attend the St Leger as 'like coming home',[54] he was in a sense paying tribute to the racing fraternity's democracy of enjoyment. He might be the guest variously of Lord Sefton (for the Grand National), the Duke of Richmond (at Goodwood), the Duke of Westminster (at Eaton Hall for the Chester races), Leopold de Rothschild (at Palace House, Newmarket), and of numerous others, but at the racecourse – as owner or spectator – he was as subject as any man to that unforgiving leveller, the caprice of fortune. 'I am happiest when I have no public engagements to fulfil,' he once told his eldest daughter, the Duchess of Fife, '. . . when I can, like plain Mr Jones, go to a race-meeting without it being chronicled in the papers next day that "His Royal Highness the Prince of Wales has taken to gambling very seriously, and yesterday lost more money than ever he can afford to pay".'[55] And racing brought out the best in the Prince in the way of generosity. Richard Marsh's *Reminiscences* is full of praise for the Prince's 'thoughtful consideration' of everyone involved with his horses. When a horse (Rosemarket) cut Marsh's face with his teeth, for example, the Prince promptly expressed his concern – as he did when 'that erratic customer Diamond Jubilee' bit a stable lad's thumb clean off.[56] And everyone who had a hand in Persimmon's Derby victory (which won the Prince £5,450) was rewarded, Marsh receiving a cheque for £800. Lord Marcus Beresford informed him: 'HRH . . . wishes you to give Crisp, the man who "did" Persimmon £100, £50 also to Leach, the head lad, and £50 to Prince, the travelling head lad, in commemoration of the event.' It was left to the trainer's discretion to spend £100 on the stable-lads 'in any way which you consider best'.[57]

Diamond Jubilee's Derby success was the climax of the Prince's racing career up to his accession. In the year following the Queen's death on 22 January 1901, no horses ran in the colours of the King, but were leased instead to the Duke of Devonshire. There would be one further Derby victory for him, when Minoru won the classic by a short head in 1909 – the last racing summer of the King's life.

The Prince's most competitive years of yacht racing (1892–6) were underscored by a leitmotif of smouldering irritation: the rivalry of Kaiser Wilhelm II, his nephew. This tedious relative might adore his grandmother, Queen Victoria, crave English brands of tea and count Kipling and P.G. Wodehouse among his favourite authors, but his strutting nationalism – greatly provoked by his mother Princess Victoria's promotion of English superiority – was dismissed as ludicrous posturing in her homeland. (Such was the Kaiser's distrust of the Prince's sister that on inheriting the throne in 1888 he put her under virtual house arrest 'to prevent state or secret documents being conveyed to England'.)[58] The Prince tolerated his nephew's overblown mannerisms, as well as his cussedness. One late afternoon when the wind died on them while they were racing each other round the Isle of Wight, the Prince was concerned not to arrive late at Osborne for a dinner the Queen was giving in the Kaiser's honour. 'Prepare to abandon race and return by train,' the Prince signalled from his racing cutter *Britannia*, only to receive the reply from his nephew's *Meteor I*, 'Race must be fought out.' As the Prince feared, they did not return to Osborne until 10 p.m., by which time the dinner was ending. While the Queen's grandson offered their apologies, the Prince, it was said, stood at a distance behind a pillar.[59]

The first of the Prince's yachts, acquired in 1866, was a modest cutter unsuited to racing. His second, the 205-ton racing schooner *Hildegarde*, won the Queen's Cup at Cowes in 1877 with the Prince on board; his third, the *Formosa* (bought in 1879) gave him another Queen's Cup victory in 1880, and within two years he was Commodore of the distinguished Royal Yacht Squadron at Cowes. His purchase in 1892 of the racing cutter, *Britannia*, built by the renowned marine architect George Lennox Watson, gave the Prince unrivalled and nigh-predictable success, until the Kaiser's ambition – and bountiful purse – usurped his mastery. (*Britannia* and her crew of twenty-eight won twenty-four of forty-three races off the British Isles in the 1893 season alone; in her career as a whole, when the Prince sailed on her every day of the Cowes Regatta, she won 122 times from 219 starts, with twenty-five second or third prizes. She served, too, for many years as the Prince's home on the Riviera.)[60]

No sooner was the Kaiser's new *Meteor II* cutting through the waters of the Solent – a Watson commission built on the same lines as *Britannia*, yet on a larger scale – than the Prince knew he was outplayed. For the 1897 season he was content to sail *Britannia* on the Solent for pleasure and he did not race again. Two years earlier he remarked: 'The Regatta at Cowes was once a pleasant holiday for me, but, now that the Kaiser has taken command there, it is nothing but a nuisance. Perhaps I shan't come at all next year.'[61]

Yachts had been a considerable drain on the Prince's resources, and his decision to sell *Britannia* to the 'Bovril' tycoon, John Lawson Johnston, in the autumn of his rival's 1897 domination was 'painful', but realistic. However, he was able to buy her back when he became King – for sentimental reasons alone.[62]

6

'He Is No Better;
He Is Much the Same'

The Prince reached the age of thirty with the mood among royal advisers decidedly glum. In Gladstone's opinion the Queen was 'invisible' and the Prince 'not respected',[1] a sorry conjunction against a background of 'disgruntled loyalism' in the nation at large. Since the death of the Prince Consort in 1861, the satirical magazine *Tomahawk*, for one, had been mining a rich seam of discontent with the Queen's absence from royal duties – presenting images of a vacant throne with orb, sceptre and crown laid aside, or draped in discarded royal robes, the carved arm-rests in the form of dejected lions. An illustration of 1866 casts Buckingham Palace as a stylized 'Gothic' ruin overrun with rats.

This landmark year of 1871 created a particular *frisson* of alarm at home and abroad. From late March, until the Versaillais meted out a brutal suppression three months later, the Paris communards had returned much of Paris to the working class. In England a less ideological, therefore cruder, republicanism fed off platform agitation in centres as diverse as Sheffield, Exeter, Norwich, Birmingham and Sunderland. In London a loose affiliation of radical malcontents was as prepared to abuse the royal family as they were to break down the railings round a royal park, which had happened at Hyde Park in 1866, when the Home Office enforced prohibitions on public meetings there. Fired by debating hall rhetoric, crowds overwhelmed all of London's public spaces in the course of 1871, making for a sense of crisis that engravings of the scenes published in the press served to worsen.[2] The normally circumspect *Pall Mall Gazette* was adamant, warning by September of 'republicanism of a very revolutionary form flooding in'.[3] (Provocatively, a provincial newspaper reported a fire at Warwick Castle in December alongside news of a riot in Derby.)[4]

Riding the bandwagon in Parliament, the Liberal MP Sir Charles Dilke resisted Civil List payments to undeserving royalty, the immediate target being a government-funded dowry paid at the time of Princess Louise's marriage in March to the Marquis of Lorne. (Once the republican hullabaloo died down, the Marquis was much in the Prince's company.) At a November meeting of the Republican Club in London, the radical atheist and future MP Charles Bradlaugh – a scion of 'the good old English political tradition of cussedness',[5] who would refuse to take the oath required of a sitting MP – had the Prince directly in his sights:

> I have lately . . . declared my most earnest desire that the present Prince of
> Wales should never dishonour this country by becoming its King. My opinion
> is that if four or five years of political education are allowed to continue in
> this land, that worthy representative of an unworthy race will never be King
> of England. My thorough conviction is that neither his intelligence nor his
> virtues, nor his political ability, nor his military capacity – great as all these
> are for a member of his family – can entitle him to occupy the throne of
> Great Britain. I am equally opposed to his ever being Regent of England. I
> trust that he may never sit on the throne or lounge under its shadow.[6]

Meanwhile, popular disloyalty was indiscriminate. The title of an anonymous pamphlet attacking the Queen's allowances – *What Does She Do with It?* (written, it was discovered, by the statesman George Otto Trevelyan) – was appropriated for chalking on walls in poor areas of the city and as the subject of satirical handbills. It was widely believed that the Balmoral recluse was failing in her public role as monarch and must be hoarding her generous Civil List allowance. And, as salacious conjecture would have it, did her dependence on her gillie, John Brown, whose name she heard called by onlookers during those rare public appearances, not point to the exchange of sexual favours?[7] No wonder, then, that for much of 1871 the Queen 'stood like one of Landseer's red deer at bay', as the royal biographer Elizabeth Longford concludes.[8]

Nor had the Prince's recent behaviour tempered the 'spirit of democracy'.[9] When the Queen wrote the previous spring of 'a painful, lowering thing',[10] she was reprising his appearance as a witness in a divorce court to explain his familiarity with Lady Mordaunt (née Moncreiffe), whose denunciation for adultery with others of her acquaintance was effectively a judgement upon her sanity. His association with her had 'show[n] an amount of imprudence', his mother regretted, 'which cannot but damage him in the eyes of the middle and lower classes'.[11] *The Times* thought him to be under a 'cloud of obloquy'. As Lady Mordaunt's husband, Sir Charles, saw matters, his wife had been receiving letters from the Prince, which, though they were innocent of passion, 'far exceeded the bounds of propriety' for being addressed to her without his knowledge. Eighteen in number, they were found secreted in her desk, together with a handkerchief bearing the Prince's initials, a lock of hair and a Valentine, this last received before her marriage.[12]

They first met at Moncreiffe House, the parental home at Bridge of Earn, near Perth – where the frequent visits of young men to the schoolroom (Harriet was the fourth of eight daughters) had led a governess to resign. In November 1865 the seventeen-year-old paid her first visit to Sandringham, and there followed an exchange of photographs: 'I shall be only too happy to receive another photograph from you if you will kindly send it to me,' the Prince wrote in December. Flowers taken from a bouquet which the Prince had sent her on the morning of a ball held the following June were pressed for keeping with his letters. In September she announced her engagement to Sir Charles Mordaunt of Walton in Warwickshire; they were married on 7 December in Perth, the day before the Prince returned from the nuptials in St Petersburg of his sister-in law, Princess Dagmar. The Prince, whose wedding gift to Lady Mordaunt was a diamond and emerald horseshoe ring, soon resumed writing to her, ostensibly thanking her (on 13 January 1867) for carrying out a somewhat surprising commission when she and Sir Charles had been together in Paris: 'I am very sorry,' he told her, 'that I should have given you so much trouble looking for a ladies' umbrella for me at Paris . . . If there is any commission I can do for you there it will give me the greatest pleasure to carry it out.'

If the Prince was merely trifling, he did so with uncommon care, behaving as if Lady Mordaunt were more to him than a convenient distraction. Indeed, when news reached him that Princess Victoria's son Sigismund had died from meningitis, it was to Lady Mordaunt that he promptly sent a note regretting that he would not have the pleasure of her company that evening. As in conducting all his *amours*, the Prince matched impeccable discretion with opportunity. Although he could rely on Sir Charles to be regularly away from home on parliamentary business, or shooting pigeons at Hurlingham, it says much for the Prince's contriving that only once – so the court established – did Sir Charles find the Prince alone with his wife in their Chesham Street drawing room. He invariably came by public hansom at least once a week, staying for up to an hour and a half; he had the assurance of complete privacy. Between times, a footman conveyed letters to and from Marlborough House. (Lady Mordaunt insisted that her used blotting paper should always be burnt.)[13]

Meanwhile, Lady Mordaunt was alleged to be indulging carnal dalliances that would lead to divorce proceedings, Sir Charles citing Lord Cole and Sir Frederick Johnstone as co-respondents. There had been a hysterical confession: 'Charlie, I have been very wicked,' his wife claimed. 'I have done very wrong . . . With Lord Cole, Sir Frederick Johnstone, and the Prince of Wales, and with others, often and in open day.' By the time Sir Charles signed a petition for divorce on 27 April 1869, on grounds of adultery, his cause was burdened by counter-claims alleging that Lady Mordaunt was prevented by insanity from being a reliable party to the suit.

Sir Charles had been slow to read the runes, even as his wife was more and more in the company of the Prince's friends; her brother-in-law, Lord Dudley, had long before spoken to him about the Prince's predatory sexuality. Nor had Sir Charles inquired too closely into the 'irregularities' his wife brought to the attention of her physician, Dr Priestley, during the London season of 1867. He could see she was becoming highly strung and easily given to hysterics – conditions he hoped would be mitigated by a summer spent in Switzerland. Meanwhile, the servants could hardly fail to notice how adeptly she found time in the day to be alone with her former male acquaintances both at home and in the country; but they were Sir Charles's guests, too, and he tolerated them. In early November – by which time she was expecting a child – Lady Mordaunt spent a night or two of dubious chastity at the Palace Hotel, Buckingham Gate, mostly in the company of a Captain Farquhar, who was using an assumed name. Before leaving she was taken ill: she was suffering a miscarriage. On 30 November she heard again from the Prince, having purchased from him a pair of white ponies, a transaction that presaged a violent unravelling of the suspicions Lord Dudley had long urged upon Sir Charles. 'I . . . trust that they will suit you, and that you will drive them for many a year,' the Prince told her.

In intense heat the following July, Sir Charles cut short a fishing trip to the Norwegian fjords, reaching Walton a day earlier than expected, having already signalled his intention to cut short his stay abroad by a fortnight. (Lady Mordaunt had cleared the house of her friends only the day before.) He arrived to find his wife practising her skill with the white ponies, trotting her carriage in front of the house with the Prince of Wales looking on admiringly. At once all sense of proportion in interpreting the Prince's ill-advised presence evaporated. As soon as her visitor had departed in haste for Moreton-in-Marsh station, a groom led the ponies on to the lawn, where Lady Mordaunt was forced to watch as the creatures were shot; the grooms, it seems, ignored an order to have the carriage burnt.[14] Lady Mordaunt would prove cruelly vulnerable to her husband's deepening distrust, while the frail hold she had kept on her emotions – if only for the sake of appearances – became no longer worth the fight.

The premature birth of a child on 28 February 1869 caused a dismal predicament. Did the nurse think it fundamentally diseased? Lady Mordaunt asked. And could she be sure it was an eight months baby? If so, the mother decided, the boy will have been conceived with Lord Cole 'in the last week of June when I was in London and Sir Charles in Norway'. When the child contracted ophthalmia, Lady Mordaunt feared it might be a gonorrhoeal discharge of the eyes, brought about through carnal association with Sir Frederick Johnstone, who was said to be 'a very diseased man'. The child, meanwhile, did not interest her: her physician, Dr Orford, attested how she would shrink from him 'in great dread'.[15] By 8 March she could contain her agitation no longer, having settled on what she would say to her husband. 'Charlie, you are not the father of the child,' she informed him. 'Lord Cole is the father of the child, and I myself am the cause of its blindness.' It was then (before Sir Charles left her to the ministrations of Dr Orford) that she implicated both Sir Frederick Johnstone and the Prince in her philandering.

To what extent Lady Mordaunt was tapping the truth in what she confessed to, or was engaged in a perverse act of emotional self-immolation, was the substance of the court's deliberations that began in February 1870. If she was insane when the petition for divorce on grounds of adultery was served on her – as her father, Sir Thomas Moncreiffe (the counter-petitioner), sought to establish – then she was unfit to defend the suit; the more so if her madness had followed immediately upon the birth of the child, and before her admission of adultery. Eminent medical men propounded a number of diagnoses, among them hysteria, puerperal mania, catalepsy and sheer lunacy. Set upon having her thought mad, they mustered evidence at variance with the opinion of Dr Orford, the family physician, who knew her best and thought her to have been sane, both before and after the birth of the child. There had been much in her subsequent behaviour to suggest she was doing no more than acting a part: her frequent refusal to answer questions; the unwarranted fits of laughter; the periods of vacant expression when in company; the statuesque pose she would adopt when standing silent in the middle of a room; and how, when greeted, she would proffer her left hand. Yet – so the court decided – the plea of madness swept such fine discrimination aside. In truth, little grasp on sanity remained to Lady Mordaunt after weeks of medical interrogation, during which she was denied the ameliorating comfort of her friends. As the Mordaunts' cook, one Florence Stephens, averred disarmingly in court, her mistress had every reason for believing the postman must be dead.[16]

The Prince's few moments in court – a performance of exemplary reserve, underpinned by assurances that the judge, Lord Penzance, would protect him from any 'improper questions' – belied his anxiety beforehand, as he told the Queen on 17 February:

> I shall be subject to a most rigid cross-examination by Sergeant Ballantine, who will naturally try to turn and twist everything that I say in order to compromise me. On the other hand, if I do not appear, the public may suppose that I shrink from answering these imputations which have been cast upon me. Under either circumstance I am in a very awkward position, and you can easily imagine how I am worried, dearest Mama.

In public, meanwhile, Princess Alexandra never flinched, but remained at the Prince's side for all his engagements. The Queen's letter of support drew a reply of childlike filiality: 'I cannot sufficiently thank you', he wrote, 'for the dear and kind words which you have written to me . . . I shall remember all the kind advice you have given me, and hope to profit by it.'[17]

The publication of the eighteen 'unexceptional' letters Sir Charles had found secreted in his wife's desk barely lowered the expectations of the public gallery, who would witness the first appearance of a Prince of Wales in a court of law since the reign of Henry IV.[18] In taking the oath, the Prince was not required to put the Testament to his lips, but instead pressed his hand within its pages. He answered to a line of questioning that sought merely to confirm that he was a Moncreiffe family friend. Lady Mordaunt's counsel asked:

I believe your Royal Highness has for some years been acquainted with the Moncrieffe family.

I have.

Were you acquainted with Lady Mordaunt before her marriage?

I was.

On Lady Mordaunt's marriage did you write to her and make her [a] wedding present?

I did.

Previous to her marriage had she visited Marlborough House when your Royal Highness and the Princess of Wales were there?

She had.

And has she gone to the theatre with both your Royal Highnesses?

She has.

We are told that she was married at the end of 1866. In 1867 did you see much of her?

I did.

And in the year 1868?

I did also.

Were you acquainted with Sir Charles Mordaunt?

I was.

Have you frequently met him?

I have.

With Lady Mordaunt?

With Lady Mordaunt.

Your Royal Highness knows Hurlingham?

I do.

Have you been in the habit of meeting Sir Charles there?

I have.

On one occasion, I think in June 1868, there was a pigeon match there between Warwickshire and Norfolk?

There was.

I believe your Royal Highness and Sir Charles were captains of each county?

I believe so.

Was Lady Mordaunt there?

She was.

With her husband?

She was.

And in the course of that match did you speak to Lady Mordaunt at times when Sir Charles was by?

I believe so.

We have heard in the course of this case that your Royal Highness uses hansom cabs occasionally. I do not know whether this is so.

It is so.

I have only one more question to trouble Your Highness with. Has there ever been any improper familiarity or criminal act between yourself and Lady Mordaunt?

There has not.[19]

It was an act of exculpation performed with formidable brevity; there was no cross-examination. The Prince stood down, so *The Times* recorded, to a burst of applause which Lord Penzance 'promptly repressed'.[20] A week later he was booed as he took his seat at the theatre. (Among those quick to discern the whiff of deceit was the Prince Consort's one-time equerry, Sir Henry Ponsonby, who fancied London to be 'black with the smoke of burnt confidential letters'.)[21] The firebrand *Reynolds's Newspaper*, which earlier had rebuked the Prince for being 'an accomplice in bringing dishonour to the homestead of an English gentleman', doubted 'whether the Queen's successor will have the tact and talent to keep royalty upon its legs and out of the gutter'.[22] Gladstone, with republican vehemence in mind, thought it timely to point up a lesson from history. Within hours of the courtroom examination (on 23 February) he was writing to the Prince out of concern that there should be no 'revival of circumstances' – he was recalling the behaviour of his titular predecessor, George IV – to bring down further, self-inflicted criticism upon the royal family. 'Even suspicion,' he warned, 'would produce much of the evil attaching to proof, and such nearness to the Throne as that of Your Royal Highness for this purpose is almost identical with its possession.'[23] Gladstone wanted the Prince's time better occupied. It irritated him that the Queen had resisted all attempts to employ the Prince more closely in matters of state. For his part, the Prince chafed, complaining to his mother of the wanton motives of those who had levelled 'gross imputations' against him.[24] Gladstone was soon regretting how 'things go from bad to worse'[25] with the Prince, whose gambling activities had been reported at length in the pages of *Reynolds's Newspaper*. And when, in November 1871 (the year of the Paris Commune), foul drains did their worst by infecting the Prince with a near-fatal bout of typhoid fever, the cynics tended to agree with his brother, the Duke of Cambridge, who believed the republicans to be routed at last. 'Heaven has sent this dispensation to save us,' he told the Queen.[26]

Keeping vigil at the Prince's bedside meant witnessing a miserable conjunction of timing and symptoms. 'There can be no hope,' the Queen confided to her journal on 13 December. The illness was entering its fourth week and the following day would mark the anniversary of the Prince Consort's death. 'There will be superstition in it,' the *Pall Mall Gazette* observed, 'and however foolish the feeling, there is real anxiety about tomorrow.'[27] Unrelieved fever brought embarrassing ravings and delirium. The Prince hurled pillows at his doctors, would fail to recognize the Princess (calling her 'waiter'), or, abusing her, would accuse her of breaking her marriage vows. His revelations were so raw at times – 'very dreadful',[28] Lady Macclesfield thought them – that the Princess was kept from the sickroom.

Returning from Abergeldie to Sandringham in late October, the couple had stayed some days at Lord Londesborough's residence near Scarborough, where the water supply was contaminated with typhoid bacteria. Little more than a week after the Prince's illness was confirmed (on 23 November) a fellow guest at Londesborough Lodge, the Earl of Chesterfield, died, as did the Prince's groom soon afterwards. The first bulletin on the Prince's condition told of a 'febrile attack . . . unattended by danger',[29] while in the sickroom Princess Alice was increasingly asserting herself, with little regard for Princess Alexandra's wishes. 'We are furious at seeing our Princess *sat upon*,' Lady Macclesfield complained, 'and spoken of as if she had not sense enough to act for herself.' Princess Alice had nursed her father in his final illness and expected to have her way again, begrudging the time the Prince wanted to be alone with his wife at his side. 'How Princess Alice is to be rooted out it is not easy the see,' admitted Lady Macclesfield; she thought the Prince's sister 'the most awful story-teller I have ever encountered, meddling, jealous, and mischief-making'. But it was Princess Alexandra who came close to exhaustion, while the strain only increased her deafness. At best she would doze a little in the Prince's dressing-room close by; when doctors thought her presence might excite the Prince too much, she was known to crawl unseen into his room on her hands and knees.[30]

There was heightened alarm at the end of November, and the Queen was sent for. The Princess, who had been selflessly composed throughout, was for a while 'almost distracted with grief and alarm' at the Prince's ravings.[31] On 2 December he rallied, the Queen departed for Windsor, and the Princess and her sister-in-law were able to refresh themselves by taking a sledge ride across the heavy Norfolk snows. It was a brief remission. That night the Prince's fever was critical: as Lady Macclesfield reported the opinion of his doctors (Sir William Gull, the Queen's physician, and the fever specialist, Sir William Jenner), were the Prince not to rally within the hour 'a very few more must see the end'.[32] The Queen gathered up family members (Princes Leopold and Arthur, the Princesses Louise and Beatrice, Princess Alice's husband Prince Louis of Hesse, and the Duke of Cambridge) and returned to Sandringham. Lady Macclesfield soon despaired of having quiet in the House, so apt was 'this extraordinary family . . . to squabble and wrangle and abuse each other'.[33]

By 10 December, a Sunday, much of the country was alert to the prospect of the Prince's demise. A day earlier the *Telegraph* had reported the 'Dangerous Relapse', while some believed him already dead.[34] In deepest Radnorshire, at Clyro, the Reverend Francis Kilvert told his diary how 'contradictory telegrams have been flying about, and we did not know whether to mention the Prince's name in the Litany or not'. He continued:

> Mr Venables [Kilvert's rector] read prayers, and when he came to the petition in the Litany for the Royal Family he made a solemn pause and in a low voice prayed 'that it may please Thee (if he still survive) to bless Albert Edward, Prince of Wales'. It was very impressive. But this suspense between life and death is terribly sad.

Before the afternoon service a prayer for the Prince's recovery had arrived by telegraph, composed by the Archbishop of Canterbury – 'the first prayer', Kilvert said, 'that I ever heard of as coming by telegraph'. (Clyro, like Sandringham, was experiencing the intense cold: Kilvert returned home at dusk from visiting parishioners, 'crazy with face ache, weak and wretched'; the Prince, he added, was 'in every one's mouth'.)[35] The Princess, when she felt she could be spared, was also out at dusk, in order to pray alone in Sandringham's church of St Mary Magdalene. On this Sunday she had a note handed to the priest (the Reverend William Lake Onslow) before the morning service, one never intended for publication, yet it appeared in *The Times* the next morning: 'I must leave, I fear, before the service is concluded,' she told the Rector, 'that I may watch by his bedside. Could you not say a few words in prayer in the early part of the service so that I may join with you in prayer for my husband before I return to him?'

The same newspaper reported the Prince's strength 'terribly diminished', as 'all England' waited with heavy apprehension.[36] Villagers at Sandringham hardly dare look to see if the church flag was lowered, Mrs Cresswell recorded; they 'lingered about the roads not asking now how the Prince was – it seemed too late for that'.[37] In a couplet famous for its bathos, the future Poet Laureate, Alfred Austin, exactly captured this helpless expectancy:

> Across the wires, the electric tidings came,
> He is no better; he is much the same.

The Queen's journal entry for 13 December (the eve of the late Prince Consort's anniversary) was her record of a portentous day, written, as it will surely have been, after Dr Gull had given his opinion that the Prince was 'on the very *verge* of the grave':

This really has been the worse day of all . . . The first report early in the morning was that dear Bertie seemed very weak, and the breathing very imperfect and feeble. The strength, however, rallied again. There had been no rest all night from the constant delirium . . . Sat on the sofa, but so he could not see me. It was very distressing to hear him calling out and talking incessantly quite incoherently . . . Returned to Bertie's room, and, whilst there, he had a most frightful fit of coughing which seemed at one moment to threaten his life . . . Poor Alix was in the greatest alarm and despair, and I supported her as best I could.[38]

The Prince then passed a quiet night, Dr Gull reported 'some abatement of the gravity of the symptoms', and by the afternoon (many thought miraculously) he was sitting up and asking for a glass of ale. By Sunday (17 December) the latest telegram read out to the congregation at Clyro confirmed that 'the symptoms continue to be favourable'.[39]

There was a brief relapse at the turn of the year, after which a slow recovery was assured. Almost at once royal advisers, Sir Henry Ponsonby among them, reawakened their unduly optimistic hope that the Queen would encourage the Prince to mark 'a turning point in his life' by undertaking desirable employment, be it in philanthropy, the arts and sciences, the army, in foreign affairs, or (citing Gladstone's preference) as her representative in Ireland for part of each year. Replying to Ponsonby's memorandum (on 19 December), the Prince's Private Secretary, Francis Knollys, scoffed at the notion, fearing that 'with his disposition, [the Prince] might become irretrievably disgusted with business of every description'. Knollys cited by way of example the Prince's connection over several years with the South Kensington museum for which he had never shown 'any special aptitude'.[40]

Gladstone's proposal to hold a thanksgiving service for the Prince's recovery at St Paul's Cathedral met with reservations from the Princess and blunt opposition from the Queen, who for so long had avoided public appearances, let alone grand ones. The Princess was understandably concerned at making 'too much of *an outward show* of the most sacred and solemn feelings of one's heart', but, believing that the public 'had been so entirely *one* with us in our grief', she persuaded the Queen to accept the '*claim*' of the people 'to join with us'.[41] In the event the Queen enjoyed the occasion, and when the state landau, the first of nine carriages, in which she sat with the Prince and Princess, reached Temple Bar, the Queen raised her son's hand with hers and kissed it, to the delight of the 'dense masses'.[42] The Queen found St Paul's 'stiflingly hot' and the sermon 'too long'; the Prince, still unable to walk unaided, had difficulty in kneeling.[43] He revealed, *The Times* said, 'an extent of caducity ill-suited to his youth'.[44] Indeed – as Tennyson perceived – the contrast of streets decked overall in flags and bunting, and of joyous crowds, with the faltering spontaneity of a pale, drawn Prince was a lesson in fickle mortality:

> When, pale as yet, and fever-worn, the Prince
> Who scarce had pluck'd his flickering life again
> From halfway down the shadow of the grave,
> Passed with thee thro' thy people and their love,
> And London roll'd one tide of joy thro'
> Her trebled millions . . .

Recording how clergy and others on the Sandringham estate had duly presented an address to the Princess before she returned to London for the public thanksgiving, Mrs Cresswell conceded the wider efficacy of the Prince's returning health – 'how one touch of nature made all England kin', as she put it.[45]

7
Unparalleled Opportunities

Five years on, the Prince was embarrassed again, this time by complaisant letters addressed to a woman – Lady Aylesford: an ill-disposed Lord Randolph Churchill had read them and discerned their 'undue familiarity', which Lord Cairns, the Lord Chancellor, considered to be an opportunity for blackmail.[1] Among the Prince's staff, Sir Henry Ponsonby thought them innocent, although peppered with the kind of 'chaff' that Lord Randolph chose to misrepresent.

What unravelled owed its origins in part to the Prince's choice of friends to accompany him to India in October 1875. In an entirely male entourage of eighteen were names from the inner circle of the Marlborough House set, Lord Charles Beresford and Lord Carrington – to whose inclusion the Queen had objected in vain – and the hard-drinking Lord Aylesford (known as 'Sporting Joe'), who rode his horses 'with hands of gossamer', but was singularly without such a reputation in his consideration of women. It was Lord Randolph Churchill's contention that the invitation to Lord Aylesford was a discreditable manoeuvre on the part of the Prince, who well knew that his friend's absence would leave the way clear for Churchill's elder brother, the Marquess of Blandford, to pursue his passion for Lord Aylesford's wife, Edith, without inconvenience. (She had borne her husband two daughters, but as yet no son and heir; Lord Blandford's wife, Bertha, daughter of the Duke of Abercorn, had provided him with three children.) As it was, Lady Aylesford had not objected to her husband accompanying the Prince. With him gone, the 'pretty, foolish, vulnerable'[2] wife took herself to a family house, Packington Hall, for the winter, while the eldest son of the Duke of Marlborough (with his hunters) found accommodation nearby, and was provided with a key to an disused doorway at the Hall.

The scandal, when it broke on the Prince's party (on 21 February 1876), received ominous mention in the Prince's diary: 'Letters!!!' he grumbled. A letter from Lady Aylesford told her husband that she intended to elope with her lover, who would, for her sake, desert his wife. The Prince's feelings were unequivocal: Lord Blandford was 'the greatest blackguard alive', he told Lord Aylesford, before seeing his guest depart aloft in a howdah for the railhead at Bareilly. It was a judgement Lord Aylesford would freely exploit when he reached England six weeks later. 'He has gone home broken-hearted at the disgrace, and the misery it all entails is terrific,' Lord Carrington recorded.[3] Lord Aylesford's daughters, meanwhile, awaited their father's return at the home of their grandmother, the Dowager Lady Aylesford, to whom their mother had penned a spurious justification that trampled on the innate regard of a mother for her son:

> I do not attempt to say a word in self defence, but you can imagine I must have suffered much before I could have taken such a step: *how* much it would be impossible to tell you . . . you do not know, you cannot know, how hard I have tried to win his love, and without success, and I cannot live uncared for. I do not ask you to think unkindly of your son; I know you could not do it, but for God's sake be kind to the children, and do not teach them to hate their wretched mother, let them think I am dead, it will be the best.[4]

The Prince was loath to interfere between friends, who seemed set upon working up a scandal that was sure to tarnish those in its vicinity. But he had written those letters, and they would be used to enmesh him. Through the influence of her sisters, Lady Aylesford was made so thoroughly fearful of the ostracism that would follow if her husband were to obtain a divorce that she was compelled to bring the Prince's letters into play. Her lover passed them to his younger brother, Lord Randolph, who intended to publish them unless the Prince would use his influence with Lord Aylesford to have him abandon the divorce. With the Prince still not returned from India, Lord Randolph took a provocative course: he called on Princess Alexandra at Marlborough House. He did not arrive alone, but took with him an 'excitable'[5] Lord Alington, an Aylesford family friend who could be relied on to echo whatever opinion Lord Randolph served up – and Lady Aylesford herself. (Lord Alington afterwards regretted the part he played, calling it a 'fearful mistake'.)[6] Thinking in her deafness that she had heard a friend's (Lady Ailesbury's) name announced, the

Princess was at first confused, then shaken by Lord Randolph's gravity. 'He [*sic*] was determined by every means in his power,' he assured her, 'to prevent the [divorce] case coming before the Public', and 'he had those means at his disposal'. Playing up the significance of the Prince's letters, he claimed they were of a 'compromising character' sufficient to ensure that the Prince 'would never sit upon the Throne of England'.[7] Then, on the point of leaving, he scratched at the scar of the Mordaunt case. Were Lord Aylesford to sue for divorce, the Prince would undoubtedly be subpoenaed to give evidence in court. It was an impetuous, cowardly performance by Lord Randolph, which infuriated the Prince, who heard of it in Cairo as he made his way home; indeed, it lost Lord Randolph Churchill all social intercourse with the Prince for some eight years – albeit two further years would elapse before the Prince (in May 1886) could bring himself to enter the Churchill home.

On Lord Randolph's departure from Marlborough House, the Princess confided in Sir William Knollys and then shared her anguish with the Duchess of Teck (who had arrived unexpectedly), explaining to her the circumstances that had brought the putative divorcee to her drawing room. Her favourite cousin was adamant. The Princess should go immediately to the Queen, who, when she was told what had occurred, would 'understand and entirely excuse you from any indiscretion'; the Duchess felt sure that the Court Circular could merely record that she had been with the Queen that day.[8]

The Prince's response to Lord Randolph's brutality was headstrong. From Cairo he dispatched Lord Marcus Beresford to demand a meeting with pistols on the channel coast of France, a challenge Lord Randolph took as an insult, since the heir to the throne could not possibly be allowed to endanger himself in such an illegal action. By 19 April, with Lord Hardwicke (representing the Prince's interests in England) and Disraeli both working to dissuade Lord Aylesford from suing for divorce, the Queen had the measure of the Prince's position. In an exchange between their respective Private Secretaries (Sir Henry Ponsonby and Sir Francis Knollys) she expressed

such perfect confidence in the Prince of Wales, that His Royal Highness's disclaimer of any evil intentions is sufficient to convince Her Majesty that the letters are perfectly innocent. But the publication of any letter of this nature would be very undesirable, as a colouring might easily be given and injurious inferences deduced from hasty expressions. The Queen, therefore, regrets that such a correspondence, harmless as it is, should be in existence . . . [H]ad there been any probability of a public scandal into which his name could be dragged by these villains, she would have agreed in thinking it advisable that he should not return [to England] until a frank explanation had been publicly made. But as it is to be hoped that there is no prospect of any such misfortune, Her Majesty hopes that, conscious of his innocence, he will discard all thoughts on the subject and enjoy the welcome he will find on his return.

Before the Prince disembarked at Portsmouth on 11 May 1876, the Princess joined him at sea off the Needles, while their family waited at Portsmouth. He had asked to see her '*first* and *alone*', a necessary privacy, which gave them time to assess the implications of the scandal into which they were both being drawn. Within an hour of reaching Marlborough House their strategy was evident: they would brave the limelight that evening and attend a gala performance of Verdi's *Un Ballo in Maschera* at Covent Garden. In the event, the audience barely held its breath: after a seven-month interval these acolytes of celebrity sensed that the couple meant business as usual, and expressed their pleasure in standing ovations between the acts. What Sir Bartle Frere (the leader of the Prince's Indian tour) described as the 'idolatry' commonly lavished on the Prince would not be lightly abandoned merely because he courted embarrassment; he was simply living as most plain Englishmen of the age would have done, had they the benefit of rank and *éclat*.[9]

The following day (12 May) Lord Aylesford bowed to unrelenting pressure and abandoned his divorce, although the Prince remained in high dudgeon. The first letter Lord Randolph Churchill wrote by way of apology (on 12 July) was ignored by the Prince; another, whose wording received the approval of the Queen, Disraeli and Lord Hartington, was formally acknowledged by the Prince in September ('However ungraciously done, it was *done*,' deplored Sir Henry Ponsonby),[10] by which time Lord Randolph was two months into temporary exile in America. Lady Aylesford and her lover were now settled in France, but without her children, while Lord Blandford had formally deserted his wife (an elder sister of Lord Ernest Hamilton). Lord Aylesford took himself to America, purchased a ranch at Big Springs, Texas, and would succumb to alcoholism: a cowboy related how he woke in the morning 'to find the [whisky] bottles lying around thick as fleas, the boys two deep on the floor snorin' like mad buffaloes and the Judge [Lord Aylesford] with a bottle in each hand over in the corner'.[11]

Although the Prince's rejection of Lord Randolph was absolute, his admiration for Churchill's American wife, Jennie (née Jerome), amounted to a complementary meeting of temperaments: hers altogether delightful and affectionate (the Countess of Warwick thought her 'like a marvellous diamond [whose] . . . host of facets seemed to sparkle at once');[12] his increasingly affected by periods of gloom, particularly after he became King. The eventual thaw in relations with Lord Randolph began on 8 March 1884, when they were dinner guests at the home of the Attorney General, Sir Henry James, in Wilton Crescent. Another dinner – at which Lady Randolph dispensed melting reconciliation – took place in June at the Café des Anglais in Paris. But two further years would elapse before the Prince would condescend to cross the threshold of the Churchills' residence in Connaught Place. By then Lord Randolph was syphilitic, although his wife did not know it: he had already deserted her bed by the time she took the Austrian Prince Karl Kinsky for a lover. At the summer general election, Lord Randolph's political ascent was confirmed when he became Chancellor of the Exchequer and Leader of the House of Commons in Lord Salisbury's Conservative government, offices that he would relinquish suddenly in December at the onset of a harrowing physical decline.[13]

Lady Randolph's efforts apart, there were other promptings which brought about what was officially described as 'a full and formal reconciliation'. Writing to his younger son, Prince George, on 18 May 1886, the Prince said that he 'thought it best', after so long a time, to 'be on speaking terms' again. But Lord Randolph's breathless rise to high office counted a good deal more. 'The Prince is always taken by success,' the prominent Conservative, Sir Stafford Northcote, told his diary by way of explanation.[14]

Inside the gates at Hyde Park Corner stands a nude bronze of Achilles, cast in martial pose, his sword pointing towards the Duke of Wellington's old residence, Apsley House. Sir Richard Westmacott's statue, erected in 1822 as a memorial to the Duke's victories, was subscribed by a group of patriotic women who had no prior knowledge of its design. Although they were momentarily disconcerted by the sculptor's immense vision of muscle, thigh and barely adequate fig-leaf, there was felt to be no lasting incongruity of subject and setting. Hyde Park, for all its display of effortless elegance, was a competitive sexual arena, and the Achilles statue on its grassy knoll at the end of 'The Ladies' Mile' (a cousin of

Rotten Row) became a hub in the predatory ritual of promenade. Here the most stylish of the *demi-monde* vied for attention – women such as the one-time Liverpool whore Katherine Walters (known as 'Skittles'), whose poise on a horse caught the breath of the Prince and his set in the early years of his extramarital promiscuity. So perfectly, indeed, did the one-piece riding habits (of her own design) sheathe her matchless figure that all believed her naked beneath. Count Albert de Maugny considered her a potent afflatus:

> Hers was a particular style reminiscent of London and Hyde Park, which was at once both startling and ultra smart, and which electrified the onlookers and gave them crazy thoughts. One was obliged to respond and vibrate at the same time . . . She shone in this manner for two or three years without seeing her star fade or her prestige diminish for a single instant.[15]

The Count was writing of a time well before the onset of discretion narrowed the range of the Prince's sexual attentions to a series of trusted mistresses older than himself. Yet a marble nude of a nymph (by J.E. Boehm), for which 'Skittles' was the model, long continued to occupy a niche in the Marlborough House library; and the Prince was still paying her an annual allowance and visiting her in Paris after he became King. Later, as her health began to fail, Francis Knollys was instructed to collect and destroy some 300 of the Prince's letters to her. (In the record of the Prince's many practical jokes, his play on her name is a cherished one: 'Skittles' had once been Lord Hartington's mistress, so on a visit to Coventry the Prince asked the Mayor to be sure to include a bowling alley in the itinerary – an arrangement that left Lord Hartington baffled. 'His Royal Highness asked especially for its inclusion, in tribute to your lordship's love of skittles,' the Mayor explained.)[16]

It goes without saying that the women who slept with the Prince felt themselves honoured. Any fumbling uncertainties in royal lovemaking were no doubt allayed by the Prince's finely tuned courtesy, and friendship usually outlasted passion. He conducted his liaisons by the rules of a game that could never condone the deflowering of maidens. Nor were young married women considered to be 'in play'. In keeping with the prevailing double standard, promiscuous men expected to bring virgin brides to their marriage beds, women who were ripe for producing heirs and a string of siblings for the nursery. Thereafter it was expedient not to expect sexual fidelity in a wife. Her procreative duty done, a degree of premarital quickening could resume – the glance first, in response to an inviting look, 'then the careful game of modest recoil and soft innuendo', as the Society memoirist Anita Leslie remembers it.

In London during the three-month season, the customary time of this libidinal interplay was the tea invitation (the so-called *cinq-à-sept* appointment), which had its strict proprieties. Hats, gloves and sticks were laid aside not in the hall, but on a table, or perhaps the floor, in the drawing room itself – indications of visits soon ended. It was usual for husbands to be absent. Servants were kept strictly from the room unless a bell-pull called them – a necessary injunction when a string of convenient departures might leave a favoured caller alone with his hostess.[17] But carnal desire could not easily contend with practicalities: as the writer Juliet Nicolson reminds us, undressing a woman laced in a corset was 'an undertaking similar to the capture of a fortress'.[18] (By the end of the century the loose and lacy tea-gown had been widely adopted.)

Less open to hasty indignities were the sleeping arrangements at country house gatherings, where a lover's strategy depended on the host's allocation of bedrooms. Time an assignation unfavourably and a husband might leave his dressing room for another's bed, only to pass, in some freezing corridor, a fellow guest bent upon a tryst of his own. Indeed, it was every host's concern that scandal should be avoided. (Lord Charles Beresford admitted to choosing a wrong door on one occasion, whereupon he leapt into the bed shouting 'Cock-a-doodle-doo' and found himself between the Bishop of Chester and the Lady Bishopess.) Of the Prince's mishaps one must suffice, which occurred not in an English country house but at the Château de Mello (south of Paris), the residence of the Prince de Sagan and his lascivious wife, Princesse Jeanne. The fifteen-year-old heir to the title – who deeply resented his mother's dalliances – entered her boudoir one day to see the Prince's clothes laid aside on a chair. He promptly snatched them up, then tore through an open French window to the great fountain and drowned them there. As servants in due course fished them out, the Prince mustered a little dignity and drove away in borrowed dress. It appears that the boy was taken in hand at some grim institution.[19]

There was little that pleased the Prince so much as the *odore di femmina*. 'What tiresome evenings we shall have,'[20] he once remarked to his Private Secretary at the prospect of dining without feminine company while the Princess was mourning the death of her father. He rarely enjoyed men's talk over the port after the women had withdrawn, finding it a poor substitute for the rustle of silk and the sharp-witted, teasing pleasantries of the drawing room where he could flirt, although never so pressingly as to ruffle his dignity. Hesitancy in a woman the Prince found regrettable; rejection he merely noted, before plying for satisfaction elsewhere.

It was at a late supper party after the opera (on 27 May 1877) that the Prince exchanged overtures with his 'first openly recognised mistress'.[21] Lillie Langtry, on her own admission, said little while she measured what was required of her. But what undoubtedly caught the Prince's breath on this first encounter was an impression of bashful beauty, charged with erotic invitation – attributes which the artist Sir Edward Poynter wonderfully evinced in his portrait, *Mrs Langtry*. Indeed, she possessed 'a frightening combination of attributes', as a playful George Bernard Shaw affirmed some years later: 'She has no right to be intelligent, daring and independent as well as lovely' – qualities (along with charm) that Oscar Wilde endorsed, maintaining that they were 'far more formidable weapons' than even her unrivalled beauty.[22] Looking back condescendingly on this period from the perspective of the 1920s – when the pomp of her later theatrical fame and fortune had already faded – she merely ascribes an arch *naïveté* to herself as she recalls her entry into Society shortly before this first supper with the Prince:

[W]e rattled up to Lady Sebright's house . . . in a humble four-wheeler. Being, of course, in deep mourning [for her younger brother Reggie], I wore a very simple black, square-cut gown (designed by my Jersey modiste), with no jewels – I had none – or ornaments of any kind, and with my hair twisted carelessly on the nape of my neck in a knot, which later became known as the 'Langtry'. Very meekly I glided into the drawing-room, which was filled with a typical London crush, was presented to my hostess, and then retired shyly to a chair in a remote corner, feeling very un-smart and countrified. Fancy my surprise when I immediately became the centre of attraction, and, after a few moments, I found that quite half the people in the room seemed bent on making my acquaintance.[23]

Pre-Raphaelite artists would portray her as an incarnation of perfect beauty, a quality the painter Walford Graham Robertson hailed as 'a vision' of natural 'loveliness'.[24] In John Everett Millais's well-known portrait – the likeness which gained her the sobriquet 'the Jersey lily' (because of her lily-white complexion and the island home of their respective childhoods) – she wears the same black gown that she wore at the Sebrights', and to supper with the Prince. The artist portrays her with her hair duly coiled in a knot at her neck, a gardenia at her collar and holding a Guernsey lily.[25] For Millais again, she is his model for *Effie Deans* in a scene from Sir Walter Scott's *The Heart of Midlothian*; and notably among the wider Pre-Raphaelite coterie, she sat for George Frederick Watts (*The Dean's Daughter*) and for Edward Burne-Jones (*The Golden Stairs*).[26] She was indeed 'the lovely Mrs Langtry'[27] who walked 'like a beautiful hound set upon its feet',[28] although it would be a mistake to suppose that she belonged to the gallery of wan, ethereal maidens of Pre-Raphaelite imagination: she was of quite a different mould – full-breasted and wide-hipped, much to the Prince's taste in fact, who liked his women fleshy. And she was entirely in possession of her charms in the company of men. In the Prince's company she spoke her mind and readily stood up to him (he abhorred flattery), traits which a far from genteel vicarage upbringing will have encouraged. Lillie was the youngest but one among six brothers; her father, William Corbet Le Breton, Dean of Jersey, was a lecher, who once made her break off a passionate romance by admitting that the youth was his illegitimate son; her mother, although she would live a long life, regularly took to her bed with unexplained illnesses.[29] Lillie's cuckolded husband, Edward Langtry, bore his humiliation as honourably as his ill-temper allowed. He had turned his second wife's head through the mistaken appearance of worldly success ('To become the mistress of the yacht, I married the owner, Edward Langtry,' Lillie wrote),[30] but the Belfast shipping business he inherited never prospered for him, and he soon declined into alcoholism.

The demise of the black gown coincided with Lady Dudley's ball in June 1877, when Langtry appeared in a 'striking creation' (her words) of 'white velvet, classically severe in line, and embroidered in pearls'. And now that she rode alone with the Prince in Hyde Park in the early morning and in the evening before dinner, her many admirers (spoken of as the 'Langtry Lancers') were invariably put to flight. By the autumn, country house hosts were expected to have Langtry's name on any guest list headed by the Prince. Meanwhile, a deferential press took no public interest in the Prince's affair until the following autumn, by which time the foundation stone of the house that legend says he paid to have built for her in Bournemouth had been laid for almost a year.[31]

The timing of this royal house-building ignored the constraints affecting ordinary mortals. The London Stock Exchange had crashed at the prospect of war with Russia, as Disraeli (in support of Turkish interests) had ordered the British fleet to sail through the Dardanelles to anchor off Constantinople – the first warmongering to be labelled 'jingoism' ('We don't want to fight, but, by Jingo if we do/We've got the ships, we've got the men, we've got the money too . . .').[32] With strikes commonplace at home in shipyards, mills, mines and factories, builders' masons, in pursuit of shorter working hours and better wages, had done little work since midsummer.[33]

The Red House (leased in the name of one Emily Charlotte Langton) had the appearance of a half-timbered, bourgeois residence in mock-Tudor red brick, and was deceptively spacious. The dining hall was a two-storey space, incorporating a minstrels' gallery in the medieval manner and a grand fireplace in dark wood; there was a large bay window with stained glass above, featuring a pair of swans in amorous display and a teasing inscription: 'They say – What say they? – Let them say.' (The Red House, after all, was a love nest.) The story goes (one for which, it must be said, the Prince's most recent biographer, Jane Ridley, has found no evidence confirming arrangements for accommodating the Prince)[34] that decorating the panels of the Prince's bedroom, with its vast Jacobean bed, was an erotic mingling of sunflowers and red-hot pokers. In contrast – as expressing a necessary mark of social distinction – Langtry's suite of rooms was plain, but had a wide view of the sea from a balcony above the garden. From these quarters (linked by a discreet passage and stairs to the Prince's) she would pass through double doors near the head of the stairs and descend to their guests, before leading them in to supper.[35] Langtry, then, in her memoir (*The Days I Knew*) asks us to picture a decidedly self-conscious semblance of bourgeois domesticity in a context that was faintly sham. Indeed, the walls of the house carried legends that defied the transience of such royal arrangements – '*Dulce Domum*' ('the sweet [sound of the word] home') and 'The Kingdom by the Sea' among them; one, on the outside wall of the Prince's suite, read: *Stet Fortuna Demesis* ('May fortune attend those who dwell here')[36] – a quaint optimism, given how Langtry, indeed any royal mistress, might soon expect to lose the privilege of the royal four-poster.

But these were the days of her easy triumph. Langtry was counted among the 'Professional Beauties' whose photographs were the first to make a commodity of the female form. 'My portraits were in every shop-window, with trying results,' she wrote, 'for they made the public so familiar with my features that wherever I went – to theatres, picture-galleries, shops – I was actually mobbed.' The *Illustrated London News* once paid £132, her weight in pounds, for a single advertisement, and she famously endorsed Pears' Soap in the popular press.[37] Soon the Langtry knot (hair loosely knotted at the nape), the Langtry bonnet and Langtry shoes were fashionable accessories. Yet Society could never regard her as quite the thing, even while it connived at her self-promotion. So long as she maintained the full confidence of the Prince, her want of breeding and the uncertainties of a bankrupt marriage could be accommodated, but Society's sanction was fickle and its jealousies not easily silenced: she might defy the spectre of eclipse for a while, but her means were frequently audacious. A case in point was Langtry's presentation at Court in May 1878, which crowned her bid for formal recognition, and which the Prince had worked hard to secure. Such an event meant tedium for the Queen, who rarely stayed the distance: instead, Princess Alexandra would acknowledge innumerable curtsies late into the afternoon. But on this occasion Langtry's reputation and a dash of curiosity kept the Queen at her station. (Langtry avoided much of the public gaze beforehand by coming late to the line of open carriages making halting progress down the Mall.) That morning the Prince had sent her Maréchal Neil roses, an 'immense bouquet' of pale yellow that complemented the garlands of her dress – a gown of ivory brocade, whose train hung from the shoulders (in the style of the Empress Josephine) and was lined in the same pale yellow,[38] the entire effect neither overstated nor rash.

But her presentation day was an opportunity like no other to assert the role the Prince had asked of her, and she did not let it pass. She opted for a theatrical gesture that she knew was sure to goad the hostility of her detractors, who must endure her social pretensions while she had the Prince's support. Owing to her ageing eyesight (and doubtless a little boredom), the Queen, through the Lord Chamberlain's office, had expressed disappointment with the paucity of feathers adorning the headdresses worn on presentation days: she wanted them to 'be at least visible to the naked eye'. Langtry responded by adopting three towering white ostrich plumes above her veil, in explicit allusion to the Prince's crest and its motto, '*Ich dien*' ('I serve').[39] When her turn came to make her curtsy, the Queen extended her hand in a 'rather perfunctory manner' and with 'not even the flicker of a smile on her face', Langtry recorded. She would gloss in her memoir how, when they met later at a Marlborough House ball, the Prince 'chaffed me good-humouredly on my conscientious observance of the Lord Chamberlain's order'. 'At all events, I *meant* well,' she added – a comment scarcely well intentioned, since (her biographer's extrapolation) 'people who really mean well do not find it necessary to highlight their intentions with italics'.

Fearful of being taken for a falling idol, and defying the limits of her income, Langtry now abandoned restraint, particularly in matters of dress – 'my colossal extravagance', she called it – as she competed for attention among Society women who 'changed their gowns as a kaleidoscope changes its patterns'. Yet the Prince expected no less: 'That damned dress again!' he exclaimed ill-temperedly when she once wore a dress of silver and white to successive balls.[40] And as his infatuation ebbed, she provoked the more. The story goes that at a charity fête held at the Royal Albert Hall, when Princess Alexandra was of the party, five shillings were asked of those who would receive a cup of tea from Langtry's hands, and a guinea if she were to take the first sip. When, without being asked, she put to her lips the cup she had poured for the Prince, he asked for another: 'I should like a clean one, please,' he said. Drinking from it, he said no more, then paid a couple of sovereigns.[41] Blatantly insulting to the Princess was Langtry's later appearance at a fancy-dress ball dressed as Pierrette, when she knew the Prince would be dressed as Pierrot.

By the spring of 1880 Langtry was falling into ill-suited liaisons. She had met, for example, the twenty-five-year-old Prince Louis of Battenberg and soon believed herself pregnant by him: there was talk of a financial settlement, after which she felt royal ranks begin to close against her. (The daughter, Jeanne-Marie, born to her on 8 March 1881, was an illegitimate forebear of the present Prince of Wales, being half-sister to both Lord Louis Mountbatten and Prince Philip's mother, Princess Andrew of Greece.) While Langtry was carrying Prince Louis's child, her income was diminished (so she admitted) almost to 'vanishing point', since no money was coming to her from her husband's impoverished properties in Ireland. By November she was back in Jersey ('Is beauty deposed, or has beauty abdicated?' surmised the *New York Times*),[42] where she remained until a chance invitation to appear in a charity production brought her to London again. She made her professional stage début in May 1882 at the Haymarket Theatre.

Although a successful theatrical career (in America as well as in Britain) restored her pecuniary fortunes, it put paid once and for all to winning Society's approval. Yet the Prince never dropped her and rarely missed her opening nights, liking to spend part of the performance in her dressing room. 'I may have many faults,' he once admitted, then added: 'No one is more alive to them than I am; but I have held one great principle in life from which I will never waver, and that is loyalty to one's friends, and defending them if possible when they get into trouble.'[43] Indeed, early in her stage career his engagement diary noted her performances on 28 January, 13 February and 15 March (1883), when he would have travelled up to London from Sandringham.[44] Furthermore, the former lovers continued to hold supper engagements, and were often together on race days. (As a racehorse owner herself, Langtry's most successful thoroughbred was the Australian colt, Merman, winner of the Ascot Gold Cup, the Jockey Club Cup, the Goodwood Cup and the Cesarewitch.)

When Langtry ended two years of professional engagements in America in 1885, returning to live permanently in London, the Prince merely resumed the personal attentiveness that was his forte. In August that year he wrote:

> Our stay here is nearly at a close I am sorry to say as we leave for London on Monday – It would be a great disappointment to me if you were unable to come on Wednesday as I had so looked forward seeing [sic] you as it may be a *very* long time ere we meet again – I thought we might have gone to the Gaiety that evening to see the new Burlesque and had a little supper afterwards wh. would have been charming.[45]

Just as there were other men in Langtry's life, so the Prince's attentions were seldom reserved for one woman alone. For a period in the mid-1880s, according to his uncle, the Duke of Cambridge, the Prince (now in his forties) adopted 'a strange new line of taking to young girls and discarding married women'.[46] One of them, Julie Stonor, a Catholic commoner and orphaned daughter of a one-time lady-in-waiting to the Princess, was also the subject of Prince George's boyish attention;[47] another was an American *ingénue*, Miss Chamberlayne (called 'Chamberpots' by the Princess), who, for example, found herself, according to one observer, 'entirely' occupied by the Prince at a party in 1884. These and the young Margaret (Margot) Tennant, later Countess of Oxford and Asquith, and a Miss Duff, formed what the political diarist Edward Hamilton, a friend of the Prince, spoke of as 'H.R.H.'s virgin band'.[48] And doubtless there were any number of hasty encounters, as there was with the Marquis of Headfort's daughter, Mrs William ('Patsy') Cornwallis-West. The story goes that when, with a too-ready tongue, a young daughter of a labourer on the Duke of Westminster's estate relayed how she had seen the Prince 'lying on top' of Cornwallis-West in the woods, the girl's father struck her a violent blow and told her that she would be killed if she repeated the story.[49]

Among the many assessments of the Prince, none better distils his sentiment in female friendship than the reminiscences of Frances (known as 'Daisy'), later Countess of Warwick, the consummate mistress of his late middle age. Throughout the 1890s Daisy Brooke's merits went unchallenged: beauty, presence, vivacity, a quick mind and an indefinable fascination that seemed not to depend on beauty or wit.[50] Describing the impression she made one night at the opera (on 6 May 1891) *The World*'s correspondent saw 'her profile . . . turned away from an inquisitive world, but I made out a rounded figure, diaphanously draped, and a brilliant, haughty, beautiful countenance'. In the Prince's letters to her she was his 'darling Daisy Wife', an endearment she felt to be perfectly sincere from a man who could be 'unduly sentimental'. She writes of qualities in his letters that she found 'rare indeed in royalty':

> The writer always makes light of his own troubles and discounts his own qualities and ability. He was, if anything, too humble about himself, and was always ready to praise other people and willing to believe that they were better than he. He would give the most detailed care to the consideration of other people's problems and troubles, was always ready to help and was full of wise counsel. Every letter reflected a kindly, generous, loyal nature. He gave to his private friendships the practical insight that might so well have served the State.

All of which was irresistible to women. But his 'deep desire for harmony', as she understood, was also a vulnerability. When she wrote that 'no appeal was ever made in vain to his good feeling',[51] she was alluding – no doubt with regret – to a time when she, too, had presumed upon his good nature. Seeking to mitigate the consequences of a rash act of jealousy, she found that she had kindled a deeper resonance in the Prince than sympathy alone.

Lady Brooke had once been Lord Charles Beresford's mistress, a role in which she had claimed exclusive carnal rights. Indeed, when she heard that his virtuous and unprepossessing wife was pregnant again with their second child (another daughter, after a ten-year gap), Lady Brooke succumbed to outrage at what she took for infidelity. Her riposte was an unscrupulous letter addressed to her lover, which Lady Charles Beresford opened while her husband was away in France – a missive her brother-in-law (Lord Marcus) knew 'ought never to have seen the light of day'.[52] Lord Charles must join her on the Riviera, Lady Brooke insisted, before claiming, as a *coup de théâtre*, that one of her children was his. Lady Charles promptly entrusted the letter to George Lewis, the London solicitor of first choice whenever the aristocracy had secrets to protect, while Lady Brooke, clearly shaken by her own audacity, appealed to that 'good feeling'. The Prince on private visits to the Brookes' country house, Easton Lodge, near Dunmow in Essex, would '[throw] aside for a few hours the heavy trappings of his state to revel in his love of nature'. Walking with Lady Brooke through her 'Garden of Friendship',[53] he melted at her entreaties. (Her garden, she later enthused, provided 'balm for sympathy, and the bluebell for constancy; the basil plant for hatred . . . and the foxglove that spells sincerity'.)[54] No sooner had she hurried to the Prince at Marlborough House to urge him to recover the letter (like 'Beauty in Distress', Lady Charles Beresford opined)[55] than the folly of past entanglements with awkward letters was unwisely forgotten. The Prince 'was charmingly courteous to me', Lady Brooke recorded in her memoir, telling her he hoped his friendship would 'make up in part' for the loss of her lover; and before she left, he was 'looking at me in a way all women understand'.[56]

True to his word, the Prince called on Lewis, disturbing him in the middle of the night; he was shown Lady Brooke's letter, which the solicitor refused to part with as it rightly belonged to his client. Nor was Lady Charles Beresford the slightest bit awed when the Prince also went to see her: she had no intention of destroying the letter, she told him, although she would consider returning it to Lady Brooke were she to agree to stay away from London for the entire season. When the Prince visited her a second time, he was intent on threat: if Lady Charles would not relinquish the letter, he insisted, her own 'position in Society!! and Lord Charles's would become injured!!!!'[57] And ostracized she was – in spite of determined defiance – while the Brookes were invited to every house where the Prince was present. As a triumphant Lady Brooke crowed in a fit of shabby point-scoring, 'when that sign of the Prince's support didn't stop the angry little cat, the Prince checked her in another way. He simply cut her name out and substituted mine for it and wrote to the hostess that he thought it would be better for me not to meet the angry woman till she had cooled off and became reasonable.'[58]

Lady Charles's boycott incensed her husband, who called on the Prince (on 12 January 1890, before taking up a naval command in the Mediterranean), whereupon he came close to blows: 'Really, Lord Charles, you forget yourself,' the Prince rebuked, upon falling heavily on to a sofa.[59] From that moment mutual rancour simmered for some eighteen months until, humiliated, Lady Charles gave up her London house in the summer of 1891 in favour of the continent. But by then the nine-month perturbation caused by unconnected events at Tranby Croft in Yorkshire had further damaged the Prince's popularity. This was the *cause célèbre* of September 1890, known as 'The Baccarat Case'. As the Queen confirmed: 'the light which has been shed on his habits alarms and shocks people so much'.[60]

The gaming scandal that condemned an arrogant womanizer, Lieutenant-Colonel Sir William Gordon-Cumming, to some forty years' exile on his Scottish estate at Altyre and at the ancestral castle of Gordonstoun, came of a ruthless closing of ranks by members of a house party who feared exposing the Prince to unfavourable opinion. The setting was the country residence, Tranby Croft, of a socially ambitious shipowner, Arthur Wilson, the host preferred by the Prince for the St Leger meeting at Doncaster in place of Christopher Sykes, whose regular entertaining of the Prince at Brantingham Thorpe had brought him to the verge of bankruptcy.[61] (A family death kept Lady Brooke away.) It was a stay which the Prince abandoned early, on learning of Gordon-Cumming's cheating at the card table, whereupon he moved to the 10th Hussars' mess in York for the last day of racing.

A table was laid for baccarat on both evenings, a game widely played in society in the privacy of its houses, although it was ruled illegal for being one of chance rather than skill. (In the subsequent court hearing, Gordon-Cumming's leading counsel, the Solicitor-General Sir Edward Clarke, called it 'about the most unintelligent mode of losing your own money, or getting somebody else's, I ever heard of'.) As the authors of a study of the scandal lucidly explain, the game is simple:

> Four packs of cards, that is 208 cards altogether are shuffled and placed in front of the banker. He deals two cards to the player on his right, two to the player on his left, and takes two himself. The object of the players is to make

up as nearly as possible the number nine, tens and court cards not counting – perhaps a three and a five, or a four and a five: for this purpose they may each ask for another card but by doing so they may spoil the hand by exceeding the number nine, so it is customary to ask for another card only if the first two add up to five or less. Similarly the banker may also take another card, his decision depending partly on the amount of money that has been staked on one side and on the other. The rest of the players hold no cards but simply bet on those held by the players on either side of the banker.

On the first evening the table was an improvised arrangement (since the Wilsons had rarely, if ever, played the game) of whist tables of differing heights, placed together and covered with a tapestry cloth that made it difficult to distinguish the counters. Indeed, Gordon-Cumming suggested placing the stakes on sheets of white paper for better identification, although only he did so. The Prince used his own counters, a leather set of different colours and patterns that carried the Prince of Wales's feathers in gold on the reverse and ranged in denomination from 5s up to £10. It appears that Gordon-Cumming alone wagered at all heavily, doing so according to the system known as *coup de trois*, whereby he compounded a winning coup by adding another £5 stake to the next, together with his winnings from the previous one. What followed was a run of cards advantageous to him, as well as the suspicion that, by sleight of hand, he was adding to his stake after favourable cards had been dealt him by placing counters beyond the white line that ran round the table, inside which a stake was deemed to be in play. Then it was that the Wilsons' son, Stanley, whispered to Lieutenant Berkeley Levett (a subaltern in Gordon-Cumming's regiment, the Scots Guards): 'This is too hot! The man next to me is cheating!' When the Prince later commented upon his success, Gordon-Cumming looked to the record he had kept of his play, saying, 'Why sir, I could not help winning with such a tableau as this.' As to Stanley Wilson's claim that first evening, this was never verified by the other participants: Wilson himself conceded that he had not always been able to give close attention to Gordon-Cumming's play, yet believed two further £5 counters had been added to the one laid before the cards were dealt him. But as yet no player had spoken to the Prince of his concern. For the next evening he merely requested a better table, one that was properly covered with green baize. When the time came, he drew a chalk line round it himself at the correct distance of six inches from its edge.

By the morning of Tuesday 9 September two further members of the party had been alerted to the suspicion: Mrs Wilson and Stanley's brother-in-law, Lycett Green. That evening, having watched Gordon-Cumming's play closely, Green believed the likelihood of cheating to be confirmed, and the following morning he spoke with Lord Edward Somerset on the train taking the party to the Doncaster racecourse for the St Leger. Soon the senior courtier of the party, Lord Coventry, knew of the accusation, as did Lieutenant-General Owen Williams (Lady Aylesford's brother), a friend of both Gordon-Cumming and the Prince. 'Shocked and overwhelmed with a sense of calamity' that the Prince had shared a game with a cheat – and what this would mean for his reputation – Lord Coventry did nothing to examine the accusation before persuading his informers that he and General Williams should go at once to the Prince; had Lord Coventry bothered to look into the matter with a degree of care, he would surely have recognized that there was no clear agreement as to what the players believed they had seen. (Mrs Wilson, for one, told of seeing an errant counter not *placed* over the line, but pushed there with a pencil.) As Sir Edward Clarke posited in the course of the hearing, Gordon-Cumming's accusers sought to serve the Prince best by a peremptory assumption of the defendant's guilt:

> There is a strong and subtle influence of royalty – a personal influence, which has adorned our history with chivalrous deeds; and has perplexed the historian with un-knightly and dishonouring deeds done by men of character, and done by them because they gave their honour as freely as they would have given their lives, to serve the interests of a dynasty or conceal the foibles of a prince.

This was the daunting influence, Sir Edward Clarke believed, that had governed the actions of Lord Coventry and Lieutenant-General Owen Williams.

The Prince was informed that the evidence was 'absolutely conclusive': neither man believed Gordon-Cumming 'had a leg to stand on'.[62] And it appears that the Prince took them entirely at their word without testing their narrative for himself, a fairness he surely owed to a man who had been his guest at Sandringham. Gordon-Cumming, although he hotly denied the accusation, appeared cowed when a document was presented to him for signing, to which the Prince and nine other (male) members of the house party had put their names. It ran:

In consideration of the promise, made by the gentlemen whose names are subscribed, to preserve silence with reference to an accusation which has been made in regard to my conduct at baccarat on the nights of Monday and Tuesday, 8th and 9th September, 1890, at Tranby Croft, I will on my part solemnly undertake never to play cards again as long as I live.[63]

Before setting out on foot next morning for the railway station, he found little comfort in the reply to a letter he had left for Lieutenant-General Williams: 'we [The Prince, Lord Coventry and Lieutenant-General Williams, who signed it] have no desire to be unnecessarily hard on you'.[64] His accusers, of course, believed they had Gordon-Cumming on the run. His letter admitted the difficulty any man of 'unstained' character would have in 'com[ing] well out of an accusation brought by numbers' against him, and how he shrank therefore from instigating 'a full and thorough investigation'.

All of which confirms how royal sway is a power to unman the staunchest personality: Gordon-Cumming, after all, had served with exemplary courage in the Zulu War (he had been the first to enter Cetewayo's kraal when it was overrun after the Battle of Ulundi) and with the Guards Camel Corps against the Mahdi's tribesmen in the Sudan. (In peacetime he invariably stalked his tigers on foot.)[65] This was the man whom the Prince and his friends so effortlessly preferred to browbeat with claims of 'overwhelming evidence' against him, which it was 'useless to attempt to deny'. Even the promise of secrecy – so essential to them all – was rated expendable by one of the signatories (Lycett Green), who had been quite prepared to denounce Gordon-Cumming publicly at the Doncaster races had he not agreed to sign their document.[66]

What developed was a concerted attempt in the New Year to have a military court inquire privately into Gordon-Cumming's conduct, an outcome that was sure to prejudice the civil action for slander that he now intended to bring against his accusers – in the course of which the Prince would undoubtedly be compelled to give evidence. But their ploy failed, leaving the Prince exposed. Gordon-Cumming's legal team were not to be deflected, but prevailed upon the Judge Advocate-General to persuade Sir Redvers Buller (the Adjutant-General) to suspend the inquiry he had ordered. 'I hear that the Prince of Wales is condemning my action . . . in loud and unmeasured terms,' Buller told Sir Henry Ponsonby on 13 February, adding that he was 'satisfied that I have done my duty with discretion'.[67] Then, to the fury of the Prince, an attempt on

20 February to have the executive committee of the Guards' Club conduct its own inquiry was well defeated. Had Sir Redvers Buller not vacillated, the Prince complained, there would have been no question of a civil action coming to trial. In a note to his Private Secretary he fulminated: 'Should Cumming, by any legal quibble, win his action, I think nearly every officer would leave the Regiment.' By March the Prince was telling Prince George how 'the whole thing has caused me the most serious annoyance and vexation'.[68] For her part, the Princess remained blindly loyal throughout. She assured Prince George after the hearing closed how right he was 'to think that as usual Papa through his good nature was dragged into it and made to suffer, for trying to save with the others together this worthless creature, who since then has behaved *too abominably* to them all' – a case of the Princess's own palpable dislike for Gordon-Cumming chiming with vehement duty (in the same letter she wrote of 'that brute' and 'vile snob').[69]

The hearing, at which the jury found against Gordon-Cumming, opened on 1 June 1891 and lasted seven days, during which the Prince was granted a seat apart on the left of the judicial chair. The *Pall Mall Gazette* thought the scene reminiscent of 'a theatre at a fashionable matinée, so filled were the galleries with opera glasses'. The Prince's testimony from the witness box on the second day was delivered a little hoarsely, but rapidly:

Your Royal Highness [began the Solicitor-General] has known Sir William Gordon-Cumming for twenty years?

I have.

Am right in saying for the last ten years at least, he has enjoyed Your Royal Highness's favour?

Certainly.

He has been a guest at your house?

On several occasions.

And did that friendship – intimacy – continue unimpaired and undisturbed up to the 9th or 10th September of last year?

It did.

. . . It was not, I believe sir, until the evening of the 10th that any communication was made to you in regard to the alleged bad play?

No.

May I ask by whom the communication was first made to Your Royal Highness?

By the Earl of Coventry.

... May I ask if Your Royal Highness remembers whether the statement made to you by Lord Coventry purported to be the statement of an individual, and, if so, whether that individual was named?

Of individuals.

Of whose?

Of three gentlemen and two ladies.

Then, in the first instance, it purported to be a statement to which all five of them could speak?

Exactly.

I believe Your Royal Highness did not see any of the five persons mentioned until after Sir William Gordon-Cumming had had the honour of an interview?

I did not.

At that interview Sir William Gordon-Cumming emphatically denied the charge?

He did.

On his own admission, the Prince had not inquired into the evidence for himself, nor seen Gordon-Cumming's accusers in person before they demanded he sign, above the Prince's signature and theirs, the undertaking never to play cards again. It was then that a cockney juryman (one Goddard Clarke, a city liveryman) interrupted the Prince as he stepped from the witness box: 'Excuse me, Your Royal Highness, I have a question or two to ask you.' They were questions many in the gallery wished had been asked by counsel:

Are this jury to understand that you, as banker on these two occasions, saw nothing of the alleged malpractices of the plaintiff?

No; it is not usual for a banker to see anything in dealing cards, especially when you are playing among friends in their house. You do not for a moment suspect anything of the sort.

What was your Royal Highness's opinion at the time as to the charges made against Sir William Gordon-Cumming?

They seemed so strongly supported – unanimously so – by those who brought them forward, that I felt no other course was open to me but to believe what I was told.

The second question should not have been allowed him, since it invited opinion and was not an attempt to clarify evidence. If the Prince's reply appears indirect, this is understandable (as Sir Michael Havers explains) given how the Prince was 'the representative of a form of government' and thus 'did not feel himself to hold a personal view'.

For the day of the verdict (9 June), when the jury found for the defendants after less than fifteen minutes' deliberation, the Prince had departed for Ascot. In his absence Lord Coleridge summed up less than justly in favour of the defendants. Havers posits, 'If Gordon-Cumming had secured a favourable verdict the Prince would have been blamed for having tried to prevent an innocent man from getting a fair hearing, instead of a guilty one. It was from this that Coleridge saved him.' We can leave the final comment to the correspondent of the American *Albany Law Journal*, whose report towards the close of the case reads as a reproach to English justice grubbily pliant to royal sensibilities:

> If five of the Prince's boon companions agree to stigmatise a sixth, it is all up with the unfortunate man in the Prince's estimation; he turns his back on him as coolly as Prince Hal turns his back on poor Jack, after he has become King in the play. Then the trial reveals the English notion of justice in that the Prince is praised for obeying a subpoena. And it reveals the extraordinary reverence of the English bar in the tenderness with which the Prince was treated on the witness stand, and the homage with which he was accorded a seat beside the judge. All this seems strange to democrats . . . [T]here will be very little sympathy in America with Sir William. He must abide the verdict of the company he trains in. It may very well be that the whole party were not in a condition to know exactly what the facts were, and it would be rather to their credit if it were so.

In a self-vindicating letter to Prince George written on 10 June, the Prince assured his son that he would 'grin and bear' the criticism widely heaped upon him in the press 'as best I may'. As a protest of unblemished behaviour in the matter, we can hardly mistake the taint of delusion. 'I have the implicit conviction that I have acted perfectly straightforwardly and honourably in the matter, thank God! The army and society are well rid of such a damned blackguard.'[70]

*

Lady Charles Beresford, who bore her social exile during this summer of 1891 knowing that Lady Brooke had been favoured with invitations to Marlborough House, prevailed upon her husband to write a letter to the Prince (dated 12 July) which she forwarded to the Prime Minister, Lord Salisbury. It was critical of the Prince's 'unasked interference and subsequent action', which he deemed insulting to his wife since it 'elevate[d] the person with whom she has had a quarrel'.[71] The days of duelling might be past, he continued, but unfavourable publicity would injure the Prince just as well; indeed, without his public apology 'the first opportunity that occurs to me I shall give my opinion publicly of Y.R.H. and state that you have behaved like a blackguard and a coward, and that I am prepared to prove my words'. Lord Salisbury, while he preferred to keep the excesses of personal quarrels at arm's length, now prevailed upon Lady Charles Beresford to withhold her husband's letter from the Prince, then trained his acuity upon Lord Charles's intemperance. He reminded him of his obligation as a gentleman to protect Lady Brooke, and not bring a woman who had yielded to him in the past into disgrace through churlish publicity. In addressing Lord Charles's 'grave' charge that the Prince had insulted his wife, he believed the husband lacked evidence: he had complained of 'a sudden cessation of acquaintance', yet

> [after the] stormy interview you had with him, in which your language to say the least was very plain, I quite understand why the Prince has fought shy of any meeting with Lady Charles. If any person had addressed you in similar language I think you would from that time forth have abstained from speaking to the third person or the third person's wife.[72]

Lord Salisbury saw plainly the flaw inherent in Lord Charles's assumption (aggravated no doubt by sexual jealousy of Lady Brooke)[73] that the Prince was treating him less than justly: '. . . the acquaintance of *no* illustrious person is necessary to one's happiness,' he told him. 'Your position in Society is in your profession and not affected by the friendship of anyone however highly placed.' Rather than have recourse to 'ill-considered publicity', Lord Charles Beresford should 'do nothing'.[74]

But the Prime Minister could not stop the circulation in the autumn of a pamphlet (titled *Lady River*) written by Mrs Gerald Paget, Lady Charles's sister – in substance an exposé (from Lady Brooke's standpoint) of her intimacy with the Prince. It was said that, because the Duchess of Manchester had given a reading from it to her guests, the Prince would not talk to her for some ten years.[75] When Lord Charles returned to London from his Mediterranean posting in December, he was still minded to threaten the Prince, something his brother (Lord Marcus Beresford) was powerless to restrain. An exchange of letters was far from conciliatory. Lord Charles iterated his wife's demand that Lady Brooke should withdraw from Society for a year, insisting that, without an apology from the Prince for his treatment of his wife, he would 'no longer intervene' to prevent wider publicity. In reply, the Prince offered mild astonishment. He was 'at a loss to understand how Lady Charles can imagine that I have in any way slighted or ignored her'. On meeting her, he had 'made a point on all occasions of shaking hands with her, or of bowing to her, as the opportunity presented'; she had, moreover, received an invitation that year to the summer garden party at Marlborough House. Lord Charles was unmoved. He thought the Prince's letter no proper answer to his demand, seeing how his behaviour towards his wife had been what he called 'a matter of common talk' during the two years he had been absent from England.[76] If necessary, he said, he would call a press conference at his home in Eaton Square and make public the whole matter, then resign his commission and leave with his wife for France. But Lord Salisbury succeeded in averting such malicious intent by means of a formal exchange of letters drafted by him and acceptable to both parties, but with the condition that Lady Brooke be temporarily excluded from Court. The Prince's letter was an expression of regret, but lacked apology. It was signed by him in London on Christmas Eve, so pressing was the crisis keeping him from Sandringham at the festive season for the only time since his marriage:

> I regret to find from your letter of 23rd instant that circumstances have occurred which have led Lady Charles Beresford to believe that it was my intention publicly to wound her feelings. I have never had any such intention, and I regret that she should have been led to conceive an erroneous impression upon the point.

Lady Brooke's inauspicious letter was eventually returned to her in March 1892, when she consigned it to the fire. When told of this by Lady Charles's brother-in-law, Lord Waterford, to whom Lady Charles had entrusted it, the Prince replied:

I have no desire to advert to what occurred at the end of last year; but I can never forget, and shall never forgive, the conduct of your brother and his wife towards me. His base ingratitude, after a friendship of about 20 years, has hurt me more than words can say. You, who have so chivalrous a nature and are such a thorough gentleman in every sense of the word, will be able to form some idea of what my feelings on the subject are![77]

The Princess of Wales's equanimity was so shaken in the summer of 1891 at the prospect of another open scandal so soon after the Baccarat Case that she determined not to return from her annual visit to her parents in Denmark on 13 October as expected, in good time for the Prince's fiftieth birthday celebrations on 9 November, but instead visited the Crimea for the coming silver wedding anniversary of the Tsar and Tsarina. To be absent on his birthday was a gesture of hurtful displeasure to the Prince, made more telling by distressing domestic events. A fire at Sandringham swept through the top floor on 31 October, damaging the dining room and its Goya tapestries. Then quite soon Prince George contracted typhoid fever, the condition that had so nearly killed his father some twenty years before. By 22 November both parents were at their son's bedside.

On 3 December Prince George's fever had passed, and in time for the announcement of his elder brother's impending nuptials: marriage seemed to offer the last hope for Prince Albert Victor ('Eddy'), now Duke of Clarence and Avondale; according to the Princess's biographer, he was 'lethargic, dissipated, impervious to education and manifestly unfitted to the high position for which he was apparently destined', yet utterly devoted to his sisters and to her. Sir Henry Ponsonby noted how the Prince constantly announced his irritation by snubbing him.[78]

The boys, who were inseparable through childhood, had joined the naval training ship HMS *Britannia* in 1877, from which Prince George would progress to a career in the service, while his elder brother was allowed to complete a course with which he was failing to contend. After this, long cruises as midshipmen in HMS *Bacchante* (1880–82) were punctuated by exchanges of letters home, their father affectionately telling Prince George on one occasion how 'you could, I am sure, see that I had a lump in my throat when I wished you good-bye . . . I shall miss you more than ever, my dear Georgy.'[79] The Princess's letters were replete with endearments, the unmistakable currency of a mother wilfully possessive of all her offspring – a failing that the Prince, who owed so much to his wife's tolerance, appeared unwilling to question. She hoped she would 'always find my little Georgie quite the same and unchanged in every respect', she wrote to him when he was already nineteen; at twenty-five, and in command of a gunboat, his 'Motherdear' (her children's moniker) signed off a letter 'with a great big kiss for your lovely little face'. Prince George, on occasions, repaid her in kind: 'I wonder who will have that sweet little room of mine; you must . . . imagine that your Georgie dear is living in it,' he wrote.[80]

Away from the family nest the royal daughters Louise, Victoria ('Toria') and Maud (many called them 'the Hags') were shyly diffident; at home they were entrapped in celibate monotony, which so strongly satisfied their mother. 'Alix found them such good companions that she would not encourage them marrying,' the Prince argued on her behalf to the Queen, adding – with a deal of complicity – that, anyway, they were not inclined to marriage. However, aged twenty-one, the eldest and shyest of them, Princess Louise, found a husband (eighteen years her senior) in the sixth Earl of Fife, and lived quietly on his estates indulging a passion for salmon-fishing. Seven years later (on 22 July 1896) Princess Maud married her first cousin, Prince Charles of Denmark, and was never reconciled to living abroad. (She became Queen of Norway on his accession in 1905.) Princess Victoria, meanwhile, endured her blighted life at home, made more miserable because she craved romance and was intelligent. The Grand Duchess Olga (her Russian cousin) saw her cast as 'a glorified maid' to her mother, of whom Prince George once wrote to his wife: 'Mama, as I have always said, is one of the most selfish people I know.'[81] For his part, the Prince was unwilling to forfeit his wife's forbearance by criticizing her domestic governance – even as he watched Princess Victoria succumb to the pitiable solace of ailments, real or imagined.

Having failed his naval apprenticeship, Prince Albert Victor ('Eddy') fared no better when sent to Lausanne to improve his French, or for that matter at Cambridge, where, separated now from his brother (lately posted to the West Indies and North American Squadron), his life ran to dissipation. An engagement in August 1890 to the Catholic Princess Hélène d'Orléans, daughter of the Comte de Paris (pretender to the French throne), soon appeared uncertain, in spite of her willingness to be received into the Church of England in disregard of the Pope's strong objection. 'It is a sad state of things and makes poor Eddy quite wretched,' his father reported to Prince George. A year later the courtship was abandoned, leaving the Prince no less exasperated at his heir's prospects, yet determined to find him a bride: 'A good sensible wife with some considerable character is what he needs most, but where is she to be found?' he inquired of the Queen. However, preliminaries were soon settled for him to marry Princess Mary ('May') of Teck the following spring. Sir Francis Knollys, for one, anticipated no opposition from Prince Albert Victor 'if he is properly managed and is told he *must* do it' for the good of the country. In the event his proposal of marriage was accepted on 3 December 1891. Then, while staying at Sandringham in the New Year, he took to his bed with influenza (on 8 January 1892), and in six days he died of pneumonia. His parents, whose relationship had never undergone so much strain as in the past year, were as one in bearing this caprice of history. 'He is broken down, and poor dear Alix . . . does nothing but cry,' the Queen reported to the Empress Frederick. To his mother, the Prince wrote: 'Gladly would I have given my life for his, as I put no value on mine . . . Such a tragedy had never before occurred in the annals of our family, and it is hard that poor little May should virtually become a widow before she is a wife.'[82] (The Princess would marry Prince George, by then Duke of York and later King George V, on 6 July 1893; their home, York Cottage, was barely a stone's throw from Sandringham House – which 'led to many little rubs which might have been avoided', the Duchess recorded.)[83]

The Prince and his former friend Lord Charles Beresford would exchange pleasantries again – at Ascot, after Persimmon's Gold Cup victory in June 1897. To 'My own lovely little Daisy' he penned an apology that credits her with timely understanding:

> . . . I hope my darling you will agree I could not have acted otherwise, as my loyalty to you, is I hope, a thing that you will never think of doubting! – Shortly before leaving Ascot today, Marcus B. came to me, & said he had a gt. favour to ask me – so I answered at once I should be delighted to grant it. He then became much affected, & actually cried, & said might he bring his brother C. up to me to offer his congratulations on 'Persimmon's' success. I had no alternative but to say yes. He came up with his hat off, & would not put it on till I told him, & shook hands. We talked a little about racing, then I turned and we parted. What struck me more than anything, was his humble attitude

and manner! My loved one, I hope you won't be annoyed at what has happened, & exonerate me from blame, as that is all I care about.[84]

But the ardour of their relationship had not long outlasted her father-in-law's death in December 1893, after which, as Countess of Warwick, her interest in good works became obsessive. She claimed that an exchange of views one day at the Fleet Street offices of the radical newspaper, the *Clarion* – where she had gone to berate its editor Robert Blatchford for an attack upon her extravagance – confirmed her conversion to socialism. (Her most eccentric scheme, perhaps, which she described in an 1897 issue of *Land Magazine*, envisaged establishing colonies of 'unmarrying women' farmers.)[85] The Prince, as she admitted in a memoir, 'had no sympathy whatever with my enthusiasm for Socialism'. As a guest enjoying sumptuous hospitality at Warwick Castle and at Easton Lodge, he would listen to her philanthropic schemes with seeming patience, but was dismissive of her belligerent Marxist posturing. 'Society grows,' he would tell her; 'it is not made.'[86]

In 1898, with conjugal rights restored, and soon to give birth to another child after an interval of twelve years, Lady Warwick was writing to the Prince and Princess by way of lowering the blinds upon her long affair. In reply, the Prince assured her that the Princess

> really quite forgives and condones the past, as I have corroborated what you wrote about our friendship having been platonic for some years . . . But how could you, my loved one, imagine that I should withdraw my friendship from you? . . . You cannot prevent my giving you the same love as the friendship I have always felt for you. Though our interests, as you have often said, lie apart, still we have that sentimental feeling of affinity which cannot be eradicated by time.[87]

In truth her friendship with the Prince would never amount to very much again. And the Prince had already found her ideal replacement in the Hon Mrs George Keppel – 'the perfect mistress for an aging man', as Anita Leslie describes her.[88]

Lady Warwick once confided in the journalist Frank Harris that the Prince 'was indeed a very perfect gentle lover'.[89] She was surely speaking not for herself alone.

8
Abroad

Until he was King, the Prince continued to be treated as a leaking vessel with regard to confidential matters of state, even those that directly concerned him. When a measure that the Queen expressly coveted – Disraeli's Royal Titles Bill of 1876 – received her assent on 7 April, the Prince was homeward bound from a four-month tour of India, entirely unaware of the Prime Minister's intention, or of the subsequent proceedings that created her Empress of India; he read of them in a newspaper. 'I think I have some right to feel annoyed,' he told Disraeli, and was little appeased by the Prime Minister's intimation that he, too, might receive an addition to his titles.[1]

The measure had had a troublesome passage through Parliament. Disraeli believed it would strengthen the fealty of the rajah class – which was 'susceptible to the influence of symbols', as one viceroy (Lord Lytton) maintained;[2] his Liberal opponent, Gladstone, readily denounced the title as imperial 'bombast'.[3] Sir Henry James, another Liberal and one of the Prince's cronies, went so far as to table a motion of censure in the Commons, which was defeated (by a majority of 334 to 226) on the day that the Prince arrived home from India: it had been a divided House. But the Queen had already accepted a degree of blame for having kept the Prince in ignorance of her wishes, and his subsequent letter to her was a necessary climb-down:

> I have not the slightest wish but to receive Mr Disraeli in the kindest manner possible, and he wrote me a very kind letter on my return. I have no doubt that it was an oversight on his part not letting me know of the Royal Titles Bill, though of course I looked upon it as a slight to me, and as your eldest son also to you.[4]

But the matter evidently rankled. When the Prince assumed the title of Emperor of India upon his accession, he declined to use his mother's full appellation 'V.R.I.' (*Victoria Regina et Imperatrix*), choosing instead to initial his documents 'E.R.'[5]

A familiar reluctance to accord him a fit role was manifest in discussions about his official status on the tour. The Queen expected Disraeli and Lord Salisbury, the India Secretary, to consult her about every detail of the Prince's programme and took little notice of his wishes. She insisted that the Prince was not to be cast as her formal representative, which would have prejudiced the status of her Viceroy, Lord Northbrook, who was adamant that his precedence should not be compromised. Lord Salisbury was forthright. 'There is . . . some real danger that if the Queen's own Son is put in a position of obvious inferiority, the true relation of the Viceroy to the Queen will be misunderstood or ignored,' he told the Queen's Private Secretary. 'I fear that in such a case the prestige of H.M.'s Dynasty will be lowered.' In the event, Lord Northbrook accepted a compromise: the Prince might hold levees, but only at those stages of the visit when the Viceroy was not accompanying him.[6]

While Lord Northbrook was seeking to protect his status, sections of the English public were expressing their displeasure at the cost of the venture. Addressing a large gathering in Hyde Park, the radical firebrand, Charles Bradlaugh, decried the expenditure and wished the Prince godspeed, albeit 'on a longer journey' than to India; at a time of severe recession at home he thought that working men across the country would view askance a costly exchange of gifts with Indian princes. Even members of the royal household were inclined to belittle the significance of the tour, Henry Ponsonby among them. 'The object of [the Prince's] mission is amusement,' he told Lord Salisbury privately – who added: 'and to kill tigers'.[7]

Unlike generations of young men who would spend the voyage out to India (invariably by P&O steamship) being closely groomed for the gratuitous superiority demanded by the colonial service, the Prince relied on finely tuned social acumen and greeted India with an open mind. Needless to say, the arrangements from the outset were largely congenial. A trio of his private friends (the Duke of Sutherland, the Earl of Aylesford and Lord Carrington) relieved the tedium of the voyage. HMS *Seraphis*, a troopship converted at considerable expense, passed muster as a floating palace and afforded the Prince a choice of port and starboard bedrooms, the better to catch the fickle breezes. The royal apartments on the upper deck, comprising reception room, drawing room and dining room, were decorated in white, blue and gold throughout, and provided with gilt mirrors, mahogany fittings and solid oak furniture; a glass and panelled *fumoir* (smoking room) was designed for his use on the quarterdeck. Below decks were housed the farm animals that provided fresh milk and meat, as well as horses from the Prince's stables and a store of countless gifts and medals needed for ceremonial presentation; here, too, was space for the gallimaufry of trophies that would accumulate in the course of a seventeen-week tour.

The occasions of pomp and circumstance were invariably demanding of the Prince's stamina, none more so than the celebrations in Bombay to mark his thirty-fourth birthday on the first full day of the tour. Encased – as he often was – in field marshal's uniform and plumed helmet, and wearing the collar of the Garter and the sash and jewel of the Star of India, he bore the heat of the day which the tempo of fans (punkahs) would barely alleviate. Twenty-four native princes were presented in order of precedence, punctuated by an interminable firing of salutes (as many as twenty-one guns for the twelve-year-old Maharaja of Baroda), the ceremony overflowing into the afternoon following a two-hour morning audience for lesser guests.[8]

The searing round of formalities fed his impatience with the snobberies of caste, founded, as they were, on conventional notions of white racial superiority and manifest in arrogance towards the native population. A mere six days into the tour he was expressing his concern to the Queen in a letter from Poona:

> What struck me most forcibly was the rude and rough manner with which the English 'political officers' (as they are called, who are in attendance upon the native chiefs) treat them. It is indeed much to be deplored, and the system is, I am sure, quite wrong. Natives of all classes in this country will, I am sure, be more attached to us if they are treated with kindness and with firmness at the same time, but not with brutality and contempt.

The Prince wrote in similar vein to Lord Salisbury, a complaint that proved to be of some influence. Almost immediately the Foreign Secretary instructed the government in India to 'check the arrogance' displayed by English military and civilian officers, while Disraeli was soon informing the Queen that a Mr Saunders (the Resident in Hyderabad) had been 'recalled in consequence of his offensive behaviour to the princes and people'.[9]

Doubtless the Prince will have felt justified in discounting the antipathies fomented some eighteen years earlier (in May 1857): mutual blood-letting had then defined the sepoy mutiny at Meerut and its aftermath of atrocities at military stations (notably Lucknow, Allahabad and Cawnpore) across Bengal, Oudh and the north-western provinces. Conduct that had generated 'pathological animus'[10] towards the native population left the British unable to establish a relationship with her subject people that was not marked by suspicion, or managed with patronizing tolerance. ('There is one terrible cry of vengeance', Macaulay told his diary, to account for the folk-myth savagery with which the Mutiny was suppressed; the narrative, moreover, of 'that dreadful military execution at Peshawar, forty men blown at once from the mouths of cannon, heads, legs, arms, flying in all directions', was received with 'almost universal'[11] approval at home – a reprisal which an eyewitness saw repeated with such 'force of habit [that] we now think little of them'.)[12]

No wonder, then, that royal amity raised a few hackles, given how entrenched racial intolerance was in the decades that remained to British rule. As the founder of the international Boy Scout movement, General Baden-Powell, bluntly attested in *Indian Memories*:

[A]s a rule the niggers seem to me cringing villains. As you ride or walk along the middle of the road, every cart or carriage has to stop and get out of your way, and every native, as he passes you, gives a salute. If he has an umbrella up he takes it down, if he is riding a horse he gets off and salutes. Moreover they do whatever you tell them. If you meet a man in the road and tell him to dust your boots, he does it.[13]

But it was rare for the Prince to have the freedom to meet native Indians face to face. At Lucknow, where he spoke with veterans who had defended the Residency during the Mutiny, one elderly man was led away sobbing with emotion because the Prince had grasped his hand, after which others in varying states of raggedness spoke with him in turn. When he met a group of Thugs at the prison in Jabalpur – members of the fraternity whose waxwork images had memorably engaged his boyish interest at the Great Exhibition – the grimmest of them divulged that his tally of murders amounted to sixty-seven; as the Prince was about to leave, the prisoners begged to be granted a better monthly allowance. Not unexpectedly in a land of treacherous susceptibilities, arrangements sometimes gave offence. When a banquet was held in the Prince's honour in an island (Elephanta) cave off Bombay, which housed carvings of Hindu deities, it was reported as being a violation of a sacred site. The press was angry again when the Prince, who had asked to see inside a Bengali home, was offered hospitality in the women's living quarters.[14]

Incidents like these made no lasting stir, whereas affronts to the ruling caste's rigid 'dignity of precedence' rankled – indeed Albert Grey (later 4th Earl Grey) told of 'cries of protest from the mighty' on occasions when wanton affability might subvert the rules. If in the course of a ball, Grey reveals, the Prince bestowed attention on the pretty wife of the Commissioner's 'underling' rather than on his own dull spouse, 'poor honest Jones' is penalized unjustly for having a giddy wife and finds his promotion retarded. On one occasion the Prince asked for a comedian, Charles Mathews, to be invited to a dinner given by Lady Clarke (he was appearing locally in a farce, *My Awful Dad*). 'Calcutta was furious' because the Prince sat on the veranda 'chaffing' and smoking alone with Mrs Mathews, while the 'official Indignants kick[ed] their feet in impatience and envious rage'. This slight persisted from dinner until the Prince took his leave in the early hours of the morning.

One single example will suffice to describe the singular honour that the native princes felt had been accorded them by the presence of the Sovereign's heir within their suzerainties. According to Grey, one half of a sofa on which the Prince had sat in the Maharaja's palace at Benares was afterwards carefully covered with tissue paper, so that 'the impress of the royal and broad seat of H.R.H. is ever hereafter to be preserved as a holy and sacred relic'.[15]

Of the twin totems of virility – big game hunting and shooting – the tour had plenty, described variously by *Reynolds's Newspaper* as 'sickening spectacle' and 'gross amusement'. The Prince killed his first tiger – a female pregnant with three cubs – in the company of the Maharaja of Jaipur. His first elephant (hunted in Ceylon) was merely wounded. The party had pursued the beast through dense vegetation until it fell, seemingly dead, whereupon the Prince (his clothing quite torn in the chase) hacked off its tail for a trophy. Then, as Lord Charles Beresford danced a hornpipe on its rump, the old tusker struggled to its feet and wandered off before a fatal shot could be fired. Ready game included bear, cheetah, leopard, black buck and boar, and on one occasion a prized flying fox (a bat of five-foot wingspan, rarely to be seen in daylight).[16] The Prince vaunted his enjoyment in letters to his young sons. 'I have had great tiger shooting,' he told them on 23 February 1876 – 'the day before yesterday I killed six, and some were very savage. Two were man-eaters.' He added: 'two little bears and an armadillo got loose in Mr Bartlett's tent last night and frightened him so he did not know what to do . . . !'[27] The jungle leeches, he told them earlier, were 'very bad, and climb up your legs and bight [*sic*] you'.[17]

The greatest carnage was orchestrated. Carcasses were laid to lure big cats to the hunting grounds; boar would be driven by hundreds of beaters towards 'a fusillade of guns and spears'.[18] At a shooting camp in the shadow of the Himalayas during February and early March, 1,000 riding elephants were employed in support of some 12,000 coolies and soldiers who acted as beaters and servants in vast tracts of forest for the benefit of just twenty sportsmen.[19] They were entertained with staged animal combats involving elephants, rhinoceros and water buffalo; tigers would be released into enclosures stocked with black buck. (On one occasion an elephant blind in one eye and lacking a tusk was rendered immobile. 'I will let him go,' the Nepalese Prime Minister suggested, 'if the Prince expresses a wish that he be set at liberty, but I hope to be able to offer his Royal Highness the [other] tusk' – an offer the Prince accepted.)[20]

When Lord Lytton visited HMS *Seraphis* as she passed through the Suez Canal on her homeward voyage, he marvelled at the collections on which the party's taxidermist (Mr Bartlett again) was exercising his skill. Live animals and birds, exotic plants and innumerable curios burst from every available space, the soon-to-be appointed Viceroy reported to the Queen, while wild beasts walked the decks 'with the most amiable expressions . . . [and] apparently disposed to fraternise with every visitor'. (A good part of the collections was put on public display at the London Zoological Gardens and the South Kensington Museum.)

By the time he reached London the Prince had covered some 10,000 miles (7,600 of them on land) and borne the routine of official engagements without surrendering geniality or grace; indeed, the success of the tour was widely credited to the Prince's personality. *The Times* believed he had 'completely dissipated' the doubts of those who had questioned his competence.[21] The Viceroy's Agent in Central India (Sir Henry Daly) described as 'miraculous' the degree of respect he won from native chiefs, while Lord Napier was struck by the admiration of his native army officers and men who, being subject to 'an indefinite authority', felt that their idea of a Prince had been realized. (In a gesture worthy of his catholic affinities, the Prince had invited a Sikh and an Afghan serving with the 11th Bengal Lancers to join his tour as orderlies; at their own request they accompanied him to England and were the forerunners of Indian officers who, in rotation, attended him as King.)[22]

More than this, the Prince had asked important questions of white complacency. A mischievous Lord Lytton ventured: 'Anglo-Indian society is mortally offended with the Prince of Wales for not having sufficiently appreciated its superiority to everything else in creation.' Lytton thought the ruling caste to be decided in its opinion that the Prince had directed him to 'to snub and aggravate the whites, and pet and spoil the blacks'.[23]

No one underestimated the Prince's ambassadorial instincts more than the Queen. She ridiculed his capacity for discretion whenever he sought to intervene in state affairs or diplomacy, leaving senior politicians at a loss how to secure him an apprenticeship in statecraft. 'Not to be thought of . . . Quite out of the question . . . Never to be considered,' was her way of dismissing an early attempt to have the Prince represent her in Ireland.[24] Disraeli, whose judgement the Queen trusted unerringly, would sometimes feed the Prince 'tit bits of Cabinet secrets'[25] without her knowledge. But only after the spat induced by the Royal Titles Bill would she allow him to see official papers with any regularity – dispatches, she told Disraeli (who broadly shared her misgiving), 'it would be best *not* to refuse to send' as long as they were 'not very confidential'.[26] Yet despite her obfuscation the Prince fostered considerable diplomatic goodwill, particularly with regard to the French. He keenly encouraged the monarchist (if factious) government of the Third Republic to pursue compromise, being on convivial terms with the staunchest anti-republicans (known to him through the French Jockey Club), as he was with those diplomatists of good blood who chose to serve the new Republic in the belief that monarchy would be restored before long; he met, too, the firebrand republican, Léon Gambetta, whose fierce anti-Prussian sentiments chimed with diehard monarchists and the Prince himself. As the historian Gordon Brook-Shepherd appreciates, 'He was about the only person, and certainly the only distinguished foreigner, who managed to keep a foothold in every social and political camp in Paris at the same time.'[27] Among the numerous envoys the Prince entertained in London were successive French Ambassadors, nominees of Louis, Duc de Decazes (Minister for Foreign Affairs), who sought to promote Anglo-French *entente* with an enthusiasm the Prince readily shared. All this stirred the Queen's Teutonic prejudices. 'A new intimate alliance with France, especially with Republican France, the Queen would strongly deprecate,' Colonel Ponsonby told the Foreign Secretary, Lord Derby on 17 August 1874. She believed Germany, Austria and even Russia to be 'far more useful, natural, and good allies for England', and iterated the Duke of Wellington's suspicion of the French in peacetime – that they should be offered 'Plenty of friendship, but no love'.[28]

The Prince (who spoke excellent French) happily imbibed the '*sociabilité*'[29] provided by hostesses such as the Princesse de Sagan and the Comtesse de Pourtales: he was not a clubbable man as London understood the term, yet the eclectic social chemistry of a Parisian *salon* – a gathering without emulation and presided over by a gifted, independent woman – appeared to minister to the whole man. Sometimes his Francophile enthusiasm got the better of political judgement. On being recalled from the French Embassy in London in the summer of 1874 on account of a pro-monarchist motion he had proposed in the National Assembly, the Duc de La Rochefoucauld-Bisaccia invited the Prince to visit his château on the Loire. When the Prince learnt that the Duc's Loire valley neighbours were eager for him visit them as well, he was happy to oblige them, a prospect which made for unfavourable comment in the Republican press. He had taken insufficient account of recent party strife, Disraeli counselled, and should modify his plans by agreeing to pay 'some act of marked respect to the Chief of the French State' as he passed through Paris. In the event the Prince agreed to do so while travelling incognito as the Earl of Chester, and so ensured that his visits 'to personal friends at their country seats' should be regarded as unexceptionable.[30]

Four years later, in 1878, a diplomatic initiative redounded to his credit. He was often in Paris that summer as President of the British section of the International Exhibition, but troubled by shades of opinion hotly antagonistic to Britain's ceding of Cyprus under the terms of a defensive alliance with the Turks, a move intended to counter-balance the prospect of Russian intervention in the Balkans. Gambetta and his supporters raged at the French government's tepid acceptance of events, which they saw as being detrimental to French influence in the Mediterranean and to colonial interests in Egypt in particular. Public excitement, as the Foreign Secretary, Lord Salisbury, understood, threatened 'a crisis . . . of no little delicacy.'[31]

The Prince read the runes with evident clarity. In the spirit of *entente* and their common wish for a successful Exhibition, he invited Gambetta and a representative of the British Ambassador to lunch with him at the Café des Anglais. It was an unlikely convergence. Gambetta (who had lost an eye in childhood) struck the Prince as 'so vulgar in his manner and so careless in his appearance', yet when they talked 'the captivating charm of his eloquence made me forget the physical repulsion with which he inspired me.'[32] The chemistry was propitious: the Prince assumed the mantle of diplomatist, ably plying his guest with assurances as to British intentions, to the Republican's evident satisfaction. 'I hear from other quarters that Gambetta was extremely pleased with the interview,' the British Ambassador, Lord Lyons, duly told Lord Salisbury. 'I am assured also that the Prince of Wales acquitted himself with great skill.'[33] Having briefed the French Foreign Minister (M. Waddington), the Prince returned to London, where his diplomacy received 'all too rare and appreciative recognition'[34] from the Foreign Secretary. 'If the leaders of French opinion had definitely turned against us,' Lord Salisbury opined on 24 July, 'a disagreeable and even hazardous condition of estrangement between the two countries might have grown up . . . Your Royal Highness's influence over M. Gambetta, and the skill with which that influence has been exercised, have averted a danger that was not inconsiderable.' For his part, the Prince was 'beyond measure pleased' to have been of use; 'nobody would have deplored more deeply than I should that any estrangement between the two countries should occur'.[35]

The success of the International Exhibition belonged to a sunny upland of Anglo-French concord, before two decades of colonial rivalry imperilled hopes for a formal *entente cordiale* that would not be secured before April 1904. It provided a rare opportunity for the Prince to commit himself wholeheartedly to leading a project of some months' duration, whose success would reflect his business acumen, attention to detail and perseverance. 'I find I shall have a great deal to do with the Exhibition,'[36] he told the Queen in March of a commitment that would define a portion of his daily routine for some eight months – until 10 November when the Exhibition closed. (It was said that he wrote at length and almost daily to one member of the British Commission, a body composed of his own nominees.)[37] As was appropriate for an *Exposition* given in the main to science and the arts, the Prince dealt directly with British manufacturers and was able to change the minds of owners who were reluctant to show their paintings in the gallery of British Art. Writing to the Queen shortly after the grand opening (on 1 May), he felt his 'hard work' had been 'amply rewarded'; he told her how almost all of the British section had been completed on time, a boast that 'no other country' could claim. He added: 'I think I have seen everything we have to show and talked almost with every exhibitor . . . The Exhibition as a whole, that is, as far as I can judge, is very fine and quite immense.' (It covered, in fact, some sixty-six acres on and around the Champ de Mars and attracted thirteen million visitors; Alexander Graham Bell's telephone and Thomas Edison's phonograph were notable exhibits – as was an eccentric gallery of four hundred indigenous individuals, a kind of human zoo brought to Paris from around the globe.)

The Queen had welcomed the Prince's enthusiasm without reservation, but decided against travelling to Paris herself – a position that all but a very few minor members of European royal houses shared since they, too, were unwilling 'to pay personal court to the Republic'.[38] When cries of 'Vive la République' sounded from the crowd as the Prince passed in procession to the formal opening, he gamely acknowledged them. At a banquet given by British exhibitors in his honour, he proposed the health of the President of the Republic (Marshal MacMahon), and in a speech (on 3 May) delivered partly in French, he glossed over past difficulties, while exciting far-fetched expectations:

> I am glad to think we should have met here this evening in a country and a city which have always received Englishmen with hospitality, and that though, not many years ago, there was a time when we were not so friendly as we are now, still that time is past and forgotten. The jealousy, which was the cause of the animosity, has now, I feel sure, ceased for ever, and I am convinced that the *entente cordiale* which exists between this country and our own is one not likely to change.

A plan was soon in place for building an under-sea railway between Dover and France – the Prince inspected the preliminary borings in March 1882 – but the will to proceed foundered on political distrust of Britain's immediate intentions in Egypt. The hapless Anglo-French administration was failing to address nationalist aspirations, and the loss in June of fifty European lives in riots at Alexandria gave aggressive imperialists in Gladstone's cabinet reason for war. By September British troops (under General Sir Garnet Wolseley) had secured unilateral occupation of Cairo. The forty-one-year-old Prince (as

Colonel-in-Chief of the Guards Regiments) had offered to serve in the field, but had had to accept the Queen's inevitable veto. While appreciating his 'gallant wish to see service,' Sir Henry Ponsonby told him on her behalf, 'the imperative demands of public duty' made it 'inexpedient and unwise' for the Prince to accompany the expedition 'as a spectator – and impossible for your R.H. to be attached to it on duty.' But knowing that his proposal 'would be heartily appreciated by everyone', she was only too glad to make it 'generally known'.

The following year he cancelled his annual spring visit to Paris at a time when anti-royalist agitators were taking to the streets and Anglo-French relations were at a low ebb following Britain's incursion into Egypt's neighbouring province of the Sudan – a move that the French were watching 'with no friendly eye'.[39] What followed was a chapter of imperial hubris that culminated in the culpable failure (in January 1885) to proceed with proper haste to relieve General Gordon's predicament in Khartoum before the hordes of the Mahdi overran him – an outcome that effectively consigned the British to remain in Egypt for the next seventy years.[40] 'For the sake of my friends who have not seen active service,' the Prince had written to Wolseley on 5 December 1884, at a time when equivocation was informing military thinking, 'I hope that your surmise about accomplishing your mission *without* fighting may not come true, though perhaps I ought not to say so'.[41] (In a letter to Gordon's sister, the Queen told how keenly she felt 'the *stain* left upon England' by a 'cruel, though heroic, fate'.)[42]

Although the Prince saw no Foreign Office dispatches until Lord Rosebery became Foreign Secretary in 1886 – and not until 1892 was he trusted with his father's key to Foreign Office boxes or shown Cabinet minutes[43] – he would exchange letters with Disraeli (now Earl of Beaconsfield), writing at one point in support of his Indian tour companion, Sir Bartle Frere, then High Commissioner in South Africa. Many thought Frere had been too ready to resort to war with the Zulus, who promptly inflicted a grievous defeat at Isandlwana in January 1879. In one exchange the Prince expressed confidence that Frere (and General Lord Chelmsford) 'would come out of it with flying colours', while Lord Beaconsfield reported 'very meagre', dispiriting news from Chelmsford himself. With Frere's sphere of influence about to be confined to the Cape Colony once Lord Wolseley's nomination – as High Commissioner in the adjacent territories and Commander-in-Chief in Chelmsford's place – was confirmed, the Prince knew his friend would find his position severely prejudiced. Indeed, when Chelmsford chose to resign rather than serve as second-in-command, the Prince encouraged Frere to follow the General's resignation with his own. In a letter to him in September 1879, the Prince, who understood his feelings, expressed himself unsure 'whether you can well retain your present important post with dignity to yourself'. Writing again in October, the Prince strongly cautioned him – but to no avail – that his staying on would likely incur further unjust injury to his reputation. 'Ministers wish me to remain,' Frere declared, although he admitted that he had reaped 'nothing but abuse for my share in the wars'. In outcome, Frere remained at his post until recalled early in Gladstone's new ministry, formed in March 1880. True to a friendship, the Prince invited Sir Bartle and his family to join him at Abergeldie on their arrival in England.[44]

On 3 June 1896 Kaiser Wilhelm made a gesture of racial solidarity with the Boers, the so-called Kruger telegram, which he sent to the Boer leader congratulating him on repelling Dr Jameson's opportunist raid into the Transvaal (a curtain-raiser, as it proved, to subsequent war). It was a curt example of the growling we associate with the Prince's nephew. The country winced and learnt to trust him less; the Prince knew him well enough not to be unduly surprised at the intervention. Ranked alongside the Kaiser's powerful leadership of some 50 million subjects, the modest influence accorded to the Prince in matters of state left him conscious of a handicap, which can only have been compounded by a lack of common interest (the Cowes Regatta apart): raffish Marlborough House and Potsdam presented cultural antipoles.[45] The Kaiser's generous patronage – in music and literature, science and archaeology – encouraged intellectuals of a breed the Prince shunned, whose achievements (as Lady Warwick attested) did not entitle them 'to our recognition . . .'[46] Indeed, men of learning are conspicuously absent from the narrative of the Prince's life.

The temper of estrangement had been confirmed in Vienna in the autumn of 1881 by an episode of crass ill will. The Prince had written twice requesting the date proposed for his nephew's state visit to the Austrian capital and had been ignored. The Kaiser had no intention of brooking other royal guests at the Viennese Court while he was there; nor was he going to have the Prince enjoy the least limelight himself. (His uncle had already sent to Berlin for his uniform as Honorary Colonel of the Blücher Hussars.) The Prince, who received the Emperor, Franz Joseph, and Crown Prince Rudolph at the Grand Hotel on 10 September, learnt that the Kaiser would arrive on 3 October, and adapted his plans so as to be in the city for the duration of the visit. Then came the 'most disagreeable communication'[47] delivered by the British Ambassador, Sir Augustus Paget, informing the Prince that his nephew refused to meet him. Lord Salisbury attributed this humiliation to the Kaiser's objection to the unwelcome questions the Prince had raised about German intentions, comprising the long-confiscated Hanoverian territories (namely Alsace-Lorraine and North Schleswig) and the restitution of sequestrated properties belonging to the Duke of Cumberland (the ex-King of Hanover's heir).[48] The Prince was trumped. He would withdraw to the Carpathians as guest of the King and Queen of Rumania, but return to Vienna as soon as the Kaiser departed, to bid the Emperor farewell.[49]

England's turn to welcome the Kaiser came in August 1889 – for what was a carnival of naval and military reviews, gala dinners and frostily competitive yachting in the Solent which, by the Prince's dismal reckoning, defeated all prospects of *rapprochement* then and in summers to come. ('One cannot have enough hatred for England,' the Kaiser once told an ambassador – this from the grandson who, hurrying to the Queen's bedside from Berlin, would insist upon closing her eyes in death.)[50] The Kaiser did not race his yachts in person after 1895, claiming that he was 'finished with England'.[51] However, he returned for a five-day visit to his grandmother in November 1899, when, with outright war in progress in South Africa, there was talk, briefly, of German disengagement from pro-Boer propaganda and, unconvincingly, of an Anglo-German alliance.

On returning home, the Kaiser hectored about Britain's failing military campaign in Africa and how it should be better conducted. In a letter to the Prince on 4 February 1900 – at a stage when Ladysmith, Mafeking and Kimberley were still under siege (the latter until 15 February) – he quoted England's defeat at the hands of the Australian cricket team the previous summer, when, he said, the home country 'took the latter's victory quietly, with chivalrous acknowledgement of her opponent'. The Prince was unblinking in his reply on 8 February:

> I am unable to share your opinions, which . . . liken our conflict with the Boers to our Cricket Matches with the Australians, in which the latter were victorious and we accepted our defeat. The British Empire is now fighting for its very existence, as you know full well, and for our superiority in S. Africa.

We must therefore use every effort in our power to prove victorious in the end!

Antipathy towards Britain's way with the Boers was demonstrated by an alarming incident on 4 April, when four pistol shots were fired from the footboard of their carriage as the Prince and Princess were leaving the Gare du Nord at Brussels. The assailant, one Jean-Baptiste Sipido, a sixteen-year-old apprentice tinsmith and member of an anarchist club, spoke of the Prince when questioned as 'an accomplice of [Joseph] Chamberlain [the Colonial Secretary] in killing the Boers'.[52] In making light of the incident, the Prince merely welcomed Sipido's unskilled marksmanship. 'Fortunately Anarchists are bad shots,' he commented; 'the dagger is far more to be feared than the pistol . . .' What appeared to bother him more – he expressed himself 'a little surprised and hurt' – was Parliament's failure to offer a formal vote of sympathy. It had not been thought necessary, Lord Salisbury told him after the matter was raised in Cabinet, to recall an adjourned House of Lords 'to have a special sitting with proper notice'.[53]

Writing to the Queen early in 1887, his forty-fifth year, the Prince defended his enjoyment of continental pleasures, describing them as beneficial to his health amid 'ever-increasing duties'. He took it 'rather hard' that she should disparage 'the round of gaieties I indulge in at Cannes, London, Homburg and Cowes'. He enjoyed Cannes 'excessively' for its climate and scenery; Homburg, he said, ministered to his health.[54] Of Paris and its enticements he made no mention.

A city that was no less familiar to him than it was in the years of his youthful dalliance, *belle époque* Paris – both real and fabled – boasted no rival in Europe as a promoter of erotic pleasure. The Prince found it irresistible. Its crowning pleasure palace, the Moulin Rouge, founded in 1889, glowed fiery red across the sexual squalor of Montmartre from the illuminated vanes above the entrance.[55] Here the can-can dancer Louise Weber confirmed her record of audacity: '*Ullo, Wales! Est-ce que tu vas payer mon champagne?*' she hazarded one night.[56] The proprietor of Le Chat Noir cabaret, Rodolphe Salis, once jested across a crowded house: 'And how is that mother of yours?'[57] The Prince was amused. Nearby one entered the Cabaret de l'Enfer (Hell) 'through a gaping Devil's mouth', where female employees went naked and the men were dressed as skeletons; its counterpart, the Cabaret du Ciel (Heaven), served 'ambrosia of the gods' (strong German beer), brought to your table by angels in scanty white attire.[58] In after years, supposed relics of the Prince's carnality would become objects of fascination to visitors: at Le Chabanais, his favourite brothel, could be seen the chair from which he made his overtures;[59] and – somewhat grotesquely – at a Left Bank bordello whose past *modus operandi* was later replicated in waxwork, there hung a contraption of hoist and stirrups, said to have been installed for his use in surmounting the impediment of obesity.[60]

In the 1890s, as progressive bronchial weakness could no longer be ignored, the Prince adapted the pattern of his continental visits to benefit from either bracing or thinner air. He never forsook the Riviera, where the spring Battle of Flowers at Cannes continued to amuse him (he once attended as the Devil, dressed in scarlet and with horns), or cruising in the Mediterranean, but yearned more for Homburg, Baden or Biarritz. From 1898 he favoured the newly fashionable Marienbad (in Bohemia) for its altitude and quiet setting. There were unconvincing attempts to restrain the extravagant eating habits of a lifetime, an intention no longer supplemented by earlier 'sporadic enthusiasm'[61] for tennis, golf and fencing. But it chimed with the discreet attentions of the one 'bachelor girl' who succeeded in satisfying him for any length of time with mere platonic diversion. Miss Agnes Keyser was a stockbroker's daughter of middle age, who was wedded to an independent career as a nurse. She would have him revert to the diet of the nursery. Her attempts after the outbreak of the Boer War to establish a nursing home for officers at her residence in Grosvenor Crescent had come to the notice of the Prince, who was instrumental in setting up a trust fund for what became King Edward's Hospital for Officers, which she ran as matron. Miss Keyser cared little for society, and there appears to have been no man in her life. The Prince would dine with her regularly and alone, even as King – an arrangement that attracted no publicity. She ministered to his ailments, heard his worries, and fed him wholesome Irish stews and rice puddings in keeping with her nanny-like devotion. Joined by her sister and a few military inmates, they would complete their evenings at the bridge table. As he pondered new responsibilities, it was with Miss Keyser that he dined on 18 January 1901 while awaiting confirmation that the Queen lay dying, and before travelling by early train to be at the Queen's bedside at Osborne House.[62]

Another bridge partner invited to Miss Keyser's table was the Hon. Mrs George Keppel – the last *amante* to grant him her favours when his sexual athleticism was all but spent. She combined adornment, charm and unremitting tact. 'My mother began as an atmosphere,' wrote her daughter Violet;[63] another daughter, Sonia, knew her to be invested with 'a brilliant, goddess-like quality'. Indeed, as a pre-eminently decorative addition to his circle she appeared to meet all the Prince's requirements:[64] 'ripe curves' (Sonia again) clothed without regard for the size of her dressmaker's bills; a flawless, alabaster complexion; humour and discernment; but above all an unfailing desire to please, unaffected by the implicit uncertainties of her role and matched always by irreproachable diplomacy. Moreover, her husband, the Hon. George Keppel (a Gordon Highlander of dwindling income), was ever the uncomplaining *mari complaisant*. According to the Prince's niece, Princess Alice of Albany, Princess Alexandra appeared to encourage the liaison.[65] Preferring, when not ensconced at Sandringham, to spend time in her native Denmark, the Princess had much reduced her public role in the years before the accession, so it no doubt suited her to tolerate a woman who was able to keep the Prince in good temper and allay his boredom which distraction alone could moderate. But it was tolerance made bearable by distance: at close quarters the chill could be palpable. Princess May had cause on one occasion to comment on her mother-in-law's dislike of Mrs Keppel's expected arrival at Cowes: 'How annoyed [she] will be'; Prince George feared that 'peace and quiet' would not be maintained.[66]

In Mrs Keppel's company the Prince had eyes for no other and appeared fretful when she left his side, for he relied on her to relieve the tedium of managing the flow of conversation. In general conversation he 'likes to . . . [inject] remarks at intervals, but he prefers to listen to others rather than to talk himself', she explained. She was expected to keep him amused and smooth away irritability. As Osbert Sitwell remembered, her talk (her voice was deep and throaty) 'was lit by humour, insight and the utmost good nature'[67] – attributes which, Sir Edward Hamilton conceded, made her 'a most useful and valuable institution' because her presence was guaranteed to lift the Prince's mood.

Meeting by arrangement for the first time at a dinner party given by Georgiana, Lady Howe (the Duke of Marlborough's daughter), at her house in Portman Square, the pair spent much of the evening in conversation on the top landing or seated on the stairs – which 'rather shocked people', their hostess recalled.[68] There quickly arose an understanding between the twenty-nine-year-old Alice Keppel and the Prince (now fifty-six), which was 'unclouded until the end of King Edward's reign' (his biographer's summation)[69] – an indispensable companionship ('She sits next to him at dinner irrespective of rank,' a courtier confirmed), suffused by Mrs Keppel's compliant sensibility.

Her young daughters, meanwhile, were left to make sense of their elders' romantic dissembling by trial and error. As recalled through the lens of hindsight, Violet's childhood naïvety loses nothing in her telling:

> Once upon a time there was a little girl who was usually exhibited when coffee was served. Her interest was centred mainly in the *canards*, those lumps of sugar grown-ups would dip into their coffee for her, a favour she used to ask of a fat, bald gentleman who smelt of cigars and eau-de-Portugal, whose fingers were covered in rings and to whom one curtsied endlessly. One day she took advantage of a lull in the conversation to inquire, 'Mama, why do we call Grandpapa "Majesty"?' A glacial silence ensued in which you could have heard a pin drop: 'No more *canards* darling, you don't look terribly well. Alfred, take Mademoiselle upstairs.'[70]

The Diamond Jubilee celebrations of 1897 had not been without intimations that the Prince's long apprenticeship was drawing to a close. The Queen's heart was weakening, her eyes clouded with cataracts, and on account of acute lumbago the Service of Thanksgiving on 22 June was held in the open below the steps of St Paul's. The long-reclusive monarch, dressed in black *moiré* embroidered a little in silver, rode the six-mile route in an open landau beneath a fitful sun; the Prince and the Duke of Cambridge rode behind her. 'The cheering was quite deafening,' she told her journal, describing an occasion that was as much a fanfare for the imperialist dream before the unedifying conduct of the Boer War 'tarnished the gilt of empire'.[71] (Kipling's contemporary poem, *Recessional*, told of 'all our pomp of yesterday' being 'one with Nineveh and Tyre'.) In the spring the Prince presided over the Privy Council for the first time, and the following year – in opposition to the Queen's wishes, who had never liked her Prime Minister – he was a pallbearer at Gladstone's funeral in Westminster Abbey; upon departing, he stooped to kiss Mrs Gladstone's hand.[72]

A fractured kneecap sustained the following spring (of 1898) from a fall on a spiral staircase at Baron Ferdinand de Rothschild's house, Waddesdon Manor, severely reduced the Prince's activities for some six months; a courtier (Victor Mallet) observed how the 'discipline of an invalid existence' benefited his general health and drew him closer to the Queen and his children. Princess Alexandra, meanwhile, was filling her time with convenient distractions. When not in Copenhagen nursing her mother through the last weeks of her life, she was at Sandringham – where she could forget Mrs Keppel's dominance of the Prince's time in London and the Riviera – or in the Mediterranean, sailing without him aboard *Osborne*, the Queen's yacht. Mallet, in fact, expressed alarm at the Princess's restlessness: 'Her one idea is to be constantly travelling; she looks ill, so do her daughters, and I hear she dreads the possibility of reigning.'[73] Princess May concurred. It did 'not look good' that her mother 'so constantly . . . leave[s] *him* alone as she does'.[74]

For his part, there was much to dispirit the Prince as the century drew to a close. He made a number of visits to his eldest sister, the Empress Victoria, who was dying of spinal cancer, and of whom he was particularly fond; in July he attended Prince Alfred's obsequies in Coburg following his death from heart failure (he too had a cancer). And with Mrs Keppel pregnant with her second daughter (Sonia), hospitality in her absence had lost much of its attraction. By November Princess Victoria's condition had become 'heartbreaking' (the Queen's description). Then, in early December, the Queen's physician, Dr Reid, raised with the Prince the matter of the Queen's own 'enfeebled' health and descent into dementia. So familiar was her reigning that her physicians had been slow to admit the onset of her demise, a hesitance the Prince now shared. He asked that 'no [further] statement whatever' should be added to the *Court Circular* of 17 January, which had confirmed the rumours of the Queen's condition. However, within two days, an equivocal bulletin was issued from Osborne merely reporting the Queen as having 'not lately been in her usual health'. The Prince arrived there on the evening of 20 January, a matter of hours before the Queen asked that he be told of her illness. 'Would your Majesty like him to come now?' Dr Reid inquired of her, to which she replied, 'Certainly, but he needn't stay.'[75] Then the Queen rallied, which allowed the Prince and other members of the family to return briefly to Marlborough House. They were at Osborne again the next morning. The final summons brought them to the bedside the following afternoon (22 January) and they remained there (the Kaiser among them) into the early evening when, peacefully, the Queen died. The previous day she had had the strength to put out her arms to the Prince, who embraced her: 'Bertie!' she whispered – whereupon he broke down.[76]

King Edward VII barely hesitated to take the helm. Seeing the Royal Standard flying at half-mast aboard the royal yacht *Alberta* as it conveyed the Queen's coffin from the Isle of Wight to the mainland, he asked to know the reason why. Receiving the faint-hearted reply of the officer standing beside him on the bridge of the escorting vessel that the Queen was dead, he offered the retort: 'The King of England lives.'[77]

EDWARD VIII

9
Weighed in the Balance

When Queen Alexandra wrote to her worried daughter-in-law in July 1901, she was seeing a good deal of her six-year-old grandson Prince Edward (known to the family as David), the future King Edward VIII. His parents, the Duke and Duchess of York, were two months into a five-continent Empire Tour that would not see them return until the autumn – too long a time, his mother fretted, to have her son exposed to his grandparents' unbridled spoiling. Nor had letters from her girlhood companion and governess lightened her concern. Charged with superintending the boy's first education, the elderly Madame Bricka told how she had twice been left in London when the family returned to York Cottage, Sandringham – 'lest she should spoil the fun',[1] as her pupil would recall in a memoir (*A King's Story*) half a century later. As Queen Alexandra explained the decision to the Duchess of York, a royal physician, Dr Francis Laking, had 'particularly asked' that the Prince might enjoy more of the company of his siblings for a while – Princes Albert, known as 'Bertie' (b. 1895), and Henry (b. 1900) and Princess Mary (b. 1897) – 'as *we all* noticed *how* precautious [*sic*] & *old-fashioned* he was getting – & quite the *ways* of *a single child*!' It had done him 'a great deal of *good*'.[2] Then idyllic high summer invited neglect of schoolroom routines, with expeditions to Virginia Water ('Little David caught his first fish and danced about with joy,' Queen Alexandra recorded) and hours of play which the grown-ups watched from the shade of trees.[3] 'It's all right. Let the children stay with us a little longer,'[4] the King encouraged, his easy way with them effortlessly eclipsing the 'quarter-deck manner' of their father.[5] '(Come in, there is nobody here,' the young Prince once told a visitor to York House, the family's London home, ' . . . nobody that matters, only Grandpa.')[6]

Elsewhere in her letter Queen Alexandra reassures a mother clearly at odds with her child's curiosity. The Duchess knew Prince Edward to be so full of questions that were 'sometimes difficult and awkward to answer' that he must be removed from the sole charge of nurses, an arrangement that Queen Alexandra readily endorsed: 'I agree with the *latter*,' she wrote, while pointing out that he did not raise matters 'more wonderful than *most children*'; indeed his siblings were asking 'just as many funny things' as was their brother. The Duchess, it must be said, had little appetite for the lessons of young motherhood. She consigned childbearing to unspoken memory, making no concession to the family's pleasure in the arrival of a new member. 'She ... does not wish it remarked or mentioned,' the Empress Frederick wrote in the course of one lying-in, and thought her 'very unmaternal'.[7] Indeed, unexceptional infant behaviour merely confused her. When one morning the two-year-old Prince was particularly restless (her term was 'jumpy'), the Duchess resolved the predicament by having him taken from the room, then wrote to the Duke: 'What a curious child he is.'[8] A close observer at Sandringham perceived the nub of the matter: 'The tragedy was that neither [parent] had any understanding of a child's mind', the Countess of Airlie, a former Lady-in-Waiting, recalled in a memoir. King George V and Queen Mary treated their young offspring with conscientious devotion – more so, the Countess thought, than did most parents in that era – yet they 'did not succeed in making . . . their children happy'.[9]

On the evening of 23 June 1894 the Duke of York was seated with a copy of *Pilgrim's Progress* in the library of White Lodge in Richmond Park, the London home of his wife's parents, the Duke and Duchess of Teck, trying to take his mind off the imminent birth of his firstborn. At ten o'clock, as he confided to his diary, 'a sweet little boy'[10] was born, whom his grandmothers would pronounce to be 'a most beautiful, strong and healthy child'.[11] Time was hanging heavily. The Duchess had chosen to have their first child at the home of her parents because it offered respite from the London heat, but the arrangement was uncongenial to the Duke. 'I am very fond of dear Maria,' he told his wife in due course, 'but I assure you I wouldn't go through the six weeks I spent at White Lodge again for anything.'[12] He could never abide unpunctuality (and hers was no exception), and he was exasperated by her thoughtless interruptions that left the couple anxious to be alone. Now they must weather the pressing congratulations that always greet the promise of monarchical succession – in this instance a reign as Edward VIII that would last a mere eleven months less ten days, the briefest since Jane Grey's fateful nine days as Queen in July 1553. *The Times* was expansive:

> The young Prince is heir to a noble inheritance, not only to a station of unequalled dignity, but more than all to the affection of a loyal people, which it will be his office to keep and to make his own. Our heartfelt prayer is that he may prove worthy of so great a trust.[13]

As telegrams poured in from the royal houses of Europe, on one day alone some 1,500 well-wishers recorded their names in a book provided in a marquee on the White Lodge lawn. Among Europe's royal houses, the Duchess's aunt Augusta, Grand Duchess of Mecklenburg-Strelitz, admitted to being all 'in a *twitter*'; she longed 'to *squeeze* everybody who comes in my way', she told her sister, Princess Mary Adelaide. When the Grand Duchess learnt the good news by telegram from London, she recalled how she had gone down 'mentally . . . on my knees, tears of gratitude and happiness flowing, streaming, and the hugging *followed*'.[14]

In honour of his late brother's (Prince Eddy's) memory – but to Queen Victoria's dismay – the Duke of York chose Edward rather than Albert for his son's first name; as he needed to remind her, it 'is indeed a *sacred* name to us'.[15] Wearing the robe of Honiton lace made for Princess Victoria's christening, and maintaining exemplary quiet, the third in direct line of succession was christened Edward Albert Christian (after his grandmother's father) George Andrew Patrick David. In a striking record of the event, four generations posed for the photographer, the child's grandfather (later Edward VII) and father (later George V) standing behind the Queen's chair, as she looks upon the future Edward VIII laid across her lap. Within six weeks the Duchess had left for St Moritz and the Duke of York for Cowes. 'I was sure you wld miss yr sweet *May* & tutsoms baby very much & it was a pity she had to leave you for St Moritz, but never mind once in a way does not matter so much,'[16] commented Princess Alexandra from Sandringham.

The parental home was a seat of prosaic domesticity. 'Until you have seen York Cottage,' the future Duke of Windsor pronounced, 'you will never understand my father.'[17] Despite its cramped, airless accommodation (kitchen smells would hang about the house), primitive plumbing and numerous rooms that were little more than cubicles, it more than contented the Duke for some thirty-three years. (Small rooms were a happy reminder of his cabin at sea and were a convenient excuse for limiting hospitality.) Indeed, the Cottage was wholly suited to making a virtue of dull privacy. The Duke's retreat was his library, the windows darkened by its northern aspect and outside shrubberies, a degree of gloom unrelieved by the scarlet cloth that decorated the walls. Here he read *The Times*, wrote his letters and arranged his famous stamp collection. For her part the Duchess was no less content with arrangements sympathetic to a woman of quiet habit and mind, who respected her husband's preferences, seemingly without demur (never would she allow herself, or her children, to forget that 'their father is also their King').[18] Some commentators, not surprisingly, displayed a measure of incredulity. From the perspective of Sissinghurst, the diarist Harold Nicolson disparaged 'a glum little villa . . . the rooms inside, with their fumed oak surrounds, their white over-mantels framing oval mirrors, their Doulton tiles and stained glass fanlights, are indistinguishable from those of any Surbiton or Upper Norwood home'.[19] The future Archbishop Lang (alluding perhaps to Barchester's charms) reflected on how the young couple 'might have been a curate and his wife in their new home'.[20]

At an extremity of the house was nanny's realm, the day and night nurseries where the children ate their meals, learnt their early lessons and slept with a nurse for company – a chastening arrangement familiar to countless well-born children whose nurture was largely remote from mother-love. Nanny made the rules and dispensed her discipline and, if she did so kindly, she would win a measure of affection. Yet a mother, however remote, rarely lost tenure of her child's heartstrings, although her aching absence often imbued her with qualities she could not own;[21] commonly, in this play of dual loyalties, the focus of affection was apt to be blurred – to the point where the child would undergo some emotional conflict.

As the Prince recalled, his parents' association with their young children was restricted to 'a fixed and regulated pattern'[22] of visits to the drawing room during the after-tea hour, meetings prepared for in a frenzy of washing, brushing and attention to dress.[23] At first it was a disheartening experience. His nanny was a neurotic woman with a sadistic line in subverting maternal love. At the threshold she would 'pinch and twist'[24] the child's arm till he bawled, whereupon the Duchess, clearly dismayed at the greeting, would have him removed from the room, rather than have him given into her arms. It was a cruelty that went unnoticed for some three years, only coming to light when the nanny suffered a nervous breakdown and was dismissed. It was a surprising ignorance to have existed in a cramped house busy with comings and goings of private secretaries, equerries and ladies-in-waiting. However, it was widely assumed that what went unheard and unseen in nursery provision was thought satisfactory. Nursery servants, after all, were employed to screen children from their parents as well as to look after them: as an exponent of nannydom admits, to keep them out of sight and mind 'except on such occasions as [they] could be used as adjunct[s], toys or decoration'.[25] (The attention of this sacked employee to the wants of the Prince's younger brother, Albert, was so negligent as to be thought the likely cause of chronic stomach trouble in later years.)[26] The disgraced nanny was replaced by the humane and adored 'Lala' Bill, previously an under-nurse who had three siblings under her wing after Princess Mary was born (on 25 April 1897).

With calm re-established, the Duchess would gather her children round her 'on little chairs' in her boudoir during the hour before dinner, to talk and read to them. 'She would be in *négligée* resting on the sofa,' the Prince recalled. 'Her soft voice, her cultivated mind, the cosy room overflowing with personal treasures were all inseparable ingredients of the happiness associated with this last hour of a child's day.' And with a lady-in-waiting playing the drawing-room piano, she delighted in teaching the children songs from the *Scottish Song Book* and others such as 'The Camptown Races', 'Oh, My Darling Clementine', and 'Funiculi, Funicula'. She also taught them crocheting, a diversion which the Prince would employ to while away periods of tedium when soldiering in France during the Great War.

The transition from nursery to schoolroom occurred early in 1902 with two appointments: the elevation of Frederick Finch, the nursery footman, to nursemaid, and the engagement of Henry Hansell as the boys' first tutor. The thirty-year-old Finch, for whom the Prince (now aged seven and a half) would develop the deepest regard, would prove indispensable to him, becoming successively his valet and butler. 'Finch . . . who travelled with me, concocted the pitiless remedy for my first hangover,' the Prince recorded, 'and never hesitated to address unsolicited advice when, in his opinion, the developing interests of his young master required it.'[27] (When Finch became ill in retirement, the Duke of Windsor wrote to him: 'What a pity you didn't let us know instead of selling some of your things. Anyway, I enclose check in the amount of £100, which I hope will pay for the doctor's bills.')[28]

On his own admission, the Prince could be refractory. 'That boy is impossible. If you don't give him a thrashing, I will,' resolved 'Lala' Bill, after the Prince had persisted in disturbing his sister's rest one afternoon, on which the 'muscular' Finch promptly marched him off to the bedroom and spanked him. 'You just wait! I will tell Papa what you have done,' the boy cried, more out of hurt pride than pain, as Finch left the room 'with the air of a man who had performed a distasteful but inescapable duty'. Nor did the Duchess offer the slightest comfort: Finch had been right to punish him; he must go to him and make his apology.[29]

Hansell was a muscular Christian in the mould of Charles Kingsley and Thomas Hughes (famous for *Tom Brown's Schooldays*), whose writings and example would inform the late-Victorian cult of manliness in the public schools – of muscle as against brain, flesh as against spirit.[30] The cult had originated with Thomas Arnold of Rugby's ideal of 'godliness and good learning', although he was never comfortable with the pedantry of his acolytes. Exuding benign virtue from every pore, Hansell offered little in the way of intellectual rigour or stimulus to the imagination.[31] He possessed 'only the most rudimentary sense of humour', the Prince's official biographer acknowledged; 'pedestrian in mind, aesthetically unaware, Hansell represented everything that was most philistine and blinkered about the English upper middle classes'.[32] His own academic journey was unremarkable: he took a second in history at Magdalen College, Oxford, then taught at Rossall and Ludgrove, before tutoring Prince Arthur of Connaught and easing him into Eton. His compensations were of a sporting kind: a fondness for cricket and football, along with shooting, golf and sailing (Hansell was born and bred on the Norfolk Broads at Wroxham). 'Mider' (in origin a mispronunciation of 'Mister'), as the Princes called him, raised few barriers to being liked. They spiked his complacency with their pranks; they would come upon him looking oddly disengaged, staring blankly into space,[33] and they laughed at his comical stride when he shared their games of football.[34] But his report books spell out the uninspiring minutiae of the daily grind. 'The work in simple division sums is most disheartening,' he wrote in July 1903. 'Both boys must give a *readier* obedience,' he complained on an earlier occasion; 'I often describe them to myself as obedient boys at the second time of asking.'[35] A Sandringham memory has them fleeing York Cottage during schoolroom hours to hide in the branches of a tree, whence they could watch their tutor making a satisfyingly fruitless search for them.

To his credit, Hansell pressed the wisdom of having the Princes educated at a preparatory school such as Ludgrove, where they would know peer-group competition and a degree of rough and tumble. But the Duke of York would have none of it: rather, the Princes should have a tutor's sole attention as he and his brother had known (who were spared the sophistry which Baron Stockmar had heaped on their grandfather, Edward VII). Hansell duplicated what he could of boarding school ethos in his school for two – straight-backed school desks, a blackboard, grammars and copybooks and a plethora of wall maps and textbooks. The Princes would be at their desks wearing Eton jackets, collars and ties at 7.30 a.m. for three quarters of an hour's preparation (homework) before breakfast, returning to the schoolroom until luncheon, after which was an hour's break in the fresh air, when they might take a walk or kick a football about on the lawns. A further hour of lessons preceded tea.[36] Saturday was designated a half-holiday.[37]

Their father was increasingly irritated by the inadequacy of Hansell's narrow prescriptions. Exasperated that Prince Edward was unable to calculate the average weight of stags recorded in the Abergeldie game book, he appointed a tutor in mathematics. Others followed. The Princes established battle lines with Princess Mary's French governess, when she insisted that French be spoken at meals (Prince Edward called them 'humiliating ordeals'), thwarting her with sullen monosyllables. Following her came Gabriel Hua, their father's former French tutor, who was appointed a member of the household, ostensibly as librarian. On one occasion this bald, black-bearded Frenchman fell victim to English conspiracy in the matter of frogs' legs: he had so praised their merits as adornments of French cuisine that a young threesome, with their mother's connivance, looked to Sandringham's lake to provide a sample of the 'succulent delicacy'. It being the spawning season, they had to content themselves with tadpoles, which the cook broiled for serving on toast. No sooner had the footman passed M. Hua the dish than his knife and fork were upon it, and a large piece was in his mouth. 'No, no! That special savoury is not meant to be eaten at all,' cried Mama. Whereupon Princess Mary 'stammered out . . . the awful truth', and M. Hua, with wounded pride in his eyes, bowed curtly and strode from the room. 'I am afraid,' the Duchess glossed, 'that between *grenouilles* [frogs] and *têtards* [tadpoles] a French gourmet draws a fine line.' When Prince Edward searched out M. Hua and offered the family's apology, his French tutor returned to his dinner.

While speaking French was never among the Duke of York's accomplishments (he would make mischievous play by mispronouncing items on a menu) the German language, being the mother tongue of many of his relations, mattered more. Professor Eugen Oswald, a man of 'strong guttural accent', who had taught him briefly at Heidelberg, was employed again to good effect: Prince Edward wrote of studying diligently and profiting from the hours he passed with this wizened, elderly man, recalling that he memorized such verses as Uhland's 'Das Schwert' and Goethe's ballads 'Der Sänger' and 'Der Erlkönig'.

Shortly before the Prince's ninth birthday a window opened twice weekly on the excluded world that was other children: Miss Walsh's dancing class. The family had exchanged their London home (York House, St James's) for Marlborough House, the King and Queen having moved into Buckingham Palace. In the Marlborough House dining room, or at one of the great London houses, 'the doyenne of the Victorian dancing-mistresses' put the class of some two dozen children (all in Eton suits and dresses tight at the waist) through their steps; in no way did Miss Walsh admit a sense of fun, yet the three older siblings were grateful to be 'lifted . . . out, if only briefly, from our walled-in life in London'.

The Prince would not adjust easily to the noise of London and he missed the freedom to roam 'to the limits of our physical capacity' which he enjoyed in the country; and he would write of the awe that the House's grand spaces, with their martial association, induced in a boy accustomed to Sandringham's snugness:

> What impressed me most about the interior decoration were the La Guerre mural paintings on the walls of the great saloon and the two main staircases, depicting the great Duke of Marlborough's victories. These fascinated me, for around the heroic and commanding figures of the Duke and his generals lay the debris of battle: dead and dying soldiers and horses and shattered canon. The agonized expression of some of the wounded redcoats, painted with fine realism, haunted my boyhood dreams of a warrior's life; and the pathetic glint in the eye of a maimed animal is still imprinted on my memory.

The Prince remembered his free hours spent in the garden for a cramped version of cricket, for which netting was rigged to keep balls out of the shrubberies where the foliage, like so much else in London, tended to be blackened with soot. Sometimes Finch, sometimes the Duke could be persuaded to bowl, but no one matched Hansell's zest for a game that would later fill 'interminably long, dull afternoons' when the Prince joined the Royal Naval College at Osborne. The children were also taken on outings of an educational kind, which went some way to tempering the sameness of schoolroom fare. These ('sometimes hard on our feet and harder still upon the resources of our curiosity'), which Hansell conducted to London's historical and cultural landmarks, he would frequently extend to satisfy a morbid appetite (so the Prince thought) for searching out the finer expressions of ecclesiastical architecture. Passively following Hansell's 'retreating figure through a succession of vast, dank, eerie naves and cave-like crypts', the Prince would find himself longing for the sunlight outside. (This was still the era when royal children and their escort could expect to walk incognito through the streets; later, as vexatious publicity attached to his every movement, the Prince would recall 'with wonder and appreciation' the special worth of this boyhood freedom.)

Weighing Hansell's legacy as educator, the Prince's disappointment was unrestrained:

> On looking back over those five curiously ineffectual years under him, I am appalled to discover how little I really learned. He could scarcely be said to have possessed a positive personality. If he harboured strong views about anything, he was careful to conceal them. Although I was in his care on and off for more than twelve years I am to-day unable to recall anything brilliant or original that he ever said.[38]

To the diarist Harold Nicolson he was equally forthright. Hansell was a 'melancholy and inefficient' man, the Prince told him, who 'never taught us anything at all. I am completely self-educated'[39] – damning confirmation of a propensity for mismanaging the education of a future king. The Duchess, who had been blind for so long to a governess's shortcomings, was no less myopic with regard to Hansell's performance. Owning little in the way of intellectual curiosity herself (a magpie enthusiasm for collecting artefacts burgeoned much later in life), she formed her opinion of Hansell's proficiency after sitting in for a while on his history lessons. 'I must say Hansell teaches it well & they really answer the questions very nicely – taking a real interest in what he tells them,' she told her Aunt Augusta on 3 September 1905, when the Prince was aged eleven. Two years later she writes complacently to the same correspondent: 'We have taken no end of trouble with their education & they have very nice people round them so one feels all is being done to help them.'[40]

Like his grandfather before him, the Prince never acquired the habit of reading for pleasure, a gap that was exposed a number of times in adult life – when, for instance, he returned from a weekend as guest of Lady Desborough and drew his Private Secretary's attention to a copy of *Jane Eyre*, which she had pressed him to read: 'Look at this extraordinary little book . . . have you ever heard of it?' he asked. Wishing to settle an argument, he once asked Thomas Hardy whether he had written *Tess of the D'Urbervilles* – 'I was sure it was by somebody else,' he told him.[41] (Interestingly, at about this time the Eton housemaster and famous diarist Arthur Benson was spelling out the deadening effect of a teaching model confined largely to the classics. 'We do nothing to train fancy, memory, taste, imagination,' he wrote in 1898. 'We do not stimulate. We only make the ordinary boy hate and despise books and knowledge generally; but we make them conscientious – good drudges, I think.')[42]

Constantly rubbing shoulders with parents unsuited to sharing much of themselves did little to settle a highly strung temperament in the making, or to enable the Prince to achieve a proper sense of his own worth; denied the kind of family support that might have persuaded him to accept his inheritance and its duties, he would grow irreversibly to resent them. He merely added to a deficit 'of talents wasted, of promise unfulfilled, and of opportunities thrown away'.[43] Although ten-year-old boys can say strange things, Lala Bill perceived his insecurity some three decades before the trauma of the Abdication: 'Do you remember,' she wrote to Queen Mary, 'when he was quite young, how he didn't wish to live, and he never wanted to become King?'[44]

The Duchess's limp attempts to soften the Duke's forbidding attitude towards his children invariably wilted before his will to prevail. She held him too much in awe. The Prince knew her to be 'a different human being'[45] (his words) when away from his father, yet she failed to relate to him credibly, or to provide the emotional ballast he needed – which put him in need of surrogate relationships for the rest of his life. Indeed, she acknowledged her failure as a mother when her eldest son was little more than a babe in arms: 'I really believe he begins to like me at last, he is most civil to me'[46] was her pathetic gloss on the doubts she harboured.

A pattern of strained encounters between father and son was peppered with 'a vast preponderance of "don'ts" ', the place of reproof invariably the library whither the Prince was summoned by a footman ('His Royal Highness wishes to see you in the library'). This occurred with greater frequency once Princess Mary had her own governess, whom she sought to please with tales (her 'sweet tyranny')[47] of her brothers' wrongdoing. The Duke subjected every grain of his own temperament to the same exacting analysis that he applied to his sons, whose conduct he monitored minutely – a rigour he sustained through implacable regard to conformity, good manners and punctuality, which he believed were inseparable from the highest sense of duty. He insisted, too, on a deal of discretion. An appointee who came to know Windsor well once jested, 'There is a blackbird on the lawn. But for God's sake don't quote me.'[48]

So duty-bound was the family ethos that the Prince could never indulge the sense that a day might belong to him alone.[49] His father had a highly tuned facility for keeping him on his toes, made the more oppressive by the hectoring banter that passes for humour, but leaves the child shamefully bewildered. An example cited by the Duke's biographer, though not directly attributed to him, namely 'Where have you been? Cutting up the paths with your bicycles, I suppose,' is surely of its kind.[50] (Typical of the Duke, too, were the asides intended to cut people down to size – the Sandringham shooting guest, for example, who, when asked for his day's tally of woodcock, received the riposte: 'And how many did you miss?') Explaining to the Prince, who was six at the time, how his newborn brother Henry had come into the world, the Duke relished a little cruelty. The child had flown in at the window, he told him, so it had been necessary to cut off his wings – a brutal imagining that would keep the Prince awake at nights.[51]

Such banter as this amused a man with little in the way of interests to offer his children, apart from sporting ones – a trait the Duke shared with many of his class, who were not disposed to equate manliness with the cultivation of mind and spirit. Wholly lacking an appreciation of the arts, yet surrounded by the cultural artefacts that accumulate in royal residences, the Duke contented himself with folk songs at the piano, and being woken by the piping of a kilted retainer. No provision appears to have been made to foster the artistic or literary sensibilities in his children.

Dull stuff indeed as viewed from the perspective of late-imperial high Society – but gloomily evocative of the seismic insecurities undermining the confidence of Europe's royal houses, which were compounding the Duke's 'deep-seated loathing for change'.[52] (His own reign would witness the disappearance of five emperors, eight kings and eighteen more dynasties.)[53] At home, the mood in factories, and the slums in particular, was unremittingly glum despite the modest efforts of Asquith's consecutive Liberal administrations (which straddled George V's accession) to address the gross (and growing) disparities between rich and poor, large numbers of whom were barely surviving 'above the level of the destitute'. As a measure of industrial unrest, between 1907 and 1912 the count of working days lost through strikes rose from some 2 million to 40,890,000 working days.[54] Furthermore, the intimidation of the suffragette movement would become more violent. 'The argument of the broken pane of glass is the most valuable in modern politics,'[55] Emmeline Pankhurst told an admiring audience in 1913, the year in which the King and Queen were assailed by suffragette petitioners in the Mall on their way to the State Opening of Parliament. No wonder that the new monarch longed for life to be as it had always been – or that, poring over his stamp collection in the shuttered library at Sandringham, he could pretend it was so.

Weathering the influence of a mother unsuited to parenthood and of a father whom he would lose the will to please had its price. The Prince acknowledged that he had known brief periods of childhood happiness, but he chiefly remembered 'the miserableness I had to keep to myself' – a judgement he expressed in the years of bitter exile in France, which it would be wrong to deem sour on that account. ('A *wretched* childhood' was the epithet he used in discussion with the collaborator with whom he recorded his memoirs.)[56] An observer of the Prince's predicament was Alec Hardinge, a Private Secretary, who thought it 'a mystery why George V . . . was such a brute to his children'; likewise the royal librarian, Owen Morshead, was struck by the House of Hanover's propensity for trampling on their young.[57] In a well-known comment whose reliability has been questioned, but hardly deserves to be rejected outright, Lord Derby reported the Duke as telling him: 'I was frightened of my father, and I am damned well going to see to it [the expletive being entirely in character] that my children are frightened of me.'[58]

All of which enhanced the children's love of the outdoors, although they would have to make do with their own company. The three eldest siblings would bicycle with Finch to neighbouring villages, especially to Dersingham to buy sweets at the village shop, or to Wolferton, with its promise of a downhill race at full speed towards the station to watch the train come in. At Frogmore House, Windsor, they made use of the wide drives, racing their bicycles to the bridges that crossed the lake. The Sandringham village schoolmaster, Walter Jones, would take Princes Edward and George on nature rambles, walking them off their feet until, with aching legs 'and not too sure of making it' home, he would chide them 'for not being quite the big, strong boys he thought we were'. On rare occasions – at Mr Jones's instigation – they were allowed contact with the village boys to play football games bristling with social distinction, during which, but for the schoolmaster's whistle, there would have been no sparing the Princes 'bloody noses, barked shins, black eyes, and other usual bumps and bruises of strenuous youth'; it was a 'mixing-up process . . . only intermittently pursued', the Prince recalled.

Yet even in the great outdoors you might never be far from reminders of your inheritance. At Balmoral, where the family were on holiday each summer, the hills and crags around were topped with memorial cairns that witnessed to royal contiguity; at Windsor and at Frogmore, Queen Victoria had 'bronze and marble tokens of remembrance' placed throughout the grounds. The Prince would liken Osborne House to 'a family necropolis' because the interior alcoves displayed life-size white marble statues of his great-grandmother's dead and living relations.[59] To a young boy acutely aware of what was expected of him, these signatures of heredity were forbidding. And at an early age he recognized the chilly servitude which his great-grandmother's presence (he was 'frankly terrified in her company')[60] produced in family, courtiers and servants alike. How, for instance, as the silent ritual of her summer breakfasts unfolded, a kilted attendant would lead her low-slung carriage towards a distant summerhouse (which turned conveniently on rollers to be out of the wind), while a lady-in-waiting walked alongside. Indian waiters (*khidmatgars*) then helped her into her wheelchair and served the meal.[61] No doubt the Prince foresaw in routines of this kind the attentions he would be expected to receive, and which so discouraged him in later years. No one more than his great-grandmother personified the royal way of doing things, where nothing was left to chance, and to which end her instructions were legion:

Mahomet Buksh and Abdul Karim should wear in the *morning out of doors* at breakfast when they wait, their *new* dark blue dress and always at lunch with any 'Pageri' [pagri] (Turban) and sash *they like* only not the *Gold ones.* The Red dress and gold and white turban (or Pageri) and sash to be *always worn at dinner in the evening* . . . As I often, *before* the days get too short take the tea out with me in the carriage, they might do some extra waiting instead, either *before* I go out, or when I come in. Better before I go out, stopping half an hour longer and should wait *upstairs* to answer a handbell. They should come in and out and bring boxes, letters, etc. *instead* of the maids.[62]

National events brought home to the Prince the inescapable demands of royal ceremonial, none more so (when aged six and a half) than the Queen's funeral day (22 January 1901) with its 'interminable waits' in the freezing cold and an abiding impression of 'Princesses sobbing behind heavy crêpe veils' – obsequies the Prince would describe as 'mournful beyond description'. Then (on 22 June 1911) the pomp of the Coronation, with its public reprise of like destinies: on his knees in Westminster Abbey to do homage to his father, now King George V, the Prince swore: 'I, Edward, Prince of Wales, do become your liege man of life and limb, and of earthly worship; and faith and truth I will bear unto you, to live and die, against all manner of folks. So help me God.'

There was, then, discernible hesitance in the Prince in these early years, which boyish high spirits could not entirely mask, a trait which belied his adventurousness as a young man, when physical challenge – and strenuous exercise in particular – were a means suited to taming his devils. He was reluctant at first to ride or play golf, understandably so in the latter case, since his father would not agree to his sons having lessons: 'If we let those boys on the fairway, they will only hack it up,'[63] he told the famous professional, Ben Sayers. Yet his father could admit 'How funny [Prince Edward] is about trying anything new like hockey. We must try to get him over it.' (Golf he came to love, but he was never to overcome the faulty swing he developed as a novice.)

How did others view this boy of very fair looks, burgeoning charm and lively, quick-witted responses? Queen Victoria thought him 'a delightful child, so intelligent, nice and friendly';[64] the Aga Khan praised the 'limpid clarity' of his expression.[65] Close observers perceived the discomfort that often pricked him when reference was made to his exalted inheritance. An uncritical royal watcher, the second Viscount Esher, recognized 'the look of *Weltschmerz*' in the twelve-year-old's eyes, no trace of which could he attribute to any of his

There was a great deal of bad words: Prince Albert Edward *(right)*, aged twelve, and his brother, Prince Alfred, with their tutor, F.W. Gibbs

A hub of family informality and clutter: Sandringham House, Norfolk, which the Prince of Wales acquired in October 1862

He gives you his blessing: Queen Victoria in mourning dress seated before a bust of the late Prince Consort in 1863, the day that the Prince and Princess of Wales *(behind)* were married

Anything that moved received the royal salute: The Prince of Wales standing over the carcass of a wild Chillingham bull, *c.* 1879

Bashful beauty, charged with erotic invitation:
Lillie Langtry, the Prince of Wales's
mistress, in her prime

*Belle époque Paris boasted no rival as a
promoter of erotic pleasure*: Le Ciel
(Heaven) and L'Enfer (Hell), adjacent
cabarets in Montmartre, Paris, the
city that the Prince of Wales enjoyed
at the height of its allure

The tragedy was that neither parent had any understanding of a child's mind: The future George V with *(from left to right)* Prince Albert, Princess Mary, Prince Edward and Prince Henry, at Sandringham in 1902

A timetable which leaves you never alone and therefore never quiet: Prince Edward as a naval cadet, 1908

It all depends whether you develop into a strong, healthy man or remain a sort of puny, half-grown boy: Aged eighteen, but looking far younger, the Prince of Wales strides out with his tutor, Henry Hansell, at Auteuil, Paris, in 1912

I feel such a swine having a soft comfortable life out here: The Prince of Wales standing between his friends Rosemary Leveson-Gower *(left)* and Diana Capel *(right)* at the Duchess of Sutherland's hospital in France during the Great War

Exposing himself to unnecessary risks: The Prince of Wales takes a fall at the Arborfield Cross point-to-point in 1924

My own sweet Angel: Freda Dudley Ward, the first of the two great loves of the Prince of Wales's life, with her children, 1918

I looked upon her as the most independent woman I had ever met: Wallis Simpson, who would monopolize the Prince of Wales's life, dressed for her presentation at Court in June 1931

Hanoverian ancestors; as the Prince's biographer, Frances Donaldson, lucidly puts it, 'he quite early acquired an air of wistfulness, as though something in the view from his elevated position had permanently blighted his hopes'.[66]

Setting aside the inclination of eminent phrenologists to tell what you wish to hear, Bernard Holländer's reading of the young Prince's cranium (in June 1904) was strikingly prescient. He concluded that the Prince lacked self-confidence and sufficient power of concentration to show his talents to full advantage; moreover, a dislike of public appearances and a reluctance to accept responsibilities meant that he would not find it easy to be King.[67]

Each year in advance of King Edward VII's birthday on 9 November, the Prince recalled, Sandringham House would spring to life at his arrival and in anticipation of the celebrations. At the wave of a wand, it seemed, the prospect of visits at dusk to the brightly lit house was real once again, where the saloon would thrill with house guests and Strauss's light airs play from the balcony – irresistible conviviality which the Prince would liken to 'being given open-sesame to a totally different world', a 'tantalizing glimpse' of unbuttoned gaiety that in later life he made his own. There were many times when his grandfather subverted an undertaking to have the children return to York Cottage by seven o'clock – and it being late, their evening would end, predictably, with admonishment, on these occasions soon forgotten. And always there had been the pleasure of the Sandringham House Christmas to look forward to – more of a family gathering, but done with no less panache for that: 'Dickens in a Cartier setting', as the Prince acclaimed it.[68]

10
'The Navy Will Teach David'

The 'Navy way' is the only way, all others being wrong. So determined the Duke of York, who set the Prince on a course that was unlikely to make a rounded man of him. A naval education condemned him to narrow horizons as if 'an iron ring' (the Prince's words) had been thrown around his prospects;[1] he claimed that his father's monomania so dominated the life of his brother and himself as to ensure that their 'characters and outlook . . . developed along more stereotyped lines than those of our contemporaries at public schools'. Moreover, life at the Royal Naval College, Osborne (which the Prince joined aged twelve and a half in May 1907) – unlike a public school education – was a recipe for the kind of attenuated relationships of which the Duke approved, since boyish friendship could so easily encourage a sense of equality, which his grandparents had warned was 'a luxury which princes were bound to deny themselves'.[2] However, he need not have worried, as two preliminary years' training at Osborne, followed by a similar period at Dartmouth, were an effective bromide. When you are commanded to move at the double from pillar to post to fulfil a timetable which leaves you 'never alone and therefore never quiet'[3] (so the Prince told Hansell), the prospect of mooning about with friends is absurd. Indeed, none of his Osborne contemporaries would rank as his friends in later life, when the lessons he might have learnt through friendship would continue to pass him by.[4]

The College prospectus did its best to promote another Eden:

The approach to the main entrance from East Cowes is by a magnificent wide thoroughfare, about a mile and a half in length, called York Avenue: a steadily rising sweep of hill, carpeted with brown sand, and flanked by beautiful sylvan estates, from amidst the foliage of which peep forth elegant villas. Indeed

Osborne College is set amidst truly Arcadian surroundings, and the first impression of the new arrival must needs be one of a tender and delightful landscape.

But, as cadets learnt to their cost, Osborne's insalubrious accommodation – much of it jerry-built – belied the boast that its 'situation, upon a high plateau, is one of the healthiest that could possibly be conceived'. Shortly before the Prince joined, criticism was voiced in the House of Commons about the 'alleged unhealthy conditions',[5] and the College authorities agreed to build an isolation hospital, which was completed during the Prince's second year (in 1909). In 1906, from a roll of 450 cadets, there were 670 reported cases of infectious diseases and 359 non-infectious. During the Prince's time at Osborne, cases of infectious disease were considerably lower, but non-infectious disease was rife: 446 cases in 1908 and 509 in 1909. Apart from common childhood illnesses and influenza, there were incidences of typhoid, bronchitis and pneumonia. In addition, the College was renowned for occurrences of conjunctivitis ('pink eye') – 'your eyes were always running and being bandaged up', a cadet recalled – but these were considerably reduced once it was decided to change the water in the boys' plunge-baths regularly. Notwithstanding, Osborne housed a far greater number of vulnerable thirteen and fourteen year olds than any public school possessed; ill health was unquestionably the product of unsuitable accommodation and cheek-by-jowl routines.

The buildings, which *Truth* magazine unfairly described as looking like 'a combination of a workhouse and stable', had been hastily erected, the builders having used materials of poor durability. The walls of the wooden-framed dormitories, termed 'bungalows', were constructed of uralite, 'a brownish, compressed, felt-like material',[6] and the cavities filled with asbestos; 'the structure of the dormitories . . . had already deteriorated so much by the time I joined that we could kick holes in the outer walls without hurting our feet,' the Prince recalled.[7] Floors were of concrete covered with paving, and the heating system ran on steam. Many window frames let in the rain. Two months before the Prince arrived, an MP was suggesting uralite to be a source of infection and was urging a rebuilding, with brick, of the entire College. In response, the Admiralty sought confirmation that the material was 'free from irritant properties'. (After some of the asbestos was removed in 1911, the accommodation was even more difficult to heat.)[8]

The Prince remembered his bare dormitory ('my orbit shrank to a hard, iron bed and a black-and-white sea chest') for its communal routines and close association, an arrangement wholly alien to him: 'the seclusion of my previous existence . . . rolled up like a curtain', as he put it. Woken abruptly by a bugle call at six o'clock (six thirty in winter), he heard next the cadet captain's gong bringing the dormitory to their knees for ninety seconds of prayer, and again for brushing the teeth. (To leave your toothbrush pointing other than eastwards was known to incur punishment.) Before dressing there was the arctic plunge-bath. 'Today I have only to close my eyes,' the Prince wrote, 'to see again that pathetic crowd of naked, shivering little boys, myself among them, being herded reluctantly towards the green-tiled pool in the first morning light.'[9] Ninety seconds were allowed for dressing – 'the whole thing was a great rush, very exciting', according to one cadet. As a Director of Naval Education acknowledged candidly, 'the boy of sensitive, poetic spirit' and 'the ruminating young philosopher' were not types the Navy had in mind.[10]

The Prince had failed Osborne's written entry examination by a few marks (his grasp of mathematics was still weak), but passed the *viva voce* test impressively: five candidates for the sixty-seven places received lower marks than he had. The papers were an 'ordeal' that ended his 'cloistered boyhood', he recalled, and for which he had 'crammed far into the night'. Three months later (in May 1907) the Prince of Wales was escorting his son to Cowes in the Admiralty yacht, calming him the while with stories of his early naval life and wishing him always to 'remember that I am your best friend';[11] two days later he wrote to say he believed the Prince 'would have a very jolly time of it'.[12]

There was no time to take stock, only 'gongs for doing this, gongs for doing that',[13] and transfers from one activity to the next, always at the double, whether there was need for haste or not.[14] As the Prince described it, the curriculum necessarily addressed the needs of seafarers at the expense of the humanities, where his natural aptitude lay: 'Priority was not unnaturally given to mathematics, navigation, science, and engineering. Instead of Latin and Greek we learned to tie knots and splice rope, sail a cutter, read and make signals, box the compass, and master all the intricacies of seamanship,'[15] much of which added to his apprehension when the time came to hand each term's confidential report to his father on returning home on leave. On the first occasion his father gave him the benefit of the doubt (he had been greeted at Frogmore by a large banner above the entrance reading: '*Vive l'amiral!*')[16] Thereafter there were a number of library attendances. 'David, I am sorry to have to tell you that you have a bad report. Read it' – the fault, during his second term being once again mathematics, which had pursued him to Osborne 'in all its hideous aspects'. Such was his trepidation as he awaited the summons about his third termly report that he burst into tears before his father had time to speak. 'Come, David . . . you have quite a good report this time; and I am pleased with the progress you have made.' Over time the Prince would learn to present his failures 'in the best possible light', this being the least self-deprecatory way of owning the truth that his father's approbation was not for him.[17]

The need to improve the status of engineering as a naval discipline (and likewise of engineering officers) explains the fifteen periods a week assigned to it, markedly more than the subject next in importance, mathematics. In the workshops at Kingston, Isle of Wight, the course taught pattern-making and fitting, use of a lathe, moulding and casting, as well as copper smelting – in all 'a pretty tough [introduction] . . . in which you always came away with your fingers all mangled', a cadet acknowledged.[18] (On a visit some years later to the Ford Motor Company in America, the proprietor was surprised by the Prince's 'intimate knowledge of engineering'; time spent at Osborne with 'grease on his face' and 'the steel filings in his hair' had not been forgotten, a witness commented.)[19] Much of the academic teaching was unremarkable, an exception being Professor Callender's championing of naval history ('First class. Old Geoffrey Callender's classes were a gift in themselves,' a cadet remembered). To the Prince's liking there was a great deal of physical recreation: gymnastics in 'Nelson', the College hall (used also for parades in inclement weather, for Sunday church, theatricals and lectures), soccer, cricket, cross-country running and hockey; swimming in the Solent, sailing and pulling an oar in a double-banked cutter on the Medina River. Osborne's prominent feature – and test of courage – was its sailing mast, which a cadet was expected to climb at least once in his career. 'We all climbed the rigging,' one recalled, 'the most intrepid going over the futtock shrouds which I personally saw no point in attempting, rather like a fly on a wall upside down. Most of us got on to the platform through the lubber's hole';[20] those who fell were caught in the net below. In so active a life the only time to call one's own was Sunday afternoon, when cadets could wander through the College woods and down to the sea, the world beyond being strictly out of bounds.[21]

The Prince appears to have been no better treated than the majority. When a young cadet asked his name soon after joining the College, he replied: 'Edward'; to which his inquirer understandably rejoined, 'Edward what?' 'Just Edward, that is all,' the Prince told him – for so he was in the world he had known until then.[22] Being quite small for his age he acquired the nickname 'Sardine', an apt schoolboy antithesis to Prince of W[h]ales, the title not yet conferred on him.[23] He was clearly fitting in. On one occasion, for mild insubordination to a cadet captain (Osborne's term for 'prefect'), his fair hair was dyed red with ink just before 'quarters' (evening parade), for which he took the rap for being an absentee, his name duly appearing on the Defaulters' List. The three days' punishment he was given comprised 'alternately going round the stable yard at the double [while] carrying a rod across the back of my shoulders', and facing the seamanship room wall for an hour. He recalled also a mock-Caroline execution, when, with hands tied behind his back, he was left for some time with his head held tight by the weight of a sash window lowered across his neck. He remembered, too, a contrasting and undeserved kindness of the matron when he feigned sickness on account of 'feeling miserably hungry'. Having confessed this through malingerer's tears, she prepared for him 'a sumptuous tea of buttered eggs, fresh bread, and jam'.[24]

Corporal punishment was the leitmotif of College routine, more strenuously so than was the case in the public schools although the Admiralty did not admit it. A caning was administered for incurring the displeasure of a cadet captains' tribunal, which exercised power by administering three 'cuts' if the culprit had accumulated three 'ticks' for minor offences – for not having his clothes laid out immaculately on his sea chest, for example. More serious breaches of the disciplinary code were dealt with by the Term Officer, one of six hand-picked from the wardrooms of the whole Navy, whom cadets saw more as demigods than housemasters.[25] 'Official cuts' were a brutal, if infrequent, assertion of the Navy's historic brutalities under the Naval Disciplinary Act. On one occasion during the Prince's time the College Captain had the punishment meted out to his own son Mervyn (Alexander-Sinclair) in the presence of the full complement of his term, seemingly for a succession of petty misdemeanours. 'What lasting benefits such harsh physical correction ever bestowed on boys was doubtful,'[26] the Duke of Windsor concluded. A former cadet recalled the punishment inflicted in the compulsory presence of boys, most of whom were not fourteen years of age:

The worst thing about this was the appalling ritual which accompanied it. The first thing [the boy concerned] had to do was to report sick in the morning to see whether he was fit to undergo the punishment. Then at about nine o'clock in the morning he was paraded in special clothes, physical training kit actually, in front of the Captain, the Commander, the staff, his whole term and then his punishment was read out and how many he'd been awarded. He was then thrown over a vaulting horse, his wrist was held by a surgeon, and a beefy Petty Officer then proceeded to give him the ordained number of strokes with a cane about four, five feet long. It was very painful. It was not called cuts for nothing. I believe in the old days the Petty Officer used to get half a crown each time he drew blood – I suppose that's where it got its name ... The only good thing that came out of it was that we did have an absolutely exceptionally good senior cadet ... as far as we were concerned he said to all the rest of us ... 'We've got to be there, but you are not to watch this.' So directly the punishment commenced we all just looked down. I hope the fact was not lost on ... our officers.

As Osborne's historian concludes, it was the College's 'primary aim' to inculcate naval discipline into adolescent boys; that it did so to 'an undesirable degree' can only have suppressed initiative and original thought in those it sought to mould into 'uniformly recognisable' officer material.[27]

During his last term, when his brother Prince Albert joined the College, the Prince was able to mentor him in a brotherly fashion, which entailed subverting the code that forbade a senior cadet being seen in the company of a junior: they would meet at some distant spot beyond the playing-fields and the Prince would try to advise him. It was evident that his brother 'was beset by the same new-boy difficulties that had nearly overpowered me'.

When the Prince transferred to Dartmouth in May 1909 for the last two years of his shore training, Osborne's cadet captains who had preceded him there (and were granted authority again) had had time to hone their tyranny. One of them, who thought his charges slackers, summarily reduced the time for getting into pyjamas each night to thirty seconds, failure resulting in 'harsh application of the gong rope'. To avoid the outcome, cadets took to removing beforehand clothing that would not be visible on evening prayer parade; yet still the odds were unfavourable, for, the Prince recounted, as soon as we were through the big doors, a stampede began. We tripped in the passage and fell up the stairs in our frantic struggles to reach the dormitory and get undressed and pass the cadet captain, standing by, watch in hand, under the gun. Every evening produced a few minor casualties; and we fell into bed panting and scared, waiting for the delinquents to be called for punishment.

When the Prince mentioned the 'awful rush here' in a letter to his mother, she hoped that he would 'get accustomed to the rush which I believe is rather trying . . .' Did he have time to clean his teeth at night, she asked, 'for Langhurst always says this is so important & I want to know?' Some few weeks elapsed before the Term Lieutenant rescinded the order, but not the cadet captain's authority.

The play of events so interrupted the Prince's Dartmouth career as to leave him disappointed with its outcome. On the verge of returning there on 6 May 1910 after a leave 'unmarred by a single melancholy note', King Edward VII had taken to his quarters with bronchitis and a weakening heart. 'I have wired your Captains that I want you both to remain with me here,' their father told his sons. 'Your grandpapa is very ill, and the end may not be far off.'[28] The public ordeal of the funeral day (20 May), which saw them marching behind their father as the cortège climbed the hill to St George's Chapel, Windsor (the lying in state had lasted thirteen days),[29] merely postponed for the Prince a daunting sense of his raised status – that after his father he would in turn become 'by the Grace of God, of Great Britain, Ireland, and the British Dominions beyond the Seas, King, Defender of the Faith, Emperor of India'. By law of succession he was now Duke of Cornwall and the inheritor of a considerable fortune from Duchy estates in London and the West Country, which he did not recall giving ' rise to any particular satisfaction at the time'; back at Dartmouth, he welcomed the weekly shilling paid uniformly to all cadets.

The Prince spent his sixteenth birthday at Windsor on 23 June, when 'in a conversation lasting but a minute'[30] his father told him of his intention to create him Prince of Wales. The next day, the day of his confirmation by the Archbishop of Canterbury (Dr Randall Davidson), the King belatedly acknowledged that, for the purpose of grooming an heir apparent, a naval education had its limitations. Dartmouth, he said, would arrange a course in Civics for him ('such a useful subject for me to learn', the Prince agreed)[31] in place of some engineering classes, and he was to read serious newspapers, the *Morning Post* and the *Westminster Gazette*, although the former was promptly changed for *The Times* at his father's insistence, who believed 'the views and opinions expressed are much sounder in every way'.[32] At a time of constitutional crisis precipitated by inconclusive moves to limit the authority of the Upper House, the *Gazette* had his thorough approval:[33] 'You should always try and form moderate opinions about things, and never extreme ones, especially in politics,' he advised.[34]

The Prince's final term at Dartmouth gained him privileges, but fell short of bringing him the satisfaction that senior boys feel they have earned. Both he and his brother (newly transferred from Osborne) succumbed to measles and were sent to convalesce at Newquay, from where the Prince returned to the College, but only in time to make hasty farewells. With the Coronation planned for June, his father informed him without warning that he would have to miss the training cruise, which for every Dartmouth entrant was the goal of their cadet life, and preceded their receiving the dirk and insignia of a midshipman. 'No cadet yearned for this proof of success more than I,' the Prince recorded in later life. 'For four impressionable years we had grown up together with one common goal – to go to sea. Now that that goal was within our grasp, it was my fate to have it snatched away.' Indeed, on a number of fronts the contours of his life were being shaped by his new status. He wrote of 'having to take part' in his first official function on 29 March 1911, when he presented a silver oar to the town of Dartmouth, symbol of the Duke of Cornwall's ancient rights over the waters of the Dart. Furthermore, familiar surroundings were being exchanged for new. The family had moved from Marlborough House to the labyrinthine arrangement of Buckingham Palace, a residence he said assailed him with 'a curious, musty smell' whenever he entered it. He was never happy there. Then Frogmore was relinquished for Windsor Castle and Abergeldie for Balmoral; of Windsor he wrote: 'within those ancient, grey, Castle walls, quite without realizing how, I arrived at the end of my boyhood'.

In preparation for the Coronation on 22 June 'a very real' difficulty arose. Although the Prince of Wales takes precedence over the peerage, not being of age he could not wear a peer's robes (or take his seat in the House of Lords), a dilemma the King addressed by investing him with the Order of the Garter on 10 June, as the Prince told his diary:

After Papa & Mama had gone into the Garter Room, I waited outside in the Rubens Room till Uncle Arthur [Duke of Connaught] & Cousin Arthur had come for me. Then I fell in between the two & we walked in & up the room, bowing three times. Then Papa put the garter, riband & george [*sic*], & star on me, & then I went round the table shaking hands with each knight in turn. I kissed both Papa and Mama's hands.[35]

The King recorded how he 'nearly broke down when dear David came to do me homage, as it reminded me so much [of] when I did the same thing to beloved Papa. He did it so well.' No doubt to the Prince's more pressing satisfaction, he learnt that morning that he was gazetted a midshipman, his father awarding him his dirk.

At Caernarvon Castle in July the limelight was his alone for the ceremony of his investiture as Prince of Wales. This required a deal of parental effort to persuade him into a 'preposterous' outfit of white satin breeches, mantle, and surcoat of purple velvet edged with ermine. (His contemporaries now at sea would quite understand that a Prince is 'obliged to do certain things that may seem a little silly', Queen Mary believed.)[36] He delivered lines in Welsh, taught him by Lloyd George, which he had practised many times, calling them to Hansell across the garden at Frogmore; the worthies of Chester complained that, since the Prince was also Earl of Chester, their city should have been host to the ceremony; and a witness described the casting, which so embarrassed the Prince, as 'the incarnation of all the Fairy Princes who have ever been imagined'.[37] The heir to the throne had gratified some 10,000 of the Welsh under a blazing sun, only to feel 'desperately anxious to be treated exactly like any other boy of his age'.[38] No amount of adult experience would reconcile him to receiving homage with any degree of comfort. Commonly it induced enervating alarm.

Sensing his son's prickly state of mind, George V sent him to sea without delay, to serve as the junior midshipman aboard the battleship *Hindustan* for a taste of what the average midshipman took three years to learn. 'Not the smallest exception or discrimination has been made in his favour,'[39] reported the Captain (and his father's one-time shipmate), Henry Campbell, an assessment that would not have borne scrutiny, for the Prince ate with him regularly, and they lunched ashore variously with the Lords Mar, Rosebery and Mount Edgcumbe during an itinerary of south coast ports and a spell with the Home Fleet in the Firth of Forth. But he was learning the ropes. Rising at six o'clock for drill, he kept watch and served in a turret during battle practice; he ran a picket boat and worked filthily in the coal bunkers – all for 1/9d (9p) a day. He told Captain Campbell: 'if I have learnt nothing else since I have been with you, I have learnt what inconvenience is and what it means to be really tired'.[40] Then at Portland his naval life ended with the ship's company singing 'God Bless the Prince of Wales' and 'Auld Lang Syne' as he went ashore. 'I only wish it was possible for you to continue serving in what I consider the finest service in the world,' his father had written to him at sea.[41] At York Cottage the King was 'well aware' that what the Prince was about to hear would disappoint him.[42] He was destined for Oxford.

11
'Learning . . . of Men'

In the autumn of 1912 the eighteen-year-old Prince of Wales was photographed walking briskly across a Paris park beside his strikingly tall tutor – a diminutive figure in bowler hat and overcoat, looking much younger than his years and sporting a cane a little long for his stature. The following spring the King was still blanching at his son's immaturity and expressing himself with crushing directness: 'You are just at the critical age from now til [*sic*] you are 21 and it is most necessary that you should develop properly, both in mind and body. It all depends . . . whether you develop into a strong, healthy man or remain a sort of puny, half grown boy'[1] – a monstrous airing by his father of an inadequacy that troubled the Prince daily, leading him to pursue manhood with excessive concern, but with little prospect of pleasing the King. Physical development appears to have been checked at Osborne (he was growing little body hair); this had stemmed not improbably from a complication (orchitis) of the mumps virus he contracted there, which produces painful testicular swelling in adolescent boys, and in extreme cases can lead to sterility. (Whether or not there was truth in the conjecture within court circles that something had gone 'wrong with his gland' serious enough to affect his capacity to father children, as his sexual life prospered he would fail to do so both in – and presumably out of – wedlock.)[2] As for the university education to which the Prince believed himself ill suited, but for which his father wished him to prepare in the autumn of 1911, his time at Oxford would fire the masculine resolve which he was determined to make his own.

The departure of the King and Queen on 11 November to attend the Coronation Durbar in India presented the Prince with his first opportunity to enjoy

Sandringham somewhat on his own terms ('I no longer stood for being ordered about in quite the same way as before'). And there was time to value relationships, particularly with Prince George (the future Duke of Kent), his younger brother by eight and a half years, who was not yet away at school; he realized that Prince George had qualities akin to his own and 'we laughed at the same things', the Prince recalled. Most evenings he would walk over to Sandringham House to play cards or do jigsaws with his grandmother, whose company he enjoyed for 'the warmth and understanding of her approach to human problems'. The Big House was quiet now, but it was as if his grandparents' personalities still reigned there.

Meanwhile, shooting was becoming the Prince's sporting pursuit of choice. 'I love shooting more than anything else,' he wrote to his father in January 1912. He was grateful to have been allowed 'to shoot so much here' that his shooting had 'very much improved'. A reply he received during the King's homeward voyage rehearsed what became a familiar discontent – that the Prince was wasting opportunities to engage in more vigorous pursuits:

> Judging from your letters and from the number of days you have been shooting, there can't be much game left at Sandringham, I should think. It also seems a mistake to shoot the coverts three times over, I never do that unless a few more cocks have been killed. I can't understand Bland wishing to do so. You seem to be having too much shooting and not enough riding or hunting. I can't understand why you didn't hunt when Sir C. Fitzwilliam came expressly for that, and Bertie and Harry [the King's third son, later Duke of Gloucester] went out. What on earth were you doing? You must learn to ride and hunt properly and you have had such good chances this winter at Sandringham. I must say I am disappointed.

Yet shooting would provide the Prince with some rare, contented hours in his father's company – long, unplanned 'small days' on foot with dogs and keepers, when the King was 'in his element' and able to put aside the cares of State. There were days of carnage, too. On one occasion, during six hours in the field on the estate of a Fleet Street baron who was out to impress, the King accounted for some 1,000 birds and the Prince more than 300. 'Young and unused to firing as I was, my left arm ached from lifting my gun, my shoulder from the recoil, and I was deaf and stunned from the banging,' the Prince recalled. As they drove back to London the King told him, 'Perhaps we went a little too far to-day, David.'[3]

Before the Prince went up to Oxford, a four-month spell in France – the country he was destined to adopt – was a well-meaning attempt on the part of another tutor, Maurice Escoffier, to conquer the Prince's reluctance to speak the native tongue. He wrote essays for him in French about the places they visited and lost something of 'a very John Bull intonation'[4] which he had acquired at Dartmouth; his tutor, meanwhile, was gaining greater mastery of English than his pupil did of French.

His host (the Marquis de Breteuil) found the Prince wanting in presence – as did others – but open, frank and abounding in charm. Society pleasures either overawed him or made little impression. 'Few wasted more than a word with me,' the Prince recalled of a salon ('a pretty heady mixture') at the Breteuils' Paris house: 'a bow, a charming phrase, and off they would dart to exercise their powers of logic and exposition on some gifted compatriot.'[5] Of an informal dance held in his honour he told his diary, 'I danced once or twice but it bores me to a degree.' At 10.15 he was in bed. Raymond Poincaré (Prime Minister and future President of the Republic) was surprised to see him treat the choicest food 'with complete indifference'.[6] He played tennis and golf with the Breteuils' sons and their friends, attended swimming parties and the races, and drove about France with his tutors. If, as he acknowledged, parts of the itinerary appeared to be giving more pleasure to his party that to him, a four-day 'naval interlude' with the French Mediterranean fleet aboard the battleship *Danton* was memorable for stirring pride in naval traditions. And looming all the while was the prospect of Oxford, which he expected to be 'a dreary chore to be finished with the least possible effort and as quickly as possible'.[7]

As Lord Esher discovered, the abrupt ending of the Prince's naval career had been a hard knock, which had added to the capricious tension between inherited obligation and personal interest. Speaking with him at Balmoral after his return to England in the autumn, Esher was aware of sadness – 'the sadness of the world's burdens' so recently stirred by a few days restored to the service he loved – as he wrote on 20 September:

> We talked for about an hour and a half alone. I let him have his say about the Navy; he is devoted to his old profession. How is it possible to have been so long a sailor, and not have got 'imbued with the spirit of it'? That was his

question. His memory is excellent and his vocabulary unusual, and above all things he thinks his own thoughts too. He has opinions, and strong ones on naval matters, and he aired them all in grave fashion – views on types of ships, on a sailor's education, on strategy and naval policy. He told me of his friendly relations with the officers and men with whom he had served, how he loved to talk with the men of their homes and their pleasures and their troubles. He was full of the 'responsibility' of midshipmen and young lieutenants, and eloquent on the merits of such a training. I asked him how if he were charged with the education of a Prince of Wales, he would plan it. This riddle he is going to think over.

'It is a charming mind,' Esher wrote in conclusion (who took long walks alone with the Prince on three occasions) – 'grave, thoughtful, restrained, gentle, kindly, perhaps a trifle obstinate and sombre for so young a lad.'[8]

He believed himself 'not a bit above the average' by any measure of cleverness (the Prince was excused taking Responsions, the entry examination), but Oxford would require more of the 'daily plodding drudgery'[9] he associated with study; he would knuckle down as best he could, but not at the expense of enjoying the first flush of independence. It was a compromise reflected in one of numerous notes he wrote to an Oxford contemporary, Frank Heilgers:

> There seems to be some fate, that I should always be engaged when you are kind enough to come & see me!! I was awfully sick this morning, cooped up with the old Professor, when I was longing to have a talk with you. What I really want to ask you is would you care for a ride tomorrow morning only I want to start at 7.00? I hope it isn't too early but I have work at 9.00.[10]

Oxford's 'formidable outlay of intellect' might fail to make the Prince studious, but the balance of his days there – which became increasingly irksome – gave every encouragement to learn from life. 'All the time he was learning more and more of men, gauging character, watching its play, getting to know what Englishmen are like,' the President of Magdalen, Sir Herbert Warren, would claim in valediction.

Magdalen was chosen for being mercifully free of cliques: nor was it over-conscious of rank (although Sir Herbert was a raging snob). Needless to say, the majority of undergraduates were public-school men linked by friendships established as schoolboys, which added to a sense of isolation made more acute by the attentions of the press. Until 'the vulgar commotion'[11] abated, the Prince kept largely to his rooms in 'Cloisters', which left the field to the tourists. Of these, the over-inquisitive sort, who lingered beneath College windows hoping to catch sight of the Prince, were likely to have pitchers of water emptied upon their heads by irritated fellow-undergraduates. (Local guides got up the story that the College deer park had been restocked to enable the Prince to do a little stalking.)

Meeting strangers was torture to him at first, and in company he would stand constantly fingering his tie. But this intense shyness would pass. Being spared the restrictive supervision that had been his grandfather's lot at Oxford – he long had the measure of his past tutor Hansell (who occupied rooms beneath his own) – and declining the close companionship of Lord Derby's son, Edward Stanley, whom his father sought to foist on him, the Prince was soon attracting friends of his own choosing. 'He was a delightful addition to a dinner-party,' one of them told *The Times*, 'most attractive in the quiet and humble part he took in the conversation, but full of humour and with opinions at once decided and sane.' Moreover, with hospitality of this kind he was developing a shrewd (and necessary) judgement of motive, as his biographer Hector Bolitho explains: 'He was stubborn when necessary, and when his time at Oxford came to an end he had enough will-power to cope with the thick-skinned and the pompous. Servants and little people were safe with him, but humbugs were likely to suffer at his hands.'[12]

Oxford's best were engaged to tutor him, among them Sir William Anson, the Warden of All Souls, whom the Prince both liked and admired, and who taught him constitutional law; also Charles Grant Robertson (history) and the Reverend Lancelot Phelps (political economy). It was to Sir Herbert Warren ('an awful old man') that he read each week the meagre essays he took no pleasure in composing – except for the best of them, about the explorer Captain Scott. He would recall reading *Scott's Last Expedition* while on holiday at York Cottage, and how the labour of reading the book had 'kept him up until 1 a.m. for almost a month'; Lord Rosebery, the former Prime Minister, to whom the King sent the essay, felt able to call it 'really admirable'.[13] Composition was no less a bane to him in his second year. Writing to Frank Heilgers on 3 February 1914, he told him:

Thanks very much for your note. I should love to dine with you tomorrow night. The only thing is I have, as usual, one of these cussed, d-d, unfortunate essays unfinished & it must be shown up Thurs. evening. So I hope you wont think it very rude of me to ask you if you don't mind my not turning up till 8.00. I have a lot of stuff to read up before I can write more & am hard at work now. As I hope to hunt Thurs, to-morrow is my last chance. Hope you don't mind. Thanks so much for asking me.[14]

'It was impossible not to like him. He is clean looking and jolly, with no side at all,'[15] recalled a contemporary (Robert Barrington-Ward), when the Prince was thoroughly used to spending evenings in the rooms of his friends and giving entertainments in return. He smoked with them, played cards and roulette, and tested his capacity for alcohol. He acquired a banjo, to which he became devoted, and suffered his neighbours to hear him practise on the bagpipes. After bump suppers, a little hell-raising, or twenty-first birthday celebrations ('the carrying out of those who could no longer walk by those who thought they could'),[16] the Prince would link arms with friends and sing beneath the President's windows on their way to bed.

Inasmuch as clothes disclose the inner man, an emerging taste at this time for comfortable informality, loud colours and two-toned shoes held a mirror to life as the Prince would have liked it to be. His father, who invariably wore a frock coat when receiving official guests and expected the Prince to wear a morning coat when visiting him, was understandably provoked, but rarely wilfully so, by a style that became the man. (Years later, when as Duke of Windsor he was exiled in France and had no one to please but himself, a secretary recorded seeing him on one occasion in the garden of his house in Paris wearing crimson trousers, a blue shirt, and red and white shoes; on another day he sported bright blue trousers with a canary shirt and blue shoes.)[17] It was during these Oxford years that the King asked 'with magnificent irrelevance' as the Prince came in to breakfast one day, 'Is it raining in *here*?' – the object of his father's scrutiny being the fashionable turn-ups to the Prince's trousers, which his father evidently thought could have no possible purpose but for crossing puddles.[18] Although clothes became immensely interesting to the Prince, he always dressed – as Osborne had taught him – without fuss; indeed, his valet once estimated that he could undress, have a bath, and be in tails and Garter star within three minutes.[19]

Increasingly the Prince was punctuating his diary with feelings that would become blacker the further he progressed into his second year. 'I'm absolutely fed up with the place and it has got on my nerves,' he wrote in December 1913; by January he was feeling 'pretty rotten'; on returning for the spring term in April he confided: 'Back again in this hole!'[20]

With the King still harping on his failings, the Prince was throwing himself into physical activity to ease his *angst*, often driving himself to extremes that surprised his friends, even those who were unaware of how diffident he could be. When the King had appointed a Major William Cadogan, a skilled horseman, to be his equerry at Oxford, charged with training the Prince to perform better in the hunting field, the Prince had accepted instruction 'with bad grace'. He recorded, for instance, how a long, uneventful day in the field at Sandringham had left him 'soaked through and petrified with cold. And then they wonder why one does not like hunting!'[21] At Oxford, Cadogan's instruction looked as if it might fail. 'I went out for an hour's ride [with Major Cadogan] . . . It is very dull & and I only do it because Papa wants me to,'[22] the Prince complained in his diary, after his father assured him that people would call him 'a duffer'[23] if he could not ride well. Yet once Cadogan had won through, the Prince did little by halves: 'Got back at 5.15 after 7 hrs. in the saddle!!' he recorded after his first day out with the South Oxfordshire Hounds; '. . . it was a successful day'.[24] Later he told a friend: 'I now have plenty of confidence and jump everything!!'[25] He was soon pursuing physical distraction at will, setting himself challenges that confirmed a love of hard exercise, sometimes to the point of seeming a driven man. A contemporary recalled an occasion in November 1914 when they revisited Oxford to go out with the beagles:

> The Pragger [the Prince] wore a muffler and heavy cap all the time we were out. There was a long stretch of walking, with the farmer and his sons on horses to scout out the hares, and a number of village people in the rear. But when the hounds did strike the scent, the Pragger was at the front in a jiffy, and there he remained all the time. With my running shoes and all the force I could put into it, I could not possibly keep up with him, nor could anybody else.[26]

It increasingly alarmed the King that the Prince was eating frugally and taking himself on gruelling cross-country runs, as well as playing a good deal of squash, football and golf: 'Do smoke less, take less exercise, *eat more* and rest more,' he urged him.[27]

At intervals the Prince was called from Oxford to learn the ropes of Court ceremonial and practise 'the subtle art of talking to the right people about the right things', as was required of him during the official visit of the Archduke Franz Ferdinand and his wife Sophie only seven months before their assassination at Sarajevo. But no sooner was he introduced to State entertaining than it began to pall; much that appeared 'exciting and colourful' to him as a boy now sat uncomfortably with the social tone that was influencing him at Oxford. He despaired of the State visit of the King and Queen of Denmark in the spring of 1914, thinking 'What rot & a waste of time, money, & energy all these State visits are!!'[28] He called his first Court 'a bum show' whose etiquette was 'intolerable'.[29] Yet these private feelings in no way clouded his performance – as subtly they would come to do – although there were observers reading the signs correctly even then. 'The Prince of Wales seems over-burdened with his duties which he performs with meticulous precision,' noted Lord Crawford. 'Poor boy, somehow he made me feel very sorry for him . . . If only he would bolt with a ballet girl, say for twenty-four hours!'[30]

The Prince had spent the Easter and summer vacations of 1913 visiting various blood relations in Germany, who offered their hospitality out of earshot from Kaiser Wilhelm's anti-British mania and the strident militarism that would soon sweep aside the authority of European monarchies through the agency of war. As guest of King Wilhelm and Queen Charlotte of Württemberg he sat through enormous meals, the strain of them little relieved by afternoon drives around Stuttgart, during which his uncle needed to be constantly roused by jabs of the Queen's elbow. The Prince toured Count Zeppelin's airship plant at Friedrichshafen; at the grand ducal court at Neustrelitz he spent evenings in the company of his aged aunt Augusta, mother of the Grand Duke of Mecklenburg-Strelitz, who 'croaked' to him for the benefit of his German and spoke of the day when George IV (her uncle) had patted her on the head. With Major Cadogan for company, he slipped the leash of stuffy Court society and the watchful eye of his German tutor, Professor Feilder, to sample the night life of Berlin ('a night of dancing not on the Baedeker schedule'),[31] which was often 'wild and uncontrolled' and possessed a homosexual subculture 'of astonishing frankness'.[32] (Exasperated by statistics for drunkenness in the city – which showed that drink was responsible for 1,600 suicides that year – Kaiser Wilhelm II had gone teetotal. Multiplying his regulations, he prohibited singing or whistling in the street, strolling more than three abreast or swinging a cane or umbrella.)[33]

Long after the event the Prince recalled the courtesy call he was obliged to pay the Kaiser, whom he knew distantly from his visits to England:

> Arriving in the late afternoon, I was taken at once to the Emperor's room. He was sitting in uniform behind an extraordinarily high desk; and in greeting me he rose in a most curious manner, as if dismounting from a horse. Upon drawing closer I saw to my astonishment that he had risen from a wooden block shaped like a horse's body; to this was girthed a military saddle, complete with stirrups. Noting my startled expression, the Emperor smiled and explained condescendingly that he was so accustomed to sitting on a horse he found a saddle more conducive to clear, concise thinking than a conventional desk chair . . .
>
> The next day when I re-entered his study to take my leave, he was again astride that incredible saddle, his face, with upturned moustache, bent over a document. He expressed the hope that I had learned something of the German people from my stay, adding that, despite all the terrible things my country thought about them, he and they really were not so difficult to get along with. And at this impressionable age I believed him. Kaiser Wilhelm played all parts. He was impatient [and] haughty, equally eager to please, to frighten, or to astonish; paradoxically stubborn-minded and weak-minded, and, above all, truly humourless.[34]

In September the Prince returned to Germany to represent the King at the wedding of ex-king Manuel of Portugal to Princess Augusta Victoria of Hohenzollern held at Sigmaringen. A photograph shows him accompanying the Duchess of Aosta in the wedding procession while looking fiercely disengaged: military swagger – and the masculine uncertainty it masked – embarrassed him at a time when concern for manliness was rife far beyond any private exchanges between the King and his heir. 'Never before had so many uniforms been seen on the street or so many duels fought, never before had there been so many classified advertisements for treatments [alleged to cure] male maladies and weak nerves,' affirms an historian of the continental scene. (As portrayed by the contemporary Austrian painter Alfred Kubin in his *Salto Mortale*, sexual coupling is a nightmare vision of emasculation in which a pitiably inadequate naked male dives headlong off the thighs of a gigantic woman towards the vagina.) Although martial posturing was widely viewed in Britain with downright suspicion, the collective male libido could appear similarly insecure. London newspapers advertised discreet corsets and innumerable panaceas for manly vigour; one could learn bodybuilding through magazines, and fitness studios could be found on high streets; a famous strongman, Eugene Sandow, flaunted his body before crowds and counted the King among his friends.[35] These were febrile times. If male superiority was not exactly under siege from suffragette sympathizers and their not-to-be-outdone Society acolytes, most certainly it was vulnerable.

In June 1914 the spectre of passing another year at Oxford was removed when the King agreed that the Prince should prepare to serve with the army, although what unravelled was a catalogue of dissatisfaction with roles he would find barely worthy of manly ambition. He had already attended two summer camps under canvas at Aldershot with the Oxford Battalion of the Officers' Training Corps, before being attached for the month of July to the 1st Life Guards, with whom he would hone his horsemanship. From 9 to 11 each morning he paraded with the recruits: 'We were put through the most bone-jarring exercises – mounted sword drill, riding bareback, jumping fences, and vaulting off and on horses at the canter,' the Prince recalled. The evenings provided his first taste of a London Season. He wrote in his diary:

> Tuesday, 7 July, 1914 – Buckingham Palace, London . . . to dine with Ld. & Lady Londesborough . . . After dinner a lot more people arrived & there was a dance. I stuck out to the bitter end & got back at 2 a.m . . . . I enjoyed it immensely; my 1st ball in London!
>
> . . . 8 July . . . to the Duke of Portland's house . . . my dancing is improving. I got in at 4.
>
> . . . 9 July . . . I was up again at 6.00 & walked to barracks . . . on to the Lady Salisbury's ball . . . I have now become fond of dancing & love going out!!
>
> . . . 10 July . . . I've had no more that 8 hrs. sleep in the last 72 hrs.!!

Indeed, in that last summer before the Great War the Prince was fast shedding the reserve which, until then, had peppered his diary, where parties were dismissed as being 'a great strain' and dancing was 'a thing I hate'.

The eve of war (3 August 1914) found the Prince alone, thrashing a ball about a London squash court for want of something useful to do. The 1st Life Guards were already preparing to embark for the front, but he must remain in London, the King ordered, until 'suitable employment'[36] could be found – a disheartening check, given his strong desire to serve as a combatant. Watching with his parents the massed crowds of his countrymen airing their patriotism in front of the Palace long into the night, his self-esteem was shaken. To his brother Prince Albert he wrote:

> I am as good as heartbroken to think I am totally devoid of any job whatsoever and have not the faintest chance of being able to serve my country. I have to stay at home with the women and children, a passenger of the worst description!! Here I am in this bloody gt palace, doing absolutely nothing but attend meals . . . Surely a man of 20 has higher things to hope for? But I haven't apparently! Oh God it is becoming unbearable to live this usual life of ease and comfort at home, when you my dear old boy, and all naval and army officers, are toiling under unpleasant conditions, suffering hardships and running gt risks with your lives, for the defence and honour of England . . . At such a time you will picture me here, depressed and miserable and taking no more part in this huge undertaking than Harry and George, 2 irresponsible kids who run about playing inane games in the passage. However, enough about my rotten self, for I am a most bum specimen of humanity, and so must not be considered.[37]

Three days later the languishing was over. The Prince was gazetted to the Grenadier Guards (his non-regulation height of 5 ft 7 inches – 'I was a pigmy among giants'[38] – was overlooked) and detailed to the King's Company, briefly at Warley Barracks in Essex, then in London. He welcomed being treated as an ordinary officer in conditions that were decidedly rugged: accommodation at Warley lacked furniture and carpets; the officers' mess he thought 'a filthy hole'.[39] He told Frank Heilgers:

Of course I am most frightfully bucked to be in the Brigade of Gds. & joined the 1st Grenadiers here a week ago where they are mobilized. We were training hard all last week to get the reservists fit; co. training, full days etc. & we sweated too in the gt. heat. But this is a godless spot, & these barracks unfit for human habitation!! However the officers are a very nice lot, & have been very nice to me so that I feel quite at home. Then we are living under war conditions & are practically on active service, so that one can't think of comfort!![40]

It was naïve, of course, to think he could escape an inevitable consequence of his birth and be allowed to risk his life in a war that many thought would be over by Christmas. When the battalion was hastily granted forty-eight hours' leave in mid-September, before embarking for France, the Prince was immediately transferred to the 3rd Battalion, also at Wellington Barracks. 'Lord Kitchener does not want you to go to France just now,' the King told him, an explanation the Prince was soon challenging in an interview he secured with the new Secretary of State for War. This 'immense, fierce-looking man', who left the impression that 'all the slow, stubborn purpose of Britain' was concentrated in his features, treated the Prince's gambit with an evenness of mind it scarcely deserved. 'What does it matter if I am killed?' the Prince insisted. 'I have four brothers.' Lord Kitchener's steely gaze settled the matter, in the short term at least: 'If I were sure you would be killed, I do not know if I should be right to restrain you. But I cannot take the chance, which always exists until we have a settled line, of the enemy taking you prisoner.'[41] The Prince watched the Guards march off from the barracks and told a friend: 'I am a broken man. It is terrible being left behind!!'[42]

Two months would elapse before he could set foot in France, during which he did duty with the King's Guard at Buckingham Palace and followed the progress of hostilities with an appetite for thinking the worst of the enemy. Being excluded from the fray was a deep hurt that played out in outbursts of invective to an audience of friends and relatives: the Germans were guilty of 'savage barbarism'[43] and 'infamous conduct', and when words failed him he would pepper his letters with obscenities.[44] ('One can't be surprised at anything those German buggers do. One really can't believe we are fighting European christians . . . I am a great advocate of the principle of taking no prisoners or as few as possible!!'[45] – this after the first poison gas attacks were reported in the Ypres sector.)[46]

The static nature of the Western Front after the first Battle of Ypres in

November – Kitchener's 'settled line', along which success would be measured by the ratio of yards gained to lives lost – lessened the risk in having the Prince join the staff of the Commander-in-Chief of the British Expeditionary Force, Field Marshal Sir John French. The General Headquarters at St Omer, a small provincial town in the Pas-de-Calais some thirty miles from the front line, presented a benign gloss on the business of war. All but the heaviest artillery bombardments sounded distant, while the town was so well provisioned that the officers (of distinctly Boer War vintage) could indulge 'their food and their comforts'. Yet a number of friends and brother officers had lost their lives by the time the Prince reached St Omer on 16 November, among them his equerry, Major Cadogan, two equerries to the King and Prince Maurice of Battenberg (a cousin)[47] – losses which compounded his sense of being a supernumerary.

With the King wanting the Prince 'to gain practical experience of the vast machinery employed in the conduct of a Campaign', he was attached to the various sections at HQ and attended briefings. 'You will find him an attentive, silent listener, absolutely reticent and discreet,' French was told.[48] In effect, the Prince found his time inadequately filled with carrying dispatches and performing low-grade administrative tasks, not a few of them created merely to keep him occupied; otherwise, as he put it, he 'sloped along astern, looking a bloody fool and very much in the way'.[49] None the less, his private feelings aside, the benefit to morale in having the Prince of Wales on board could not be gainsaid. As Lord Esher noted in his journal: 'The King sent for me in the afternoon: he had just heard from the Prince of Wales, who has been motoring all through the French lines in Alsace. He has seen all the French generals and was extraordinarily well received. This must have done a great deal of good.'[50]

Persistence would get the Prince close to the front line, albeit in stages. Briefly in March 1915 he was attached to General Charles Munro's 2nd Division at Béthune, some five miles behind the front positions, only to be withdrawn before the Neuve Chapelle offensive. Even so, while at Béthune he was witness to sniper fire and shelling. A breezy letter (dated 1 March) will not have eased the King's concern:

Dearest Papa,
    . . . Here the Germans are rather close so I didn't go into the front trench proper tho. I managed to see the enemy's trenches as well as a lot of their dead . . . I spent a grand 10 minutes spotting thro. my stalking glass for an

officer who had his rifle aimed on a certain spot in a German trench where men could be seen frequently passing & standing. Whenever I saw a man I told him & he fired!! I never saw one drop but the bullets must have gone fairly close for the men used to disappear v. hurriedly!! . . . So I spent a most wonderful 2 hrs. this morning; 2 hrs. that I shall never forget.[51]

Back at St Omer the Prince revisited the theme of his own adventure. 'Of course I never went near the fighting; kept right away as usual!!' he told Marion, Lady Coke, the first of the married women to fill the role of confidante.[52] And when at last he broke loose from GHQ and was attached to the 1st Army Corps, again at Béthune under the new command of General Munro, the pattern of his days took on little of the sedentary character he chose to report unfairly to his father, when he told him (on 19 May): 'As regards myself it's always office work of various kinds & and I never see anything or go near the front . . . I shall have to remember the war by the various towns & places far back which were headquarters of generals I was attached to, of meals, etc!!' In truth, as he would admit in a memoir, he was making regular 'surreptitious forays'[53] up to the front to visit friends in the Guards regiment. Nor was he deskbound. He told a friend in June: 'I am out a gt. deal and never get into a car if I can possibly help it, doing all my work riding, biking or on foot.'[54] As if to avenge a distaste for the accident of birth, he plied his father with a distorted picture of his war, so compounding the myopic, self-defeating cast of mind to which he was becoming increasingly prone, his earlier recall from Béthune having been a reminder of 'how wretched it is to be the Prince of Wales!!'

Meanwhile, his coming of age (on 23 June) passed without fuss (his memoir is silent on the subject). 'It was a sad and depressing occasion, with this ghastly war on and so many of one's friends killed. In fact I did my utmost to forget it altogether,' he told Lady Coke. His increasingly jaundiced opinion of the military and political figures who frequently dropped in on GHQ contributed to his gloom. Winston Churchill, whom a year earlier (as First Lord of the Admiralty) the Prince had cast as hero for advocating an increase in the size of the Navy, he now recast as villain for being an 'interfering politician'.[55] Churchill's frequent visits to France were burdening the military and causing, according to Kitchener, 'profound friction between French & himself, & between French's staff & his staff, which it is most desirable to avoid'.[56] After Churchill's sacking in May, due in the main to his failing strategy in the Dardanelles, the Prince, in a letter to the Queen, was calling him an 'intriguing swine'. Nine days later (on 16 June) he was dismissive also of Fisher, the First Sea Lord: 'Thank God both Winston and Fisher have gone,'[57] he remarked to a friend, Godfrey Thomas. (It was Fisher's eighth resignation in six and a half months.)[58] Writing to the Queen in July, the Prince regretted the continuing strife between Kitchener and French and its effect on the conduct of the war. 'It does seem a disgrace that people in high positions can't put away all thoughts for themselves at such a time!!' he told her. He thought French 'far from clever'.[59]

In the course of duty, the Prince was aware of logistical failings, particularly a shortage of high-explosive shells and field radios, which had made for strategic stalemate during the Second Battle of Ypres in the spring, and put paid to a summer offensive; human reserves were severely depleted as well. (By the autumn the Germans were producing more than ten times Britain's daily tally of some 22,000 shells.)[60] The Prince laid much of the blame for the shortages in France on the failing campaign in the Dardanelles: 'It makes me sick to think of 10 ruddy DIVS [divisions] killing old Turks instead of Boches!!' he told Thomas.[61]

The twin demons of impatience and impulse were placated, as they were at Oxford, with doses of physical exertion. He would regularly take six-mile walks through difficult terrain before breakfast. 'The Prince eats little and walks much: we eat much and walk little,' admitted a brother officer, Oliver Lyttelton;[62] 'he is simply full of vim . . . and as wiry as a cat,' wrote another.[63] Lyttelton recalled an occasion when they were to dine together with Desmond FitzGerald, then commanding the 1st Battalion Irish Guards and a 'great friend' of the Prince. They would travel in the Prince's grey Daimler, Lyttelton supposed. Arriving in the staff office at about 6.30, the Prince said, 'By the way, you have got a bicycle, I suppose? If you haven't you had better get one, because we ought to start. Dinner is at 7.30.' Lyttelton continued:

> It was still very hot when we set out. 'I never get off,' said HRH as we faced a mile or two of hilly road. 'It is one of the ways that I keep fit.' I was in good training, but after a mile I had sweated through my Sam Browne belt and had begun to entertain some republican inclinations. However, we had a gay and delightful evening: the Prince was happy, and in the highest spirits; we had replaced our lost tissue with some old brandy, and free-wheeled home to our cage like schoolboys.[64]

In hindsight, the Prince thought the time spent on the seat of his bicycle provided the greater part of what he learnt about war, while the perspective which bicycling gave contributed to 'the profound effect' the war years had on him:

> My duties constantly took me back and forth between the various units; and, although entitled to a staff car, I seldom used one within our area. The cars of the brass hats honked infantrymen off the road into ditches, splashed them with mud, and, even under the best of circumstances, were an irritating reminder of the relative comforts of life on the staff.
>
> My green Army bicycle was a heavy, cumbersome machine. But on it I must have pedalled hundreds, even thousands, of miles, collecting material for reports, inspecting camps and ammunition dumps. My brother officers laughed at me for preferring this hard way of getting around, but they missed the point.[65]

On leave in August, the Prince had an unwelcome taste of the attention that would accompany his movements after the war. Arriving by train at Dunrobin for an informal visit to the Duke of Sutherland, his party was unexpectedly greeted by 'rows and rows of people in kilts', and to his silent fury the route to the castle was lined with troops. Ending their holiday with a few days stalking at Abergeldie, where Princes Harry and George were also staying, the party anticipated the further attention they received by waving, yelling and bursting into song as they drove to the railway station at Ballater. 'We were all dirty, sweaty and dishevelled, and must have looked like a lot of tramps,' Thomas recalled.

The highlight of the leave was a visit by the Prince to the fleet at Scapa Flow, which the King had been reluctant to grant, knowing the emotion it would probably arouse. It was a frequent gripe of the Prince that the army officers he met barely acknowledged the Navy's contribution to the war, and it grieved him much to hear 'my beloved service' disparaged. Sea-fever, after all, was in the blood. On 18 August he told his diary: 'How I long to be back at sea again and infinitely prefer being a sailor to a soldier!!'[66]

The renewed, but soon thwarted, Allied offensives at Loos that began on 25 September saw the British use poison gas for the first time, a move intended to compensate for the failure to resolve the shortage of artillery shells. But the winds were fickle and the gas cylinders unreliable. There were many friendly casualties. Under 'the heaviest concentration of [French] artillery fire in history', the Germans evacuated their forward trenches, and so 'rendered much of the French bombardment useless'. The infantry assaults, in which Kitchener's New Army units made their first substantive appearance, were conducted in sodden conditions over ground broken by the Allied shelling. At the reckoning, the British had suffered more than twice the casualties they inflicted – some 60,000 men.[67] The Prince's view of events was entirely consistent with the explicit catalogue of mortality that we associate with some parts of the fighting on the Western Front. Having joined Major General (later Field Marshal) Lord Cavan's Guards division shortly before the Loos offensives, the Prince accompanied him on a tour of his divisional front line after the fighting had begun. His diary entry for 29 September reads:

> Then commenced probably the 4 most interesting hrs. of my life!! We walked along the rd. to le Rutoire, a solitary ruined farm on the open ground which stretches towards Loos, but there was a battery in position half way which was being shelled & we were driven to an old communication trench by a big shell which burst 40 yds. from us!! No more above ground strolls for us after that & we had a muddy progress to H.Q. 1st Gds. Bde. in the ruined farm . . . & after a short pow wow . . . forward to an observation sta . . . To get there we had our original system of trenches round 'Triangular Fence' to traverse & then climed [sic] out over our front parapet into what was 'No man's land' & crossed over to the original German front line past 'Lone Tree', which we got down into, due S. of the 'Bois Carree [sic]'. In so doing we were able to see exactly what the assaulting parties of the Div. had to undertake on the morning of the 25th: they had to charge a good 300 yds. across the open towards & past 'Lone Tree' after the gas had been turned on!! Of course the dead lie out unburied & in the postures & on the spots as they fell, & one gets some idea of the horror & ghastliness of it all!! . . . Those dead bodies offered a most pathetic & gruesome sight; too cruel to be killed within a few yds. of yr. objective after a 300 yds. sprint of death!! This was my first real sight of war, & it moved and impressed me most enormously!!

Then occurred the incident which signalled his withdrawal from the front line and an immediate transfer to the XI Corps staff:

We emerged near Vermilles church, a muddy pair, for it was one continuous wallow in a foot of mud the whole way in the trenches. We found our car all right but had a bad shock when we were told that Green [my driver] had been killed by a burst of shrapnel!!!! We went into No. 4 F.A. dressing sta. close by and saw the poor man's body; he was hit in the heart & death must have been instantaneous. I can't yet realise that it has happened!! . . . This push is a failure . . . I have seen & learnt a lot about war today.

In a letter to the Prince written on the King's behalf on 1 October, Lord Stamfordham, the King's Private Secretary, apportioned no blame for the danger to which he had been exposed, but counselled proper regard for the extra burden placed upon the High Command in having him do duty in the combat zone. 'Make it as light for him [Lord Cavan] as you can Sir!' he urged. The Prince hankered after active service because he wanted to make common cause, as he saw it, with his generation's 'rendezvous with history', but it was not a defensible perspective, given his importance to the country, and it exposed a fragile sense of duty that would not stiffen with age. 'Manifestly I was being kept, so to speak, on ice, against the day that death should claim my father,' he glossed – a case of youthful sour grapes evoked in a memoir and without qualification.

Nor was special recognition to his liking. To have been granted service medals of the French and Russian Orders and to be expected to parade them in the presence of men who properly deserved them did little for his self-esteem and made him feel a sham – a scruple his father dismissed outright. 'Get both the ribbons sewn on your khaki at once,' the King told him when he heard that he was choosing not to wear them. The Prince duly apologized for looking at the matter from what must have seemed 'a wrong & foolish point of view', while in private he deplored his status afresh.[68]

Late in October, during George V's visit to the First Army and with the Prince in attendance, the King was thrown from Sir Douglas Haig's mare while inspecting a detachment of the Flying Corps, the animal rolling on him twice and crushing him. The Prince recognized at once that only the soft ground had saved his father from death. He watched over him during the painful drive to the château at Aire, before leaving for London to reassure the Queen. An officer recalled how the Prince met the crisis 'anxious but excited, efficient although he was deeply sympathetic'.[69] When the King was returned to the Palace, a fracture of the pelvis was not immediately diagnosed and he never fully regained freedom of movement;[70] as a result, intermittent pain told upon his nerves and temper for the rest of his life.[71]

With General Haig's appointment on 17 December to command the British Expeditionary Force in Sir John French's place, the Prince's life fell into a routine that he was happy to interrupt at his own suggestion in the spring of 1916. The King reluctantly agreed that he should visit allied forces in the Middle East, despite the threat from submarines in the Mediterranean ('D—n the risk of . . . torpedoes,' the Prince told Stamfordham, 'it is such rot, isn't it? But all these family fears have to be considered!')[72] He would be back in France in May, when the attrition centred on Verdun was still unresolved, before the mutual slaughter on the Somme, and later at Arras and Messines, further intensified at Passchendaele (between July and November 1917), where the territorial gain was 'a few miles of liquid mud'.[73]

Shadowed before it began by the 'fearful blow' of losing his greatest friend Desmond Fitzgerald ('he was that to me') in a training accident with a hand grenade, the Middle East interlude tended to reinforce the contrariety of the Prince's position. As he told Lady Coke, 'I feel such a swine having a soft comfortable time out here.'[74] That said, the fetters of irritation loosened a little in the heat. The brief camaraderie of the seasoned Anzac troops lately evacuated to Egypt after the abortive Gallipoli campaign, whose vitality and raw frankness overwhelmed him, immediately ignited his admiration for the loyalties and oxygen of Empire. He bathed with them, ate with them, shared their jokes[75] – and was moved by the 'marvellous imperial spirit' of men who were fighting neither for themselves nor for their own country. For their part, the Anzacs would form a line and cheer him whenever he appeared. 'Some of them gazed at him with tears rolling down their cheeks,' Queen Mary was told.[76] (So warm was his affection for Australia by the end of his visit there in 1920 that he declined to say good-bye: 'she can never be far from my thoughts, wherever I may be,' he told the crowds in Sydney.) The Prince was apt to assume that the applause he won was owing to his royal blood alone and would balk at its easy excesses, when plainly he was victim of his own success. Having met the Prince in April and on numerous occasions after the war when the Prince was actively supporting the Toc H Christian movement, 'Tubby' Clayton, its founder, recognized innate merit when he saw it:

The Prince's natural shyness and reserve no longer impeded him. He had in 1916 won a place of his own in the esteem of all ranks in or near the line; he knew what he could do, and did it with cheerful tact and most unfailing energy . . . And what he said was never strained or formal. This was the beginning of his development as a conversationalist . . . It is not generally fluidity which makes his talk so versatile. It is because of his undimmed, never-wearying attempt to find out facts, which he sorts discerningly and puts into his astonishing memory. From this store the facts have an odd habit of popping out at the right moment . . . All sorts of conditions of men thus become attached to the Prince with a kind of loyalty and appreciation, which is essentially personal and has nothing to do with his unique position.[77]

Had he been able to separate public and private activities, the Prince's six-week respite from France might have been more pleasurable. Maintaining a front as heir to the throne was, he complained to Godfrey Thomas, 'what ruins my life and ever will!!!!' His wish to visit Khartoum as a common tourist was not granted; he was taken round ancient sites in the company of an eminent Egyptologist ('he . . . nearly killed me with his detailed descriptions')[78] till he had no wish to see one ever again; more than anything he craved a few hours in which to visit the bazaars to do some shopping for his parents. But he did have the opportunity to drive a golf ball from the summit of a pyramid.

Back in London, the Prince submitted a brief but well-received report of some 1,200 words on logistical deployments in the Canal Zone, before joining the 14th Army Corps staff under Lord Cavan in May. When the Corps was committed to front-line action for the Passchendaele offensive, the Prince had his closest call when an observation post in a ruined church came under fire. He recorded crouching for an hour in a dugout with the Welsh Guards during friendly fire from a French battery. Irresistibly, he was aware of being within range of 'indescribable mass carnage', as he put it, and could iterate the fascinating, widely held affinity with sacrifice: 'There could be no finer death, & if one was spared how proud one would feel to have been thro it . . .' he wrote. On 31 July he described his circumstances to the King after the preparatory artillery phase was ended and before the British advanced the next day, when the toll was 27,000 casualties:

What the ground must be like tonight I shudder to think and we have completely obliterated all roads W. of Pilckem by shell fire . . . I'm writing this in the office as I'm on watch or night-duty as they call it & it's very cold and damp & still pouring in sheets the rain making a depressing pattering noise on the tin roof of the hut!! The telephone is ringing fairly often so I don't suppose I shall get much sleep tonight . . . But *how* thankful I am to think I am not living forward tonight & am sitting back here in comfort when one has been forward & seen what it's like in the line now!! The nearest thing possible to hell whatever that is!!!![79]

For much of the eighteen months (from May 1916) he spent with the 14th Army Corps in France, the Prince was subject to despondency and was often lonely. 'I could not face . . . any company. I wanted to be alone in my misery!! I feel quite ready to commit suicide and would if I didn't think it unfair on Papa,' he told his diary on 19 August, having again been denied a visit to the front line. A growl, perhaps, although coming early in this further phase of the Prince's service in France, was indicative of an inward and detrimental mindset. But for the close companionship of Claud Hamilton and the faithful Piers 'Joey' Legh (who would serve the Prince for twenty years and accompany him into exile after the abdication), the unrewarding aspects of his work would have been gloomy indeed. For their part, his friends were able to speak their mind when this proved necessary – when, for example, the Prince persisted with his routine of punishing runs or flirted publicly (so Hamilton recognized) with members of the Voluntary Aid Detachment – criticism which the Prince took in good part. And they arranged that he should lose his virginity at a brothel in Amiens – to Paulette, whom he thought 'A heavenly little woman of the kind'.[80]

A first flight in an aeroplane and an artillery course brought changes of scene, the tedious gunnery drills and a poor diet fortified with weekly hampers from Fortnum and Mason, which he shared with others in the mess. 'You know I attach very little importance to my food,' he told the Queen, although 'I like the small amount of food that I eat to be good.'[81] Meanwhile, Lord Stamfordham was failing to persuade the King that the Prince should be making more of these 'valuable and important' years by returning to London, where he would absorb the influence of leading men other than soldiers, get 'some useful reading' done and begin to accustom himself to 'speaking in public'.[82] When he did have time at home early in 1918, ostensibly to visit defence factories, the King intervened: the British Fifth Army was just then in retreat before Ludendorff's searing offensive, which threatened to become a rout. Looking up from his war maps one evening, the King exclaimed: 'Good God! Are you still here? Why aren't you back at your Corps?' His father could not have him seen around London when the Army had its back to the wall.

The Prince had been with Lord Cavan in Italy since November 1917, when the 14th Army Corps was sent to bolster a failing campaign against Austrian and German forces. For almost a year, once their advance was halted, 'we froze in winter and sweltered in summer at our headquarters in the Venetian Plains, without any significant advances or retreats,' the Prince recalled.[83] In May 1918 he delivered a speech in Rome during the third anniversary celebrations of Italy's entry into the war, his 'little touch of boyish shyness' pleasing the crowds; the Queen acknowledged a 'wonderful success . . . I feel prouder of my dearest son than ever.'[84] And, at Foreign Secretary Balfour's insistence, he called on Pope Benedict XV, telling the Queen that he declined to kiss the Pontiff's ring. The Prince did not return to London for his parents' Silver Wedding festivities on 6 July, by which time German resistance along much of the battlefront was already weakening.

The remainder of the Prince's military service endeared him to the Dominion and American troops with whom he spent a good deal of time, first with the Canadian Corps ('real, husky stout-hearted fellows for whom I've a great admiration')[85] when the Armistice was signed at Mons; then with the Anzacs and with General Pershing and the 2nd US Army at Coblenz, who paraded 20,000 men to welcome him. 'I'm just crammed full of American ideas,' he told his father.[86]

Coming home in February 1919 'was like a reprieve from an interminable sentence', he recorded in looking back on a conflict he described as 'a relentless slugging match, contested with savagery and in animal-like congestion'.[87] Addressing his audience when he received the Freedom of the City of London in May, he took stock of his military service, seemingly unclouded by the tally of its frustrations: 'The part I played was, I fear, a very insignificant one, but from one point of view I shall never forget my periods of service overseas. In those four years I mixed with men. In those four years I found my manhood.'[88]

12
'A Desolating Gift'

Little by little an anxious and bewildered Prince would lose the will to reconcile private misgiving and public duty – an impasse capable of making him wretched. It was to mother figures that he turned to solace the pain. He met, while on leave in late February 1918, the married woman who would contend with much pitiful maundering for some sixteen years – Mrs Freda (Winifred) Dudley Ward. He was soon addressing her in letters variously as 'My Angel!!'(26 March), 'My own sweet Angel' (17 April) and 'Beloved Angel' (22 April); on 1 May she was 'My own beloved angel', whose snapshots in a leather frame ('my most precious possessions') never left his pocket and whose favourite scent he was dabbing nightly on his pillow. By August 1919, when the Prince was at sea on the way to his first foreign tour, which he feared 'will only be an existence', he was telling her how 'when I'm in Canada I shall miss my very own darling beloved little mummie so terribly & all her comfort & advice'. He had been making a distinction between his 'deep-down' feelings for her and the crushing dejection he often experienced 'on top'; he told 'My very own darling precious little Fredie' on 31 May:

> It was marvellous hearing your sweet voice on the telephone this morning & to know that you aren't too fearfully 'ang-wy' with your poor little David for everything . . . you did make your little boy so hopelessly happy (deep down) although I even left you in a depressed mood & am no better today!! I just can't cheer up somehow darling, everything & still more the future does look so hopelessly black & I'm so hopelessly despondent about it all.[1]

Theirs had been a chance first meeting in the course of an air-raid warning, Mrs Dudley Ward and her escort having taken shelter in the doorway of a house in Belgrave Square, where dancing was in progress. The emergency over, they were invited to join the guests, one of whom was the Prince. (It is a consummate irony that the brother of their unexpected hostess, Mrs Maud Kerr-Smiley, was Ernest Simpson, whose wife would abruptly displace Mrs Dudley Ward in the Prince's affections in mid-1934.) A fine judge of grace on the dance floor, the Prince monopolized Mrs Dudley Ward for the rest of the evening. He was overwhelmed, while she at no time would lose her head: '. . . be like Mrs Keppel. Be discreet,'[2] Lord Esher (her husband's uncle) would advise, and, indubitably, she was. Indeed, Cynthia Asquith's oft-quoted brutal dismissal – 'a pretty little fluff'[3] – was so much nonsense. Being tirelessly tactful and discreet, Mrs Dudley Ward was well suited to restraining the Prince's relentless devotion. And, taking her pleasures freely, she never compromised the warmth and stability of her home, which provided familial comfort to the Prince. He in turn became devoted to her two young daughters. ('Darling your 2 sweet babies [Angie and Penelope] were so divine to me tonight & it makes me so happy when they play with me,'[4] he would tell her in June 1919.) The daughter of a Nottingham lace-manufacturer, Freda had married, aged nineteen, her elder by sixteen years, William Dudley Ward ('Duddie'), a Liberal Member of Parliament and Vice-Chamberlain to the Royal Household, whose complaisance came of early love grown cold: after five years of marriage they were living more or less separate lives.

As the Prince's affection ripened, earlier infatuations could be dismissed as puppyish. The motherly Lady Coke, his confidante while in the army, had been flattered to receive his endearments ('You . . . have absolutely changed my life,'[5] he told her in May 1917); she dispensed copious maternal balm, but not, it is thought, sexual favours. (A note in Lady Donaldson's copy of her biography, *Edward VIII*, records Viscount Coke's son telling her that his father had occasion to fire a warning shot across the Prince's bows.)[6] Then, with the advent of Freda Dudley Ward, the Prince turned savagely against her for failing to keep her distance. He wrote on 27 December 1920:

> Oh! & Fredie darling who should I run into at the meet but Lady Coke who had come over with a bunch from Holkham!! And the little bitch made a dead set at me during the few moments I was in the house for a drink!! Christ! How I loathe that woman & she didn't get any change out of me.

The following day the Prince was incensed at seeing a photograph in the *Daily Mirror* showing Lady Coke standing close to him, he, mounted, exchanging words with Queen Maud of Norway. 'Fredie darling I'm just livid & wild about that bloody snap . . . in which that — — little bitch Lady Coke is to be seen standing in front of me! A thousand curses on her,' he wrote that evening from York Cottage. All year he had been upbraiding himself for his naïvety. 'I must have been mad to run after her,' he had confessed that January, 'which I own I did until I met YOU Fredie darling, though you know there was never any love about it & I was merely a silly ignorant & green little boy!!'[7] It would not be the only friendship he would discard, having wrung from it what suited him.

Mrs Dudley Ward had put others in the shade – notably Rachel Cavendish (whom the King judged favourably), Portia, the Earl of Cadogan's daughter, and Rosemary Leveson-Gower. The Prince, who had met Portia Cadogan at Windsor in the spring of 1915, fashioned an intense relationship with her until his Oxford contemporary, Edward Stanley, claimed her for himself in June 1917. This had occurred mere days after the Prince had tentatively discussed marriage prospects with the Queen, who settled his mind as to family expectations. 'How depressed I am,' he told his diary. 'I suppose it's Portia having gone West, for of course that talk with Mama has cheered me up and taken a big weight off my mind.' Portia Cadogan had been the Prince's golf partner; she had danced and dined with him regularly; she had accompanied him to the theatre and enjoyed protracted farewells. 'It was divine,' he told his diary on one occasion, 'particularly as I'm madly in love with her!!'[8] Yet – cruelly jealous of all but present passion – he would write to Freda Dudley Ward in September 1919:

> you must have had a bl—d— afternoon with those betas & though you thought Edith Hillingdon [Portia Cadogan's sister] nice, guess she isn't really & of course I can't even think of Portia Stanley without going mad!! Don't you trust that gang an inch, sweetie, it's not worth it & there's nothing to them; I think I know them better than you do & I was once in their clutches & now that I'm quit of them I've forgotten them!!

The Prince's brief romance with Lady Rosemary Leveson-Gower (they met in France where she was nursing wounded soldiers) prompted what could be taken for a frank gloss upon the sexual inadequacy that had cast its shadow since youth. He wrote to Mrs Dudley Ward at the time of Lady Rosemary's engagement to the future Lord Dudley: 'As regards Rosemary's engagement it's a relief to MOI, darling, though I can't help feeling a little sad; TOI knows how I used to feel about her, that she was the only girl I felt I ever could marry . . . Still I just can't bear the thought of having to marry, beloved, though TOI knows that & the reason!!'[9] As to marrying her, it was out of the question (the Queen explained), for there was 'a taint in the blood of her mother's [the St Clair-Erskine's] family' on account of an alleged strain of madness.[10]

'But who exactly was I?'[11] It was the self-absorbing dilemma sapping the Prince's resolve once grinding duty laid siege to his personality: the gaps in his uncertain nature would never be filled. Male confidences – which might have offered ballast – were shallow; reflection he invariably subordinated to practical matters; and the life of the soul went unnourished. When Lady Airlie spoke with him on her own ground soon after he had put aside his khaki, in no sense was he composed. 'He sat for over an hour on a stool in front of the fire smoking one cigarette after another and talking his heart out. He was nervous and frustrated, pulled this way and that,' she remembered.[12] Before long he was roundly disabused of what came most naturally to him. Having experienced 'the levelling process of Osborne, Dartmouth, and Oxford, and the democracy of the battlefields'[13] (his words), a life set apart was not easily reconciled with an instinct for being hail-fellow-well-met when the mood was of his choosing and duration.[14] If this was the Prince's way of helping to bring the monarchy nearer the people, the King would have none of it. The war had made it possible for him to mix with all manner of people, but he should not act like them. 'Remember your position and who you are,' the King insisted, an injunction the Prince had 'dinned' into him again and again. When asked for his advice, a courtier of long experience, Sir Frederick Ponsonby, was similarly direct: 'If I may say so, Sir, I think there is risk in your making yourself too accessible . . . The Monarchy must always retain an element of mystery. A Prince should not show himself too much. The Monarchy must remain on a pedestal.' When the Prince cited the stirrings in the country of a less rigid social order, Ponsonby insisted: 'If you bring it down to the people it will lose its mystery and influence.'

'I do not agree,' the Prince said. 'Times are changing.'

Ponsonby's reply was severe. 'I am older than you are, Sir; I have been with your father, your grandfather, and your great-grandmother. They all understood. You are quite mistaken.'

What the Prince perceived was a seismic shift in the social realities around him: the Victorian and Edwardian matrix that Ponsonby urged could be dismissed because it appeared to ignore 'the seemingly reckless desire for change'[15] with which he was broadly in sympathy. He was only too aware how Lloyd George's 1918 election promise to provide a land fit for heroes was alarmingly short of fulfilment, with the result that many thousands of British men and women, who had contributed to the war machine in many and various capacities, 'were struggl[ing] to make sense of what they had done'.[16] The Prince later wrote:

> As I began to move about the country, it dawned on me that people were discontented and disillusioned. The service men not yet discharged were angry over the clumsy demobilization programme; those who had been demobilized were disgruntled over the lack of jobs and homes; the disabled were bitter over inadequate disability pensions. There were strikes and demonstrations disturbing in their frequency and prevalence. And the trouble had infected the armed forces, leading to small, local, socialist-inspired mutinies at certain supply ports.

And he recounted the occasion when the King reviewed some 15,000 honourably discharged and disabled soldiers in Hyde Park, among them men who saw it as an opportunity to express their grievances before the King in person. There was a sudden commotion at the rear of the ranks as banners of protest were unfurled; men broke ranks; and swiftly the King was surrounded and cut off from the Prince and his brother Prince Albert, being in immediate danger of his horse taking fright. In the charged atmosphere the men closest to the King merely attempted to shake his hand. Once the police had restored calm, he lightly dismissed the matter: 'Those men were in a funny temper,' he remarked dryly, when he returned to the Palace.[17] (The occurrence bore scarcely a whiff of insurrection to compare with the shooting in Russia of the Romanovs on the night of 16–17 July 1918, which left many believing the King culpable for not having tried hard enough to rescue his cousins and give them domicile in England – for fear, it was said, of upsetting British socialists.)[18]

The first of the Prince's provincial tours, in June 1919, and numerous others interspersed between foreign visits gave closer understanding of working lives in Britain than was possible to his predecessors. 'One can't help seeing the work people's point of view,' he told the Queen in February. The tours began on 10 June with a four-day visit to his Duchy of Cornwall properties; in South Wales (from 19 June) he was shown slum dwellings and descended 1,000 feet down a Rhondda Valley coal-pit, where he responded to a message from the miners chalked on a wall ('Welcome to our soldier Prince') by chalking his own ('Thank you. Edward, Prince').[19] These were gentle enough introductions to the art of 'stunting' – the term he coined for official appearances – which, in writing to Freda Dudley Ward, he cast as daunting tedium. 'I started my sordid day at 6.00 a.m. when I had to step out of the train at Newton Abbot & look happy & pleased with a loyal "reception!!" ' he wrote of his arrival in the West Country. 'Gud!! But it was some strain sweetheart & the same thing happened at another little town called Ashburton,' then signed off his account of the day: 'Christ! What I think of my life, beloved, & my prospects for the future are so much worse . . .'[20] This was commonly his tone when voicing the incompatibility between private feelings and public duty.

The Prince provided a good deal of practical help at a time of widespread hardship – for example, by investing in new machinery for the Cornish tin mines, forming farming cooperatives and improving the housing stock in his London estates at Kennington.[21] Furthermore, while he had no wish to commit to campaigning on social issues, his speeches could deliver conviction. In a Mansion House speech delivered when he had returned from Canada and the United States, he took stock of the prevailing malaise:

> A year had passed since the Armistice, and in many parts of the world millions of people are still torn by conflict, haggard with want, and almost broken by despair. I am certain that there never was a time when the world looked so anxiously to Great Britain for an example of confidence and steadiness. I am certain, too, that the restoration of peace and happiness in the whole world depends more largely upon that example than upon anything else. We did our duty quietly and thoroughly as a nation in the War. What is our duty now? It is to show the world that we can work at our social, economic, and industrial problems with a general fairness and sympathy, striving wholeheartedly towards our goal. That goal is happier conditions of life, to ensure that every man and woman in the country may enjoy the just proceeds of their labour, and that every child born into the country may have a fair sporting chance.

Our present problems will never be solved by hatred or by violence. They can only be solved by common sense, and above all by goodwill. The world is feeling rather lost at the present time, and it is up to us, the British nation, and to all the nations of the Empire, to show the way. I feel sure that we will show that way, and that we can.[22]

(When the Prince asked Winston Churchill for advice about composing and delivering speeches – a task to which he invariably gave meticulous care, but which he never came to enjoy – the Churchillian response was characteristically robust: 'If you have an important point to make, don't try to be subtle or clever. Use a pile driver. Hit the point once. Then come back and hit it again. Then hit it a third time – a tremendous whack.')

As he embarked on his twenty-sixth year in July 1919, the Prince received his father's consent to establish an independent household at his early childhood home, York House, the rambling adjunct to St James's Palace, north-facing accommodation which invited little in the way of ostentatious living. The Prince often preferred to eat his meals alone or with intimates in front of the first-floor sitting room fire rather than use the larger dining room below; the compact arrangement of sitting room, bedroom and bathroom had all the convenience of bachelor quarters within the 'veritable rabbit warren'[23] of the greater Palace. The trusty Finch served him there as major-domo ('without whom I'm completely lost & perfectly helpless').[24] Crucial to the efficient conduct of the Prince's affairs was the office space available to his recent appointees. Godfrey Thomas left the Foreign Office to be his Private Secretary and would serve the Prince for some seventeen years until the abdication. Thomas fulfilled Lord Stamfordham's criteria for the post, and more: 'Someone with brains, with some Colonial knowledge: a facile pen – a nice fellow . . .'[25] The Prince was soon addressing him as 'my greatest friend and the one man I can trust and who really understands me'.[26] As equerries the Prince appointed Lord Claud Hamilton, his aide during the war, and his brother Grenadier, Piers 'Joey' Legh. The temperaments of both men would all too soon be tested when the Prince undertook a series of Empire tours that assailed his spirit and his patience. Meanwhile there were numerous figurehead roles thrust upon him. 'I foresee a good deal of work ahead,' Lord Stamfordham warned in a letter of 22 December.[27] The King wished him to take over the Presidency of the King Edward VII Hospital Fund and that of the Royal College of Music; he succeeded the King as

Chancellor of the University of Wales and was elected a trustee of the British Museum. Between the late winter of 1919 and early spring, as his biographer Frances Donaldson neatly garners, his engagements were greatly increased:

> He visited Belgium and France, reviewing troops in both countries, and in Paris visiting the Queen of Italy and dining with [the Premier and his wife] M. and Mme Poincaré. He became President of a great many hospitals, of the RSPCA and of the Royal National Lifeboat Institution, he was elected a fellow of the Royal Society, a member of the Jockey Club, and he was initiated as a Freemason . . . He received the Freedom of the Cities of London and Plymouth. He visited the New Zealand Force and part of the Australian Fleet and he took the salute at Australia House on Anzac Day. He visited ex-servicemen at Rhondda and lunched with Mr Lloyd George at the House of Commons. Among the speeches he made were one to the Canada Club on the part of the Canadian troops in the war and another to the Canadian Officers' Club; he made a speech to the Grenadier Guards' Old Comrades Association at Chelsea Barracks, to the Printers' Pension Corporation at the Connaught Rooms and to the Fishmongers' Company at Fishmongers' Hall.[28]

And all the while there loomed the Empire tours which his father's Private Secretary, Lord Stamfordham, loaded with ominous significance:

> I am hopeful that you will not think my views exaggerated when I say that your visits to the Dominions will be made or marred according as you do & *say* the right thing. The Throne is the pivot upon which the Empire will more than ever hinge. Its strength and stability will depend entirely upon its occupant . . . Every year [the Dominions] will expect more and you ought to go well equipped as to their history and politics.[29]

At 4.30 p.m. on 5 August 1919 the Prince sat in his cabin aboard the fast battle-cruiser HMS *Renown* moored in Portsmouth harbour and wrote to Mrs Dudley Ward in tones by now familiar. 'God! I'm miserable, beloved one, waiting till we sail at 6.00 . . . this trip will only be an existence though I'm going to work so hard to try to make it a success & I shall be so busy that I think the time will go quickly!!' Taking up his pen again at 11 p.m. he concluded: 'Now I must turn in as I am dead beat & no wonder, though it's such a joy to think that the last bed I got into in England was yours'; his party was some twenty strong, yet he would face 'the great blank' of her absence 'feel[ing] so so terribly lost & lonely'. Yet the voyage passed pleasantly enough. The Prince killed time sprinting around the deck, playing 'medicine ball' and getting in some revolver practice. The wardroom was soon 'a cheery crowd & we've been bear fighting and playing vewy wough games',[30] he told his lover. Two appointees he admired from the outset, although they would prove uneasy partners: Rear-Admiral Sir Lionel Halsey ('the old Salt'), his Chief of Staff, whom he found to be 'tolerant and understanding',[31] and Lieutenant-Colonel Edward Grigg (later Lord Altrincham), a political adviser well versed in imperial affairs, whom Halsey would find generously endowed with a clever man's assertiveness. 'Of course it really is everything to have a man like Grigg to keep one up to the mark,' the Prince would report.

The point of arrival on 11 August – the fishing community of St John's, Newfoundland, where the Prince was invited to pass under a triumphal arch built of drums of cod-liver oil hung with strings of dried fish – he thought 'a little pip-squeak place' and the Governor of Newfoundland 'the completest old dud & his wife is beyond description!!' Yet he was 'bucked' by a warm reception, he had spoken 'quite effectively' at a lunch club and shaken hands with 500 guests at a garden party. But in what became a leitmotif of irritation, he was appalled by the homage paid to formality and was determined to put his own stamp on the tour at an early stage.[32] He looked on 'State drives in horse-drawn landaus with mounted escort, mounted military parades, civic lunches, official dinners, sightseeing detours to notable landmarks'[33] as being out-of-date, pompous components of his father's tour some eighteen years earlier, and he was determined to reduce their number. ('I'm so glad that I'm not pompous & royal by nature,' he told Mrs Dudley Ward. 'As I guessed, it isn't wanted & won't go down on this side [of the Atlantic].') Instead, the Prince would set his store by open, public reception, with no barriers as to who might shake his hand. He called this 'pump handling',[34] by which he inaugurated what is a familiar aspect of royal walkabouts today.

After Quebec and Montreal, where the Prince won the approval of French Canadians by delivering addresses in their tongue, Toronto gave startling meaning to 'meeting the people'. The crowds were increasingly 'uncontrolled, almost ferocious in their determination to satisfy their curiosity about me,' he recorded, breaking through police lines to snatch at his person for souvenirs and risking life and limb if carriage horses should take fright. 'I simply cannot understand what has come over the Canadian people, Sir,' pleaded the civil servant (Sir Joseph Pope) entrusted with ceremonial arrangements of the kind that had served the King during his tour in 1901. It took 'a spectacular incident' to have Canadian officials abandon the use of horses altogether. The occasion was a parade of some 27,000 veterans, which required the Prince to ride down the ranks. 'But, General [Burstall], do you think it's a good idea for us to ride on this occasion? You know the veterans. They are not going to keep their ranks once I appear. God knows what this horse will do. Frankly, I am for using a motor.' But the Prince had asked in vain. Before long 'the human mass engulfed me', he recalled, his horse mercifully held by the crush as if in a vice. Then the Prince was 'passed like a football' over the heads of the men towards the platform, which he reached to roars of cheering and with the crumpled notes of his speech intact. That evening he expressed the hope that he had seen the last of horses at public events. 'I was afraid you were going to say that, Sir,' the General answered. 'I shall send out the necessary orders.'[35]

Toronto had delivered a foretaste of the many gruelling days that would strain the Prince to breaking point in New Zealand and Australia the following year. As he described in letters to Mrs Dudley Ward, he had never encountered so punishing a schedule, having spoken at least half a dozen times on 26 August alone – formally, for example, at lunch and at the city hall, and in impromptu fashion at a dinner, even though he had been told there would be no speeches. He had shaken over 2,000 hands in one hour outside the city hall. The next day he visited four hospitals in the morning ('with hundreds of limbless & disabled men to talk to which kills me more than anything else as you know . . . & it took over three hours'), then attended a university degree ceremony, a garden party and a yacht club dinner (a dry one, owing to Prohibition). On 28 August, following the unruly veterans' parade (during which he had decorated 200 officers and men), came a three-hour motor drive round the city 'which has left me in a state of collapse despite a wet dinner at Government House!!'[36] That night the Canadian Pacific Railway conveyed him westwards towards Ottawa.

According to Godfrey Thomas, the Prince was squandering opportunities to relax between engagements; growing more restless as a result, he smoked more and would insist on keeping later and later hours with members of his staff.[37] 'One's head almost reels at the amount you are doing & I feel angry at the amount of handshaking and autograph writing you seem compelled to face!' the Queen wrote from Balmoral in early September.[38] By then the bone of the centre knuckle of his right hand was so bruised and swollen ('it gives me such hell to be gripped') that for a week he was shaking hands with his left. Nor did long train journeys altogether shield him from public attention. Travelling west from Ottawa (where the city women dropped his cigarette butts – 'well, you can guess where, angel!!'[39] he told Mrs Dudley Ward) to Montreal, North Bay, Sudbury, Nipigon, Port Arthur, Fort William and Winnipeg, then through the prairies to Edmonton, Saskatoon, Alberta and Calgary and across the Rocky Mountains to Vancouver,[40] he was expected to speak ad lib to gatherings of local farmers and miners at countless country stations, then pass among them and pump more hands. 'It's been a weary day in the train,' he recorded on 4 September, 'only two [half-hour] stunts in small towns, though I've always got to be on watch for small stations & people to wave to!! . . . I feel I just have to show myself on the stern walk, though it means doing so every 10 mins!!' Regrettably, many of the leisure hours planned for him took little account of his preferences. Besides a little golf, which he welcomed ('though of course it's impossible to hit the ball when one's nerves are in the state that mine are nowadays!!'), he was offered shooting and fishing, which suited his entourage, but not the strenuous exercise he thrived on. He complained of 'a mouldy day's fishing' on the Nipigon River and finding himself 'the only mug of the party' for hooking no fish and failing to shoot 'hopelessly wild' duck. He would spend fruitless hours sitting with his gun on the train's viewing platform, hoping 'for a shot at a duck or something'. A single energetic day on the Bar U Ranch near Calgary proved exceptional, as he told Mrs Dudley Ward:

I enjoyed it all & got a huge amount of exercise . . . I started with an 8 mile run at 8.00 4 miles out to a dried-up river & back & at 10.00 we rode off to the 'round-up' of cattle which was an amazing stunt; I rode a nice locally bred horse in a 'stock' saddle . . . we were in time to help the cowboys and Indians round up the last odd hundred of cattle & they collected close on 2,000 head I guess . . . I got lots of hard riding doing my best imitation of a cowboy chasing refractory calves which wouldn't be driven into the kraal to be branded etc . . . I was walking fields for prairie chickens for 2 hrs after lunch though neither Legh (who was with me) or self shot anything!! Still it was all fine exercise.[41]

Smitten by this brief insight into ranch life, he began negotiations to purchase 2,000 adjoining acres, although in the event they were never profitable.

Despite the fretting, he accepted that no Prince 'had ever stumped a Dominion in quite [this] way'. He was getting impressions of Canada far more instructive than anything he was learning in the company of civic functionaries;[42] he liked the people and esteemed their aspirations. By early September he was assuring Mrs Dudley Ward that he was 'thoroughly bitten'[43] with the place. 'I do not regard myself as belonging to Great Britain and only in a lesser way to Canada and the other Dominions,' he told his audience on one occasion. 'On the contrary I regard myself as belonging to Great Britain and to Canada in exactly the same way.'[44] The Dominions were no longer colonies, but sister-nations of the British nation, he insisted. And in answer to his father's concern that he had set a precedent and would be obliged to adapt the attribution to suit other Dominions, the Prince saw no difficulty: 'Of course in India there would be no question of it as I happen to have been born a white man and not a native.'[45]

When the King had expressed dismay at the mobbing that the Prince was undergoing at his major appearances, implying that his demeanour was inviting loss of dignity, the Prince did his best to defend the new zeitgeist. 'They just go mad & one is powerless!!' he wrote on 23 September. 'It's all so different out here & as I said before so much more is expected & one thing above all others that won't go down & which one has to be careful not [to] put on is "side" & pompousness. You can trust me not to let down your position or mine either.' By mid-October the King was penning a rare expression of appreciation for 'the splendid success' of the tour, which he ascribed in great measure 'to your own personality & the wonderful way in which you have played up'. But from reports he was receiving he feared that the Prince was overburdened with engagements ('these people think one is made of stone,' the Prince wrote, '& that one can go on for ever'); his father hoped he might 'take things easier'[46] for the remainder of the tour.

With very little to content him, the Prince was becoming emotionally dependent on the mailbag bringing letters from Mrs Dudley Ward. On 19 September he wrote:

> Fredie darling guess I must have fallen asleep last night as I took your 2 divine
> letters to bed & read them over & over . . . I was on the verge of tears reading
> all the divine things you say to me sweetheart & I did want you beloved one

& just held out my arms (I did really!!) though alas nothing happened & I felt more hopelessly lonely than ever.

She had just sent him a seal for his letters bearing the impress of a spider, which he kept on his watch chain, but sometimes held it in his hand as a talisman as he delivered difficult speeches: ('your darling little "thpider" seal . . . gave me marvellous comfort & inspiration'). Although he admitted that her letters could effect in him 'a marvellous change' for the better, the gaps between them invited wilful delusion. He wrote on 20 October:

> I feel such a vewy vewy pompous little boy knowing that I belong to my precious beloved little Fredie & am as much a 'married man' as I ever shall be, far more so, & consider myself as such & am the happiest man in the whole world to have such a lovely precious darling darling little 'wife'!! That's my life in a nutshell baby mine.

It appears that Mrs Dudley Ward's thoughts on all this remained discreetly her own, as befitted a lover and confidante to the heir to the throne. If, on reading his outbursts, she knew that she must act a little dumb, no doubt it was uniquely flattering to be the sole recipient of such blunt confessions. Here, in late September, is the Prince larding his predicament:

> Christ what I think of life sweetie & being caged as I am; the fact that every second of my life since we left London has been public is getting rather on my nerves . . . & I feel like a caged animal!! . . . it maddens me never to be out of the public eye & to have to lead this eternal official existence without the break of a second.

A month later 'a lonely fagged out & stale little boy' was voicing a preference which, at a critical point in the future, would have ominous consequence:

> What an unnatural life for a poor little boy of 25 . . . I do get so terribly fed up with it & despondent about it sometimes & begin to feel like 'resigning'!! And then I should be free to live or die according to how hard I worked though I should have you all to myself sweetheart & should only then be really happy and contented.[47]

And so the darkening of his soul progressed. Not until he returned home in November did he trouble himself with what was becoming plain to Mrs Dudley Ward – that in private circles their relationship was no longer being regarded as one between friends.

After Canada came brief visits to Washington and to New York. Despite his eagerness to be home, this initiative was the Prince's own and was welcomed by the Americans, with whose forces he had warmly associated in the war. Because President Woodrow Wilson was stricken with paralysis, the King was set firmly against the visit, although he left the decision to the Foreign Office, whose consent was given. Once the motorcades rolled, the Americans fell in love with the Prince: 'blue eyes, fair hair, easy smile and little-boy-lost look' were winning attributes of a Prince Charming figure who captivated them.[48]

In Washington he was taken to the sick President's bedside at the White House ('this was the most disappointed face that I had ever looked upon') and to Mount Vernon to lay a wreath on George Washington's tomb. He met war veterans at the Red Cross headquarters and was greeted by 2,000 cadets at the Annapolis Naval Academy, who yelled their unscripted greeting 'in perfect cadence and unison: NAV-EE, NAV-EE, NAV-EE, NAV-EE, NNNN, AAAA, VVVV, YYYY, NAV-EE, PRINCE, PRINCE, PRINCE'. And for the first time he experienced the blaring sirens of a motorbike escort conducting him to and from a suburban railway station. For the return leg it was clear to all that the outriders, steering their erratic courses, were very much the worse for wear. During their long wait they had fallen in with a party of Revenue agents who had raided a premises for bootleg liquor, then shared the loot. That evening the outriders thanked the Prince personally for sparing them dismissal: 'One of the few occasions in my life that I ever used my position to defeat the normal processes of the Law,' he told his memoir.

He arrived in New York at the Jersey City Pier, and was carried across the harbour to Lower Manhattan by admiral's barge to a cacophony of horns and whistles from 'scores of vessels', while the street cleaning department's brass band played from an accompanying tugboat. Then, in the back of an open motor, the impresario of all that was taking place, Mr Grover Whalen, asked, 'All set, Prince?' and they were heading up Broadway's 'steep-sided canyon' to a snowstorm ticker-tape welcome. After this he was granted the Freedom of the City, whose touchy Irish constituents neither gave nor took offence. In a hectic three days he reviewed the troops and cadets at West Point; he visited the sixty-storey Woolwich Building (then the world's tallest) and the grave of the former President Theodore Roosevelt at Oyster Bay; he heard Caruso and Rosa Ponselle at the Metropolitan Opera, attended Mrs Whitelaw Reid's ball (he had danced evenings away all across Canada), and before *Renown* sailed for home on 21 November he had reviewed 5,000 Boy Scouts drawn up on the river bank and held a farewell luncheon party on board. Something he carried home in his head, along with memories of 'that great new country that baffled us at that time', was a song he had heard at the *Ziegfeld Follies*: 'A Pretty Girl Is Like a Melody'. 'What's that damn tune you are whistling all the time?' the King asked. The Prince explained: 'Oh, I'm sorry if it bothers you. It's just something I picked up in America.'[49]

The chilly reception he received from the King on 23 December, as the family gathered for the Sandringham Christmas, left the Prince feeling like 'a guest in a strange house'. He faced two weeks without seeing Mrs Dudley Ward, who was at her parents' house in Nottinghamshire, and he had only the company of Princes Albert, Henry and George to distract him from the oppressive rituals. 'Sweetheart the crash came this morning,' he wrote to her at Lamcote on Christmas Eve, 'I mean the cross-questioning re YOU & ME that we've been awaiting, though it was a double-barrel one angel as not only did my mama talk to me but the King did too!!' He managed to play down the more piquant rumours, and believed he had satisfied the King that what had come to his ears 'was entirely idle female gossip'.[50]

Compounding Mrs Dudley Ward's absence was the anguish that was feeding off it. On Christmas Day he wrote to Godfrey Thomas:

A sort of hopelessly lost feeling has come over me and I think I'm going kind of mad!! . . . I'm simply not capable of even thinking, let alone make a decision or settle anything!! I've never felt like this in my life before . . . How I loathe my job now and all this press puffed empty '*succès*'. I feel I'm through with it and long and long to die . . . You'll probably think from this that I ought to be in a mad house already, tho' this isn't necessary yet: I'm still quite sane and very much in earnest, but I don't know for how much longer!! Of course I'm going to make a gt effort to pull myself together, and it may only be that I never realised how *brain* weary I returned from the 'Other Side' . . . But my brain has gone and I can hardly think any more . . . What you must think of me, and you and all the staff have been and are working so desperately hard for me . . . How can I ever try to thank you, my dear Godfrey?[51]

His mood was unrelieved when writing to his lover that evening:

I'm getting absolutely no rest here beloved one & am worried to death with every sort & kind of complex brain-racking problems!! . . . I'm sure I'll end in a madhouse soon as my brain really is going & I feel so hopelessly & utterly lost; my brain hasn't really recovered from Canada yet & I don't think it ever will!! . . . I'm really getting quite frightened about myself.

On 29 December, with a week of his stay at Sandringham remaining, his theme to her was the same. 'If I can't talk & unburden my soul . . . then I get thinking & brooding & that is fatal & something in my tired brain seems to snap & I feel I'm going mad!!'[52] Replying to the Prince in early January, Thomas showed he had the measure of him, and did not hesitate to take him to task:

It is inconceivable to me that anyone who has got such sound, if perhaps somewhat exaggerated ideas about health from the point of view of exercise . . . should be so utterly insane and unreasonable about the elementary rules of health as regards other things. How you survived Canada I cannot imagine . . . You are highly strung and nervy to begin with. You never allowed yourself a moment's rest the whole time. You sat up every night, often quite unnecessarily, till godless hours . . . You smoked far too much and you drink a great deal too much whiskey.

Thomas expected the Prince to be 'bloody minded, irritable and impossible' when he embarked in due course for Australia, unless he should manage a change of heart; without one he feared the Prince would 'crack up' before he reached the Panama Canal. He should let off steam sometimes rather than mope; his was bound to be a 'more or less bloody life', but it should be given 'a chance. It's certainly a life worth fighting through, not one to chuck away.'[53]

The Prince complained of days trapped in a 'pompous secluded & monotonous groove' enlivened only by rounds of golf on the short Sandringham course and at Brancaster, and an evening with Queen Alexandra at Sandringham

House, when the King 'looked rather sour' throughout. Paternal disapproval encompassed his brothers as well, so 'we're all in the same boat', he told Mrs Dudley Ward. Sundays meant morning church ('we trudged off . . . muttering foul oaths & talking filth . . . in the wake of H.M.'s firm stride') and a family stroll round the grounds; there might be golf, but no shooting. They found solace in unruly games of billiards and late-night confidences:

> I've been giving them some of my early experiences in Paris etc. which you've heard so often! But I think it's rather a good thing to talk to Harry & George about all that, don't you, darling, as of course they are both going to get far more chances of getting themselves into trouble than I ever did & they are both very hot by nature!!

(The Prince would be instrumental in helping Prince George, a bisexual, end his dependence on drugs in the autumn of 1929.) But it was Princess Mary's predicament that the Prince thought 'the greatest tragedy of all', for the way the King was 'imprisoning her at court' and ruining her chances of marriage.[54]

Returning to London in mid-January, the Prince had to accept unfavourable decisions. The Colonial Office had dismissed out of hand his plea for a three-week postponement of his departure for New Zealand and Australia; and he was thwarted over a key appointment. He wanted Admiral Halsey as chief of staff, but Grigg was given the role, chosen for his superior political acumen. Godfrey Thomas would continue as Private Secretary and Piers Legh, his equerry, was engaged again. A newcomer was the Prince's high-spirited nineteen-year-old cousin, Sub-Lieutenant Lord Louis ('Dickie') Mountbatten, who would instigate 'many an unexpected diversion'.[55]

A concurrent bone of contention was the timing of a tour of India, which the King expected the Prince to make almost immediately after his return from Australia, ostensibly to open the country's new constitution in the autumn. This was an unpalatable prospect which the Prince, to his father's considerable annoyance, had first raised with Lloyd George, suggesting that Prince Albert should go in his place. Lady Lloyd-George recalled the Prince begging the Prime Minister 'to get him out of it'. (As we shall see, the Prince was in serious need of rest after his Australian tour and his departure for India was delayed until October 1921.)

Meanwhile, by way of distraction, the Prince was taking to the hunting field – 'I started off to pilot the Prince but before we had gone very far he was piloting me,' recalled a member of the Pytchley Hunt – and winning games of squash at the Bath Club off a handicap of seven (the equivalent of 30-love at lawn tennis), with Mrs Dudley Ward looking on.[56] In addition, a series of public engagements were occasions for speaking warmly of Canada and the Commonwealth ideal.

All too soon he was penning lines to Mrs Dudley Ward in the train to Portsmouth, from where the *Renown* would sail on 16 March:

> I gather you've written something about ties & that I mustn't feel I'm bound to you, darling. Well, let me tell you again, Fredie darling mine, that it's the feeling that I am so so fastly tied to you that's going to keep me going the next 7 months & keep me going straight.[57]

Lord Curzon was one who witnessed the ritual of departure at Victoria, with 'crowds of cheering people' seeing the reluctant traveller off. The twenty-six-year-old Prince was all uncertainty. Curzon recorded: 'In a little tight naval uniform which clung close to his figure he did not look above 15, quite a pathetic little person.'[58]

HMS *Renown* sailed for the southern hemisphere via Barbados, the Panama Canal, San Diego (California), Hawaii and Fiji. Comforted to have 'Fredie's picture gallery' of photographs displayed all round his cabin, the Prince filled her absence with ferocious exercise between landfalls and at each one was disappointed that no letter from her awaited him. On 20 March he wrote:

> I had my game of squash this afternoon & other exercise & I'm shortening up on my food to get thinner, sweetie, which you'll be pleased to hear!! I'm no good on these official trips if I don't keep myself terribly fit & I can only do that by eating little, working hard & taking lots of exercise . . . how you've spoiled me these last 4 months till I've become such a blasé little David & it's not till I've left you that I realise how much you've changed me & improved me since my return from Canada!! It's amazing darling one & I've become more of a man & less of a boy . . . if only we could live together I would become of some use perhaps & have a will of my own & be strong!!

Camaraderie and high jinks would lighten the mood. A romp ended in Admiral Halsey's cabin being drenched with a power hose; Lord Claud Hamilton was de-bagged at the Prince's instigation ('he's such a boob really & never plays any games or does any of the things a man of 30 ought to do'); there was music-making after dinner ('I tried to be cheery & beat the jazz drum for a rag orchestra they've organised!!'),[59] and a canvas bath was rigged on deck for salt-water bathing, photographs of which irritated the King when they appeared in the press. At Balbao, a suburb of Panama City, the Prince partnered a pretty storekeeper's daughter on the dance floor to the disappointment of 'more patrician daughters'.[60] And the natives of Panama were unsparing: 'In frantic supplication we fling ourselves at the feet of Almighty God to shower His blessings upon Your Highness,' they told him.[61] In Hawaii, feathered dancing girls performed for him at a feast. On 17 April *Renown* 'crossed the line', King Neptune initiating some 600 novices, both officers and men, in a two-hour ceremony of smeared faces and salt-water ducking. Suva, on Fiji Island, was reached on 20 April. (In the pictorial record of innumerable guards of honour that the Prince of Wales would inspect in the course of duty, it is quaintly striking how the men of Fiji were as short as him in height.)

By now tensions were surfacing over Mountbatten's unguarded familiarity with the Prince – whom he alone, of all the staff, called 'David' – and particularly because of his informal manner with him in public. 'We are more or less inseparable & are in & out of each other's cabins all day (he's generally in mine),' the Prince admitted, 'and when we sleep on deck our beds are always next to each other!!' Admiral Halsey reprimanded the young cousin, albeit sympathetically, but failed to turn the tide of general disfavour towards him. In a letter to Mrs Dudley Ward telling of Mountbatten's disposition, the Prince raised the prescient question, 'Oh! why is it that anybody who gets involved with me or who I get to know & like suffers & must finally regret it all?' It was at this stage, too, that a grave want of balance entered his correspondence with Mrs Dudley Ward, as was evident in a wildly naïve and confused outpouring, which, given his past performance, she probably chose to ignore. (It goes without saying that, had she recorded her feelings at this time, they would surely have remained private.) While at sea on 18 April the Prince wrote:

I've been doing a hell of a lot of thinking this last month at sea angel & I'm quite quite decided!! Of course there are terrible obstacles for both of us; we know we are both 'up against it' & as I think it all over soberly it would be a d—d shame to even ask you to take on the job of wife to the P. of W. In fact I don't think I could ever summon up the courage to ask you to & I know you would hate it all as much as I should!! It just would not be fair on you sweetheart though who knows how much longer this monarchy stunt is going to last or how much longer I'll be P. of W. I dread to think how you'll curse me for writing like this but I just can't help it as I love you so so desperately. It's doing me worlds of good getting this off my chest which I've bottled up ever since our tragic parting . . . I feel it stronger than ever the thought (I can almost say knowledge) that one day we really will belong to each other!! It's by far the most marvellous thought that could ever come to me & I'm nearly going mad just writing it down!! Oh! if only I could see YOU & talk to YOU . . . though I know you'll say 'why the hell didn't he say all this before when we were together?' . . . But as regards the marriage part I'm absolutely decided now, sweetie; YOU are now the one & only thing that matters to me in my life & it will always always be the same with me in the future!! I don't want to live & I'm not going to live if I can't live with YOU my sweet precious beloved darling little Fredie, my vewy vewy own lovely blessed little angel. I don't care a damn for the rest of the world which means absolutely nothing to me. Oh! how much better I do feel after all that sweetheart.[62]

By now the Prince was the consummate actor, able to satisfy the demands of public attention – until, that is, he could no longer be sure of masking the dissonance within. His apparent skills were 'a desolating gift'.[63] 'The programme was my master; I did my best to obey,' he wrote in retrospect. 'Two days here, three days there, any number of one-night stands – much of the time I was like a man caught in a revolving door.'[64] It was altogether a transient and disconnected experience, teaching him little about the pulse of established sympathies and behaviour; to be dispensing brief and kindly interest to all and sundry – a depressingly unfulfilling occupation for any man palpably lacking personal happiness – was leaving a smaller and smaller part of himself wanting to be Prince of Wales.

The Prince and his party went ashore at Auckland on Anzac Day, 25 April 1920, and were immediately engulfed in complex and arduous programmes[65] that ignored his express wishes. It had been agreed that there would be no engagements before 10 a.m. and three half-days a week assigned for recuperation.

'The mere thought of the programme they insist on my carrying out is staggering
. . . Christ only knows how far gone towards insanity we'll all be at the end of
it when we go to Australia!!' he told Mrs Dudley Ward.[66] Writing to Lord
Stamfordham, Admiral Halsey declared, 'I do not believe any human being
could go through with all that was proposed.' Godfrey Thomas told the Queen
that the Governor General, Lord Liverpool ('a pompous, interfering ass,' the
Prince thought him), can only have approved the itinerary if he intended to
'break the Prince down' before ever he reached Australia.[67] By 4 May, according
to Edward Grigg, the Prince was 'showing profound dejection'.[68]

The New Zealand crowds were more restrained than those he would
encounter in Australia, yet the Prince was no less idolised. Boys would take
toothpicks from his table as souvenirs; girls would pat his pillow when they
toured the royal train.[69] Eight thousand Maoris performed their *haka* at Rotorua,
draped him in a mat of kiwi feathers, then kept him standing in vain for an
hour near the site of hot geysers, waiting for one to blow. State Governors loaded
the itinerary with undue demands – parades, speeches, hand-shaking, luncheons,
dinners and civic parties – severally at Wanganui, Napier, Wellington, Nelson,
Reefton, Christchurch, Dunedin, Lyttelton and places between. 'It's a rotten
way of seeing a fine country like N.Z.', the Prince griped, '& I shall have to
quit without having seen any of the up-country life or anything that might be
the least instructive.' Meanwhile, his commentary to Mrs Dudley Ward rehearsed
all too familiar lines: 'we've had a bad evening too darling . . . 2 ghastly
concerts and a civic supper party in a huge marquee where there were 3,000
people!! Oh! & I forgot a big school I had to visit after the parade!! Christ! How
dead I am beloved & no chance of rest till Saturday.'

The *Renown* left Lyttelton for Melbourne on 22 May with a gale and heavy
seas coming on, putting paid to four days' peaceful respite until stunting
recommenced. Written between bouts of seasickness, the day's letter to Mrs
Dudley Ward contained an extravagant tirade against the King:

So my morale is low tonight sweetie though there wouldn't be any morale at
all if it wasn't for YOU . . . YOU are more my all & everything in life than
ever & there's not a single thing that I wouldn't do for you my beloved including
die for you!! Doing things for you is my only pleasure in life . . . Christ! how
I loathe & despise my bloody family as Bertie has written me 3 long sad
letters in which he tells me he's been getting it in the neck about his friendship

with little Sheilie [Sheila, Lady Loughborough] & that TOI et MOI came in for it too!! But if H.M. thinks he's going to alter me by insulting you he's making just about the biggest mistake of his silly useless life; all he has done is to infuriate me & make me despise him & put me completely against him & I'll never forgive him for insulting you as he has!! God! damn him! though in a way he's done me good sweetheart by his extra display of foulness to Bertie & me as it's cured me of any weakness that was left in me!! Christ! I'll be firm with him when I get back & tell him to go to hell & leave me alone as regards my friends; I'll have whatever friends I wish & what is more I won't have them insulted or I'll bloody well insult him!!

Meanwhile, Lord Louis Mountbatten's loose tongue (he was appointed to the tour chiefly on account of his ability to keep the Prince cheerful) was compromising relations with others of the staff, as the Prince recorded on 9 May:

Dickie has been in my room as usual & he's been telling me lots of interesting things about the staff etc ... Even Joey is rather hard but Grigg, Claud, & [Captain] Dudley North are the worst offenders in this respect & according to Dickie say the foulest things behind my back!! Christ! how I loathe the first 2 named though Dudley is a good fellow really; but he's certainly become rather a courtier after nearly a whole year's contact with the P. of W .... but of course one can't collect a staff indiscriminately as I have without having one or two hostile members; of course if only the hostile members had any guts they would chuck their [h]ands in on our return but they're far too big snobs to do that sweetie & it's hard for me to give them the sack though I long to drop Grigg & Claud!![70]

An Australian welcome was nothing if not boisterous. Most alarming was what the Prince called 'a mass impulse' to touch some part of the Prince of Wales's person, but failing this, a blow to the head with a folded newspaper sufficed; his party came to regard knocks and bruises as part of the daily rounds.[71] On one occasion the hood was torn from the Prince's car and the running boards trampled away.[72] His personal detective and bodyguard, Sergeant Burt, mitigated the worst of many an over-enthusiastic encounter, 'his massive frame taking the first shocks' and opening a path for the Prince with a firm 'By your leave', accompanied by a determined forward thrust.[73] (This 'marvellous man!!' who was 'anything else you wanted him to be!!'[74] served the Prince until his retirement through ill health in 1931.)

Australians might hate formality (so Melbourne's Governor-General, Sir Ronald Munro-Ferguson, advised the Prince), yet the formal progresses through the cities could be stiffly ceremonial. 'Look! Horses again,'[75] the Prince despaired when he saw the barouches drawn up at the Melbourne pier for the eight-mile drive through the city, where some half-a-million people lined the streets – Ferguson, the Prime Minister (W.M. 'Billy' Hughes) 'and hundreds of other bearded men . . . in cocked hats till I thought I would die!!'[76] ('Oh! Percy, where did you get that hat?' someone called out.)[77] A hat, so the Prince learnt, might be a politician's downfall. These were hot-blooded times in Australian politics, and Hughes, who had broken with most of his Labour colleagues in 1916 to form a national government, was anxious not to provoke the militant working class or the anti-monarchists (many of them from sizeable Irish communities in the big cities), a sensitivity to which the Prince was creditably alert throughout the tour. What, then, of Hughes's hat? At the head of carriage processions the Prince would hear the Prime Minister being 'chaffed, cheered and damned'[78] close behind him. In Sydney, Hughes insisted on having a large hatbox with him, which he placed on the floor of the carriage. With the procession under way, he whipped off his silk topper 'with almost a conjuror's deftness', exchanging it for a well-worn soft hat from the box. 'You can't be too careful,' he told his fellow travellers. 'That top hat might cost me thousands of votes.'

The many 'sly' additions to an already bursting schedule – made more intolerable by the exploitative determination of private people to entertain him in the evenings – began to invite the arbitrary selectivity that would come more and more to be held against the Prince: to leave a party early because he was mindful of the next morning's programme was to disappoint his hosts, who had spent weeks preparing the evening in his honour.[79] And when, occasionally, he showed a determination to have things his own way, an excuse might not be plausible as was clear when he absented himself from a ball on account of the weather making roads impassable, roads which other guests had travelled. One of them opined that the Prince 'had found the Bell girls in Boonah' to his liking and had not wished to leave them.[80] (At Gilgandra, where he failed to appear, they ceremoniously counted him 'OUT!' – as one would a boxer – by way of disapproval, only to count him back in favour when he returned to repair the slight.)[81]

He illustrated his predicament in a letter he wrote to Mrs Dudley Ward on
1 June:

> I'm far more dead than alive tonight sweetheart so can only scribble a few
> lines to say I love you . . . I got through the naval parade all right at 9.30 A.M
> . . . . it was a fearful strain trying to address over 1,000 men at that hour &
> I've lost my voice, though not badly . . .
>
> I did have the rest of the forenoon free & played squash though I was
> stunting again at 1.30; first a huge but marvellous schoolchildren's demonstration
> followed by a visit to 800 badly wounded men at a hospital, which entailed
> miles of 'driving' & there were addresses en route!!
>
> Then $1/2$ hr to change & I attended a naval Jutland dinner . . . I was at a
> vast 'smoke night' for returned men at 8.30 whom I had to address . . . the
> hospital ball at the Town Hall which followed was a worse bullfight than on
> Saturday night & I was almost killed in my efforts to dance with the Lady
> Mayoress!!
>
> On top of it all I was fool enough to go to a private party about 11.00
> which some nice people had well-meaningly & kindly organised for me & of
> course we had to go though it was silly. But isn't that a staggering day Fredie
> darling.[82]

Little wonder, then, whether at Melbourne, Sydney, Perth, Brisbane, Adelaide,
or in the vast lands between, that punctuality slipped, 'an unguarded moment'
of 'utter fatigue' would be taken for boredom or bad manners, and blunders
magnified.[83] And so, writes Frances Donaldson, the Prince slogged on – 'never
for long at one place, while he had to speak, lunch, dine, receive addresses, shake
hands, smile, wave, for day after day, week after week at a time'.[84]

At home, meanwhile, the royal affair continued to be the subject of gossip.
In 'long yarns' with Prince Albert, Mrs Dudley Ward was measuring the wisdom
of bringing her intimacy with the Prince to a close in favour of a more platonic
arrangement. Such was the substance of her letter that reached him on 24 June,
a most tenderly couched one, as he acknowledged (for 'being sweeter to your
petit amoureux than you've ever been before'), the gist of it being that 'we
must make the greatest sacrifice of our lives & give up our LOVE!!' Coming
from a grown man, the Prince's slushy response is hardly credible.

It now seems a superhuman task to me to even live through the night my sweetheart, though perhaps a real good cwy when I get into bed will help me as of course I can't let myself go till I can bury my head in your little pillow. Oh! Oh! Oh! Oh! I'm cwying already sweetie & you know how I can cwy.

Two days later he resolved to leave discussion of their futures ('to readjust and re-set ourselves') until his return home – the most important thing being 'to carry on as usual with camouflaged "smiles" and cheeriness!!'

You say that we've so often tried to make resolutions when we've been together & have always failed; that it will always be useless to actually discuss changing our lives!! But sweetheart you know perfectly well that never have we really faced the facts before, at least I know I never have . . .

And of course when you bring in sweet little Penelope & Angie darling I just can't discuss your suggestion at all for as you say they are our care (& how I love the way you say our) & you know how devoted I am to them.

Meanwhile he would continue to rely on their correspondence and use the next three months 'to practise getting a hold on myself & keeping my feelings under control'. He owned that 'no doubt I've got blacker days ahead of me in my ghastly & loathsome career as P. of W. but they'll never be blacker than these last 3, anyway I'll never feel them as much'.[85]

A highlight of the tour was the Weigalls' hospitality in Adelaide ('real live people instead of boobs', he called the Governor of South Australia and his wife). Lady Weigall was a confidante of Mrs Dudley Ward and he could talk with her freely; 'it cheered him up no end,' Godfrey Thomas recorded. He craved her cosseting;[86] she would cook him eggs and bacon in the early hours of the morning and keep him from his bed with 'priceless yarns' (she 'doesn't care a d–mn what she says which is vewy refreshing & we feel better already!!') As pleasant diversions he worked cattle all day at a bush station in Queensland – longing 'for a week here instead of only a weekend' – and hunted kangaroo and emus on a New South Wales sheep station. Expecting a lukewarm reception from the 'red flag' element in the Western Australian goldfields, he found his day there 'one of the most trying of the whole trip'. He travelled the Trans-Australian railway across 300 dead straight miles of flat plain, stopping at tiny little stations to meet the few railway employees and their families. About the aborigines gathered to meet him at a wayside station the Prince was hotly disparaging, as he wrote to Mrs Dudley Ward on 11 July:

> they were the most revolting form of living creatures I've ever seen!! They are the lowest known form of human beings & are the nearest thing to monkeys I've ever seen; they danced for us & threw spears and boomerangs, though the whole interest of this native stunt (& you know how I just loathe any form of native stunt sweetie) was spoilt by the fact that they had all been transported (vermin & disease & all) over 100 miles by train for the purpose!! The authorities must think me the biggest fool God ever created if they imagined they were going to hand out to me that these filthy nauseating creatures had just drifted in from a waterless district to see me without my finding out the truth!!

Five days earlier (on 5 July) at Pemberton, South Australia, the rear carriage of the Prince's train and the carriage next ahead were derailed as a result of heavy rains on an unballasted track. Both of them had turned over on their sides on a slight embankment, the train having already slowed because a cow was obstructing the line. 'A miraculous escape,'[87] the Prince called it. He clambered out through a corridor window, then lightly brushed the incident aside: 'Well, anyway, at last we have done something which was not on the official programme.'[88] Yet in a letter to the Queen a month later he wrote, 'I live so much on my nerves nowadays that they get very easily upset and I just loathe a train now and have "the wind up me" the whole time!!'[89] There had been 'the long, long seconds from the moment we derailed, the toppling over, the being dragged along overturned till the moment we stopped, seconds of real mental agony,' he told his lover.[90]

By mid-July agreeable moments were having little influence on a state of mind that was finding people a trial, be they the women he met at parties ('a hen-faced crowd'),[91] the press corps or his staff. 'I never really feel well nowadays . . . it's my nerves that have really cracked up from overstrain . . . but nerves affect everything, particularly one's tummy,'[92] he told Mrs Dudley Ward. A friend (Philip Sassoon) heard much the same: 'I feel fit enough, but mentally I'm *absolutely* worn out. Thank God it's all over bar the shouting now as I really don't think I could carry on much longer without the top of my head *cracking like an egg* and making a mad house my only possible [word omitted] for the remainder of my natural life.' By now the Prince was losing his voice as well as his presence of mind. *The Times* correspondent cabled, 'Renewed sign of nerve strain . . . very disturbing.' The King, who had opposed all requests to postpone the Indian tour – the Prince was due to sail from England in November – agreed to a postponement until the autumn of 1921 only after he had received the strongest expressions of concern. Prince Albert (now Duke of York) thought the King had no understanding of his brother's difficulties; Admiral Halsey likened the Prince to a machine operating at highest pitch; Lloyd George feared a 'disaster' unless the Prince was given time at home to recuperate.[93] The King's change of mind, which he communicated by cable on 27 July, was coldly formal – 'like an official proclamation', the Prince called it.[94] In due course his father advised rest, proper eating, more sleep and less exercise, a 'lecture' the Prince dismissed out of hand. Release from mental strain, he told his father, was an outcome best achieved through a good deal of exercise and, in due course, plenty of fitting work. '*Nobody,*' he said, 'is going to make me play the invalid!!'

HMS *Renown* sailed from Sydney on 19 August, returning to Portsmouth on 11 October via Fiji, Samoa, Honolulu, Panama, the West Indies and Bermuda. Lord Louis Mountbatten recorded that, in the course of 210 days, they had visited 208 different towns and places and travelled over 45,000 miles by sea and land. The Prince had utterly spent himself in public, winning strong affection, and in due course a rare – because unqualified – plaudit from the King. Both he and the Queen rejoiced 'at the splendid success of your tour and the way in which you have won all hearts by your hard work and your own personality. I must say we are very proud of you. You are doing untold good for the Empire.'[95]

'I hope, Sir, that you will not risk your neck in a steeplechase again,' Lord Stamfordham advised after the Prince won a race at a Household Brigade meeting.[96] Duties permitting, he had promised himself an outdoor life that winter and spring of 1920–21 and was not disappointed. He hunted with the Household Drag Hounds and the Pytchley, lost his seat quite frequently and remained undaunted. In point-to-point races in the spring he came third in a field of sixteen at the Guards meeting, despite falling at the second fence. He then won a lightweight race from a field of fourteen at the Pytchley Hunt point-to-point. Riding an experienced horse (Pet Dog) on 1 April, he won the Welsh Guards Challenge Cup under National Hunt rules in the presence of his parents, the Duke of York and Prince Henry.[97] And in preparation for India, he took up polo.

The economy, after a brief respite, was verging on slump conditions once again, 26 million working days having been lost to strikes in 1920 and 85 million to be lost in 1921. Furthermore, London had witnessed the first demonstration of the kind that preceded the hunger marches that would be an indelible image of the interwar years.[98] 'Society seemed to be *en fête*,' the Prince recalled, as the great London houses offered 'a flourish of hospitality after their post-war refurbishments such as will never be seen again'.[99] He was a serial partygoer throughout the Season, finding respite whenever possible from stunting and from enervating family obligations. In one five-day period he made twenty-seven visits in the North of England, namely (as Frances Donaldson lists them) to 'Ormskirk, Southport, Great Crosby, Waterloo, Litherland, Bootle, Liverpool, Ashton-under-Lyne, St Helen's, Manchester, Salford, Eccles, Irlam, Prescot, Fleetwood, Clevelys, Blackpool, St Anne's, Lytham [*sic*], Kirkham, Mowbreck, Hale, Preston, Leyland, Chorley and Wigan'.[100] Between times he was doing little to adjust his relationship with Mrs Dudley Ward as she wished; to lose her close devotion was inconceivable. On 12 January he was able to record, 'we were loving so so much tonight & then we both got quite tired suddenly at the same moment like two little children & we wanted to go to sleep in each other's arms!!'[101]

India – uninvitingly never far from the Prince's thoughts – promised a resumption of all that the Prince was weary of, but in the uneasy context of Britain's loosening grip on the subcontinent and the wilting confidence of those who served there. In recent, painful memory were the Punjab riots and the consequent banning of assemblies that culminated in General Dyer's demoniac massacre near the Temple at Amritsar on 13 April 1919 (379 killed, 1,500 injured in ten minutes' shooting), and its cruelly repressive aftermath. Since then, the will to oppose British rule was being sustained by Gandhi's campaign of passive resistance, a strategy that would encompass organized boycotts of the Prince's tour, although the government attempted to spike these by offering the crowds free food and elephant rides.[102] ('We go from cold to frost,' Halsey would record at worst, when a mere thousand Indians turned out to greet the Prince in Allahabad. In Peshawar, where threats were made to assassinate the Prince, he was furious to think he might be taken for a coward because his procession had been diverted through back streets – 'the blackest rage I ever hope to see him in', according to Mountbatten.)[103]

The Prince disembarked at Bombay on 17 November wearing the uniform of a naval captain and the blue ribbon of the Star of India, to be met by the Viceroy, Lord Reading, the Governor of Bombay, Sir George Lloyd, and numerous Indian princes. Rarely on his own terms, this shy embodiment of the Crown's mystique was playing once again to the exasperating rules of etiquette and ceremony. His first public words, which he added to the King-Emperor's formal message, naïvely challenged the detachment so smugly absolute in British India. 'I want you to know me and I want to know you,' he said. 'I want to grasp your difficulties and to understand your aspirations . . . I feel some awe at the difficulty which I may experience in getting to know India.'[104] It was a stiff task. White officialdom was alarmed by his democratic manner: how he spoke in public as to his fellow-men, winning the regard of native Indians despite Gandhi's prohibitions – 'he was far more interested to find out all about them than about his own countrymen,' recalled the tour's official historian.[105] And as if impervious to the anti-British uproar outside their Native State borders, gilded princes spared no effort, least of all their wealth, in honouring the heir to half the world with fabulous, if disquieting, hospitality such as he 'imagined existed only in books'.[106]

At times his progress amounted to a sumptuous demigod's triumph. The Maharaja of Baroda's elephants were painted with gold, the carriages made of silver. 'The nobles who salaamed before [the Prince] moved over a golden carpet; they wore apple green dappled with gold, and their robes were laden with jewels and orders . . . the Princes and the people moved, like fabulous butterflies, over the lawns and marble terraces.' By the water palaces of Jag Mandir (in Rajputana), lit by myriad flickering oil-lamps, the Prince was rowed across the lake, then carried, accompanied by torchbearers, in a golden chair up to the banqueting hall. As he drove into the country in Mysore, field workers 'ran to the roadside to salaam and to kneel in the dust as he passed'.[107] At Poona his path was strewn with gold and silver coins for him to tread on.[108] In the Native States, he recorded, it was as if Mahatma Gandhi's 'menacing influence' was set at naught.[109]

There were moments when, precipitately, he loosed the reins of protocol so that he could be among the people. Attending the Madras races, he left the stand to stroll in the teeming public enclosure. At Lucknow he insisted on walking among some 4,000 of the poor, later telling Mrs Dudley Ward that this had made him feel 'one up' on the officials and police whom he thought over-assertive: 'All I can say is "God help the Viceroy"!!'[110] if the Crown's representative was subject to the same level of protection as himself. He also spoke before 25,000 Untouchables in Delhi after their spokesman had intervened on their behalf.[111] 'Drop those barriers and let the people in,' he demanded just before his train pulled out of Bombay, upon which (as an eye-witness eagerly described) 'like the sweep of a river in flood the interminable multitudes rolled in and shouted and adored and laughed and wept . . . [running] alongside the royal carriage till they could run no more'.[112]

The Prince frequently complained of trying to understand India through 'interposed layer[s]'[113] of officialdom keeping him from the crowds. Yet perceived threats to his person were no small matter. When an estimated half a million people welcomed him in Lahore, malcontents were held in check by the presence of 3,000 troops, tanks and armoured cars. A reporter on the *Statesman* newspaper wrote how 'Sentries, with fixed bayonets, constantly patrolled the edge of the footways behind the cordon of infantry, even during the passage of the royal barouche.'[114] Writing to the King from Nepal on 16 December, the Prince was seeing only failure:

> Well I must at once tell you that I'm very depressed about my work in British India as I don't feel that I'm doing a scrap of good; in fact I can say that I know I am not. The main reason for this is naturally the boycotting of my visits to the various cities in British India by the non-co-operators but another reason is the police . . . no one realises better than I do that precautions have to be taken on a tour of this sort . . . But I do assure you that they (the police) are overdoing these precautions & that they have the wind up unnecessarily . . . [B]y taking too great care of me they aren't helping me. I'm hardly ever allowed even to drive through the bazaars & native quarters of the cities & and the crowds if there are any lining the routes through the European quarters are herded together into pens like sheep & guarded by constables who face 'outboard' (with their backs to me) so as to watch them. Such severe police tactics can scarcely be conducive to encouraging even loyal natives to come & see & welcome the P. of W.

It injured his mood not a little to suffocate behind the pale of various British stations as a guest in Government House or Residency, being obliged to mingle constantly with their civil and military functionaries – 'the Chief Justice, the General Officer commanding the troops, the President of the

Legislature, the Indian Civil Service secretaries, regimental officers, inspectors of police, officials of the Indian Medical Service and the public works department etc., and . . . their wives', gazing down the dinner table, as he recalled, at 'the same faces disposed [by strict protocol] in the same places as the night before'.[115]

Among the 100 Europeans and Indians who constituted the Prince's retinue, there was only one man with whom, as the tour progressed, the Prince felt he could share his private misgivings. Captain Edward 'Fruity' Metcalfe MC was a bold Irish cavalryman whose uncomplicated sympathy cemented a private relationship conducted on almost equal terms, one nourished by charm, high spirits and the lightest censure. (Metcalfe would be best man at the Prince's wedding as Duke of Windsor to Wallis Simpson in 1937.) 'He is an excellent fellow, always cheery and full of fun, but far, far too weak and hopelessly irresponsible,' wrote Halsey, who called him 'a *wild, wild* Irishman' and thought him 'not *at all* a good thing for HRH'. The Prince was aware how shocked people sometimes were by Metcalfe's familiarity of attitude – he came to refer to the Prince as 'My Little Man' – but he cared not a jot. He told Mrs Dudley Ward that his long-serving staff were 'doing their utmost to make life hell'[116] for him. Halsey would offer his resignation once again, believing that he had lost the Prince's confidence; both Godfrey Thomas and Claud Hamilton now feared to trespass beyond official matters. Only Lord Louis Mountbatten's standing was secure.

'Fruity' Metcalfe served as major-domo to the Prince's sporting interests – the polo ground providing the exertion that best reinvigorated him (a third train having been added to his retinue to transport the twenty-five ponies that were lent to them).[117] Given how equestrian prowess was esteemed in India by the indigenes and the British Army alike, news of the Prince's triumph in a gruelling point-to-point crossed India in a flash; this occurred in a four and a half mile race for lightweight hunters at the Kadir Cup Meeting. Very rough country, deep ditches (nullahs) and a river were familiar to his mount, Bombay Duck, (which had won the same race once before), but it was courageous riding that saw the Prince pass all his opponents in a field of ten.[118] (Assessing the risks of attempting such a race, *The Times* correspondent explained that it usually produced 'a lot of grief . . . One year, out of 22 runners 10 fell, one man fractured his skull, and four or five others were carried in.')[119] The Prince also took to pig-sticking and, of much less interest, was offered the chance of pursuing big game – elephant and tiger hunts, the tigers corralled to make them easy targets.

The geographical range of the tour had been immense, the sights diverse, the remembered detail emblematic. 'Curiously, the thing about India that I remember most to-day [he was writing aged fifty-five] was the smell, compounded of the myriad odours of heavily perfumed flowering trees and shrubs, of the sun-baked earth, of Oriental spices, and of burning dung, of the pungent aroma of ghee in millions of cooking-pots, of domestic animals and humanity in the mass.'[120] He had seen (although this is not all) Nepal on the southern ranges of the Himalayas, Calcutta and, by way of Burma, Madras; Bangalore and other parts of Mysore, Hyderabad, Agra and Delhi, the Punjab, Peshawar and the Khyber Pass as far as the Afghan frontier; Rawalpindi and the Sind desert and, returning to the sea, Karachi, from where, exactly four months from his arrival in Bombay, he sailed for Ceylon and on to the Malay Peninsula, Hong Kong, Japan (as guest of Prince Hirohito), the Philippines, British North Borneo, Penang, to Ceylon again (the naval base of Trincomalee), then across the ocean to the Red Sea and Suez. He reached Plymouth on 20 June, having covered 41,000 miles by sea and land.

The Prince appeared to settle upon an unflattering assessment of the tour, believing his presence in India to have had little bearing on the interplay of British and native Indian relations. As to playing the royal game according to the rules, he was – in his twenty-eighth year – well beyond pleasing. He had become dog-tired of touring – the tour's official historian thought him 'almost dead of exhaustion by the end of it'[121] – which latterly made him unconscionably careless of punctuality and often bored by hospitality, failings which many among the official British community would not forgive. The official verdict was entirely favourable. At the Guildhall banquet to mark the Prince's return, the Prime Minister, Lloyd George (in his last official act) put on record the Government's abundant approval:

Whatever our feeling for him was before he went to India, it is deeper today. It was a high act of statesmanship, carried through with inimitable gifts of grace, of tact, and of a drawing attachment which is so very much his dominant characteristic. More than that, it was a high act of courage, carried through with faultless nerve. There were many who doubted the wisdom of the visit. There was no one who was not anxious about the visit. There were difficulties, there were menaces, there was an atmosphere which gave great concern to everyone. He went there without fear. He went indomitably at the call of duty, and whatever the Empire owed to him before, it owes to him a debt which it can never repay today.[122]

It was even suggested, by way of a question put down in the Commons, that the Prince should have conferred on him the title 'Prince of India', an honour which the King had no wish to grant.[123]

13
Losing Heart

There would be further peregrinations before the 1920s were half spent – in Canada (twice) and the United States, in South Africa and South America – but for now, and between times, the siren company of freer spirits was irresistible. The 'war-fostered [upper-class] generation'[1] (the Prince's term), so many of them bereaved and wanting emotional vigour, were abandoning both tomorrow and convention in a vortex of night-club life and parties. These were the Bright Young Things (but wholly inclusive of the none too young and the none too bright), survivors of soldiering or recent products of a haphazard, unfinished education in wartime schools 'kept going by the old and the invalid'.[2] The collective mood could be capricious. By the summer of 1923 an insatiable appetite for the dance-floor had exhausted the foxtrot craze in favour of languid, melancholy alternatives, music described by Michael Arlen in his contemporary Society novel *The Green Hat* as 'played with a sensibility approaching grief'. ('Wouldn't the *Marche Funèbre* make just the cutest one-step!' quipped an American visitor.) Even femininity appeared to be under duress. ('I hate her!' an angry Glorinda tells her companion in a *Punch* cartoon of 1924: 'She says such catty things. She [has] just told me I had a pretty figure.' 'But – pardon me – why is that so offensive?' the man inquired. 'Oh, surely even you must know that figures are hopelessly out of fashion!')[3] For sure, female emancipation, both social and political, had bred a 'masculine severity in line'.[4] As the decade progressed, bosoms were flattened under straight bodices – some would bind themselves round with constricting ribbons – and dresses were hipless; colour was sacrificed to unsubtle tones and innumerable shades of green; hair was shorn at the nape, then cut short in the Eton crop. (Again in *Punch*, an elderly street flower-seller comments to another, as a smart young woman passes them: 'I don't know what they're comin' to, these days. Masculine independent young 'ussies, I call 'em. You an' me was always the fluffy clingin' sort.') For the winter of 1925–6 women were adopting a style of dinner jacket[5] – a vogue that invites mention of a third *Punch* line, delivered by a short-sighted lady peering at a person of uncertain sex. 'Excuse me,' she inquires, 'but did you say you were going up to Trinity or Girton next term?'[6]

As for male attire, the Prince was not without influence. The wearing of soft dress shirts – an introduction from America – in place of starched was widely accepted when he and his younger brother, the Duke of Kent, adopted them. When the Prince wore a white waistcoat with a dinner jacket, others copied him – and he was happy to abandon gloves for dancing. He sported berets and returned straw hats to favour. Since Oxford days (as we have seen) he had liked loud check suits and two-tone shoes. The shorts that the Prince wore at a Norfolk beagles meeting were readily taken up by fashion columns.[7]

The full splendour of country-house hospitality, as his grandfather Edward VII had known it, was now waning, for many a landowner was seeing his wealth depleted through taxation and death duties. But it would need a second world war to snuff out 'much of the old elegance' which the Prince owned and which was still 'my good fortune to enjoy'. In London, very much his haunt of choice, he received invitations during the Season – as many as four in the same evening – to parties at the various houses of distinction: Londonderry, Wimborne, Forbes, Derby, Chesterfield and Crewe. 'If the first failed to please,' he recalled, 'one could always move on to another,'[8] after which the comparative anonymity of a night-club, with its enveloping, gay democracy, could be relied on to save an unsatisfactory evening. Often accompanied by his brother, Prince George, the Prince frequented the Café de Paris, Ciro's, the Kit-Kat Club (on one occasion raided the night after the Prince was there by policemen enforcing licensing hours),[9] but particularly the Embassy Club. Here, after the theatres had emptied, every square inch of basement floor space was occupied by diners hurriedly downing a little excellent food before returning, 'as though mechanically activated',[10] to yet more dancing. The late hours were presided over by the *maître d'hôtel*, Luigi Naintre, who, the Prince recalled, had 'an unequalled sense of discretion'.[11] This was Michael Arlen's inimitable territory, in which, briefly, he cast the Prince:

Nearby was a corner-table of eight young people . . . The women had white oval faces, small breasts, blue eyes, thin arms, no expression, no blood; literally of course, not genealogically. One of them stared right into people's faces and blinked vaguely. She was lovely . . . Presently, a prince of the blood joined them, there was a little stir for a minute or two, a little laughter, and then he rose to dance with the girl of the blind blue eyes. As she danced she stared thoughtfully at the glass dome of the ceiling. She looked bored with boredom.[12]

Such wan, defiantly unromantic sophistication found expression in the syncopated rhythm of the Charleston, the knee-bending and kicking dance that the Prince mastered (as he did its successor, the Black Bottom), and which burned like a meteor in the second half of the decade. 'Everybody terribly serious; not a single laugh, or the palest ghost of a smile,' wrote a *Daily Mail* feature-writer of its English manifestation.[13] 'Youth is so terribly fleeting,' sang Noël Coward, as his generation danced the harder.[14]

The Prince had come home to a good deal of imperial posturing. Looking to the future, the ruling class was admitting that the Empire was failing to resonate with the new generation at a time of decline in British power. But much could be done to reawaken interest, with all this could mean for the nation's influence and prosperity. Films such as *Lives of a Bengal Lancer* and ceremonial broadcasts by the BBC paraded the imperial theme – as did popular songs, children's comics (George Orwell accused them of peddling 'gutter patriotism') and the plethora of patriotic images appearing on household requisites, chocolate boxes and cigarette cards.[15] Yet many were sceptical that the public mind could be influenced in this way. (Intellectuals claimed that the heroic fictions of Ryder Haggard and G.A. Henty won 'no more converts to the cult of Empire than Gothic melodrama inspired "a belief in ghosts".')[16] Indeed, emigration to the colonies was in such decline at this time that more migrants were returning to the British Isles than were leaving them.

The trump card in the campaign of indoctrination was the British Empire Exhibition at Wembley, which opened on St George's Day, 23 April 1924, with the Prince as its president. Replying to his son's official welcome, the King called it 'This great achievement' that 'will bring the peoples of the Empire to a better knowledge of how to meet their reciprocal wants and aspirations.' The colonial grandee Lord Milner spoke of the Exhibition as a 'powerful bulwark' against imperial decline.[17] Unlike its illustrious forerunner, the Great Exhibition of 1851, which trumpeted British superiority and self-interest to comprehensive approval, this time a vocal portion of the populace was inclined to reserve judgement. Nevertheless the event attracted – although at a financial loss of £600,000 – some 27 million visitors by the time it closed (after an extension into a second year) in October 1925. Many thought the Exhibition ludicrously inflated, while socialists and the left-wing press balked at endorsing a celebration of imperial expansion that Ramsay MacDonald had earlier insisted was 'only the grabbings of millionaires on the hunt';[18] Hampstead intellectuals founded a society they called the WGTW (the Won't-Go-To-Wembleys). Thousands chose easier alternatives to trailing through daunting pavilions spread across 220 acres, preferring the distractions of dance hall and floodlit amusement park, where you could rush through tunnels in a miniature train, or in small boats descend a water chute to the lake below. 'I've brought you here to see the wonders of the Empire,' says Father in Noël Coward's *This Happy Breed*, 'and all you want to do is go on the dodgems.'[19]

The Exhibition embraced the mighty: the Palaces of Industry and Engineering occupied an area six and a half times the size of Trafalgar Square; and the miniature: the architect Edwin Lutyens's hugely popular Queen's Dolls' House, presented to Queen Mary. The Indian pavilion displayed a concrete replica of the Taj Mahal, but also 25,000 miniature models of pilgrims to Haridwar. Canada honoured the Prince with a life-size statue of himself, carved out of butter (the legs were said to be too fat). On view were grain elevators, gold and diamond mines, rubber and tea plantations, ostrich farms, oil wells, native craftsmen working in leather and metal, foreign street scenes, wild creatures, exotic goods, pageants and torchlight tableaux; and from the home country, model ships fighting famous British battles – a gallimaufry housed in an orgy of architectural styles and materials.[20]

Unquestionably, the Prince's unique experience of the British abroad had left him aware of a disturbing lack of enterprise among the mercantile class. Addressing the British Industries Fair in 1926, he warned against complacency:

A trade opportunity missed is gone forever; there is no second barrel, and there are many, many people shooting. I would strongly urge British manufacturers and traders to keep always alert on the *qui vive*, with their eyes skinned for opportunities of dealing overseas. At the same time study local conditions and demands, and having found an opportunity never let it go, because someone else will seize it.[21]

The tone here conflates with an undertow of impatience, which he was failing to mask as he readjusted to home and Court life. His homogeneous sibling circle had now broken up: Princess Mary and the Duke of York were both married, she to Lord Lascelles, he to Lady Elizabeth Bowes-Lyon; Prince Henry ('Harry') was serving with the 10th Hussars, and Prince George was overseas with the Navy. Meanwhile, the 'smooth perfection' of his father's style of life – his fixed habits, the relentless and solemn formalities, the disapproving asides ('Good God, look at those short skirts; look at that bobbed hair') and harping on the mores of Queen Victoria's century ('Well, we never did that in the olden days')[22] – inhibited any chance of rapport with a parent who was first and foremost King. And punctuating the Prince's dealings with him was the inescapable failure to please, which made him distrustful of the King's friends and those among his own staff whom he suspected of having his father's ear. Nor was it lost on the Prince that, as a married man, his dutiful, conservative younger brother was winning warm approval from the King for being 'sensible and easy to work with' and ready to listen to advice and agree with his opinion – 'very different,' the King said, 'to dear David'.[23] Indeed, the brothers were drawing apart. 'All his life,' his biographer Frances Donaldson affirms, '[the Prince] tended to view his fellows as might a schoolboy, setting a demarcation line between himself and kindred spirits on the one hand, and authority and the friends of authority on the other.' His immaturity of outlook, shallow perspectives and lack of worldly knowingness meant that the tension between private inclination and public role was beyond his wit to reconcile. Writing of the Prince's 'failure to develop in depth', Donaldson writes:

> What is beyond doubt, however, is that the most important influences of his childhood and youth – his relationship with his parents, his restricted education, the arid discipline of the Naval Colleges, the lack of close contact with civilised minds, as well as the freak of birth which placed him in a unique position of isolation and pre-eminence in which if we are to believe modern psychologists, his primary function was to assuage the infantile longing of the rest of mankind for a father figure – all contributed to it.

Needless to say, paternalism, as he experienced it, invited little in the way of emulation (he would father no children), while making a life of his own, as far as this was possible, brought him no nearer to being reconciled to the hollow satisfactions of public popularity – or to a performance of his duties consistent with Establishment approval.

Among people of influence, there was suspicion tending to conviction that the Prince was not quite of the right sort. A taste for jazz and loud dressing, and want of cultural endowment were held against him for being marks of vulgarity – betrayals of upper-class shibboleths that would famously be harvested in the mid-1950s by Nancy Mitford (after Professor Alan Ross) as the U and Non-U question.[24] Nor could he mask a weak man's inconsistencies. He was known to enjoy a sycophant's manner one moment, then snub him the next.[25] An oft-quoted story records that on a visit to Magdalen, his Oxford college, the Prince put the Junior Common Room at its ease, telling the members to remain seated since he wished to be treated as a fellow member; yet on a subsequent occasion when 'nobody stirred', he upbraided the JCR for failing to pay him due courtesy.[26] All the while the shades of dejection were proving a vitiating accompaniment to keeping up appearances. On one occasion he told Mrs Dudley Ward how 'the *black*, *black*, mist came down and enveloped me irrevocably . . . and it wasn't any good making an effort to cheer up'.[27] He could usually count on 'magnetic charm' (Lord Louis Mountbatten's epithet) to ease the way, although this he deployed as if it were a weapon of calculation to be 'switch[ed] . . . on and off at will', as Lady Hardinge observed. And while there was no gainsaying a desire to please everyone, as time went on much counterfeit effort appeared to lose its worth.[28] At worst, when he failed to command his mood, he might throw in the rag altogether – which brought disappointment to many and unravelled much hard-won goodwill. After a long day of engagements in June 1923 he cried off a ball at Lord Revelstoke's house at two hours' notice. On another occasion, in Fife, he left it to the last minute to telegraph that he could not attend a ball because the Court was in mourning for the Duchess of Albany. 'It is a pity that the impression grows prevalent that he shows ill-concealed boredom with his public engagements,' regretted Lord Crawford. He felt that the Prince was 'stretching family etiquette too far'.

His personal staff maintained a broadly steady watch if, between themselves, not always amicably: at quiet times they scrapped over the meagre quantity of work to be done.[29] A new member, appointed as Assistant Comptroller under

Admiral Halsey's direction, was Brigadier-General G.F. Trotter of the Grenadier Guards, known to his friends as 'G'. The Prince's elder by twenty years, he became 'my constant companion in the things pertaining to the lighter side of the Princely rôle',[30] a man who fitted the Prince's decided taste for living life to the full. Another newcomer was Captain Alan 'Tommy' Lascelles, Assistant Private Secretary from 1921 to 1929, who at the outset spoke of the Prince in glowing terms ('He won me completely. He is the most attractive man I've ever met'),[31] but who would become aggressively disillusioned before his service ended. But it was 'Fruity' Metcalfe whom the Prince considered 'his greatest man friend',[32] whose boon companionship – one which he would largely gloss over in writing his memoir – he would defend to the hilt against mounting opposition from the King. As major-domo of the Prince's sporting interests, he was bound to attract the Sovereign's disapproval.

After 'an exacting apprenticeship' with the Pytchley Hunt in Northamptonshire riding in steeplechases and point-to-point races, and the 1922–3 season with the Beaufort in Gloucestershire, the Prince engaged Metcalfe to establish a string of hunters at Melton Mowbray, where he rented accommodation at a hunting club. He fondly remembered the Vale of Belvoir for its 'miles of undulating grassland stretching as far as the eye could see' where 'one could gallop for twenty minutes at a stretch without drawing rein'.[33] He was known for his fearless riding. An observer recalled how he rode 'about as straight a line as a man could take', wanting 'no preferential treatment at gaps'.[34] He took the pain of his falls 'without a sign'.[35] The exhilarating sport apart, it was the democracy of the hunting field that he cherished:

> In this vigorous, untrammelled company I revelled. There is no thrill to equal that of riding a good, keen horse on a line of one's own as he takes in his stride the stake-and-bound fences standing out black in the wintry light . . . In the hunting field I could forget my round of duties. I was too busy riding my horse and scanning the next fence for a place to jump to worry over my next engagement or my next speech. Besides, [hunting] satisfied the latent desire in me to excel; to pit myself against others on equal terms; to show that, at least in matters where physical boldness and endurance counted, I could hold my own. Just as my father was one of the best shots in the country, so it was my ambition to be a good rider to hounds.

To cast off duty, however briefly, for days in the company of people who made few demands and sought no favours was guaranteed to invigorate him. He described a 'sturdy and cosmopolitan' fraternity melded by the Quorn, the Cottesmore and the Belvoir:

> Intermixed with the local landed gentry, who form the sure base of any hunting community, was a lively sampling of dashing figures: noblemen and their ladies; wealthy people who had discovered that the stable door was a quick if expensive short-cut into society; a strong injection of Americans from the famous eastern hunts; ladies whose pursuit of the fox was only a phase of an even more intense pursuit of romance; retired admirals and generals; cavalrymen and Guardsmen; good riders on bad horses; bad riders on good horses. And last but by no means least were the yeoman farmers, keen sportsmen in spite of the fact that their land was often a dismal scene after the 'field' had galloped over it, smashing the fences and leaving the gates open for cattle to stray.[36]

In the same way that he was 'such a good thruster' (as a fellow sportsman called him) when riding to hounds, in steeplechases the Prince's tactic was to jump into the lead on hard-pulling horses, defying his own and the horse's ability in a heedless determination to hold it as long as he could. 'Thank God I've got 2 races tomorrow as must do something desperate, which is just what race-riding gives one,' he told Mrs Dudley Ward in April 1923.[37] The following autumn he took a bad fall at the first fence in the Army point-to-point at Arborfield Cross, which knocked him out for half an hour and left him so seriously concussed that the injury 'kept me in a dark room for a week and in bed for nearly a month'. In consequence the Prince's racing exploits were now a public issue, a question was raised in the House, and the Prime Minister, Ramsay MacDonald, had his wheedling say: 'No one in these days can do more good than you, Sir, to your people, through them, to the world, & were a serious mishap to come upon you, who could take your place? Even if someone could, it would not diminish the heartiness of the appeal I make to you.' Having weighed up 'the general feeling of the country, which you know is also the very strong opinion of Mama and myself', the King told the Prince by letter on 30 March that, in showing 'great courage and horsemanship which everyone appreciates', he was 'expos[ing] himself to unnecessary risks'; he could continue to hunt and play polo, 'but the time has come when *I must ask you to give up* riding in steeplechases & point to point races'.

Of startling concern was the Prince's interest in taking to the skies. Late in 1927 the King granted him permission to make use of a plane for far-flung engagements in Britain, but the role of passenger was never going to satisfy him, for this was the era of Lindbergh's pioneering flights and the Prince wanted to taste the new-fangled exhilaration for himself. (At the end of the First World War his father had taken a poor view of a flight he made near London, piloted one-handed by a Canadian flying ace whose wounded arm was held in a sling.)[38] The next spring the Prince was granted a personal pilot, Flight-Lieutenant D.S. Don, and was instructed in the rudiments of aviation; he began a flying log in the name of 'H.R.H. Prince of Wales; *Rank*, Group-Captain R.A.F.' They flew together in an open Bristol Fighter, then migrated to a Wapiti plane with a higher cruising speed and longer range, which enabled the Prince to visit Scotland and to cross the Channel to play golf.[39] In October 1929 the Prince bought a De Havilland Gypsy Moth and set his mind to flying solo – without the King's approval. Accompanied by Don, he practised at a deserted Northolt airstrip. Then one evening his instructor jumped from the front cockpit with his control stick in his hand and waved the Prince into the air alone; there followed 'two extremely lonely circuits of the field'. 'I've beaten you to it,' he trumpeted over the telephone to Princes Harry and George, who were themselves taking instruction. Thereafter he was content to let the element of adventure fade and commit his safety 'to experts',[40] sometimes with scant respect for their judgement. Furious on one occasion at being grounded by foul weather, he insisted on taking off. When, after some minutes, his pilot invited him to the telephone, from which he had returned from making a call, the Prince heard the stentorian voice of Air Marshal Trenchard: 'Good morning, Group Captain. I am giving you an order. You are not to fly on to Cardiff.'[41]

The Prince visited Canada in the autumn of 1923 and briefly the following year, which were opportunities to inspect his ranch. 'Our conversation is largely of sheep-dips, shorthorns and stallions,' Godfrey Thomas reported.[42] When the liner *Berengaria* docked at New York on 30 August 1924 the Prince's 'charming boy'[43] reputation, which the American press had done so much to exaggerate in 1919, was due a robust reappraisal. Having declined the services of Admiral

Halsey in favour of 'Fruity' Metcalfe and Brigadier Trotter ('a right old rip', an equerry called him),[44] he had appropriate companions among his entourage for enjoying a good time. The Prince came in holiday mood, ostensibly to watch the international polo matches between Great Britain and America to be played at the Meadow Brook Club on Long Island, but the prevailing theme as presented by the newspapers was one of frivolity.[45] Within forty-eight hours the *New York Times* had dubbed him 'the indefatigable vacationist'.

To the embarrassment of his hosts, there were times when his whereabouts were unknown. While staying for the polo with Mr and Mrs James Burden at Syosset, he telephoned to say he would not be in for dinner, then was 'whirled away' in a car to dine elsewhere; another time he was secretly 'streaking it up Long Island in one of the fastest motor boats extant'; one afternoon he managed to watch polo incognito by entering the ground through a hole in the fence, then sat swishing a stick and chewing a blade of grass well away from spectators and those who were trying to search him out.[46] He was no less inclined to let people down – as when, having got to his bed after dancing until six o'clock in the morning, he failed to appear at a morning drag hunt. Yet, according to the columnist Cholly Knickerbocker, there was no sparing 'the bank balances of the refulgent chieftains of the Long Island set' who competed to ensure that no previous visitor had been 'so persistently and extravagantly fêted' as was the Prince.[47] As he himself admitted:

> Compared to the creature comforts Americans took for granted, the luxury to which I was accustomed in Europe seemed almost primitive . . . Basically, America meant to me a country in which nothing was impossible. And the scale of hospitality purveyed on Long Island did nothing to disabuse me of this conception. Some of the parties given in my honour were fabulous. My American hosts spared no expense in demonstrating the splendour of a modern industrial republic. Not one but two orchestras and the stars of popular Broadway revues were brought out from New York in relays to provide entertainment at parties that lasted until dawn.[48]

Meanwhile, sections of the popular press were expressing concern for the soul of America's *haut monde*, blaming the Prince's visit for casting a spell at a time when thoughts were turning to the presidential election. According to the *New York World*, a leading national voice of the Democratic Party, the Prince managed, by his choice of friends and diversions, to provoke an exhibition of social climbing on the part of a few Americans which has added nothing to his prestige nor to the prestige of royalty in general. In fact, he managed to demonstrate to Americans, grown tolerant of the business of royalty, that it is, whatever his personal Democracy may be, in fact a pyramid of snobbery. A good deal of hot fuel is added to the fires of the old-fashioned republican conviction that civilization would survive if the King business were wound up.[49]

The Prince had put much of the bad press he received at the outset down to 'an unmistakably derisive . . . tone' adopted towards the game of polo for being the sport of playboys. He was forced to conclude that to be 'photographed in white riding breeches and a helmet and armed with a mallet was only storing up future trouble' for oneself. The *Chicago Tribune* thought fit to suggest that the international matches – which the British lost convincingly – were a ruse intended to harm America's standing. But it was soon apparent to those who saw him putting social convenience before strict line of duty that the Prince was handing the newspapers an open invitation to make light of respect. His staff, who knew that 'the more colourful reports'[50] would be reaching the King's desk at Balmoral, did their best to quash the more extravagant claims. No, the Prince was not in his bed until ten o'clock of a morning, Lascelles announced, nor was his stay given wholly to pleasure seeking. He had visited a high school, the Museum of Natural History, a telephone exchange and Wall Street. He was reading a book. Lascelles arranged a tea party for a group of editors, and thought it a 'howling success . . . every one of them, even the two Hearst editors succumbed to [the Prince] completely after 5 minutes' talk' – after which the column inches given to dissecting the pattern of his night hours all but disappeared.[51]

Looking to 'disarm suspicion', the Prince wrote to the King on 20 September describing his 'more prosaic activities' and how the American press 'indulges in queer & extravagant headlines *daily* which means that they are forgotten the next day. Sometimes they don't look so good . . . but being a daily habit their "bark" or . . . their "*look*" is worse than their "*bite*".' When next he saw his father, he was pointedly shown some of the clippings lying on his desk:

PRINCE GETS IN WITH MILKMAN
HERE HE IS GIRLS – THE MOST ELIGIBLE BACHELOR YET
   UNCAUGHT

OH! WHO'LL ASK H.R.H. WHAT HE WEARS ASLEEP?
PRINCE OF WALES HAS THEM GUESSING IN THE WEE HOURS![52]

The Prince spent a dispiriting week at his ranch in Alberta ('I had the flu and fever the whole time')[53] and before returning home saw more of Canada and something of the American Middle West. In Detroit, Mr Henry Ford showed him his assembly line along which cars were being constructed in sixteen minutes. From New York the Prince re-crossed the Atlantic, aware that his visit could have tested the nerve of many who looked on the American way of life with some incredulity – not least his father. He concluded that his 'doings', and the flippancy with which they had been reported, had so upset the King as 'to nullify temporarily his otherwise favourable impressions of the United States', with the result that, for the foreseeable future, he would conceive 'irremovable obstacles' whenever his family showed an interest in going there. 'If this vulgarity represents the American attitude towards people in our position, little purpose would be served in your exposing yourself again to this kind of treatment,' he told the Prince.[54]

In an important regard the Prince's stay in America marked an inauspicious turning point in his life: he was no longer prepared to tolerate the creed whereby the Prince of Wales delivers all but his most intimate life to public scrutiny and accepts that to be seen in public in any circumstance is to be deemed on duty. He expected people to accept that his private life was be treated as his to do with as he pleased.[55]

The Prince's fourth and final official tour – to South Africa and South America between March and October 1925 – would complete 150,000 miles of travel into forty-five countries, equal, he said, 'to six circumnavigations of the globe' which occupied, by the age of thirty-one, the major portion of seven consecutive years. As he later recalled:

> When I had finished poking into the corners of the world I could have qualified as a self-contained encyclopaedia on railway gauges, national anthems, statistics, local customs and dishes, and the political affiliations of a hundred mayors . . .
> The number of memorial trees I planted, if they have survived the vicissitudes of climate and the depredations of man, must today constitute a substantial forest . . . And the number of public buildings and institutions whose foundation-stones I laid would comprise, could they be brought together, a sizable city.[56]

'[H]e will not find any amusement socially I fear,'[57] remarked Princess Alice, Countess of Athlone, wife of the Governor-General of South Africa. She was writing to Queen Mary in anticipation of the Prince's five-day stay at Government House in Cape Town, a comment presaging a tour thoroughly businesslike in its management. Lord Louis Mountbatten had returned to naval duties; there was no 'G' Trotter or 'Fruity' Metcalfe to spice the Prince's recreational hours. Admiral Halsey again headed a staff that included Godfrey Thomas, Dudley North and Piers Legh, as well as a South African-born newcomer as equerry, Lieutenant W.D.C. Greenacre of the Welsh Guards. North would tell Lascelles: 'It is all work and very uninteresting work at that. The dances and evening entertainments so far have been dreadful. There simply isn't a nice-looking woman in the whole of the Union.' Thomas would find it 'the most heart-breaking' and 'soul-less' undertaking that required the Prince to work 'like a slave'.[58]

Having set his mind to the task, the Prince earned plaudits with his intention to treat all peoples as one under the Crown and by what Lord Athlone's political secretary recognized as 'his sure appreciation of public sentiment'. When he addressed both Houses of Parliament in Cape Town, he appended to the official speech some sentences of his own, which he delivered in Afrikaans to the delight of the Nationalist element. As the dinner guests dispersed that evening, he was willingly lured away to hear the Dutchmen render a selection of old folk-songs.[59] During the many train journeys he would sit at the window of the carriage for long hours, waving to the clusters of dusty natives who had walked strenuous distances for the opportunity of seeing him pass. On a day towards the end of May it was estimated that 100,000 of the Basuto were gathered in a great valley clearing to appear before him, only half of them having come on mounts. For this occasion he wore the blue ribbon of the Garter across his scarlet tunic, but occasionally he disappointed by the plainness of his dress.[60] 'He no wear feather in for him hat,' a Gambian said of him.[61]

The lands showing red on the map of East Africa harboured tribal mystique by turns no less morbid and spellbinding than was familiar to the early explorers. Before the battle-cruiser *Repulse* anchored below Table Mountain in Cape Town on 30 April the Prince had visited the Gambia, Sierra Leone, the Gold Coast and Nigeria, being the first Prince of Wales, as he said, 'ever to set foot on this steaming malarial coast of scattered settlements'.[62] At Kumasi, in the Gold Coast, he had met the Ashanti King, Prempeh, past scourge of white settlements and practitioner of human sacrifice, now returned from exile to a fine house and a British government pension; savage men of Sierra Leone 'whipped themselves with snakes before him until their arms and legs were bleeding';[63] at Kano, in the Northern Provinces of Nigeria, 20,000 Muslim horsemen, wearing chain armour or turbans and flowing cloaks, galloped past 'in serried ranks across the desert plain in a charge that would have stunned a motion-picture director';[64] almost everywhere natives would dance by way of welcome, as did 10,000 Bantus 'until the dust beneath their feet was muddy with their sweat'.[65]

There were moments when the shadow of the imperial project was real enough. He met a Boer Cabinet Minister who refused to ride with him in Johannesburg, and an Oxford-educated Afrikaner who reminded him that the legacy of 'bitterness' left by the barbaric, scorched-earth tactics employed by the British against the Boers would never be eradicated. The Prince wrote: 'And as I visited the old battlefields – Talana Hill, Elandslaagte, Colense, Spion Kop, Belmont, Enslin, Modder River, and Magersfontein – I began to understand why.' Among those who performed a war dance at Eshowe in Zululand were the grandsons of warriors who, on 22 January 1879, had fought hand-to-hand encounters with the British-led forces at Isandlwana, before disembowelling the bodies of the fallen to release their spirits. One 'grizzled old warrior of ninety', the Prince recalled, gave him 'blood-curdling imitations of the groans and cries of the dying British soldiers'.[66] But as Godfrey Thomas remarked, welcoming the Prince of Wales made common cause among the two white races in particular, to which the Prince's democratic instincts undoubtedly contributed.[67] On the day that he visited the memorial to 27,000 Boer women and children, he had left the train and galloped into town at the head of a commando of Dutch farmers. He placed a wreath of white carnations on Kruger's grave. In Pretoria, the Administrator told him, 'You have shown that you understand us; you have spoken to our people in their own tongue, thus giving recognition to their language . . . We recognise in you, Sir, if I may say so, a certain kinship of character with our own people. Ours is a simple people, big-hearted and frank.'[68] He played his ukulele for the press corps who accompanied the royal train.[69]

At the end of thirteen weeks he had visited much of Cape Province, had travelled through the Orange Free State, Natal and Zululand, and made excursions into the protectorates of Basutoland and Swaziland; he had seen the Transvaal goldfields (where he descended to 6,700 feet at the Deep City Mine) and Bechuanaland, then Southern and Northern Rhodesia. 'It has certainly been the most strenuous, the most exacting and the most difficult of your tours,'[70] the King acknowledged. On 29 July he left the British base at Simonstown for South America – the stage of the tour that would all but exhaust his endurance.

He accepted with an air of resignation that Latin Americans 'never seem to have a good reason for going to bed before 4 a.m.'. It was intended that his presence, particularly in the Argentine, would bring commercial advantage, to which end he was victim to inexhaustible hospitality and its 'moments of sheer desperation'. Between times there were aspects of carnival, among them his greeting in Buenos Aires, when clouds of doves were released, their wing-tips dyed red, white and blue,[71] and while roses, daffodils and lilies rained down on his landau.[72] After Uruguay and the Argentine came Chile, from where he arrived back in England on 16 October. With time to reflect, he came to deplore the complacent attitude shown by many Englishmen who, like Charles Dickens's Mr Podsnap, took the sweated efforts of those who were manning the Empire too much for granted: 'Although his business was sustained upon commerce with other countries, he considered other countries, with that important reservation, a mistake.'[73]

As for the Prince's own state of mind as he contemplated a more settled future – altogether he had been abroad for some thirty months since going ashore at St John's, Newfoundland, in August 1919 – the comment of an American officer who saw him late in the tour says it all: 'Talking to people he hung his head, mumbled, tugged at his cuffs or toyed with his necktie or his fly. He smoked cigarettes incessantly, with nervous little gasps. He was boredom personified – restless, impatient to be away.'[74]

The Prince described the nine-day General Strike in May 1926 as 'a skip in the gay rhythm'[75] of upper-class pleasures – a somewhat specious gloss given his open concern for issues of social hardship, which had not caused the strike directly, but did explain why so many people withdrew their labour. The miners, in particular, had been dealt an unenviable hand by the course of economic events. Post-war, with German coal withdrawn from markets, the price of home-produced coal had increased, which gave scope for wages to regain their wartime minimum level. But when German exports resumed, both prices and demand fell sharply through the first half of 1925; employers sought to cut wages and to extend the working day from seven to eight hours: with the pound strengthening, slump soon became crisis.[76] 'Not a minute on the day, not a penny off the pay,' the miners insisted, as a dispute ensued during which Sir Samuel Herbert's Coal Commission attempted to reconcile the interests of miners and of pit owners, but whose early recommendations were seen as unworkable by Stanley Baldwin's Conservative government. When the executives of the Trades Union Congress voted to stand by the miners in calling a General Strike on 3 May 1926, the government duly declared a state of emergency. Suspending his sympathy for the workingman's lot, the Prince admired the efforts of the eager upper- and middle-class volunteers ('they put on a first-class show')[77] who were determined to restore the nation's essential services. With minimal training, they drove the trains, the buses and the trams (looking fresh from the golf course, your conductor might be wearing plus-fours and ornamental stockings);[78] they abandoned their hunters for police horses, or, bellicose, patrolled the streets. The aesthete Osbert Sitwell called them 'the thug-militia of St James's'.[79] They manned power plants and factories, and in all manner of menial ways were determined to restore essential services.

As did the majority, the Prince regarded the intention to strike as an imminent threat to the realm and to the throne, an opinion he saw no reason to modify with the benefit of hindsight. In his memoir, the strike was 'a blow aimed at the constitutional foundations of English life'[80] (although he did not, as many Tories did, regard the Labour Party as proponents of revolution).[81] Before ever it was called, there were communist leaders sewing mailbags in Wandsworth Prison. 'The time is rapidly approaching when the courage and revolutionary fervour of every Party member will be tested . . . [I]n the period of the decline of British capitalist production, the most backward trade union becomes potentially a revolutionary battalion and every demand for higher wages, or even the maintenance of present standards, poor as they are, becomes a revolutionary demand,' declared the Moscow-backed *Communist Review* in February 1925, its tone not untypical of the Party's organs at the time. The Party estimated that 1,000 of its members were arrested in the course of the strike, 'and that a third of all court appearances involved Communists'.

By the ninth day the protest was withering on the vine, Lord Beaverbrook's hostile *Daily Express* reporting how trade unionists had admitted in the lobbies of the House of Commons that 'the organisation against it grows day by day'. By the end of that day the strike was called off, so paving the way for all but the coal-miners to go back to their jobs. The King told his diary: 'Our old country can well be proud of itself, as during the last nine days there has been a strike in which 4 million men have been affected; not a shot has been fired & no one killed; it shows what a wonderful people we are.'[82]

Not minding their father's injunction to lie low while the strike lasted, the Prince and the Duke of York did manage to 'make the rounds of London' each evening, and they listened to 'the acrimonious debates' in the Commons from behind the clock in the Peers' Gallery. And by way of an indirect gesture of support, the Prince lent his chauffeur and his car in the cause of seeing the government newspaper (the *British Gazette*) delivered to Wales.

The strike over, the Prince took up again the mantle of social concern to which he was not always constant. The deepening economic slump brought more and more letters from miners who had served in the war, and who looked to him as their patron, begging him to use his influence with the government on their behalf. When the north countryman Sir Alexander Leith proposed that he should visit the Durham and Northumberland coalfields, the Prince welcomed the opportunity to show the miners that they were not entirely forgotten. Baldwin, however, feared an outcome making for political embarrassment, and asked to see the Prince within hours of his departure. 'Unemployment may well be used as a stick with which to beat my Party,' he told him. The Prime Minister was surprised when the Prince told him that the tour was sponsored by a staunch Conservative and owned that this put 'quite a different face on the matter'.[83] (Not until 1925 had Stanley Baldwin, in his second term as Conservative Prime Minister, seen slum conditions for himself; when he corrected the omission, he 'as near as two pins sat down and howled'.)[84]

The American G. Patrick Thompson told in the *New York Tribune* how the Prince, together with his Private Secretary Godfrey Thomas and Noel Curtis Bennett (of the Coalfields' Distress Organisation), went north to see conditions for himself, eschewing all formality, mayoral dinners and addresses, and travelling without an equerry or police escorts. Calling on an elderly miner in the first village they visited, Curtis Bennett learnt that the miner's wife had died that morning. 'I'd like to go in,' said the Prince quietly.

> The miner's daughter was inside, a nice girl, employed as a domestic servant in a good family. The Prince caught her arm and gave it a comforting little shake.
>
> 'I understand.'

That broke the ice. It also emboldened the girl to ask . . . 'Would you come up to see my Mother, sir?'

The Prince nodded. They went upstairs.

. . . [I]n another village, they came to a row of terrible little houses. They picked one out by chance and knocked. Could he come in, the Prince asked the miner who opened the door. The man recognized him, but stood dubiously in the doorway. Then he said, 'Ay, ye can, sir. But my wife's sick, if ye understand.'

The Prince didn't understand until he got inside. And then he did. In that dreadful little bare room the miner's wife lay in the pangs of childbirth. For a moment the Prince stood looking at that twitching figure under the rough bedding.

'If ye wouldn't mind holding her hand just for a minute, she'd never forget it.' The Prince stepped up, put down his hand and the mother's sought it and clutched it.[85]

According to his cousin, Prince Christopher of Greece, the Prince returned to London tired and depressed: 'I can't get those poor fellows out of my mind,' he said, nor 'the despair in their eyes'.[86] And though he knew that his voice counted for little in national debate, certain critical remarks he made had pricked the complacency of the mine-owning élite, among them a member of Baldwin's government, Lord Londonderry, who dismissed the Prince's evident outspokenness about what he had been shown in the mining communities (the 'perfectly damnable' conditions) as a 'thoroughly stage managed point of view'.[87] What the Prince was attesting to – and it was duplicated in the Midlands, in Wales, in the Lancashire textile communities, on the Tyne and the Clyde – was, as the novelist James Hanley saw it, 'a kind of social hell with nothing special about it except the demoralization of a whole people, physical and moral,'[88] for whom funeral rites were 'the remaining bit of pageantry' available to them (J.B. Priestley's words).[89] With more than two and a half million men out of work by mid-summer 1931, Ramsay MacDonald's new National Government had been brought low by events of consequence – namely the mutiny of the Atlantic Fleet at Invergordon and the 'supposedly inflationary'[90] decision to decouple the currency from the gold standard in September. The Prince was thinking that 'unless the despair was arrested a large part of our manhood would sink into a slough of despond from which they would never rise':

In making the rounds of my father's depression-ridden realm I witnessed many grim sights – throngs of idle men everywhere, with nowhere to go. In town after town, village after village throughout the industrial areas, one would come upon dejected groups aimlessly milling in the streets or standing about the labour exchanges, and in front of the pubs they lacked the means to patronize.[91]

An influence for practical good was the National Council of Social Service, whose patron the Prince became in 1927. In response to a rally that he addressed at the Albert Hall in January 1932 ('I am thinking now of each member of the unemployed population as a single, separate personality, beset by depression, labouring under a sense of frustration and futility'), some 700 independent schemes received coordinated encouragement. Within a year 2,300 centres had been opened, each manned by volunteers, many of whom were unemployed themselves. Notable undertakings were the Welsh Land Settlements, in effect agricultural and market garden cooperatives where unemployed families lived and worked. Another, albeit small, scheme saw twenty-four men put to work in Windsor Great Park. Patronage helped, too. 'People like you ought to run clubs,' the Prince suggested to Mrs Dudley Ward, and so, in 1934, was born the Feathers Clubs (using as insignia the Prince of Wales's Feathers) and the Feathers Club Association over which Mrs Dudley Ward presided as chairman and fund-raiser for thirty years.[92]

An attempt to persuade the London County Council to build model low-rent housing on former Duchy of Cornwall land at Kennington in London was deemed impracticable. And when the Prince held a dinner party at York House to bring together 'a few leading men' with interests in housing projects to meet Ramsay MacDonald, the Chancellor of the Exchequer (Neville Chamberlain) and the Minister of Health (Sir Hilton Young), a 'steady cross-fire of criticism' levelled at the Government's housing programme condemned the initiative to failure.

Immune to the temper of widespread social strains, Court life and its archaic customs continued immutable. The Prince makes much in his memoir of the fuss that brewed in 1929 over the American Ambassador's refusal to wear knee breeches at Court. (They were still required dress even at dinner parties given for the King and Queen in private houses.) Brigadier-General Charles G. Dawes (a former Vice-President), a man of blunt and independent manner and unduly sensitive to American distrust of British airs and graces, had given an equivocal response to a mischievous enquiry by a home reporter who had asked how he intended to dress for his introduction at Court. The King was convalescing at the time, Queen Mary was to hold the levee with the Prince in attendance, and the press was agog to learn whether the ambassador would wear his breeches. 'The King is extremely upset,' the Lord Chamberlain, Lord Cromer, concluded, so would the Prince – who had met the ambassador several times in America and considered him his friend – intervene to spare the Queen embarrassment? Having, as the Prince recorded, 'more sympathy with Mr Dawes's position than it seemed advisable to divulge to the Lord Chamberlain, I proposed what I considered an ingenious solution'. The ambassador should be seen to leave his embassy and return there wearing black evening trousers over his knee breeches; he could dispense with the trousers at the Palace. However, the Prince was unwilling 'to forfeit a friendship' he valued by putting the proposition to the ambassador himself, so Lord Cromer was 'left with the hot potato'. In the event, the Brigadier-General wore his trousers, and at subsequent Court appearances they presented less of an affront.

If the Prince was tickled by the 'breeches incident', he was more often exasperated by his parents' unyielding homage to convention. 'The . . . rending of the social fabric' and 'the acceleration in change' during his father's reign 'almost outraged him', the Prince wrote. 'It would not be correct to say that [the King] rejected the twentieth century. It was only that he was determined to resist as much of it as he could.' Of Windsor Castle dinners during Ascot Week, the Prince recorded:

A few seconds before 8.30 my father and mother with the other members of the family present would start down the corridor towards the Green Drawing Room. At the door we would be met by the Master of the Household, who, as he backed across the threshold, would bow the King and Queen in. The ladies in evening gowns and sparkling jewels formed a quarter-circle on one side of the room. The men were similarly drawn up on the other. The King, his sons, a few close friends, and members of the Household would be in Windsor uniform. The rest of the men would be in black tail-coats. All would wear knee breeches. While my mother shook hands with the men, my father would repeat the same formality with the curtsying women. Then the man who had been commanded to sit on my mother's right would bow and, offering her his arm, escort her to the table while strains of 'God Save the King' issued from a grille in the dining room behind which was concealed a Guards string band that played during dinner.[93]

And, in like vein, the historian Piers Brendon tellingly conveys the 'monstrous tableau vivant of archaic custom' framed by the Palace:

There was the Honourable Corps of Gentlemen-at-Arms, bearing swords and wearing scarlet jackets heavily ornamented with gold lace and tall burnished helmets with white horse-hair plumes. There were the square-bearded Yeoman of the Guard with their halberds and maces, dressed in black velvet hats, white ruffs and scarlet doublets and tunics embroidered with royal emblems. Also performing arcane rituals were ladies of the household, equerries, gentlemen ushers, pages and footmen matched in pairs by size and dressed in scarlet coats with gold trimmings, red velvet breeches, white stockings and buckled shoes. These gorgeous flunkeys were the standard-bearers of an army of servants who dwelt hugger-mugger in 'beetle-ridden basements'.[94]

Beneath even them, as King Edward VIII later discovered, came a 'troglodytish individual' who apparently slept in an enormous, tallow-filled room in the bowels of the Palace and 'help[ed] with the candles'. The King and Queen were 'the focus of the hive's constant solicitude', King George 'conservative to the point of ossification', Queen Mary 'awesomely remote from the everyday life of the nation'.[95] During the darkest days of the slump, which so engaged the Prince's concern, she exclaimed to a group of East Enders: 'Why, why do you live here?'[96]

Of senior political figures, Stanley Baldwin stood highest in the Prince's estimation, the Tory leader who, between 1923 and 1937, was but briefly out of office as Prime Minister, or as an otherwise dominant figure, then only when the minority Labour administrations of 1924 and 1929–31 were in power.[97] Letters the Prince sent him during the General Strike demonstrated 'affection, at times near veneration', and supposedly stiffened his resolve. 'I've got great faith in Baldwin's human personality and soundness,'[98] he told the Queen, a view echoed by the left-wing intellectual, Harold Laski, who wrote of 'his power to evoke a sense of trust which transcends the division of parties'.[99] Baldwin and his wife

Lucy accompanied the Prince of Wales and Prince George on their six-week visit to Canada in the summer of 1927 to take part in the Diamond Jubilee of the Confederation. ('Those damn horses again,' the Prince muttered, seeing on arrival the open landau that was to conduct him through the streets of Quebec. 'I thought I had talked these Canadians out of this eight years ago.' Whereupon, from the carriage behind, Prince George watched the equipage rocket out of sight.)[100] The official highlight was the opening of the International Peace Bridge over the Niagara River, a much-heralded link with the United States – the occasion accompanied by a heavy police presence, coming as it did the day before two left-wing agitators were to be executed. The Prince endured five hectic days of engagements, and speeches too many for his liking. 'A speech to [Canadians] is like a good day's shooting to you,' he told the King. Mrs Dudley Ward learnt that he was burning the candle at both ends 'and I'm too old to make it now'.[101] Meanwhile, the Baldwins were getting a taste of the Prince's way when obligations were likely to bore him. Arriving punctually to dine at Government House, they passed the royal brothers, who were guests there, dressed for the squash court. Dinner had to await the end of their game, their ablutions and a change of dress.

The Baldwins travelled westwards with the Prince for some sightseeing in the Rockies, the Prince leaving them in Alberta to visit his ranch. The Prime Minister would while away the train journey with talk of 'apple husbandry [in] Worcestershire, cricket, and the revision of the Prayer Book',[102] topics altogether one with the pipe smoking, country-squire persona he liked to present. Overlooking an errant preference for squash, Baldwin told the King quite late in the tour (on 24 August) how he thought the Prince 'was at his best' and a pleasure to be with – this but four days before Captain Lascelles confirmed in a letter to Godfrey Thomas how he and Piers Legh had agreed 'it would be a real disaster if, by ill chance, he was called on to accede to the throne now'; they doubted, too, the Prince's fitness for making a better fist of things in the future – the kind of categorical judgement that Lascelles was apt to deliver.[103]

His prejudice was confirmed in the autumn of 1928 during a semi-official visit the Prince made with his second brother, Prince Harry, Duke of Gloucester, to East Africa (England was 'seem[ing] a trifle cramped' again),[104] which the Princes saw as an opportunity to go on safari once public engagements were fulfilled in Kenya. By mid-October Lascelles was 'thoroughly and permanently out of sympathy' with the Prince, in writing of the tour, who makes no mention of Lascelles being on his staff (along with Piers Legh and Brigadier-General Trotter). By Christmas Lascelles had resigned. In Nairobi the Prince was the guest of his one-time equerry, Sir Edward Grigg, now Governor of Kenya. According to Lascelles, the Prince kept late nights, behaved rowdily at a Nairobi club and was a good deal in the company of Gladys, Lady Delamere ('I guess she's a bit keen,' the Prince told Mrs Dudley Ward). The writer Isak Dinesen (Baroness Blixen) appeared to be infatuated with him, while Lady Grigg recognized his volatile humour, one moment finding him all 'sweetness and charm', then as his visit drew to a close 'the most unpleasant and uncivil guest I have ever had in my house'.[105]

After official engagements in Nairobi, the Princes pursued separate safaris, Prince Harry travelling south into Tanganyika and Northern Rhodesia, the Prince going westwards across Lake Victoria to Uganda. They planned to spend Christmas with the Athlones in Cape Town. The open-air safari life had the appeal of 'idyllic existence' laced with incidents of *Boy's Own Paper* piquancy: sudden flight from the terror of a charging single-tusked elephant; a night lost in 'almost impenetrable elephant grass ten feet high, the hunting-ground of lions and snakes';[106] an emergency in mid-October aboard the steamer SS *Baker* crossing Lake Albert when Trotter suffered a heart attack and was returned to Kampala, then home. On 27 November, at Dodoma (in Tanganyika), came news confirming an earlier Reuters message that the King was ill. His physician, Lord Dawson, then cabled that the King had suffered a relapse; further cables from Stanley Baldwin and others urged the Prince to return at once to London. Not to return, Baldwin pleaded, 'will profoundly shock public opinion'. As Lascelles coloured the moment when he read the Reuters cable, the Prince was stopped in his tracks by the spectre of possible accession. He records the Prince telling him (in an extant document dated in advance of their reaching Dodoma), 'I don't believe a word of it. It's just some election dodge of old Baldwin's.' Lascelles expostulated: 'Sir, the King of England is dying, and if that means nothing to you, it means a great deal to us' – after which Lascelles has the Prince finding distraction in seducing the wife of a British official.[107]

What bears no ill scrutiny is the urgency with which the Prince travelled home. The light cruiser *Enterprise* sailed from Aden to collect him at Dar-es-Salaam on 2 December and with barely a pause began the 4,700-mile voyage to Brindisi via the Suez Canal, completing it in eight days. There Godfrey Thomas met him and, thanks to his provision, the Prince was able to change out of his safari clothes. Mussolini lent his own train to carry the Prince across Europe and on 11 December, accompanied by Baldwin, he arrived in London from Folkestone. Lucy Baldwin's diary records her husband telling her how, from his bed at the Palace, the King asked his son: 'Damn you, what the devil are you doing here?'[108] The sixty-three-year-old King had suffered a streptococcal infection of the right lung, which by 2 December was telling on his heart – 'the mischief of the lung', Lord Dawson called it, being overshadowed by a general infection of the blood. It was, he said, 'an exceptionally big illness for any man to have'[109] before the advent of either sulphonamide drugs or antibiotics. The Prince foresaw a 'painful and prolonged' path to recovery.[110]

14
New Loves for Old

The King left London to convalesce at Bognor Regis in early February 1929, but owing to 'frequent relapses' he did not return (to Windsor) until late May: a Council of State, which he had asked the Privy Council to set up while the Prince was hurrying home, continued to conduct business in the King's name. Together with the Queen and the Duke of York, the Archbishop of Canterbury (Dr Cosmo Lang), the Prime Minister and the Lord Chancellor (Lord Hailsham), the Prince was learning something of a sovereign's burden by approving Orders in Council and government appointments. Signing himself 'Your devoted Son', he told his father on 20 February how 'we are trying to keep things going while you are still laid up & there is no reason for you to worry your head over a thing'.[1] That morning he had accepted the Japanese Ambassador's credentials and presented the King's Cup at a horse show. He was soon taking on more of the King's functions. Indeed, the Foreign Office later confirmed that in 1929 he received all who presented their credentials.[2]

Showing inconsiderate haste, Dr Lang pressed the King's secretariat to agree a date (Sunday 7 July) for a service of national thanksgiving for the King's recovery, to be held in Westminster Abbey. In the event, the sovereign, who was still a weak man, endured considerable strain in his determination not to disappoint the crowds. Legend has it that the day before the Abbey service he was 'laughing in full-chested enjoyment' at a story told him by a Labour minister when a surgical wound ruptured. The abscess was discharging as he drove to the Abbey. Only after it was drained on 15 July did his convalescence continue uninterrupted. 'Fancy a thanksgiving service with an open wound in your back,' the King had remarked to Lord Dawson.[3] The jocular minister (J.H. Thomas) observed of his sovereign's undeniable brush with mortality: 'It was his bloody guts that pulled him through.'[4]

With his father's health safely restored, the Prince returned to East Africa in January 1930 to spend four uninterrupted months on safari, this time enjoying himself more with a motion-picture camera than with a rifle. In Nairobi was an American, Thelma, Lady Furness, the Prince's *amour* (as we shall see) of some months' standing, who was on safari with her unsatisfactory husband. She was invited to join the Prince on the Governor's safari, a group some forty strong provided with every comfort for the nomadic life: 'portable bath tubs, dining-tables, wine coolers and the finest mosquito-proofed tents'. Writing some thirty years later, she evoked, as in a trance, their evenings together under the stars:

> This was our enchanted time to be together. As we sat by our own fire, now little more than glowing embers, the tropic African night would come closer and closer . . . [T]he air was like a caress, silken soft. No one could remain insensitive to the vastness of the starry sky, the teeming, fecund sense of nature at its most prodigal. As the Prince and I would feel enveloped in all this, we would instinctively draw closer as if we were the only two people on Earth; our companions became as unreal, as remote from us, as the insubstantial shadows along the jungle's edge. This was our Eden, and we were alone in it. His arms about me were the only reality; his words of love my only bridge to life. Borne along on the mounting tide of his ardour, I felt myself being inexorably swept from the accustomed moorings of caution. Each night I felt more completely possessed by our love, carried ever more swiftly into uncharted seas of feeling, content to let the Prince chart the course, heedless of where the voyage would end.

Instead of the brief farewell she expected on the last day, the Prince drove her alone across trackless country to the railway, the journey abruptly interrupted when all of a sudden he felt ill: slumped over the wheel, he was breathing in shallow gasps, then rallied a little. He was returned to Government House in Nairobi whence he cabled Lady Furness after she had sailed from Mombasa on her way home that he had been diagnosed with malaria.

They had been introduced some four years earlier at the home of the Marquess of Londonderry, then had met again at the Leicester (agricultural) Fair in the summer of 1929. 'This is the first opportunity I've had to congratulate you on the birth of your son,' the Prince told her. Shortly afterwards she was invited for cocktails at St James's Palace, after which they dined *à deux* and danced at the Hotel Splendide.

She thought her escort 'winsomely handsome . . . the quintessence of charm', his 'natural shyness and reserve' appealing to her after 'the swaggering earthiness' of her husband and the strain of a marriage long given to keeping up appearances. She had married and divorced her first husband (James Vail Converse, grandson of a president of Bell Telephones), himself a divorcee, by the age of twenty. She had married her second, the shipping magnate Viscount Furness, in 1926 and knew she was playing second fiddle to his *affaires*; having provided him with an heir, she was expected to accommodate his right as an English gentleman to be promiscuous.

Unrestrained American women were to the Prince's liking, and in Lady Furness he found a companionship of glossy elegance and undemanding intellect, attributes that would not have been out of place in the pages of an F. Scott Fitzgerald novel. Their haunts were the fashionable London nightclubs, the Embassy and the Kit Kat more often than others, not always alone but in a party of six or eight, and often Lord Furness would join them. (He 'took our friendship in stride', his wife said, 'in the sophisticated Englishman's stride'.)[5] And the Prince would attend parties at the Furnesses' house in Arlington Street and at their country seat, Burrough Court, near Melton Mowbray.

Contemplating his return from Africa in March 1930, the Prince told Mrs Dudley Ward how he felt '*sunk*' at the prospect of 'all the silly stunting' again, calling it 'artificial nonsense': he was 'getting too old' for it.[6] A bald sense of inadequacy was lending urgency to a wish to conduct more of his life on his own terms – which meant away from York House, 'the centre of [his] official life'. A solution had presented itself the previous summer when Fort Belvedere, a 'Grace and Favour' house situated on Crown land bordering Windsor Great Park, fell vacant and the Prince obtained his father's agreement that he should have it. Not long back from Africa, he moved in. ('What could you possibly want that queer old place for? Those damn weekends, I suppose,' he recalled his father saying.) Nothing answered his father's question so well as the regime he embraced for freeing an unsettled mind. He worked so relentlessly in the grounds that he begrudged losing an hour of daylight that could be put to use laying siege to acres of neglected woodland or encroaching vegetation, to paths long hidden, or to an intrusion of yew trees that darkened one side of the house, 'staining the walls with green, acidulous mould'. Weekend guests who were pressed to clear an untended patch endured 'arduous physical labour' – as did the Duke of York, who came over from nearby Royal Lodge to lend a hand. The Prince perceived 'the half-buried beauty of the place' and by hurried degrees was making of it 'a peaceful, almost enchanted anchorage':

> Down came the gloomy, encroaching yew-trees, to let in light and air. A muddy lily pond below the battlements was transformed into a swimming pool. I cleared away acres of dank laurel and replaced them with rare rhododendrons. I cut winding paths through the fir- and birch-trees, revealing the true enchantment of the woodland setting . . . I found a new contentment in working about the Fort with my own hands – planting the herbaceous borders, moving shrubs, mowing the hay in summer, building a rock garden with cascades supplied by water pumped up from a dam I had installed below Virginia Water.

It was somewhere, he said, 'I came to love . . . as I loved no other material thing – perhaps because it was so much my own creation.'

The house had been begun by the Duke of Cumberland (third son of George II) in 1750, then enlarged by the architect Sir Jeffry Wyatville (the restorer of Windsor Castle) in 1825; it had been the home of Queen Victoria's son Arthur, Duke of Connaught. With its crenellated, irregular outline, its stone battlements and bronze canons mounted in embrasures, and tall hexagonal tower, the Prince rightly described the Fort as 'a pseudo-Gothic hodge-podge' standing like 'an ancient castle in a forest'.[7] From this very private domain he flew, not his standard, but the flag of the Duchy of Cornwall.

A narrow hallway led to an octagonal hall with its floor of black and white marble. There was much panelling in the principal rooms, furniture by Chippendale, paintings by Canaletto and George Stubbs, and just ten mahogany chairs at the dining room table. Four of the six bedrooms were named after the predominant shade of their decoration ('The Blue Room', 'Yellow Room', 'Pink Room', 'Green Room'), the effect largely created by Mrs Dudley Ward.[8] And now, under Lady Furness's influence, the Prince introduced plenty of New World comfort unknown in so many English houses – as he boasted, 'a bathroom to nearly every room, showers, a steam bath, built-in cupboards, central heating'.[9]

Lady Furness, who was spending long weekends at the Fort, described her life there as 'quiet, even domestic', one of 'comfortable simplicity'. Working at *petit point*, as the afternoons darkened, to embroider a pair of fire screens, she encouraged the Prince to share her interest; his first project was a paperweight for the Queen mounted on a silver base, depicting the royal crown with her initials below. Next he stitched a backgammon table cover in the Guards' colours of red and blue. What Lady Furness called her 'most striking innovation' was the life she breathed into the set pattern of the Prince's way of doing Christmas. Out went his predictable selection of presents for his staff (the autographed pictures, cufflinks, but nothing for their wives and children); in their place were fitting items which she purchased on visits to department stores, which were presented to the staff at the foot of a Christmas tree dressed with decorations of American origin.

All the while what had been 'flirtation' was becoming 'deep-rooted affection', until Lord Furness's visits to the fort lapsed ('Duke went his way, and I went mine').[10] It was said that she was indiscreet in her comments to friends about the Prince's sexual performance, which appears to have troubled him since adolescence. At his childish suggestion they exchanged small teddy bears each time they parted; whimsically, she was 'Poppa' to his 'Momma' and, behind his back, 'The Little Man' for his lack of virility.[11] Lady Furness was at Fort Belvedere much of the time, or when the Prince had engagements they would dine quietly at York House, or at her house, and they were frequently together at parties and charity balls.

A pleasure the Prince associated with living at the Fort was the visits he made to Windsor Castle with its treasures and archives. He would show his guests round the State apartments, or browse in the library alone; a Knight of the Garter, he would sometimes occupy his stall for evensong in St George's Chapel. And he was seeing a good deal of his brother the Duke of York and his wife, Elizabeth (née Bowes-Lyon), who were regular visitors. A reticent man, in the relaxed atmosphere of the Fort the Duke could be decidedly playful. On one occasion he and the Duke threw gramophone records from the terrace to see if they would behave like boomerangs, then continued the sport in the drawing-room until a lamp 'was bowled over by a direct hit'.[12] Lady Furness remembered the time when the Princes rocked with laughter to see herself and the Duchess of York clinging desperately to kitchen chairs as they attempted to skate on Virginia Water. Also at this time the Prince was helping Prince George, nine years his junior, to establish a new life now that he had left the Navy. As part of a refurbishment of York House ('its drab, gloomy rooms furnished according to the . . . style prescribed by the Office of Works') to make it more suited to the increasing number of official and social duties that he and the Duke of York were performing, the Prince provided modest private accommodation for his young brother. 'Bertie and I, who until then had carried most of the load, were pleased to be able to count upon his reinforcement.' Ever since the Prince had helped to wean Prince George off drugs the previous winter (an addiction encouraged by one Kiki Preston, an American socialite nicknamed 'the girl with the silver syringe'), he was constantly concerned for him. (To everyone's satisfaction, Prince George's marriage in November 1934 to the beautiful Princess Marina of Greece was a supremely happy one.)

It was not the Prince's pattern of life to settle for long at home. In January 1931 he met Lady Furness in Paris before they went their separate ways, she to Africa again, he with Prince George to Spain before they sailed for a semi-official tour of South America, ostensibly to boost trade and to open the British Empire Exhibition in Buenos Aires. In Peru, the first stop, where the political atmosphere was 'explosive', talk of commerce seemed inappropriate. The place reserved at the Prince's left for the Vice-President at a British Legation dinner in Lima was empty. The Provisional President, Sánchez Cerro, explained: 'I wouldn't wait for my colleague; I happen to know that he is plotting to have me shot. But I am planning a little surprise for him; I am going to have *him* shot.'[13] Cerro was soon bound for France and exile. In the cause of promoting sales of British aircraft in the Argentine, the Prince flew his own De Havilland Puss Moth, and by the end of the three-month tour – and much travelling – Bolivia, Chile and Brazil had received royal visits.

The trip produced a mix of competent performance, dilatory timekeeping, and at worst dereliction. The Prince had polished his Spanish on the voyage out, having worked up beforehand a speech for delivery in the Argentine under Lady Furness's tuition. His equerry, Major John Aird, thought his speech to the Chamber of Commerce 'one of the best I've ever heard him make, quite natural, obviously his own ideas and criticisms which were very good to my mind'.[14] In Chile, according to the Ambassador, the Prince was 'endeavouring to subordinate himself to the task in hand' while making the most of 'extra-curricular activities; baccarat, roulette, double whiskey sodas and ladies with pasts were his favourites'. By late February punctuality was slipping by as much as two hours and he looked tired and casual. During eight days in Rio de Janeiro in April it was reported of the brothers: 'Neither their suite nor the British Ambassador appeared to have any control over them, and their conduct was marked by a desire to gratify their personalities rather than to conform to the rules which usually guide distinguished foreigners.'[15]

'Haven't I seen that lady before?'[16] the Prince asked Lady Furness, as she introduced guests at an afternoon reception on 15 May 1931 to welcome the Princes home. He had met her, she reminded him, at her house in Arlington Street. Mrs Wallis Simpson curtsied and brief words were exchanged in a wholly unremarkable passage of social ritual. It is generally accepted that she and the Prince had first met at a house party at the Furnesses' country house, Burrough Court, on 10 January 1931. Like Lady Furness, Mrs Simpson (née Warfield) was in her second marriage, to an inadequate husband, by the time she met the Prince. (She had divorced her first husband, Earl Winfield Spencer – a violent alcoholic – in December 1927, after a separation of some six years.) Having lost her father through tuberculosis when an infant, she was brought up among Baltimore society by her mother who 'existed on the charity of relations' and the rent from letting rooms.[17] Ernest Simpson, whom she married in July 1928, aged thirty-two, was American on his mother's side; he earned his bread in shipping and the couple belonged to the aspiring upper middle class. Among their American friends in London was Lady Furness's brother-in-law, William Thaw, the First Secretary at the US Embassy; it was when illness prevented the Thaws from attending the house party that the Simpsons were invited to fill the gap.

By the time Mrs Simpson was presented at Court on 10 June 1931 she and Lady Furness were close friends; Lady Furness helped her dress for the occasion and lent her the train and feathers she had worn when she was presented. Afterwards, at Lady Furness's new house (21 Grosvenor Square), the Prince met the Simpsons for a nightcap; when they left at 3 a.m. the Prince offered to drive them home to Bryanston Court in his own car. When they arrived he declined to have another drink with them as he was on his way to the Fort.[18] So ended an unremarkable episode without apparent implications for either woman. At some point Lady Furness became settled in her intention to separate from her husband and told the Prince so. When she broke the news to him at York House, she recorded, he pressed her a little closer and said, 'Oh, my darling, I am sure you have made the right decision. I am so very, very happy.'

On 20 January 1934 Lady Furness sailed to visit friends in New York and California, not returning until 22 March. It was a trip she approached with misgiving. 'Oh, Thelma, the little man is going to be so lonely,' Mrs Simpson told her, to which Lady Furness replied, 'Well, dear, you look after him while I'm away. See that he does not get into any mischief.'[19] The Prince telephoned her regularly or sent cables in their private code. While she was away Lady Furness met the twenty-three-year-old Prince Aly Khan, who pressed his attentions upon her with the devotion of a Lothario. Before the return voyage he filled her cabin with red roses, then announced that he, too, was aboard. No doubt his strategy was overwhelming given that, at his father's (the Aga Khan's) instigation, he had received the finest tuition in sexual performance in the bordellos of Cairo.[20]

At dinner on the evening she disembarked, the Prince let her know he was not ignorant of the Indian's attentions. There were stiff silences among the small talk. As a guest at the Fort the next weekend, she witnessed the Prince being attentive to Mrs Simpson, at one moment during dinner offering to her mouth a piece of lettuce held with his fingers. 'Darling, is it Wallis?' she asked him after she had taken early to her bed. Through frozen features the Prince replied: 'Don't be silly!'[21] Their relationship was at an end.

Mrs Simpson came to emotional nannydom with a major advantage over those who preceded her: she was thoroughly imbued with the matriarchal tradition of the American South, where the ambitious marriage market encouraged you to cherish and look after your man.[22] Mrs Simpson could praise; she could bolster a man's ego as deftly as she could reprimand him, something which the Prince, who liked the gentle lash of domination, came to expect of her. She commanded what amounted to a cocktail of attraction that counted more than good looks or the cut of a middle-aged figure. (On her own admission, by Americans she 'would have been considered securely [left] on the shelf'.)[23] Lady Furness found her 'not even pretty', her 'alert and eloquent' eyes being her best feature.[24] Her hair she parted centrally, 'Indian' fashion. Lord Beaverbrook described her as 'plainly dressed',[25] a taste not in the least at odds with the chic she later cultivated, which was strikingly enhanced by 'the unprecedented splendour of her jewels'. When the author Marie Belloc Lowndes expressed surprise that Mrs Simpson appeared to be wearing a 'mass of dressmakers' jewels', her guests 'screamed with laughter' for they knew them to be real. The Prince 'had given her fifty thousand pounds' worth at Christmas', they told her, 'following it up with sixty thousand pounds' worth . . . a week later at the New Year'.[26]

Accustomed to receiving from all quarters the deference that let his views go unchallenged, the Prince had found in Mrs Simpson a foil 'with vigour and spirit'. 'A man in my position seldom encounters that trait in other people,' he wrote. 'Never having believed that my offhand judgments were infallible, I always welcomed the chance to argue them – perhaps because I had so few opportunities of doing so . . . I looked upon her as the most independent woman I had ever met.' That he would never know her to be less than 'complex and elusive'[27] can be put down to the not uncommon female characteristic of adjusting her personality to changing circumstances.[28]

Mrs Simpson was every bit a new broom at the Fort. She usurped the domestic responsibilities of the housekeeper and the butler (the Prince's one-time batman, Osborne) by dictating much of the work of household employees, Osborne himself rather than a maid being required to arrange the flowers; and although Mrs Simpson was mostly at the Fort at weekends, she took it upon herself to plan the menus for the entire week. Out went the décor chosen by the Prince with Lady Furness's guidance. The long-serving Finch, the York House butler, was dismissed for insubordination, having previously received his instructions only from the Prince – and Crisp, his successor, soon followed. The general upset saw the back of the cook and a footman, and doubtless there were others. (It appears that Mrs Simpson's own household at Bryanston Court was faring no better. She wrote to her aunt, Bessie Merryman, in October 1934: 'I have had an upset household – no cook upon arrival – notice from Florence and the kitchen maid. I bribed the latter by offering her £5 more to stay. Florence goes next Thursday and I have a new one coming, also Mrs Ralph returns.')[29] As the Conservative MP Victor Cazalet observed, the Prince let Mrs Simpson dominate every situation in which they were together[30] just as she choreographed his every appearance. 'It doesn't look very pretty,' Chips Channon heard her say when making him remove a cigar from his breast pocket.

A triumph of Mrs Simpson's ascendancy was the brutal dismissal of Mrs Dudley Ward, whose elder daughter Penelope had undergone an operation for appendicitis in May. There had been complications, which meant that for the first time in some seventeen years her mother was so preoccupied with visits to the nursing home that there had been no regular contact with the Prince. Then, after her daughter had rallied, Mrs Dudley Ward put a call through to York

House. The telephonist, whose voice she knew so well, was quite unable to sweeten the pill. 'I have something so terrible to tell you,' the discarded mistress was told. 'I have orders not to put you through.'[31] The Prince and she never spoke again. His interest in Penelope and her sister Angela, who had been like nieces to him, withered too, such that their marriages went unmarked.

A line was crossed in August 1934 during Ernest Simpson's absence in the United States on business. The Prince invited Mrs Simpson and Bessie Merryman (cast as chaperone) to join him at Castille Meretmont in Biarritz for a holiday, which became more intimate in its arrangements as the itinerary lengthened. As their stay at the French resort progressed the couple would leave their party (composed of Hugh Thomas, 'G' Trotter, John Aird, the Prince's equerries, and their friends the Colin Buists) to dine alone at local bistros – Aunt Bessie's chaperonage having ended when she started on a planned motor trip into Italy. There followed an invitation to charter Lord Moyne's yacht, *Rosaura*, for sailing into the Mediterranean for what at the outset was so stormy a passage that the crew were forced to put in at Corunna after five days at sea. In her memoir, Mrs Simpson (then Duchess of Windsor) recalled how, with the wind shrieking through the rigging and the bows plunging deeper and deeper into the full fury of the gale, 'our party [Aird and Lord Moyne excepted], one by one, melted away to their cabins'. All was serene when the storm blew itself out. *Rosaura* sailed into rarely visited inlets, picnic lunches were taken ashore, and an informality of dress and conduct prevailed. 'Often the Prince and I found ourselves sitting alone on deck, enjoying the soft evening air, and that unspoken but shared feeling of closeness generated by the immensity of the sea and the sky' which amounted to a letting go the distinction 'between friendship and love'.[32] It was 'most embarrassing for others', Aird told his diary, that the Prince was following Mrs Simpson around 'like a dog'.[33]

From Corunna the party visited Santiago de Compostela, then Vigo, Tuy and Oporto. At sea again, they rounded Gibraltar and sailed on to Majorca for a brief stay before ending their trip at Cannes, from where the Prince had planned to fly at once to Marseille to see Prince Henry, who was on his way to the antipodes aboard HMS *Sussex*. However, Mrs Simpson mattered more, and Prince Henry sailed without seeing him. The couple's arrival at Cannes was quickly known, and when they went ashore at midnight to dance at the Palm Beach Club there were newspapermen and photographers in their train. Heedless of inviting yet more attention, the Prince abruptly moved into the

Hotel Miramar on the third day, only to leave well before dawn. In the interval he had given orders (at 1 a.m.) to have the staff at Cartier attend the shop, where he bought, among other items, an emerald and diamond charm for Mrs Simpson's bracelet; he then demanded the party leave their beds and that *Rosaura* put to sea, where, as the lights of Cannes slipped away, he presented the Cartier charm.

The Prince now extended the trip with visits to Nice and Genoa, before driving to Lake Como, where Aunt Bessie was staying at the Hotel Villa d'Este, for boating and golf.[34] As the holiday mood prospered, informality had become impulsive, as was evident on a visit to the Borromeo Islands where the press took pictures of the Prince wearing only a pair of shorts and sandals for a tour of the Palace; his host, Prince Borromeo, welcomed him in morning dress.[35]

Arriving in Paris on 23 September, the Prince flew to Scotland for the launching of the RMS *Queen Mary* on Clydeside. In due course the rest of the party reached Southampton to find the Prince keenly awaiting them.[36] Taking stock of how she had viewed the past weeks with the Prince, the Duchess later wrote:

The only reason to which I could ascribe his interest in me, such as it was, was perhaps my American independence of spirit, my directness, what I would like to think is a sense of humour and of fun, and, well, my breezy curiosity about him and everything concerning him . . . Then, too, he was lonely, and perhaps I had been one of the first to penetrate his inner loneliness. Beyond this point my speculations could not carry me; there was nothing else real or tangible to nourish them.

I had no difficulty in explaining to myself the nature of the Prince's appeal to me. Over and beyond the charm of his personality and the warmth of his manner, he was the open sesame to a new and glittering world that excited me as nothing in my life had ever done before. For all his natural simplicity, his genuine abhorrence of ostentation, there was nevertheless about him – even in his most Robinson Crusoe clothes – an unmistakable aura of power and authority. His slightest wish seemed always to be translated instantly into the most impressive kind of reality. Trains were held; yachts materialised; the best suites in the finest hotels were flung open; aeroplanes stood waiting. What impressed me most of all was how this could all be brought about without apparent effort: the calm assumption that this was the natural order of things, that nothing could ever go awry . . . [It] seemed unbelievable that I,

Wallis Warfield of Baltimore, Maryland, could be part of this enchanted world. It seemed so incredible that it produced in me a happy and unheeding acceptance.[37]

She was continuing to receive gifts from the Prince, telling her aunt in October how she had bought a coat and dress and some leopard skins with $200 he had given her.[38] And reflecting the progress of their liaison, the Duchess's memoir covering late November that year has her calling the Prince 'David' for the first time[39] – the name by which he was known among his family. At Christmas the Prince gave her a cairn puppy called Slipper, which they nicknamed 'Mr Loo'.

The Prince's bachelor state, with its 'sense of incompleteness and inner discontent' which he admitted was pervading his life, was a matter of such tense anxiety to his parents as to condemn any discussion of a future union to failure. He had resisted from the start any overtures to an arranged marriage, which he feared might become 'an inharmonious partnership' almost impossible to dissolve, never wavering in his resolution to await the dictates of his heart.[40] The Duke of Kent, meanwhile, had married Princess Marina of Greece, which brought an end to his regular visits to the Fort. The brothers' companionship had outlasted the Duke's tribulations over women and drug-taking, but now only Lord Louis Mountbatten among the Prince's family visited him with any regularity. Feeling in low spirits before the wedding, he was aggravated to learn that the King had had Mrs Simpson's name removed from the list of people invited to a party at Buckingham Palace in honour of the nuptials. Seemingly the Duke intervened and her name was reinstated, but the snub understandably rankled. On the day, Mrs Simpson wore a startling dress of violet-coloured lamé out of keeping with the muted tones adopted by other guests. The King and Queen 'stared at her in cold dismay'.[41] Unperturbed, the Prince introduced the woman he loved to Queen Mary and, Aird recorded, 'would have done to HM if he had not been cut off'.[42] The King would later pass judgement. 'That woman in my house!' he exclaimed in recounting the affront to the former Austrian ambassador, Count Mensdorff.

The following November the King's third son, Prince Henry, Duke of Gloucester, married Lady Alice Montagu Douglas Scott, a daughter of the Duke of Buccleuch, who had died in October, causing the ceremony to be held privately in the chapel at Buckingham Palace. 'Now all the children are married except David,' the King told his diary.[43]

For some time Ernest Simpson's pleasure in inhabiting the Prince's circle had been wearing thin. When the Prince invited the pair to ski at Kitzbühel in February 1935, Simpson offered his wife the understandable excuse that an increased workload precluded his going. After 'a rather silent dinner' during which she confirmed her wish to have the holiday without him, he retired to his bedroom and 'for the first time [she] heard his door bang'.[44]

'Can't say I couldn't live without winter sports,' she wrote to her aunt on 9 February, her third day in the Tyrol.[45] Shunning the ski slopes, she latched on to good-looking male guests – to the Prince's evident discomfort choosing to sit next to one of them at meals – and otherwise passed much of the time playing bridge, backgammon and poker with members of the party. The Prince appears to have skied unceasingly.

On 16 February the party left for Vienna, the point at which vacation acquired a political hue. Austria's pro-Mussolini government was in repressive mode, quelling socialist unrest in the days surrounding the Prince's arrival. The Prince visited President Miklas, his Chancellor and Vice-Chancellor, the trio who were in the broil of opposing Hitler's waxing diplomatic influence. Then moving on to Budapest he attended further high-level meetings with the Hungarian regime. He would continue to engage with, and be flattered by, men of Fascist sympathies at home and abroad, who were determined to gain the good opinion of the cream of British society. Lady Cunard, for one, enjoyed numerous Nazi connections, among them Leopold von Hoesch, the German ambassador in London, who at a reception introduced the Prince and Mrs Simpson to Joachim von Ribbentrop, Hitler's ambassador without portfolio. Thereafter, to mark their meeting, the smooth-talking Ribbentrop sent red roses to Bryanston Court every day and all year round. 'Fruity' Metcalfe from among the Prince's close circle was a friend of William Joyce, the man who became known as 'Lord Haw-Haw' for his broadcasts of Nazi propaganda during the Second World War. He was a member of the pro-Hitler January Club, which was funded by Mussolini through an Italian ministry led by a former lover of Mrs Simpson, the dictator's son-in-law and Foreign Minister, Count Ciano. Understandably, webs of friendship embraced members of the upper class in varying degrees sympathetic to German high-caste posturing. Fellow guests with Metcalfe at a Fascist Blackshirt dinner at the Savoy Hotel included the Oswald Mosleys (Metcalfe's wife was Lady

Cynthia Mosley's sister) and Count and Countess Paul Munster, friends of the Prince. In January 1935 the double agent Baron William de Ropp was entertained in London by the Prince and the newly married Duke of Kent, using the occasion to present a favourable picture of the German leadership. (The Duke was recently returned from visiting Princess Marina's brother-in-law, Karl Theodor, Count von Toerring-Jettenbach, whose wife Elisabeth had informed Berlin how the Duke appeared reconciled to Germany's revived militarism.)

Among the phalanx of guests who attended the Silver Jubilee celebrations in May 1935 was the ailing Kaiser's daughter-in law, Crown Princess Cecilie, and a Nazi sympathizer and friend of the Prince, Carl, Duke of Saxe-Coburg-Gotha. Apparently at Princess Cecilie's suggestion, the Prince was prepared to address a gathering of the British Legion in support of its intention to encourage overtures of friendship to war veterans' organizations in Germany. In the interests of *détente*, he expressed his desire to have the conflicts of the Great War put out of mind, a view sure to be received with suspicion by the pro-Mussolini leadership in Austria, Hungary and France. Delivered on 19 June at the Queen's Hall, the Prince's intervention and its timing were crass. Almost concurrently, German veterans were marching with swastika flags at a rally in Brighton to be addressed by Prince Otto von Bismarck who, at a dinner, delivered a message from the Prince. At the town hall the Reich League leader Klaus Korres proclaimed, 'The Prince of Wales is the man of the moment, not only in his own country, but throughout Germany. Heil Hitler!' Hermann Goering told an assembly in Nuremberg that the Germans were 'profoundly cheered' by the Prince's words.[46] The King, as well as those members of the Commons who viewed appeasement with Mussolini as being necessary to the protection of the Mediterranean and the Suez Canal, were furious with the Prince for this trespass on to political ground. (That the Anglo-German Naval Agreement allowing significant rebuilding of the German fleet had been signed only six days earlier seemed beside the point.) And there would be further sallies of a questionable character on the part of the Prince, which in his memoir he masked by reprising the cliché that 'a Prince's ... politics must remain within the constitutional pale'.[47] Using the ineffectual pseudonym of Lord Chester and accompanied by special agents and detectives for their protection from communist assassins, the Prince took Mrs Simpson with him to Cannes in July. Meanwhile, Mussolini had the conquest of Abyssinia in his sights. On 11 September the couple arrived in Budapest for meetings with

President Gömbös as news of Hitler's swashbuckling at a Nuremberg rally was appearing in the press. Then to Munich and on to Paris, where they met Albert Grégoire (Mrs Simpson's lawyer), a founder of Marcel Bucard's Fascist Franciste movement and another friend of Crown Princess Cecilie. They met the vacillating premier of France, Pierre Laval, on the most friendly terms (and would do so again in December, apparently in secret), both being present at discussions involving European diplomacy – unprecedented occasions for being held in the presence of the heir to the British throne and his ostensible mistress. On 2 October they were back in London.

George V's distaste for Mrs Simpson supposedly decided him to have the commissioner of the Metropolitan Police, Lord Trenchard, investigate her private life.[48] That a dossier had been made of the Yard's findings was widely doubted. But, regardless of any revelations, the King had been set against her for some time, and he would not have her invited to the Silver Jubilee State Ball held on 14 May 1935. In the course of a tense interview with his son the decision was reversed. Mrs Simpson should not be thought his mistress, the Prince assured his father, and he swore on his oath that he had not slept with her. Aird, for one, knew there were many who believed he had lied; the King's Private Secretary, Clive Wigram, wrote of Halsey and the Prince's staff being 'horrified at the audacity' of his claim.[49] Mrs Simpson attended the ball accompanied by her husband. She wrote in her memoir: 'As David and I danced past, I thought I felt the King's eyes rest searchingly on me. Something in his look made me feel that all this graciousness and pageantry were but the glittering tip of an iceberg . . . filled with an icy menace for such as me.'[50]

About this time the strain of triangular relations led Mrs Simpson to upbraid the Prince about his unthinking demands:

I was and still am terribly upset. You see my dear one can't go through life stepping on other people. I know that you aren't *really* selfish or thoughtless at heart but your life has been such that you have been the one considered so that quite naturally you only think of what you want and take it too without the slightest thought of others. One can arrive at the same result in a kinder way. I had a long quiet talk with E[rnest] last night . . . Everything he said was so true. The evening was difficult as you did stay much too late. Doesn't your love for me reach to the heights of wanting to make things a little easier for me. The lovely things you say to me aren't of much value unless they are backed up by equal actions. I should have come back Sat and I didn't. Then last night you should have left by 8. Then you telephone the second time – which just did finish the evening and made a row. You must have understood from my conversation the first time that I was upset and also very disappointed in a boy and that nothing you could say could help in the least – because David what are all those words if what they say isn't enough for a little sacrifice on our part to do what is really the right thing for all concerned. So far you have always come first in my actions if there had to be a choice (like Sat.). It isn't fair and cannot always be that way. Sometimes I think you haven't grown up where love is concerned and perhaps it's only a boyish passion for surely it lacks the thought of me that a man's love is capable of. Please understand I am not writing a lecture only your behaviour last night made me realise how very alone I shall be some day – and because I love you I don't seem to have the strength to protect myself from your youthfulness . . .

In writing to her aunt on 8 June she was feeling her disadvantage. People were 'grand' to her but she saw no prospect of it lasting beyond 'the duration of my length of service'. She concluded, 'I imagine anyway I am doing far, far better than Thelma on far, far less.' Then on 29 June such thoughts were banished.

I have been so gay – a dance nearly every night – and I dined at the *Londonderrys* Wednesday a dinner for 50. It really was an experience. Then on to the Dudley dance. The Prince gave a dinner last night for the Kents. Next week there are 3 more dances, Mrs Corrigan, Lady Weymouth and Lord Moyne's. That ends the dance list and only a dinner at the German Embassy left. My evening clothes will just make it. It is very amusing what one is invited to in hopes of PW. All the very best titles come across whereas no one noticed Mrs Simpson before.[51]

All the while she was making the most of a relationship she did not expect to last, the Prince was believing it had every prospect of breathing real life into a parched, often desolate birthright. He was becoming so reliant on her company that her absence unnerved him. His eyes followed her everywhere. He would strain to catch what she was saying to someone else. Winston Churchill wrote of him: 'He delighted in her company, and found in her qualities as necessary to his happiness as the air he breathed. Those who knew him well and watched him closely noticed that many little tricks and fidgetings of nervousness fell away from him. He was a completed being instead of a sick and harassed soul.' Love notes of the kind the Prince had sent to other women now betrayed a desperate intent. Aboard HMS *Faulknor* for a naval review in the Channel, he wrote (on 23 July):

> Wallis – a boy is holding a girl so very tight in his arms tonight. He will miss her more tomorrow because he will have been away from her some hours longer and cannot see her till Wed-y night. A girl knows that not anybody or anything can separate WE – not even the stars – and that WE belong to each other for ever. WE love [twice underlined] each other more than life so God bless WE. Your [twice underlined] David.

Writing from the Fort (probably in September) he pressed her not to lose heart when he was absent. Nor was he veiling a wish to consider marriage. 'WE are strong together in our purpose,' he told her, 'which is our very life and that must not, cannot fail for any reason or obstacle that may confront us.'[52] Ernest Simpson's return from a business trip to America on 18 October, where he was understood to be conducting an affair with one Mary Kirk Raffray, realized a truth. 'We were both going our separate ways,' his wife recorded; 'the core of our marriage had dissolved; only the shell remained – a façade to show the outer world.'[53]

By Christmas the Prince was describing the King as 'grown thin and bent'.[54] Neither father nor son had fashioned an opportunity to discuss the matter of Mrs Simpson, the Prince giving as his reason the circumstances filling so much of the King's time – the pattern of his summer at Cowes, Sandringham and Balmoral, Prince Henry's wedding, a general election, and the death of his favourite sister, Princess Victoria, whose passing was so great a grief that he would not face appearing in public again. For his part, the King (as if transfixed in headlamps) feared for the monarchy residing in a son who, he said, lacked 'a single friend who was a gentleman'[55] and with whom discussion on any useful subject was long foreclosed. He could not discount the prospect of a union with a married woman already once divorced, to which end his son would consider 'withdraw[ing] altogether from the line of succession' in favour of the Duke of York. There was little left that could lighten these days of waning strength.

In December the Prince watched the Duke of York's children, Princesses Elizabeth and Margaret Rose, playing beneath the twenty-foot Christmas tree in the ballroom at Sandringham, a new generation enjoying the kind of family ritual which left him feeling 'detached and lonely'. Then came the moment for which, at the age of forty-one, his disappointed life was merely the prelude. While out shooting in Windsor Great Park on Thursday 16 January he received an urgent note from the Queen informing him of his father's worsened condition. She suggested he come to Sandringham for the weekend but with nothing said that could be construed as pretext. The Prince flew to the royal estate next morning, but before landing signalled to his pilot to fly in a wide circle around it: his way of taking stock of the House, its lawns and surrounding woods which 'seemed the embodiment of [his] father's life and philosophy – secure, unchanging, apart'.[56]

He found the King, who managed a flicker of recognition, sitting before a fire in his bedroom. Later in the day the dying sovereign would write in his diary for the last time: 'Dawson arrived this evening. I saw him and feel rotten.'[57] A series of six bulletins was issued over the next two days as his cardiac weakness progressed. On Sunday 19 January the Prince drove to London to consult with Stanley Baldwin at Downing Street, after which ministers authorized a Council of State comprising the Queen and her three sons to act on the King's behalf. Shortly after 12.15 the next day, Monday – with Lord Dawson guiding his pen – the King signed the warrant in the presence of a quorum of Privy Councillors. By late afternoon his demise was near. Having dined alone, the Queen and her children gathered round the King's bed. At five minutes before midnight his life slipped away, whereupon the Queen first, then the Duke of York, took his successor's hand in theirs and kissed it. Addressing an Accession Privy Council the next afternoon he told them:

> I am determined to follow in my Father's footsteps and to work as he did throughout his life for the happiness and welfare of all classes of my Subjects. I place my reliance upon the loyalty and affection of my peoples throughout the Empire, and upon the wisdom of their Parliaments, to support me in this heavy task, and I pray God will guide me to perform it.[58]

As the King's life was moving to a close that last Saturday, the Prince penned a message to 'My own Sweetheart' which he ended with a pledge: 'You are all and everything I have in life and WE must hold each other so tight. It will all work out right for us. God bless WE. Your DAVID.'[59]

Notes

Introduction

1. A. Aspinall (ed.), *The Correspondence of George, Prince of Wales 1770–1812*, Vol. 1, Cassell, 1963, pp. 5–6.

Edward VII

Chapter 1: 'Make Him Climb Trees!'

1. George Dangerfield, *Victoria's Heir: The Education of a Prince*, Constable, 1942, p. 98.
2. Christopher Hibbert, *Edward VII: A Portrait*, Allen Lane, London, 1976, p. 17.
3. Philip Magnus, *King Edward the Seventh*, John Murray, London, 1964, p. 5.
4. A.C. Benson and Viscount Esher (eds), *The Letters of Queen Victoria*, Vol. 1, John Murray, London, 1911, p. 458, in Magnus, p. 5.
5. Cecil Woodham-Smith, *Queen Victoria: Her Life and Times*, Vol. 1, Hamish Hamilton, London, 1972, p. 184.
6. Pierre Crabitès, *Victoria's Guardian Angel: A Study of Baron Stockmar*, George Routledge and Sons, London, 1937, p. 155.
7. Crabitès, pp. 145, 147, 148.
8. Theodore Martin, *A Life of His Highness the Prince Consort*, Vol. 2, Smith, Elder and Co, London, 1880, p. 184, in Crabitès, p. 148.
9. Woodham-Smith, p. 266.
10. Dangerfield, pp. 44–5.
11. Lyttelton Letters, p. 340, in Hibbert, p. 5; also Sir Sidney Lee, *King Edward VII: A Biography*, Macmillan, London, 1925, p. 16.

12. The Queen's reminiscences, January 1862, in Woodham-Smith, p. 334.

13. Thomas E. Brown, *Attention Deficit Disorder: The Unfocused Mind in Children and Adults*, Yale University Press, New York, 2005, p. 96.

14. Lyttelton Letters, quoted in Hibbert, p. 5.

15. Magnus, p. 8.

16. Lady Lyttelton to the Queen, 9 September 1844, in Woodham-Smith, pp. 336–7.

17. Stanley Weintraub, *The Importance of Being Edward: King in Waiting 1841–1901*, John Murray, London, 2000, pp. 1, 2.

18. Memorandum by the Queen and the Prince, 4 March 1844, quoted in Woodham-Smith, p. 267.

19. Woodham-Smith, p. 335.

20. Magnus, p. 8.

21. Weintraub, p. 15.

22. Hibbert, p. 299.

23. Magnus, p. 8.

24. See Weintraub, pp. 15–17.

25. Benjamin Disraeli in Weintraub, p. 17.

26. Hibbert, p.11.

27. Crabitès, p. 148; Magnus pp. 5–6.

28. Leslie Mitchell, *The Whig World 1760–1837*, Hambledon Continuum, London, 2005, pp. 100, 118.

29. Weintraub, p. 18.

30. Gibbs's diary entries in *Cornhill Magazine*, Spring 1951, p. 986, in Hibbert, p. 13.

31. Gibbs Papers. See Hibbert, pp. 14–15; Magnus, p. 13.

32. Weintraub, p. 20.

33. Weintraub, p. 21.

34. Magnus, pp. 10–11.

35. Elizabeth Longford, *Victoria R.I.*, Weidenfeld and Nicolson, London, 1964, p. 218.

36. Longford, p. 277.

37. Hibbert, p. 16.

38. Lincolnshire Papers (Bodleian MSS Film 1120–21), in Hibbert, p. 16.

39. The Letters of Queen Victoria to her Eldest Daughter, the Princess Royal, 22 December 1852, in Longford, pp. 275–6.

40. A.N. Wilson, *The Victorians*, Hutchinson, London, 2002, p. 273.

41. A.N. Wilson, *After the Victorians*, Hutchinson, London, 2005, p. 5.

42. G.M. Young, *Victorian England: Portrait of an Age*, Oxford University Press, Oxford, 1936, p. 79.

43. Longford, p. 216.

44. Weintraub, p. 12

45. 'The Boy who "Licked" the Prince of Wales', reprinted in the *Portland Eastern Argus*, 30 May 1856, cited in Weintraub, p. 16.

46. Queen Victoria's diary, in Magnus, p. 7.

47. Longford, p. 218.

48. Queen Victoria to King Leopold, 7 March 1848, in Woodham-Smith, p. 285.

49. A.C. Benson and Viscount Esher (eds), Vol. 2, p. 218.

50. Young, p. 78.

51. Woodham-Smith, p. 327.

52. Young, 'The Victorian Noon-time', in *Daylight and Champaign*, Jonathan Cape, London, 1937, p. 168.

Chapter 2: Seeds of Approval

1. Weintraub, p. 27.

2. 31 January 1853. *The Letters of Queen Victoria*, Vol. 2, John Murray, London, 1908, p. 435.

3. Monica Charlot, *Victoria: The Young Queen*, Basil Blackwell, Oxford, 1991, p. 364.

4. Weintraub, p. 27.

5. The Greville Memoirs, Vol. 7, pp. 156–7, in Magnus, p. 19.

6. A. Ponsonby, *Henry Ponsonby*, Macmillan, London, 1943, p. 26, in Magnus, p. 21.

7. 4 August 1857. Hawarden MSS, in Weintraub, p. 30.

8. Viscount Esher, *The Influence of King Edward and Essays on Other Subjects*, John Murray, London, 1915, p. 22.

9. Hibbert, p. 21.

10. Esher, p. 14, pp. 18–22.

11. Lee, pp. 53–4.

12. Longford, p. 269.

13. E.C. Corti, *The English Empress: A Study in the Relations between Queen Victoria and*

Her Eldest Daughter, Empress Frederick of Germany, Cassell, London, 1957, p. 50; Corti, pp. 50–51, in Magnus, p. 27.

14. Hibbert, p. 25.

15. G.W. Curtis (ed.), *The Correspondence of J.L. Motley*, John Murray, London, 1889, p. 320, in Lee, pp. 64, 63.

16. Weintraub, p. 40.

17. *Punch*, 20 September 1859, in Lee, p. 74.

18. Esher, pp. 28 and 29.

19. Dangerfield, p. 106.

20. Elizabeth Gaskell to Charles Eliot Norton, 5 April 1860, in Weintraub, p. 46.

21. H.L. Thompson, *Henry George Liddell, D.D., Dean of Christ Church, Oxford: A Memoir*, John Murray, London, 1899, p. 178, in Lee, p. 78.

22. Dangerfield, p. 110.

23. Weintraub, pp. 52, 53, 62.

24. Weintraub, p. 72.

25. Lee, p. 103.

26. R.J. de Cordova, *The Prince's Visit: A Humorous Description of the Tour of His Royal Highness, the Prince of Wales, through the United States of America, in 1860*, B. Frodsham, New York, 1861, in Weintraub, p. 74.

27. Rothschild Family Archive, in Weintraub, p. 86.

28. Weintraub, p. 86.

29. Hibbert, pp. 47–8.

30. Magnus, p. 51.

31. Queen Victoria's diary, in Magnus, p. 52.

32. Woodham-Smith, p. 417.

33. Magnus, pp. 52–3.

Chapter 3: Marriage

1. The Princess Royal to the Queen, 17 December 1860, in Corti, p. 64.

2. Roger Fulford (ed.), *Dearest Child: Letters between Queen Victoria and the Princess Royal, 1858–1861*, Evans Brothers, London, 1964, pp. 356, 357.

3. Corti, p. 72.

4. Hibbert, p. 46.

5. Magnus, pp. 49, 50.

6. Dangerfield, p. 139; Weintraub, p. 113.

7. Georgina Battiscombe, *Queen Alexandra*, Constable, London, 1969, p. 33.

8. The Prince Consort to Ernest, Duke of Coburg, 22 July 1861, in Corti, p. 68.

9. Battiscombe, p. 17.

10. Roger Fulford (ed.), *Dearest Child*, pp. 289, 291, in Battiscombe, pp. 19, 20.

11. Battiscombe, p. 34.

12. Magnus, pp. 48, 49.

13. Queen Victoria's diary, in Magnus, p. 49.

14. Magnus, p. 51.

15. 11 January 1862. Magnus, p. 53.

16. Lee, pp. 139, 138.

17. Kronberg Letters, in Longford, p. 315.

18. Weintraub, p. 111.

19. Weintraub, p. 112.

20. 18 September 1862. Longford, p. 315; Magnus, p. 59.

21. Weintraub, p. 114.

22. Battiscombe, pp. 46, 44, 48.

23. A.L. Kennedy (ed.), *My Dear Duchess: Social and Political Letters to the Duchess of Manchester 1858–1869*, John Murray, London, 1956, pp. 213–14, in Magnus, p. 67.

24. Lady Geraldine Somerset's diary, 5 March 1863, in Battiscombe, p. 50.

25. Battiscombe, p. 48.

26. Weintraub, p. 124.

27. Roger Fulford (ed.), *Dearest Mama: Letters between Queen Victoria and the Crown Princess of Prussia, 1861–64*, Evans Brothers, London, 1968, p. 236.

28. Hibbert, p. 72.

29. Lee, p. 171.

30. Anthony Allfrey, *Edward VII and His Jewish Court*, Weidenfeld and Nicolson, London, 1991, p. 23.

31. Weintraub, pp. 194–5, 129.

32. A.V. Baillie and Hector Bolitho, *A Victorian Dean*, Chatto and Windus, London, 1930, p. 218, in Battiscombe, p. 56.

33. Lord Esher, *Cloud Capp'd Tower*, John Murray, London, 1927, p. 163, in Battiscombe, p. 54.

34. Battiscombe, p. 13.

35. Richard Hough, *Edward and Alexandra: Their Private and Public Lives*, Hodder and Stoughton, London, 1992, p. 123.

36. Journal of the De Goncourts, 7 March 1888, in Lee, pp. 168–9.

37. Roy Hattersley, *The Edwardians*, Little, Brown, London, 2004, p. 19.

38. Devonshire MSS, Chatsworth, CS/340/527, 12 March 1873, in Hibbert, p. 75.

39. Lee, pp. 250, 251.

40. Hibbert, pp. 78, 77, 78.

41. Battiscombe, pp. 63, 65, 80, 68.

42. Weintraub, p. 130.

43. Hibbert, p. 84.

44. Battiscombe, p. 77.

45. Weintraub, p. 144.

46. Battiscombe, pp. 83, 84.

47. Virginia Cowles, *Edward VII and His Circle*, Hamish Hamilton, London, 1956, p. 160.

48. Rupert Christiansen, *Tales of the New Babylon: Paris 1869–1875*, Sinclair-Stevenson, London, 1994, p. 17.

49. Magnus, p. 128; Allfrey, p. 43.

50. Christiansen, pp. 61, 64.

51. Allen Andrews, *The Follies of King Edward VII*, Lexington Press, London, 1975, p. 92.

52. Emile Zola, *Nana*, Oxford University Press World's Classics edition, Oxford, 1992, pp. 125, 127, 129.

53. Douglas Parmée, in introduction to Zola, *Nana*, p. viii.

Chapter 4: Marlborough House

1. Weintraub, p. 325.

2. Theo Aronson, *The King in Love: Edward VII's Mistresses*, John Murray, London, 1988, p. 8.

3. Hibbert, pp. 98–9.

4. Allfrey, pp. 52, 55.

5. Hibbert, p. 98.

6. Anita Leslie, *The Marlborough House Set*, Doubleday and Company, New York, 1972, p. 122.

7. Cowles, pp. 158–9.

8. Battiscombe, pp. 219–20.

9. Aronson, p. 19.

10. Hough, p. 109.

11. Hibbert, p. 175.

12. Constance Battersea, *Reminiscences*, Macmillan, London, 1923, p. 343, and Carrington Diary, Lincolnshire Papers, MS film 1120, Bodleian Library, in Hough, pp. 111, 112.

13. Andrews, p. 10.

14. Hough, p. 113; Weintraub, p. 140.

15. Richard Shannon, *Gladstone: Heroic Minister 1865–1898*, Penguin, Harmondsworth, 1999, p. 92, in Wilson, *The Victorians*, p. 360.

16. Magnus, pp. 162–3.

17. Hattersley, p. 31; R. Cecil, *Life in Edwardian England*, Batsford, London, 1969, p. 111, in Hattersley, p. 30.

18. Magnus, p. 424.

19. Hibbert, p. 225.

20. Hough, p. 110.

21. Magnus, p. 229.

22. Hibbert, p. 223.

23. Magnus, pp. 268–9.

24. Allfrey, pp. 37, 2.

25. Giles St Aubyn, *Edward VII: Prince and King*, Collins, London, 1979, p. 84.

26. Hibbert, p. 91.

27. Cowles, pp. 74–5.

28. Hibbert, p. 70.

29. Weintraub, pp. 201, 174, 175.

30. Allfrey, pp. 22, 24.

31. Dowager Countess Cowper to Earl Cowper, October 1874. 'Memoir of Earl Cowper' by his wife (privately printed, 1913), in Allfrey, p. 22.

32. Hibbert, pp. 172–3.

33. Magnus, pp. 63, 64.

34. Allfrey, pp. 68–9, 35.

35. Sir Algernon West, Private Diaries, 1922, p. 84, and Lucy Masterman (ed.), *Mary Gladstone, Her Diaries and Letters*, Methuen, London, 1930, p. 154, in Allfrey, p. 36.

36. G.R. Searle, *A New England? Peace and War*, Oxford University Press, Oxford, 2004, pp. 176–7.

37. R.C.K. Ensor, *England 1870–1914*, Clarendon Press, Oxford, 1936, p. 115, in Wilson, *The Victorians*, p. 427.

38. Young, p. 145.

39. Wilson, *The Victorians*, p. 428.

40. J.R. Walkowitz, *City of Dreadful Night: Narratives of Sexual Danger in Late-Victorian London*, University of Chicago Press, Chicago, IL, 1992, pp. 26–7, in Searle, p. 173.

41. Countess of Warwick, *Afterthoughts*, Cassell, London, 1931, p. 258; Richard Davis, *The English Rothschilds*, Collins, London, 1983, pp. 99–100, in Allfrey, p. 37.

Chapter 5: The Sporting Life

1. Philip Hepworth, *Royal Sandringham*, Wensum Books, Norwich, 1978, p. 19.

2. Macclesfield Papers, in Battiscombe, pp. 55–6.

3. Hepworth, p. 16.

4. Helen Cathcart, *Sandringham: The Story of a Royal House*, W.H. Allen, London, 1964, pp. 24, 25, 84.

5. Hepworth, p. 48.

6. Cathcart, p. 98.

7. Lillie Langtry, *The Days I Knew*, Hutchinson, London, 1925, p. 117.

8. Aronson, p. 135.

9. 'The Prince of Wales at Sandringham', in *Strand Magazine*, Vol. 5, 1893, p. 330.

10. Wilson, *The Victorians*, p. 384.

11. Cathcart, p. 94.

12. Battiscombe, p. 138.

13. Cathcart, pp. 114–15.

14. Mrs C.S. Peel, *A Hundred Wonderful Years*, Bodley Head, London, 1926, p. 66, in Aronson, p. 135.

15. Cathcart, p. 104.

16. Battiscombe, pp. 121, 122–3.

17. Lady Geraldine Somerset's diary, 17 April 1871, 6 April 1871, in Battiscombe, p. 123.

18. Sandwich Papers at Mapperton, in Battiscombe, p. 127.

19. *Strand Magazine*, Vol. 5, 1893, p. 327.

20. Louise Cresswell, *Eighteen Years on Sandringham Estate*, Temple Company, London, 1887, pp. 61, 26, 62, 63–4, 65, 66, 225, 67, 68.

21. Hepworth, p. 44.

22. Jonathan Garnier Ruffer, *The Big Shots: Edwardian Shooting Parties*, Debrett's Peerage, London, 1977, p. 27.

23. Cathcart, p. 138.

24. Alfred E.T. Watson, *King Edward VII as a Sportsman*, Longmans Green and Co., London, 1911, pp. 22, 44, 46.

25. Aubrey Buxton, *The King in His Country*, Longmans Green and Co., London, 1955, p. 2, in David Duff, *Whisper Louise: Edward VII and Mrs Cresswell*, Frederick Muller, London, 1974, p. 76.

26. Cresswell, p. 69.

27. Hibbert, p. 94.

28. Cresswell, pp. 70, 71.

29. David Duff, *Albert and Victoria*, Frederick Muller, London, 1972, p. 240.

30. Ruffer, pp. 27, 15, 20.

31. Weintraub, pp. 64, 227, 230.

32. Watson, p. 26.

33. Ruffer, p. 21.

34. Watson, pp. xxix, 23.

35. Ruffer, p. 32.

36. Hibbert, p. 95.

37. Ruffer, p. 133.

38. Cresswell, pp. 71, 68, 71, 78, 80, 84, 86, 93, 227, 237.

39. Edward Spencer, *The King's Racehorses: A History of the Connection of His Majesty King Edward VII with the National Sport*, John Long, London, 1902, p. 55.

40. Michael Seth-Smith, *Bred for the Purple*, Leslie Frewin, London, 1969, p. 124.

41. Lee, p. 580.

42. Richard Marsh, *A Trainer to Two Kings: Being the Reminiscences of Richard Marsh M.V.O.*, Cassell, London, 1925, p. 117.

43. Spencer, p. 60.

44. Seth-Smith, p. 132.

45. Seth-Smith, pp. 220, 138, 141,142.

46. Spencer, p. 81.

47. Seth-Smith, p. 145.

48. Seth-Smith, p. 124.

49. John Corlett in the *Sporting Times*, in Spencer, pp. 121, 123.

50. Seth-Smith, pp. 154, 154–5.

51. Seth-Smith, p. 175.

52. Hibbert, p. 143.

53. Seth-Smith, p. 178.

54. Lee, p. 579.

55. Seth-Smith, p. 183.

56. Marsh, p. 115.

57. 24 June 1896. Lord Marcus Beresford to Richard Marsh, in Seth-Smith, p.159.

58. T. Rennell, *The Last Days of Glory*, Viking, London, 2000, p. 94, in Hattersley, p. 461.

59. Leslie, p. 120.

60. Lee, p. 585.

61. Leslie, p. 120.

62. Magnus, p. 245.

Chapter 6: 'He Is No Better; He Is Much the Same'

1. Shannon, p. 92.

2. Antony Taylor, *'Down with the Crown': British Anti-monarchism and Debates about Royalty since 1790*, Reaktion Books, London, 1999, pp. 92, 85, 82, 64, 105.

3. Hough, p. 139.

4. Taylor, p. 105.

5. Wilson, *The Victorians*, p. 447.

6. Hypatia Bradlaugh Bonner, *Charles Bradlaugh*, T. Fisher Unwin, 1908, in Cowles, p. 102.

7. Taylor, p. 80.

8. Longford, p. 379.

9. Hough, p. 137.

10. Roger Fulford (ed.), *Darling Child: Private Correspondence of Queen Victoria and the Crown Princess of Prussia 1871–1878*, Evans Brothers, London, 1976, p. 262, in Elizabeth Hamilton, *The Warwickshire Scandal*, Michael Russell, London, 1999, p. 370.

11. Magnus, p. 108.

12. Hamilton, pp. 369, 142, 141.

13. Hamilton, pp. 14, 38–9, 70, 71.

14. Hamilton, pp. 111, 56, 82–3.

15. Hamilton, see pp. 102–6.

16. Hamilton, pp. 111, 116, 165, 345.

17. Magnus, p. 108.

18. Weintraub, p. 167.

19. Cowles, pp. 88–9.

20. *The Times*, 23 February 1870, in Cowles, p. 89.

21. Weintraub, p. 168.

22. Hibbert, p. 107.

23. Magnus, pp. 108–9.

24. Hibbert, p. 107.

25. T.G. Otte (ed. Agatha Ramm), *The Gladstone-Granville Correspondence 1868–1876*, Vol. 2, Frank Cass, London, p. 261, in Magnus, p. 113.

26. Cowles, p. 108.

27. Weintraub, p. 184.

28. Battiscombe, p. 114.

29. Weintraub, p. 181.

30. Battiscombe, pp. 114, 116, 117.

31. Lady Macclesfield, in Battiscombe, p. 115.

32. Hibbert, pp. 112–13.

33. Battiscombe, p. 116.

34. Weintraub, p. 182.

35. 10 December 1871. William Plomer (ed.), *Kilvert's Diary*, Vol. 2, Jonathan Cape, London, 1969, pp. 95–6.

36. *The Times*, 11 December 1871, in Battiscombe, p. 117; Hibbert, p. 113.

37. Cresswell, pp. 187, 188.

38. Hough, pp. 145–6.

39. Plomer (ed.), p. 98.

40. Magnus, p. 116.

41. Battiscombe, pp. 119, 120.

42. Hibbert, p. 115; *The Times*, in Hibbert, p. 116.

43. Weintraub, p. 190.

44. Hibbert, p. 116.

45. Cresswell, p. 198.

Chapter 7: Unparalleled Opportunities

1. Hattersley, p. 21.

2. Leslie, pp. 61, 64, 59.

3. Prince of Wales's diary and Lincolnshire Papers, in Magnus, p. 141.

4. Leslie, pp. 59–60.

5. Hibbert, p. 137.

6. Battiscombe, p. 134.

7. Magnus, p. 145.

8. Hough, p. 166.

9. Magnus, pp. 146–7; Magnus, pp. 147, 148.

10. Weintraub, p. 246.

11. Leslie, p. 64.

12. Countess of Warwick, *Afterthoughts*, p. 81.

13. Leslie, p. 169.

14. Hibbert, pp. 140, 139.

15. Henry Blyth, *Skittles: The Last Victorian Courtesan*, Rupert Hart-Davis, London, 1970, pp. 49, 55, 121.

16. Weintraub, p. 203.

17. Leslie, pp. 162, 140, 2.

18. Juliet Nicolson, *The Perfect Summer: Dancing into the Shadow in England in 1911*, John Murray, London, 2006, p. 75.

19. Leslie, p. 4, 45.

20. Sir Frederick Ponsonby, *Recollections of Three Reigns*, Eyre and Spottiswoode, London, 1951, in Aronson, p. 39.

21. Leslie, p. 69.

22. Noel B. Gerson, *Lillie Langtry*, Robert Hale, London, 1972, p. 9.

23. Laura Beatty, *Lillie Langtry: Manners, Masks, Morals*, Vintage, London, 2000, p. 38.

24. Walford Graham Robertson, *Time Was*, Hamish Hamilton, London, 1931, in Beatty, p. 46.

25. Malcolm Warner in *Millais: Portraits*, National Portrait Gallery, London, 1999, p. 211.

26. Kate Flint in *Millais: Portraits*, p. 197.

27. Frances, Countess of Warwick, *Life's Ebb and Flow*, Hutchinson and Co., London, 1929, p. 46.

28. Margot Asquith, *More Memories*, Cassell, London, 1933, p. 31, in Aronson, p. 24.

29. Aronson, p. 27.

30. Gerson, p. 20.

31. Beatty, pp. 78, 77, 87.

32. Wilson, *The Victorians*, p. 399.

33. James Brough, *The Prince and the Lily*, Hodder and Stoughton, London, 1975, pp. 167–8.

34. Jane Ridley, *Bertie: A Life of Edward VII*, Chatto and Windus, London, 2012, p. 206.

35. Beatty, pp. 88–9.

36. Brough, p. 72.

37. Flint, p. 197.

38. Aronson, p. 64.

39. Brough, p. 196.

40. Beatty, pp. 105, 106, 106 footnote.

41. Brough, p. 213.

42. Lillie Langtry, *The Days I Knew*, p. 140, and *New York Times*, 6 November 1880, in Aronson, p. 91.

43. Hibbert, p. 71.

44. Leslie, p. 71.

45. 'My Dear Mrs Langtry . . .' MS Letter from Edward Prince of Wales to Lillie Langtry, 5 August 1885, in Beatty, p. 269.

46. Aronson, p. 116.

47. Battiscombe, p. 172.

48. Hibbert pp. 151, 154.

49. Private information in Aronson, p. 80.

50. Elinor Glyn, *Romantic Adventure*, Ivor Nicolson and Watson, London, 1936, pp. 74–5, in Aronson, p. 130.

51. Countess of Warwick, *Life's Ebb and Flow*, pp. 64, 156, 154, 157, 155.

52. Margaret Blunden, *The Countess of Warwick*, Cassell, London, 1967, p. 66, in Aronson, p. 118.

53. Countess of Warwick, *Afterthoughts*, pp. 97, 4.

54. Countess of Warwick, *Life's Ebb and Flow*, pp. 82–3.

55. Blunden, p. 67, in Aronson, p. 120.

56. *Pearson's Magazine*, October 1916, in Aronson, p. 120.

57. Blunden, p. 68, in Aronson, p. 120.

58. *Pearson's Magazine*, October 1916, in Hibbert, p. 156.

59. Hibbert, p. 156.

60. 16 June 1891, in Battiscombe, p. 183.

61. Magnus, p. 223.

62. Sir Michael Havers, Edward Grayson and Peter Shankland, *The Royal Baccarat Scandal*, William Kimber, London, 1977, pp. 73, 27, 28, 29ff, 216, 33.

63. Magnus, p. 224.

64. Havers, Grayson and Shankland, p. 39.

65. Havers, Grayson and Shankland, pp. 37, 23, 78.

66. Havers, Grayson and Shankland, pp. 39, 32.

67. Magnus, p. 225.

68. Magnus pp. 226, 227.

69. Battiscombe, p. 182.

70. Havers, Grayson and Shankland, pp. 104–5, 106, 107, 108, 240, 246–7, 253.

71. Leslie, p. 134.

72. 12 July 1891. Salisbury Papers 3M, in Hibbert, p. 162; p. 162.

73. Leslie, p. 135.

74. Salisbury Papers 3M, in Hibbert, p. 163.

75. Battiscombe, p. 187.

76. Salisbury Papers 3M, in Magnus p. 235, Hibbert, p. 164.

77. 24 December 1891 and 6 April 1892. Salisbury Papers 3M, in Magnus pp. 235, 236.

78. Battiscombe, pp. 190, 139.

79. Hibbert, p. 182.

80. Battiscombe, p. 143.

81. Leslie, pp. 257, 260, 255.

82. Magnus, pp. 221, 238, 239.

83. Battiscombe, p. 198.

84. Theo Lang, *My Darling Daisy*, Michael Joseph, London, in Hibbert, pp. 164–5.

85. Weintraub, p. 358.

86. Countess of Warwick, *Life's Ebb and Flow*, pp.145, 146.

87. Hibbert, p. 168.

88. Leslie, p. 143.

89. Lady Warwick to Frank Harris, *Pearson's Magazine*, in Blunden, p. 91.

Chapter 8: Abroad

1. Lee, p. 403.

2. B. Balfour, *Lord Lytton's Indian Administration, 1899*, p. 110, in Piers Brendon, *The Decline and Fall of the British Empire 1781–1997*, Jonathan Cape, London, 2007, p. 232.

3. Longford, p. 427, in Brendon, p. 137.

4. Lee, p. 404.

5. Hibbert, p. 135.

6. Lee, pp. 374, 375, 376.

7. Hibbert, p. 127.

8. Weintraub, pp. 214–16, 220, 221.

9. Lee, p. 399.

10. Brendon, p. 132.

11. G.M. Young, *Early Victorian England 1830–1865*, Vol. 1, pp. 404–5, in David Newsome, *The Victorian World Picture*, John Murray, London, 1997, p. 108.

12. James Morris, *Pax Britannica: The Climax of an Empire*, Faber and Faber, London, 1968, p. 137.

13. R.S.S. Baden-Powell, *Indian Memories*, Herbert Jenkins, London, 1915, in Brendon, p. 125.

14. Weintraub, pp. 232, 238, 224.

15. Earl Grey Papers, MSS, pp. 216–17, in Hibbert, pp. 132–3; 130.

16. Weintraub, pp. 228, 226, 227.

17. Magnus, p. 140; 137.

18. Weintraub, p. 224.

19. Magnus, p. 140.

20. Weintraub, p. 237.

21. 26 March, 8 February 1876, in Lee, pp. 392 footnote, 393.

22. Lord Napier to the Queen, 28 January 1876, in Lee, pp. 388, 392 footnote.

23. Weintraub, p. 240.

24. Simon Heffer, *Power and Place*, Weidenfeld and Nicolson, London, 1998, p. 21, in Hattersley, pp. 18–19.

25. Francis Knollys to Edward Hamilton, in Hibbert, p. 146.

26. Heffer p. 35, in Hattersley, p. 19.

27. Gordon Brook-Shepherd, *Uncle of Europe*, Collins, London, 1975, p. 70.

28. Lee, pp. 245, 346.

29. Benedetta Craveri, tr. Teresa Waugh, *The Age of Conversation*, New York Review of Books, New York, 2005, p. 295.

30. Lee, pp. 347–8.

31. Magnus, p. 155.

32. X. Paoli, *My Royal Clients*, Hodder and Stoughton, London, 1911, p. 206, in Allfrey, p. 46.

33. Newton's *Life of Lord Lyons*, Vol. 2, p. 152, in Lee, p. 367.

34. Allfrey, p. 46.

35. Salisbury Papers 3M, in Magnus, p. 155.

36. Lee, p. 357.

37. Weintraub, p. 253.

38. Lee, pp. 358, 359.

39. Lee, pp. 360, 457–58, 470.

40. Brendon, p. 170.

41. Lee, p. 465.

42. Lytton Strachey, *Eminent Victorians*, Chatto and Windus, London, 1921 edition, p. 299.

43. Hibbert, p. 146.

44. Lee, pp. 442, 443, 444.

45. Francis Neilson, 'Edward VII and the Entente Cordiale' in *The American Journal of Economics and Sociology*, Vol. 17, 1957, p. 99.

46. Countess of Warwick, *Afterthoughts*, pp. 40–1.

47. Brook-Shepherd, p. 84.

48. Magnus, p. 210.

49. Lee, p. 651.

50. Wilson, *After the Victorians*, p. 10.

51. Brook-Shepherd, p. 87.

52. Lee, pp. 756, 759, 777.

53. 6 April 1900. The Prince to Sir Frank Lascelles, in Lee, pp. 777, 778.

54. Magnus, p. 197.

55. June Rose, *Mistress of Montmartre: A Life of Susanne Valadon*, Richard Cohen, London, 1998, p. 90.

56. Weintraub, p. 310.

57. Rose, p. 97.

58. Weintraub, p. 310.

59. Hibbert, p. 236.

60. Weintraub, p. 311.

61. Magnus, p. 177.

62. Leslie, pp. 206, 208.

63. Diana Souhami, *Mrs Keppel and Her Daughter*, Flamingo, London, 1997, p. 8.

64. Aronson, p. 210.

65. Leslie, p. 201.

66. Battiscombe, p. 209.

67. Osbert Sitwell, *Great Morning*, The Reprint Society, London, 1949, p. 217.

68. Weintraub, pp. 365, 363.

69. Magnus, p. 260.

70. Lord Esher to his son Maurice, July 1905, in *Journal and Letters of Reginald Esher*; Violet Trefusis, 'Triple Violette', unpublished memoir in French (Beinecke Library), in Souhami, pp. 61, 48.

71. Hibbert, *Queen Victoria in Her Letters and Journals*, John Murray, London, 1984, p. 335, in Brendon, pp. 209, 215.

72. Georgina Battiscombe, *Mrs Gladstone: The Portrait of a Marriage*, Constable, London, 1956, p. 229.

73. Weintraub, pp. 369, 371.

74. James Pope-Hennessy, *Queen Mary 1867–1953*, Allen and Unwin, London, 1959, p. 361, in Aronson, p. 196.

75. Weintraub, pp. 383, 385, 386.

76. Magnus, p. 270.

77. Weintraub, p. 389.

Edward VIII

Chapter 9: Weighed in the Balance

1. Duke of Windsor, *A King's Story*, Cassell, London, 1951, p. 15.

2. Queen Alexandra to Duchess of York, 19 July 1901, in James Pope-Hennessy, pp. 394–5.

3. Battiscombe, pp. 240, 241.

4. Duke of Windsor, p. 15.

5. Battiscombe, p. 241.

6. Hector Bolitho, *Edward VIII: His Life and Reign*, Eyre and Spottiswoode, London, 1937, p. 9.

7. Queen Alexandra to Duchess of York, in Pope-Hennessy, pp. 394, 299.

8. Duchess of York, 28 October 1896. Philip Ziegler, *King Edward VIII*, Collins, London, 1991 edition, p. 7.

9. J. Ellis (ed.), *Thatched with Gold: The Memoirs of Mabell, Countess of Airlie*, Hutchinson, London, 1962, p. 112, in Peter Gordon and Denis Lawton, *Royal Education: Past, Present and Future*, Frank Cass, London, 1999, p. 179.

10. Duke of Windsor, p. 1.

11. 24 June 1894. Ziegler, p. 5.

12. Pope-Hennessy, pp. 301–2.

13. *The Times*, 25 June 1894, in Frances Donaldson, Edward VIII, Weidenfeld and Nicolson, London, 1974, p. 6.

14. Grand Duchess of Mecklenburg-Strelitz to Duchess of Teck, 25 June 1894, in Pope-Hennessy, pp. 299–300.

15. Ziegler, p. 5.

16. Pope-Hennessy, p. 301.

17. Harold Nicolson, *Diaries and Letters 1945–62*, Collins, London, 1971, p. 164, in Donaldson, p. 4.

18. Pope-Hennessy, p. 391.

19. Harold Nicolson, *King George V: His Life and Reign*, Constable, London, 1952, p. 51, in Donaldson, p. 5.

20. J.G. Lockhart, *Cosmo Gordon Lang*, Hodder and Stoughton, London, 1949, p. 143, in Kenneth Rose, *King George V*, Weidenfeld and Nicolson, London, 1983, p. 97.

21. Jonathan Gathorne-Hardy, *The Rise and Fall of the British Nanny*, Hodder and Stoughton, London, 1972, p. 78.

22. Duke of Windsor, p. 7.

23. Gathorne-Hardy, p. 78.

24. Duke of Windsor, p. 7.

25. Osbert Sitwell, *Left Hand, Right Hand*, The Reprint Society, London, 1946, p. 97.

26. John W. Wheeler-Bennett, *King George VI: His Life and Reign*, Macmillan, London, 1958, p. 17.

27. Duke of Windsor, pp. 24, 25, 17.

28. 11 June 1949. Ziegler, p. 259.

29. Duke of Windsor, pp. 17–18.

30. David Newsome, *Godliness and Good Learning: Four Studies on a Victorian Ideal*, John Murray, London, 1961, p. 206.

31. Donaldson, p. 18.

32. Ziegler, p. 14.

33. Wheeler-Bennett, p. 24 and footnote (a).

34. Sir Shane Leslie to the *Sunday Times*, 23 August 1959, in Ziegler, p. 14.

35. Wheeler-Bennett, p. 25.

36. Duke of Windsor, pp. 23–4.

37. P. Gibbs, *George the Faithful: The Life and Times of George V*, Hutchinson, London, 1936, p. 19, in Gordon and Lawton, p. 177.

38. Duke of Windsor, pp. 37–9, 39, 40, 29, 42, 28–9, 29–30, 34–5, 57.

39. Harold Nicolson Diary, 20 March 1953. Nicolson papers, in Ziegler, p. 15.

40. Prince of Wales to Grand Duchess of Mecklenburg-Strelitz, 3 September 1905, 10 February 1907, in Pope-Hennessy, pp. 393, 394.

41. 28 October 1942. Sir A. Lascelles Diary LASL 1/2/1, in Ziegler, p. 17.

42. David Newsome, *On the Edge of Paradise: A.C. Benson, the Diarist,* John Murray, London, 1980, p. 68.

43. David Cannadine, *History in Our Time*, Yale University Press, New Haven and London, 1998, p. 48.

44. 10 December 1936. Ziegler, p. 18.

45. James Pope-Hennessy, *A Lonely Business*, Weidenfeld and Nicolson, London, p. 214, in Ziegler, p. 9.

46. Pope-Hennessy, *Queen Mary*, p. 392.

47. Duke of Windsor, pp. 27, 42.

48. Rose, pp. 54, 226.

49. Duke of Windsor, p. 26.

50. Donaldson, p. 10.

51. Rose, p. 55.

52. Pope-Hennessy, *Queen Mary*, p. 431.

53. Nicolson, *King George V: His Life and Reign*, p. 154, in Donaldson, p. 34 footnote.

54. Wilson, *After the Victorians*, pp. 53, 55.

55. Hattersley, pp. 218–19.

56. J. Bryan III and Charles J.V. Murphy, *The Windsor Story*, Granada, London, 1979, p. xvi, in Ziegler, p. 9.

57. James Lees-Milne, *Harold Nicolson*, Vol. 2, Chatto and Windus, London, 1981, pp. 230, 235, in Ziegler, p. 8.

58. Randolph S. Churchill, *Lord Derby: King of Lancashire*, Heinemann, London, 1959, p. 159, in Rose, p. 57.

59. Duke of Windsor, pp. 42, 43, 44, 14, 13.

60. Wheeler-Bennett, p. 19 footnote.

61. Duke of Windsor, p. 10.

62. Wilson, *The Victorians*, p. 505.

63. Duke of Windsor, pp. 13, 78, 22.

64. 28 October 1907. 10 May 1898. Queen Victoria's Diary, in Ziegler, pp. 16, 17.

65. *The Memoirs of the Aga Khan*, Cassell and Company, London, 1954, p. 244, in Ziegler, p. 17.

66. *Journals and Letters of Reginald Viscount Esher*, Vol. 2, Nicolson and Watson, London, 1934, p. 140, in Donaldson, p. 20.

67. Ziegler, pp. 17–18.

68. Duke of Windsor, pp. 47, 48, 51.

Chapter 10: 'The Navy Will Teach David'

1. Duke of Windsor, pp. 62, 56.

2. Magnus, p. 30.

3. 5 February 1908. Ziegler, p. 21.

4. Bolitho, p. 16.

5. A Retired Naval Officer, 'Life at Osborne', in *How to Become a Naval Officer, 1916*, pp. 29–30, in Michael Partridge, *The Royal Naval College, Osborne*, Sutton Publishing, Stroud, 1999, pp. 23, 24, 111.

6. Captain C.H. Drake, interview, 28 August 1987, IWM SA 9906/1/1, in Partridge, p. 116; S.W.C. Pack, *Britannia at Dartmouth*, Alvin Redman, London, 1966, p. 135, in Partridge, pp. 2, 24.

7. Duke of Windsor, p. 59.

8. Partridge, pp. 30, 32.

9. Duke of Windsor, pp. 61, 59, 62.

10. Cdr L. Gowlland, interview, 11 August 1987, IWM SA 9871/1/1, in Partridge, p. 97; A.W. Ewing, *The Entry and Training of Naval Officers*, HMSO, London, 1914, p. 1, in Partridge, p. 34.

11. Duke of Windsor, pp. 58, 59.

12. 5 May 1907. Ziegler, p. 20.

13. Cdr H.L. Jenkins, interview, 25 August 1987, IWM SA 9896/2/1, in Partridge, p. 57.

14. E.A. Hughes, *The Royal Naval College, Dartmouth*, Winchester Publications, London, 1950, p. 50, in Wheeler-Bennett, p. 59 footnote.

15. Duke of Windsor, pp. 62–3.

16. Ziegler, p. 23.

17. Duke of Windsor, pp. 63, 63–4, 64.

18. Cdr R.H. Barrett, interview, 4 August 1987, IWM SA 9868/1/1, in Partridge, p. 72.

19. Bolitho, p. 13.

20. Cdr W.D. Bradbury, interview, 21 August 1987, IWM SA 9898/2/1, in Partridge, p. 88; Cdr H.D.G. de Chair, interview, IWM SA 9905/1/1, in Partridge, p. 77.

21. Duke of Windsor, p. 65.

22. Bolitho, p. 11.

23. Ziegler, p. 21.

24. Duke of Windsor, pp. 60, 64.

25. Wheeler-Bennett, p. 40.

26. Duke of Windsor, p. 61.

27. Brig C.W.P. Richardson, interview, 13 August 1987, IWM SA 9873/1/1, in Partridge, pp. 133–4, 165.

28. Duke of Windsor, pp. 65, 66, 67, 68.

29. Donaldson, p. 34.

30. Duke of Windsor, pp. 72, 73.

31. 6 October 1910. Ziegler, p. 24.

32. 20 November 1910. Ziegler, p. 25.

33. See Rose, pp. 112–15.

34. 20 November 1910. Ziegler, p. 25.

35. Duke of Windsor, pp. 75, 76, 77.

36. Ziegler, pp. 26, 79.

37. Sir Henry Luke, *Cities and Men*, Geoffrey Bles, London, 1953, p. 208, in Ziegler, p. 27.

38. Duke of Windsor, p. 79.

39. Bolitho, p. 14, in Ziegler, p. 28.

40. See Ziegler, pp. 28–9; 2 November 1911. Ziegler, p. 29.

41. 29 September 1911. Ziegler, p. 29.

42. Duke of Windsor, p. 80.

Chapter 11: 'Learning . . . of Men'

1. George V to Edward, Prince of Wales, 20 April 1913, in Ziegler, p. 31.

2. Kirsty McLeod, *Battle Royal: Edward VIII and George IV, Brother Against Brother*, Constable, London, 2000 edition, p. 36.

3. Duke of Windsor, pp. 61, 82, 83, 74, 85, *Family Album*, Cassell, London, 1960, pp. 86, 87.

4. Hansell to Queen Mary, 16 April 1912. Ziegler, p. 32.

5. Duke of Windsor, pp. 91, 89.

6. Prince of Wales's Diary, 11 May 1912, in Ziegler, p. 33; Sir George Arthur (tr. and adapted), *The Memoirs of Raymond Poincaré*, Vol. 1, Heinemann, London, 1926, pp. 96–7, in Ziegler, p. 34.

7. Duke of Windsor, pp. 91, 92.

8. Viscount Esher, Vol. 3, pp. 108–9, in Donaldson, p. 42.

9. Duke of Windsor, p. 96.

10. 2 December 1912. Quoted in Kenneth Carlisle, *Wyken: The Life of a Small Suffolk Estate*, Snakeshead Press, Stanton, 2007, p. 90.

11. Duke of Windsor, pp. 94, 95, 93.

12. Bolitho, pp. 36, 37.

13. 18 October 1913. Prince of Wales's Diary, in Ziegler, pp. 40, 41.

14. Carlisle, p. 91.

15. Donald McLachlan, *In the Chair: Barrington-Ward of The Times*, Weidenfeld and Nicolson, London, 1971, p. 36, in Ziegler, p. 37.

16. Duke of Windsor, p. 95.

17. Dina Hood, *Working for the Windsors*, Allan Wingate, London, 1957, p. 136, in Donaldson, p. 40.

18. Duke of Windsor, pp. 81–2.

19. Ziegler, p. 166.

20. 15 December 1913, 22 January, 29 April 1914, in Ziegler, p. 41.

21. 4 December 1911. Prince of Wales's Diary, in Ziegler, p. 38.

22. Duke of Windsor, p. 102.

23. 14 January 1912. Ziegler, p. 38.

24. Duke of Windsor, pp. 102–3.

25. Prince to Godfrey Thomas, 11 March 1914. Thomas papers in Ziegler, p. 39.

26. J. Brett Langstaff, *Oxford – 1914*, Vantage Press, New York, 1965, p. 196, in Donaldson, p. 46.

27. 20 April 1913. Ziegler, p. 31.

28. Duke of Windsor, pp. 101, 102.

29. 16 July 1914. Prince of Wales's Diary, in Ziegler, p. 45.

30. John Vincent (ed.), *The Crawford Papers*, Manchester University Press, Manchester, 1984, p. 319, in Ziegler, p. 39.

31. Duke of Windsor, pp. 97, 99.

32. Philipp Blom, *The Vertigo Years: Change and Culture in the West, 1900–1914*, Weidenfeld and Nicolson, London, 2008, p. 179.

33. Virginia Cowles, *1913: The Defiant Swansong*, Weidenfeld and Nicolson, London, 1967, pp. 84, 64.

34. Duke of Windsor, pp. 99–100.

35. Blom, pp. 2, 380–1, 181–2.

36. Duke of Windsor, pp. 103, 104, 103, 106.

37. 5 August 1914. Ziegler, p. 49.

38. Duke of Windsor, p. 109.

39. 10 August 1914. Prince of Wales's Diary, in Ziegler, p. 50.

40. Carlisle, p. 99.

41. Duke of Windsor, p. 109.

42. 16 September 1914. Ziegler, pp. 50–51.

43. Prince to Godfrey Thomas, 23 August 1914. Thomas papers, in Ziegler, p. 53.

44. Prince to George V, 10 August 1914. Ziegler, p. 53.

45. Prince to W.E. Houston-Boswell, 7 May 1915. Ziegler, p. 53.

46. Michael S. Neiberg, *Fighting the Great War: A Global History*, Harvard University Press, Cambridge, MA, and London, 2005, p. 80.

47. Duke of Windsor, pp. 110, 111.

48. 14 November 1914. Ziegler, p. 53.

49. 27 January 1915. Prince of Wales's Diary, in Ziegler, p. 54.

50. Lord Esher, p. 207, in Donaldson, p. 50.

51. Duke of Windsor, pp. 112–13.

52. Prince of Wales to Lady Coke, 18 March 1915. Rose, p. 219.

53. Duke of Windsor, p. 114.

54. Ziegler, p. 59.

55. 22 December 1914. Prince of Wales's Diary, in Ziegler, p. 58; 24 June 1915, Coke papers, in Ziegler, p. 60.

56. Randolph Churchill and Martin Gilbert, *Winston Churchill, Companion Volumes,* Vol. 3, Heineman, London, 2002, p. 313, in Roy Jenkins, *Churchill*, Macmillan, London, 2001, p. 262.

57. Prince to Queen Mary, 7 June 1915. Ziegler, p. 59; 16 June 1916. Thomas papers, in Ziegler, p. 59.

58. Jenkins, p. 270.

59. Prince to Queen Mary, 7 July 1915. Ziegler, p. 61.

60. Neiberg, p. 87.

61. 16 June 1915. Thomas papers, in Ziegler, p. 60.

62. Lord Chandos, *From Peace to War*, The Bodley Head, London, 1968, p. 137, in Donaldson, p. 51.

63. Bolitho, p. 59.

64. Oliver Lyttelton, *Viscount Chandos, The Memoirs of Lord Chandos*, The Bodley Head, London, 1962, pp. 46–7, in Donaldson, p. 51.

65. Duke of Windsor, p. 124.

66. Godfrey Thomas diary. Thomas papers, 18 December 1914. Ziegler, p. 62; 18 August 1915. Prince of Wales's Diary, in Ziegler, p. 63.

67. See Neiberg, pp. 90–92.

68. Duke of Windsor, pp. 115–16, 117, 117–18.

69. Bolitho, p. 72.

70. Rose, p. 182.

71. Pope-Hennessy, p. 502.

72. 22 January 1916, in Ziegler, p. 68.

73. Charles Miller, quoted from Memorial at the Irish Peace Park, Messines, Belgium, in Neiberg, p. 269.

74. Prince to Queen Mary, 18 March 1916; 30 March 1916. Coke papers, in Ziegler, p. 69.

75. Bolitho, p. 63.

76. Prince to George V, 18 March 1916. Mary Walrond to Queen Mary, 12 June 1916. Ziegler, p. 70.

77. Bolitho, pp. 122, 72–3.

78. 2 April 1916. Thomas papers, in Ziegler, p. 71; 10 April 1916. Prince of Wales's diary, in Ziegler, p. 72.

79. Duke of Windsor, pp. 121, 122.

80. Prince of Wales's diary, in Ziegler, pp. 75, 89.

81. 7 March 1917. Ziegler, p. 78.

82. Stamfordham to George V, 21 September 1917. Ziegler, p. 80.

83. Duke of Windsor, p. 123.

84. Sir James Rennal Rodd, *Social and Diplomatic Memoirs (Third Series)*, Edward Arnold, London, 1925, pp. 360–1; Queen Mary to Prince, 2 June 1918. Ziegler, p. 82.

85. 1 November 1918. Piers Legh papers, in Ziegler, p. 84.

86. Prince to George V, 8 January 1919. Ziegler, p. 85.

87. Duke of Windsor, p. 125.

88. Edward Windsor, *Speeches by H.R.H. the Prince of Wales 1912–1926*, Hodder and Stoughton, London, 1927, p. 4.

Chapter 12: 'A Desolating Gift'

1. Rupert Godfrey (ed.), *Letters from a Prince: Edward, Prince of Wales to Mrs Freda Dudley Ward, March 1918–January 1921*, Little, Brown and Company, London, 1998, pp. 8, 20, 21, 26, 166, 169, 146, 147.

2. Donaldson, p. 58.

3. Lady Cynthia Asquith, *Diaries 1915–1918*, Hutchinson, London, 1968, p. 412, in Ziegler, p. 95.

4. 22 June 1919, in Godfrey (ed.), p. 153.

5. Prince to Lady Coke, 27 May 1917. Coke papers, in Ziegler, p. 91.

6. Donaldson papers, in Ziegler, p. 91.

7. 27 December, 29 December 1920, 3 January 1920, in Godfrey (ed.), pp. 390, 391, 243.

8. Ziegler, pp. 92, 93.

9. 21 September 1919, 19 February 1919, in Godfrey (ed.), pp. 194, 140–1.

10. 7 September 1917. Ziegler, p. 94.

11. Duke of Windsor, p. 132.

12. *Thatched with Gold: The Memoirs of Mabell, Countess of Airlie*, p. 144, in Donaldson, p. 66.

13. Duke of Windsor, p. 132.

14. Bolitho, p. 210.

15. Duke of Windsor, pp. 132, 136, 130.

16. Dan Todman, *The Great War: Myth and Memory*, Hambledon Continuum, London, 2005, p. 129.

17. Duke of Windsor, pp. 128, 129.

18. Wilson, *After the Victorians*, pp. 225–6.

19. 19 February 1919. Ziegler, p. 110; *The Times*, 25 June 1919, in Ziegler, p. 111.

20. 10 June 1919, in Godfrey (ed.), p. 151.

21. Ziegler, p. 113.

22. Edward Windsor, *Speeches*, pp. 35–6.

23. Duke of Windsor, pp. 135, 137.

24. 28 July 1918, in Godfrey (ed.), p. 63.

25. Duke of Windsor, p. 134.

26. 25 December 1919. Thomas papers, in Ziegler, p. 108.

27. Duke of Windsor, p. 133.

28. Donaldson, p. 64.

29. Duke of Windsor, pp. 133–4.

30. 5 August 1919, 6 August 1919, 7 August 1919, in Godfrey (ed.), pp. 166, 167, 169.

31. Duke of Windsor, p. 137.

32. 12 October 1919, 13 August 1919, 16 August 1919, in Godfrey (ed.), pp. 208, 171, 172.

33. Duke of Windsor, p. 138.

34. 13 August 1919, 23 August 1919, in Godfrey (ed.), pp. 171, 176.

35. Duke of Windsor, pp. 139, 140.

36. 26 August 1919, 27 August 1919, 28 August 1919, in Godfrey (ed.), pp. 177, 178.

37. Ziegler, p. 118.

38. Duke of Windsor, p. 143.

39. 8 September 1919, 31 August 1919, in Godfrey (ed.), pp. 184, 181.

40. Donaldson, p. 70.

41. 4 September 1919, 30 August 1919, 6 September 1919, 5 September 1919, 17 September 1919, in Godfrey (ed.), see pp. 180–3, 189–90.

42. Duke of Windsor, p. 141.

43. 7 September 1919, in Godfrey (ed.), p. 183.

44. Edward Windsor, *Speeches*, p. 19.

45. Prince to George V, 6 October 1919. Ziegler, pp. 119–20.

46. Duke of Windsor, pp. 143, 144.

47. 19 September 1919, 5 November 1919, 2 October 1919, 20 October 1919, 27 September 1919, 24 October 1919, in Godfrey (ed.), pp. 191, 220, 201, 221–2, 198, 214–15.

48. Martin Pugh, *We Danced All Night: A Social History of Britain Between the Wars*, The Bodley Head, London, 2008, p. 169.

49. Duke of Windsor, pp. 145, 146, 147, 148, 151.

50. 23 December 1919, 24 December 1919, in Godfrey (ed.), pp. 227, 229.

51. 25 December 1919. Thomas papers, in Ziegler, p. 122.

52. 25 December 1919, 29 December 1919, in Godfrey (ed.) pp. 230, 236.

53. January 1920. Copy in Thomas papers. Ziegler, p. 123.

54. 26 December 1919, 4 January 1920, 3 January 1920, 26 December 1919, in Godfrey (ed.), pp. 231, 244, 241–2, 231, 232.

55. Duke of Windsor, p. 152.

56. A.J.P. Taylor, *Lloyd George, A Diary*, Hutchinson, London, 1971, p. 178, in Donaldson, pp. 77, 75.

57. 16 March 1920, in Godfrey (ed.), p. 252.

58. Curzon to Grace Curzon, 16 March 1920. Curzon papers, in Rose, pp. 303–4.

59. 17 March 1920, 20 March 1920, 11 April 1920, 22 March 1920, in Godfrey (ed.), pp. 256, 258–9, 273, 259.

60. 30 March 1920. Edward Grigg diary. Grigg papers, in Ziegler, p. 125.

61. Bolitho, p. 99.

62. 17 April 1920, 18 April 1920, in Godfrey (ed.), pp. 277, 280, 279.

63. Donaldson, p. 82.

64. Duke of Windsor, p. 160.

65. Ziegler, p. 126.

66. 25 April 1920, in Godfrey (ed.), pp. 284–5.

67. 23 April 1920. 27 April 1920. Ziegler, p. 126.

68. 4 May 1920. Edward Grigg diary. Grigg papers, in Ziegler, p. 127.

69. Bolitho, p. 106.

70. 9 May 1920, 4 May 1920, 22 May 1920, 9 May 1920, in Godfrey (ed.), pp. 293, 290, 300, 292–3.

71. Duke of Windsor, p. 155.

72. Bede Clifford, *Proconsul*, Evans Brothers, London, 1964, in Ziegler, p. 128.

73. Duke of Windsor, p. 156.

74. Godfrey (ed.), picture caption, p. 343.

75. Duke of Windsor, p. 154.

76. 27 May 1920, in Godfrey (ed.), p. 309.

77. Duke of Windsor, p. 154.

78. Bolitho, p. 117.

79. Duke of Windsor, pp. 156–7, 158.

80. Letter to the author from Mr Ian Scott. Donaldson, p. 81.

81. Duke of Windsor, p. 159.

82. 1 June 1920, in Godfrey (ed.), p. 314.

83. Duke of Windsor, p. 158.

84. Donaldson, p. 80.

85. 10 June 1920, 25 June 1920, 24 June 1920, 27 June 1920, 26 June 1920, 27 June 1920, in Godfrey (ed.), pp. 319, 331, 329, 336, 333, 334, 336.

86. Thomas to Alan Lascelles, December 1950. Ziegler, p. 130.

87. 13 July 1920, 1 August 1920, 10 July 1920, 11 July 1920, 5 July 1920, in Godfrey (ed.), pp. 349, 360, 347, 348, 343.

88. Philip Ziegler (ed.), *The Diaries of Lord Louis Mountbatten, 1920–1922*, Collins, London, 1987, p. 130.

89. 4 August 1920. Ziegler, p. 129.

90. 5 July 1920, in Godfrey (ed.), p. 344.

91. 11 June 1920. Ziegler, p. 130.

92. 18 July 1920, in Godfrey (ed.), p. 354.

93. 3 August 1920. Ziegler, pp. 130, 131.

94. 27 July 1920, in Godfrey (ed.), p. 358.

95. 5 September 1920. 9 September 1920. 24 June 1920. Ziegler, p. 132.

96. Duke of Windsor, p. 162.

97. Donaldson, p. 84.

98. Pugh, pp. 13, 77.

99. Duke of Windsor, p. 162.

100. Donaldson, p. 84.

101. 12 January 1921, in Godfrey (ed.), p. 399.

102. Brendon, p. 264.

103. Halsey to Lascelles, 1 March 1922. Lascelles papers LASL 3/5/6; Ziegler (ed.), Diaries of Lord Louis Mountbatten, p. 263, in Ziegler, p. 138.

104. Bolitho, p. 145.

105. Professor Rushbrook Williams in a letter to the author. Donaldson, p. 96.

106. Duke of Windsor, p. 172.

107. Bolitho, pp. 149, 157.

108. Donaldson, p. 89.

109. Duke of Windsor, p. 172.

110. 11 December 1921. Dudley Ward papers, in Ziegler, pp. 137, 138.

111. Bolitho, p. 160.

112. Katherine Mayo, *Mother India*, Jonathan Cape, London, 1935, in Bolitho, p. 147.

113. Duke of Windsor, p. 173.

114. Bolitho, pp. 160–1.

115. Duke of Windsor, pp. 171–2, 174.

116. 6 February 1922. Dudley Ward papers, in Ziegler, pp. 142, 143.

117. Donaldson, p. 89.

118. Duke of Windsor, p. 176.

119. *The Times*, 8 April 1922, in Donaldson, p. 94.

120. Duke of Windsor, pp. 173–4.

121. Donaldson, pp. 91, 95; Professor Rushbrook Williams, in Donaldson, p. 96.

122. Duke of Windsor, p. 181.

123. Viscount Peel to Lord Reading. 6 April 1922. IO EUR E 238/5/2, in Ziegler, p. 144.

Chapter 13: Losing Heart

1. Duke of Windsor, p. 188.

2. Donaldson, p. 103.

3. Michael Arlen, *The Green Hat*, Heinemann, London, 1924, in Alison Adburgham, *A Punch History of Manners and Modes*, Hutchinson, London, 1961, pp. 288, 287, 298.

4. John Montgomery, *The Twenties: An Informal Social History*, George Allen and Unwin, London, 1957, p. 167.

5. Adburgham, pp. 313, 311.

6. Montgomery, p. 199.

7. Robert Graves and Alan Hodge, *The Long Weekend: A Social History of Great Britain 1918–1939*, Faber and Faber, London, 1940, p. 129.

8. Duke of Windsor, p. 191.

9. Graves and Hodge, p. 120.

10. Donaldson, p. 104.

11. Duke of Windsor, p. 191.

12. Arlen, *The Green Hat*, pp. 110–11.

13. Graves and Hodge, pp. 118–19.

14. Montgomery, p. 202.

15. S. Orwell and I. Angus (eds), *The Collected Essays, Journalism and Letters of George Orwell*, Vol. 1, Penguin, Harmondsworth, 1971, p. 530, in Brendon, p. 330.

16. J.M. MacKenzie, *Propaganda and Empire*, Manchester University Press, Manchester, 1984, p. 82, in Brendon, p. 331.

17. James Morris, *Farewell the Trumpets: An Imperial Retreat*, Faber and Faber, London, 1978, pp. 299, 300–1.

18. D. Marquand, *Ramsay MacDonald*, Jonathan Cape, London, 1977, p. 65, in Brendon, p. 333.

19. Morris, p. 302.

20. Brendon, p. 332.

21. Edward Windsor, *Speeches*, pp. 350–51.

22. Duke of Windsor, pp. 183, 187.

23. 26 April 1923. Ziegler, p. 171.

24. Donaldson, pp. 100, 107.

25. Bolitho, p. 213.

26. See Compton Mackenzie, *The Windsor Tapestry*, Chatto and Windus, London, p. vii, in Donaldson, p. 115.

27. 10 July 1922. Dudley Ward papers, in Ziegler, p. 164.

28. Donaldson, p. 110; Helen Hardinge, *Loyal to Three Kings*, William Kimber, London, 1967, p. 68, in Donaldson pp. 112, 114.

29. Prince to Revelstoke, 28 June 1923. Baring papers. DEP 201/18; Crawford Papers, p. 437, in Ziegler, pp. 164, 166.

30. Duke of Windsor, p. 188.

31. Lascelles diary, 29 November 1920. Lascelles papers LASL 1/1/13, in Ziegler, p. 163.

32. Donaldson, p. 90.

33. Duke of Windsor, pp. 192, 193.

34. Bolitho, p. 216.

35. Guy Paget, *Life of Frank Freeman, Huntsman*, Edgar Backus, Leicester, 1948, p. 25, in Zeigler, p. 176.

36. Duke of Windsor, pp. 194, 193.

37. Wigram to Birdwood, 3 February 1926. 6 April 1923. Dudley Ward papers, in Ziegler, p. 176.

38. Duke of Windsor, pp. 195, 196, 240.

39. Bolitho, pp. 220, 221.

40. Duke of Windsor, p. 241.

41. William Pearson-Rogers, *The Flying Prince*, unpublished typescript, p. 125, in Ziegler, p. 177.

42. Thomas to Ronald Waterhouse, 28 September 1923. Kenneth Rose papers, in Ziegler, p. 149.

43. India Office 10 MSS EUR F 112/224a, in Ziegler, p. 150.

44. Memorandum by Bruce Ogilvy. Donaldson papers, in Ziegler, p. 149.

45. Bolitho, p. 226.

46. *New York Times*, 1 and 2 September 1924, in Donaldson, pp. 125, 126.

47. Ziegler, pp. 150–51.

48. Duke of Windsor, pp. 197, 198.

49. Bolitho, p. 227.

50. Duke of Windsor, pp. 198, 220.

51. Lascelles to Legh, 21 and 24 September 1924. Lascelles papers. LASL 3/1/10 and 11, in Ziegler, p. 153.

52. Duke of Windsor, pp. 200, 201.

53. 3 October 1924. Thomas papers, in Ziegler, pp. 153–4.

54. Duke of Windsor, p. 201.

55. Ziegler, p. 155.

56. Duke of Windsor, p. 210.

57. 30 January 1925. Ziegler, p. 156.

58. North to Lascelles, 24 May 1925. Lascelles papers. LASL 3/5/12; 29 June 1925. Ziegler, p. 159.

59. Clifford, p. 136; Godfrey Thomas to Queen Mary, 16 May 1925. Ziegler, p. 157.

60. Bolitho, p. 177.

61. G. Ward-Price, *With the Prince to West Africa*, Gill Publishing Co., London, 1925, p. 43, in Ziegler, p. 156.

62. Duke of Windsor, p. 205.

63. Bolitho, p. 169.

64. Duke of Windsor, p. 206.

65. Bolitho, p. 176.

66. Duke of Windsor, p. 207.

67. Thomas to Ronald Waterhouse, 6 August 1925. Kenneth Rose papers, in Ziegler, p. 158.

68. Bolitho, pp. 183–4.

69. Thomas Boydell, *My Luck Was In*, Stewart, Cape Town, 1948, p. 326, in Ziegler, p. 159.

70. 14 July 1925. Ziegler, p. 160.

71. Duke of Windsor, p. 209.

72. Bolitho, p. 192.

73. Duke of Windsor, p. 210.

74. Bryan III and Murphy, p. 49, in Ziegler, p. 162.

75. Duke of Windsor, p. 217.

76. Anne Perkins, *A Very British Strike 3 May–12 May 1926*, Macmillan, London, 2007 edition, p. 51.

77. Duke of Windsor, p. 218.

78. Perkins, p. 206.

79. Osbert Sitwell, *Laughter in the Next Room*, The Reprint Society edition, London, 1950, p. 210.

80. Duke of Windsor, p. 218.

81. Ziegler, p. 183.

82. Perkins, pp. 77, 152, 229, 242.

83. Duke of Windsor, pp. 218, 219, 228.

84. Robert Rhodes James, *Memoirs of a Conservative*, Weidenfeld and Nicolson, London, 1969, in Perkins, p. 23.

85. Bolitho, p. 203.

86. The Duke of Beaufort, *Memoirs*, Country Life Books, Richmond upon

Thames, 1981, p. 165, in Ziegler, p. 186.

87. Londonderry to Baldwin, 1 February 1929. Baldwin papers 177/48, in Ziegler, p. 185.

88. J. Hanley, *Grey Children, 1937*, Methuen, London, p. vii, in Piers Brendon, *The Dark Valley: A Panorama of the1930s*, Jonathan Cape, London, 2000, p. 167.

89. J.B. Priestley, *English Journey*, Heinemann, London, 1934, p. 319, in Brendon, *The Dark Valley*, p. 166.

90. Rose, p. 381.

91. Duke of Windsor, p. 246.

92. Donaldson, pp. 133, 134.

93. Duke of Windsor, pp. 249, 250, 233, 234, 186–7, 184–5.

94. M. Crawford, *The Little Princesses*, Cassell, London, 1950, p. 94, in Brendon, *The Dark Valley*, pp. 159, 160.

95. M. Bloch, *The Reign and Abdication of Edward VIII*, Bantam, London, 1990, p. 94, in Brendon, *The Dark Valley*, pp. 159, 160.

96. R. Gray, *The King's Wife: Five Queen Consorts*, Secker and Warburg, London, 1990, p. 333, in Brendon, *The Dark Valley*, p. 160.

97. David Cannadine, *In Churchill's Shadow: Confronting the Past in Modern Britain*, Penguin, Harmondsworth, 2003, p. 159.

98. Keith Middlemas and John Barnes, *Baldwin*, Weidenfeld and Nicolson, London, 1969, p. 977, in Ziegler, p. 184; Prince to Queen Mary, 4 August 1925, in Ziegler, pp. 183–4.

99. H.J. Laski, *Parliamentary Government in England: A Commentary*, Allen and Unwin, London, 1938, p. 161, in Cannadine, p. 161.

100. Duke of Windsor, p. 219.

101. 3 August and 8 August 1927. Dudley Ward papers, in Ziegler, p. 187.

102. Duke of Windsor, p. 220.

103. Baldwin to George V, 24 August 1927. Cited in H. Montgomery Hyde, *Baldwin: The Unexpected Prime Minister*, Hart-Davis MacGibbon, London, 1973, pp. 283–4; 28 August 1927. Lascelles papers, LASL 3/2/9, in Ziegler, pp. 188, 189.

104. Duke of Windsor, p. 221.

105. Lascelles to Legh, 15 October 1928. Lascelles papers, LASL 3/3/13, in Ziegler, p. 193; 19 September 1928. Dudley Ward papers, in Ziegler, p. 190; 30 September and 12 October 1928. Lady Grigg's diary. Grigg papers, in Ziegler, p. 191.

106. Duke of Windsor, pp. 222, 211.

107. Baldwin papers, 177/36; 17 November 1928. Lascelles papers, LASL 7/1/2, in Ziegler, p. 192.

108. *An Unpublished Page of History, Monica Baldwin's Diary, 1937*, in Donaldson, p. 138.

109. Rose, p. 356.

110. Duke of Windsor, p. 224.

Chapter 14: New Loves for Old

1. Duke of Windsor, pp. 229, 225, 226.

2. Ziegler, p. 196.

3. Duke of Windsor, pp. 229, 230.

4. Rose, photo caption opposite p. 354.

5. Gloria Vanderbilt and Thelma Lady Furness, *Double Exposure: A Twin Biography*, Frederick Muller, London, 1959, pp. 265, 265–6, 223, 226, 262.

6. 31 March 1930. Dudley Ward papers, in Ziegler, p. 197.

7. Duke of Windsor, p. 235; see pp. 236–7.

8. Duchess of Windsor, *The Heart Has its Reasons: The Memoirs of The Duchess of Windsor*, Michael Joseph, London, 1956, p. 186.

9. Duke of Windsor, p. 237.

10. Vanderbilt and Furness, pp. 269, 278, 271.

11. Charles Higham, *Mrs Simpson: Secret Lives of The Duchess of Windsor*, Macmillan paperback edition, London, 2005, p. 66.

12. Vanderbilt and Furness, p. 281.

13. Duke of Windsor, pp. 239, 240, 241–2.

14. 14 March 1931. John Aird diary, in Ziegler, p. 213.

15. NA 033 4120 Prince of Wales 42, 33.5, 47, in Ziegler, pp. 212, 213.

16. Duke of Windsor, p. 255.

17. Ziegler, p. 224.

18. Higham, p. 77.

19. Vanderbilt and Furness, pp. 286, 291.

20. Higham, p. 87.

21. Vanderbilt and Furness, p. 298.

22. Michael Bloch (ed.), *Wallis and Edward: Letters 1931–1937*, Michael Joseph, London, 1986, p. 110.

23. Duchess of Windsor, p. 201.

24. Vanderbilt and Furness, p. 274.
25. Lord Beaverbrook, *The Abdication of King Edward VIII*, Hamish Hamilton, London, 1966, p. 34, in Donaldson, p. 162.
26. Donaldson, p. 164; *Diaries and Letters of Marie Belloc Lowndes*, Chatto and Windus, London, 1971, pp. 144–6, in Donaldson, p. 164.
27. Duke of Windsor, p. 256.
28. Donaldson, p. 161.
29. 27 October 1934. Bloch (ed.), p. 100.
30. Early April 1936. Victor Cazalet diary, in Ziegler, p. 237.
31. Robert Rhodes James (ed.), *Chips: The Diaries of Sir Henry Channon*, Weidenfeld and Nicolson, London, 1967, p. 35, in Donaldson, pp. 163, 159.
32. Duchess of Windsor, pp. 196, 197.
33. 13 August 1934. John Aird diary, Aird papers, in Ziegler, p. 230.
34. Higham, p. 105; see pp. 105–6.
35. Donaldson, p. 168.
36. Higham, p. 106.
37. Duchess of Windsor, pp. 201–2.
38. 27 October 1934. Michael Bloch (ed.), p. 101.
39. Duchess of Windsor, p. 205.
40. Duke of Windsor, p. 203.
41. Higham, p. 110.
42. 27 November 1934. John Aird diary. Aird papers, in Ziegler, p. 231.
43. Mensdorff Papers. State Archives, Vienna, in Rose, p. 392; 6 November 1935, in Rose p. 390.
44. Duchess of Windsor, p. 208.
45. Michael Bloch (ed.), p. 114.
46. Higham, pp. 113, 114, 94, 99, 111, 123.
47. Duke of Windsor, p. 257.
48. See Higham, pp. 126–9, 116.
49. 15 May 1935. John Aird diary. Aird papers; 11 May 1935. Memo to Wigram. Ziegler, p. 233.
50. Duchess of Windsor, p. 216.
51. Bloch (ed.), pp. 118, 121, 126.
52. Martin Gilbert, *Winston Churchill*, Vol. 5, Heinemann, London, 1976, p. 810, in Bloch (ed.), pp. 108, 128, 139.
53. Duchess of Windsor, p. 218.

54. Duke of Windsor, p. 260.

55. 31 October 1935. Mensdorff Papers, in Rose, p. 392.

56. Duke of Windsor, pp. 258, 260, 261.

57. 17 January 1936. Rose, pp. 400–1.

58. Duke of Windsor, p. 265.

59. 18 January 1936. Michael Bloch (ed.), p. 148.

Bibliography

Adburgham, Alison, *A Punch History of Manners and Modes*, Hutchinson, London, 1961

Allfrey, Anthony, *Edward VII and his Jewish Court*, Weidenfeld and Nicolson, London, 1991

Andrews, Allen, *The Follies of King Edward VII*, Lexington Press, London, 1975

Arlen, Michael, *The Green Hat*, Heinemann, London, 1924

Aronson, Theo, *The King in Love: Edward VII's Mistresses*, John Murray, London, 1988

Battiscombe, Georgina, *Mrs Gladstone: The Portrait of a Marriage*, Constable, London, 1956

——, *Queen Alexandra*, Constable, London, 1969

Beatty, Laura, *Lillie Langtry: Manners, Masks, Morals*, Vintage, London, 2000

Bloch, Michael (ed.), *Wallis and Edward: Letters 1931–1937*, Michael Joseph, London, 1986

Blom, Philipp, *The Vertigo Years: Change and Culture in the West, 1900–1914*, Weidenfeld and Nicolson, 2008

Bolitho, Hector, *Edward VIII: His Life and Reign*, Eyre and Spottiswoode, London, 1937

Brendon, Piers, *The Dark Valley: A Panorama of the 1930s*, Jonathan Cape, London, 2000

——, *The Decline and Fall of the British Empire 1781–1997*, Jonathan Cape, London, 2007

Brook-Shepherd, Gordon, *Uncle of Europe*, Collins, London, 1975

Brough, James, *The Prince and the Lily*, Hodder and Stoughton, London, 1975

Brown, Thomas E., *Attention Deficit Disorder: The Unfocused Mind in Children and Adults*, Yale University Press, New York, 2005

Blyth, Henry, *Skittles: The Last Victorian Courtesan*, Rupert Hart-Davis, London, 1970

Cannadine, David, *History in Our Time*, Yale University Press, New Haven, CT, and London, 1998

——, *In Churchill's Shadow: Confronting the Past in Modern Britain*, Penguin, Harmondsworth, 2003

Carlisle, Kenneth, *Wyken: The Life of a Small Suffolk Estate*, Snakeshead Press, Stanton, 2007

Cathcart, Helen, *Sandringham: The Story of a Royal House*, W.H. Allen, London, 1964

Charlot, Monica, *Victoria: The Young Queen*, Basil Blackwell, Oxford, 1991

Christiansen, Rupert, *Tales of the New Babylon: Paris 1869–1875*, Sinclair-Stevenson, London, 1994

Cowles, Virginia, *Edward VII and His Circle*, Hamish Hamilton, London, 1956

——, *1913: The Defiant Swansong*, Weidenfeld and Nicolson, London, 1967

Crabitès, Pierre, *Victoria's Guardian Angel: A Study of Baron Stockmar*, George Routledge and Sons, London, 1937

Craveri, Benedetta (trans. Waugh, Teresa), *The Age of Conversation*, New York Review of Books, New York, 2005

Cresswell, Louise, *Eighteen Years on Sandringham Estate*, Temple Company, London, 1887

Dangerfield, George, *Victoria's Heir: The Education of a Prince*, Constable, London, 1942

Donaldson, Frances, *Edward VIII*, Weidenfeld and Nicolson, London, 1974

Duff, David, *Albert and Victoria*, Frederick Muller, London, 1972

——, *Whisper Louise: Edward VII and Mrs Cresswell*, Frederick Muller, London, 1974

Esher, Viscount, *The Influence of King Edward and Essays on Other Subjects*, John Murray, London, 1915

Fulford, Roger (ed.), *Dearest Child: Letters between Queen Victoria and the Princess Royal, 1858–1861*, Evans Brothers, London, 1964

——, *Dearest Mama: Letters between Queen Victoria and the Crown Princess of Prussia, 1861–1864*, Evans Brothers, London, 1968

——, *Darling Child: Private Correspondence of Queen Victoria and the Crown Princess of Prussia 1861–1878*, Evans Brothers, London, 1976

Gathorne-Hardy, Jonathan, *The Rise and Fall of the British Nanny*, Hodder and Stoughton, 1972

Gerson, Noel B., *Lillie Langtry*, Robert Hale, London, 1972

Godfrey, Rupert (ed.), *Letters from a Prince: Edward, Prince of Wales to Mrs Freda Dudley Ward. March 1918–January 1921*, Little, Brown and Company, London, 1998

Gordon, Peter and Lawton, Denis, *Royal Education: Past, Present and Future*, Frank Cass, London, 1999

Graves, Robert and Hodge, Alan, *The Long Weekend: A Social History of Britain 1918–1939*, Faber and Faber, London, 1940

Hamilton, Elizabeth, *The Warwickshire Scandal*, Michael Russell, London, 1999

Hattersley, Roy, *The Edwardians*, Little, Brown and Company, London, 2004

Havers, Sir Michael, Grayson, Edward and Shankland, Peter, *The Royal Baccarat Scandal*, William Kimber, London, 1977

Hepworth, Philip, *Royal Sandringham*, Wensum Books, Norwich, 1978

Hibbert, Christopher, *Edward VII: A Portrait*, Allen Lane, London, 1976

Higham, Charles, *Mrs Simpson: Secret Lives of The Duchess of Windsor*, Macmillan, 2005

Hough, Richard, *Edward and Alexandra: Their Private and Public Lives*, Hodder and Stoughton, London, 1992

Jenkins, Roy, *Churchill*, Macmillan, London, 2001

Langtry, Lilllie, *The Days I Knew*, Hutchinson, London, 1925

Lee, Sir Sidney, *King Edward VII: A Biography*, Macmillan, London, 1925

Leslie, Anita, *The Marlborough House Set*, Doubleday and Company, New York, 1972

Longford, Elizabeth, *Victoria R.I.*, Weidenfeld and Nicolson, London, 1964

Magnus, Philip, *King Edward the Seventh*, John Murray, London, 1964

Marsh, Richard, *A Trainer to Two Kings: Being the Reminiscences of Richard Marsh M.V.O.*, Cassell, London, 1925

McLeod, Kirsty, *Battle Royal: Edward VIII and George IV, Brother Against Brother*, Constable, London, 2002

Mitchell, Leslie, *The Whig World 1760–1837*, Hambledon Continuum, London, 2005

Montgomery, John, *The Twenties: An Informal Social History*, George Allen and Unwin, London, 1957

Morris, James, *Pax Britannica: The Climax of an Empire*, Faber and Faber, London, 1968

——, *Farewell the Trumpets: An Imperial Retreat*, Faber and Faber, London, 1978

Neiberg, Michael, S., *Fighting the Great War: A Global History*, Harvard University Press, Cambridge, MA, and London, 2005

Neilson, Francis, 'Edward VII and the Entente Cordiale', *American Journal of Economics and Sociology*, Vol. 17, 1957

Newsome, David, *Godliness and Good Learning: Four Studies on a Victorian Ideal*, John Murray, 1961

———, *On the Edge of Paradise: A.C. Benson, the Diarist*, John Murray, London, 1980

———, *The Victorian World Picture*, John Murray, London, 1997

Nicolson, Juliet, *The Perfect Summer: Dancing into the Shadow in England in 1911*, John Murray, London, 2006

Partridge, Michael, *The Royal Naval College, Osborne*, Sutton Publishing, Stroud, 1999

Perkins, Anne, *A Very British Strike 3 May – 12 May 1926*, Macmillan, London, 2007

Plomer, William (ed.), *Kilvert's Diary*, Vol. 2, Jonathan Cape, London, 1969

Pope-Hennessy, James, *Queen Mary 1867–1953*, Allen and Unwin, London, 1959

Pugh, Martin, *We Danced All Night: A Social History of Britain Between the Wars*, The Bodley Head, London, 2008

Ridley, Jane, *Bertie: A Life of Edward VII*, Chatto and Windus, London, 2012

Rose, June, *Mistress of Montmartre: A Life of Susanne Valadon*, Richard Cohen, London, 1998

Rose, Kenneth, *King George V*, Weidenfeld and Nicolson, London, 1983

Ruffer, Jonathan Garnier, *The Big Shots: Edwardian Shooting Parties*, Debrett's Peerage, London, 1977

Searle, G.R., *A New England? Peace and War*, Oxford University Press, Oxford, 2004

Seth-Smith, Michael, *Bred for the Purple*, Leslie Frewin, London, 1969

Sitwell, Osbert, *Left Hand, Right Hand*, The Reprint Society, London, 1946

———, *Great Morning*, The Reprint Society, London, 1949

———, *Laughter in the Next Room*, The Reprint Society, London, 1950

Souhami, Diana, *Mrs Keppel and Her Daughter*, Flamingo, London, 1997

Spencer, Edward, *The King's Racehorses: A History of the Connection of His Majesty King Edward VII with the National Sport*, John Long, London, 1902

St Aubin, Giles, *Edward VII: Prince and King*, Collins, London, 1979

Strachey, Lytton, *Eminent Victorians*, Chatto and Windus, London, 1921

Taylor, Antony, *'Down with the Crown': British Anti-monarchism and Debates about Royalty since 1790*, Reaktion Books, London, 1999

Todman, Dan, *The Great War: Myth and Memory*, Hambledon Continuum, London, 2005

Vanderbilt, Gloria and Furness, Thelma, *Double Exposure: A Twin Biography*, Frederick Muller, London, 1959

Warner, Malcolm and Flint, Kate, *Millais: Portraits*, National Portrait Gallery, London, 1999

Warwick, Countess of, *Life's Ebb and Flow*, Hutchinson, London, 1929

———, *Afterthoughts*, Cassell, London, 1931

Watson, Alfred E.T., *King Edward VII as a Sportsman*, Longmans Green and Co., London, 1911

Weintraub, Stanley, *The Importance of Being Edward: King in Waiting 1841–1901*, John Murray, London, 2000

Wheeler- Bennett, John W., *King George VI: His Life and Reign*, Macmillan, London, 1958

Wilson, A.N., *The Victorians*, Hutchinson, London 2002

——, *After the Victorians*, Hutchinson, London, 2005

Windsor, Duchess of, *The Heart Has its Reasons: The Memoirs of The Duchess of Windsor*, Michael Joseph, London, 1956

Windsor, Duke of, *A King's Story*, Cassell, London, 1951

Windsor, Edward, *Speeches by H.R.H. The Prince of Wales 1912–1926*, Hodder and Stoughton, London, 1927

Woodham-Smith, Cecil, *Queen Victoria: Her Life and Times*, Hamish Hamilton, London, 1972

Young, G.M., *Victorian England: Portrait of an Age*, Oxford University Press, Oxford, 1936

——, *Daylight and Champaign*, Jonathan Cape, London, 1937

Ziegler, Philip (ed.), *The Diaries of Lord Louis Mountbatten, 1920–1922*, Collins, London, 1987

——, *King Edward VIII*, Collins, London, 1991

Zola, Emile, *Nana*, Oxford University Press, Oxford, 1992

Index

313